To Glenys – refused to

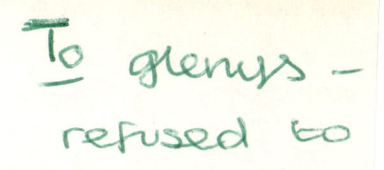

Megan Norris is a journalist with n... ence. She began her career on a large provincial evening newspaper in the UK where she went on to specialise in crime reporting.

After emigrating to Australia with her husband and two sons in 1990, Megan established a court reporting agency, supplying major news stories and features to national print and TV outlets. Now writing for women's magazines, Megan continues to have a special interest in women and children who are victims of violent crime.

She is a former winner of the EVA (Eliminating Violence Against Women) awards and is the co-author of the best-selling book *Perfect Victim*, the true story of the murder of Melbourne teenager Rachel Barber, a case she covered extensively.

As well as her sons, Megan has two grandsons. She lives in Melbourne.

lots of love

Megan xxx

Running Pink

One woman, one dog and an 18,000-kilometre run for a cause

Deborah De Williams' inspiring story

Megan Norris

The Five Mile Press

The Five Mile Press Pty Ltd
1 Centre Road, Scoresby
Victoria 3179 Australia
www.fivemile.com.au

Copyright © Megan Norris and Deborah De Williams, 2012
All rights reserved. No part of this book may be reproduced, stored in a retrieval system, or be transmitted by any form or by any means, electronic, mechanical, photocopying, recording or otherwise, without the prior written permission of the publisher.

Megan Norris and Deborah De Williams assert their moral rights to be identified as the authors of this book.

First published 2012

Printed and bound in Australia by Griffin Press
Only wood grown in sustainable regrowth forests is used in the manufacture of paper found in this book.

Cover design by Luke Causby, Blue Cork
Page design and typesetting by Shaun Jury
Map by Kristy Lund-White

Front cover photographs: Glyn De Williams
Internal and back cover photographs courtesy Deborah De Williams, except second from top, photographer Graham Tidy, reproduced with permission from *Canberra Times*

National Library of Australia Cataloguing-in-Publication entry
    Norris, Megan.
    Running pink: the Deborah de Williams Sory / Megan Norris,
    Deborah De Williams.
    ISBN:9781743006894 (pbk.)
    De Williams, Deborah.
    Breast—Cancer—Research—Australia.
    Fund raising—Australia.
    Running—Australia—Biography.
    Breast cancer patients' writings.
    616.9944900994

Some names and identifying details have been changed to protect the privacy of individuals.

The poem 'Courage Doesn't Always Roar' by Mary Anne Radmacher published Red Wheel/Weiser, LLC. Copyright © Mary Anne Radmacher http://maryanneradmacher.net. Reprinted by permission of the publisher.

Back cover photographs: Deborah with her friend Janelle Larkin, jubilant after completing her record breaking run around Australia, May 2010; Deborah and Maggie outside Old Parliament House, March 2011; Deborah at the 7000km mark near Broome, August 2010; Deborah and Maggie on being told she was Tasmanian Australian of the Year, November 2010

Contents

Running for a Cure	1
Broken Feet, Shattered Dreams	17
The Never Say Never Girl	23
Stage Zero Cancer	33
Chemo Brain	43
Maggie	47
The Bosom Buddies	55
One Journey Ends	63
Chasing Hope	65
A Black Day	79
Outback Angels	91
Freedom	103
Walk Before You Run	115
These Feet are Made for Walking	125
The Grey Nomad	133
A Silent Prayer under a Desert Moon	143
Christmas Crackers	151
The Flying Fossil	155

Cyclones and Detours	163
The Break-in	179
The Never Never	185
Crikey – Who's Crazy?	191
Bedridden	199
Running for a Cure – Again!	213
Blisters	219
Lucky Money	229
Angels and Fairies	235
Pink Pyjamas	243
Road Works	247
Completing the Loop	257
Pink X-Men	261
A Christmas Cyclone	267
A National Disaster	275
Queensland Floods	279
Meeting the Prime Minister	287
The Boob Flasher	297
Friends in High Places	307
A New World Record	313
Royal Bragging Rights	317
No Comedy Clubs in Berlin!	325
Author Acknowledgements	334
Deborah's Acknowledgements	335
List of sponsors	337
Logs	339

*For Glyn, my parents and my 'angel', Alistair,
for believing in my dream and for
helping me to make it come true.*

*And to Jan, the Facebook friend I never
had the chance to meet, for giving me
the hope to fulfil my dream.*

This book is for you.

Deborah

Courage doesn't always roar. Sometimes courage is the quiet voice at the end of the day saying, 'I will try again tomorrow.'

— Mary Anne Radmacher

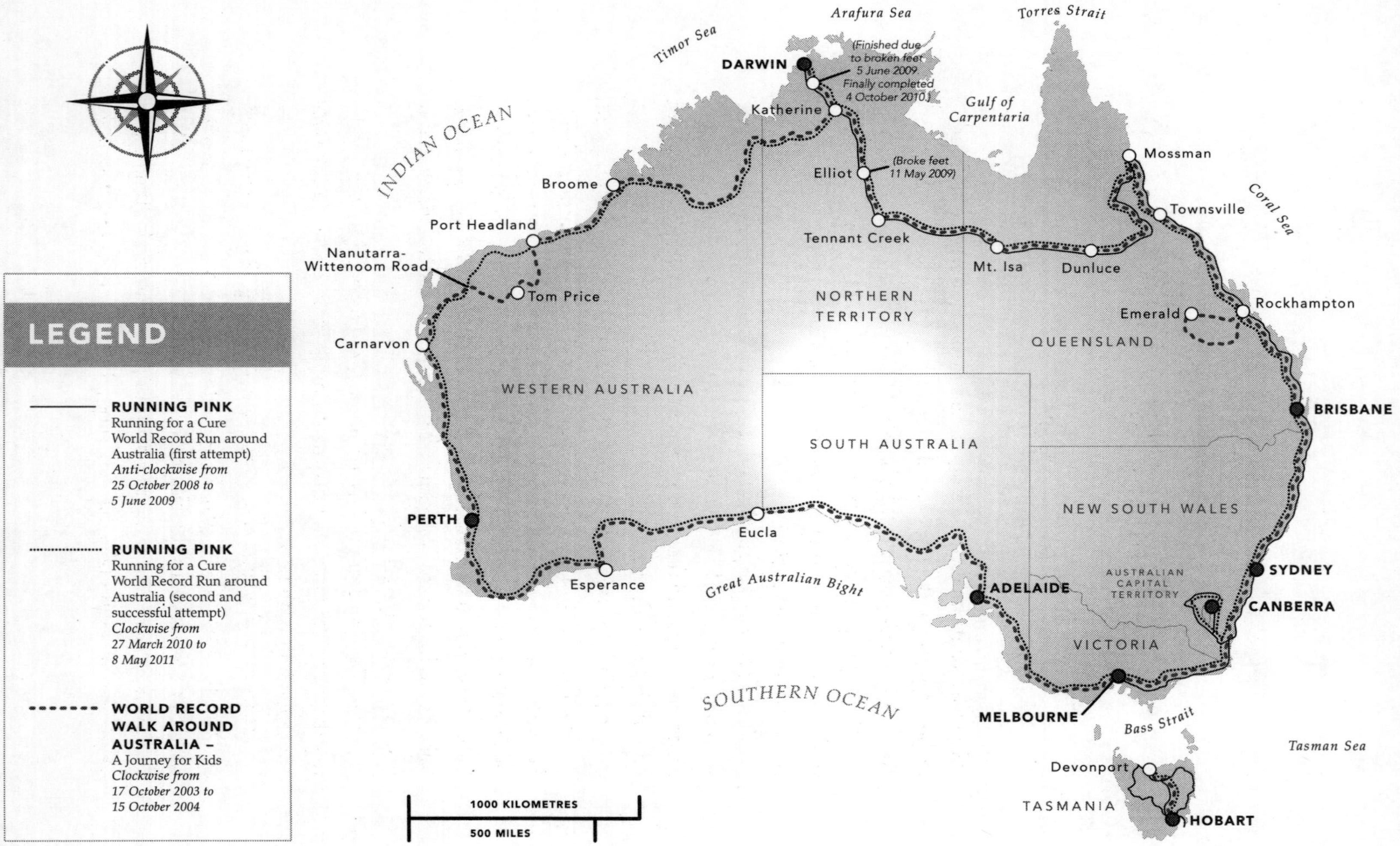
LEGEND
RUNNING PINK
Running for a Cure
World Record Run around
Australia (first attempt)
Anti-clockwise from
25 October 2008 to
5 June 2009
RUNNING PINK
Running for a Cure
World Record Run around
Australia (second and
successful attempt)
Clockwise from
27 March 2010 to
8 May 2011
WORLD RECORD
WALK AROUND
AUSTRALIA –
A Journey for Kids
Clockwise from
17 October 2003 to
15 October 2004
Arafura Sea
Torres Strait
Timor Sea
DARWIN
(Finished due
to broken feet
5 June 2009
Finally completed
4 October 2010)
Gulf of
Carpentaria
Katherine
INDIAN OCEAN
Mossman
Elliot
(Broke feet
11 May 2009)
Coral Sea
Broome
Townsville
Port Headland
Tennant Creek
Mt. Isa
Dunluce
Nanutarra-
Wittenoom Road
Tom Price
NORTHERN
TERRITORY
Emerald
Rockhampton
Carnarvon
QUEENSLAND
WESTERN AUSTRALIA
BRISBANE
SOUTH AUSTRALIA
NEW SOUTH WALES
PERTH
Eucla
SYDNEY
Esperance
Great Australian Bight
ADELAIDE
AUSTRALIAN
CAPITAL
TERRITORY
CANBERRA
VICTORIA
SOUTHERN OCEAN
MELBOURNE
Bass Strait
Tasman Sea
Devonport
TASMANIA
HOBART
1000 KILOMETRES
500 MILES

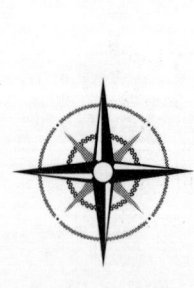

Running for a Cure

'Go easy,' cautioned the young casualty doctor, shaking his head in disbelief at the pink patient hobbling through the crowded hospital's Accident and Emergency Department towards the front entrance.

His triage nurse craned her neck from behind the central casualty desk, her eyes following the woman now limping out of the doors and across the car park.

'Is she actually *jogging*?' asked the nurse, peering after the woman who had arrived at her desk very early that morning and casting an anxious eye around the rows of patients already waiting in line to see one of the duty doctors.

Dr John Johnson nodded. 'Yep, she certainly is,' he said, resigned.

For the last few hours a subdued and dejected Deborah De Williams had lain behind the curtain of a cubicle in the casualty area of Darwin Hospital, watching the clock and waiting. Her face had looked anxious as young Dr John Johnson pinned her X-rays on the light board beside the hospital bed where she had been instructed to rest her badly injured feet.

'These X-rays don't tell us too much,' Dr Johnson had said, studying the films. 'I think we need to do bone scans so we know what we're dealing with here.'

Deborah shifted uneasily on the bed, groaning. She'd seen enough of Darwin Hospital already, she thought, staring miserably from her feet, to the X-rays, to the clock.

It was already two p.m. and from the moment she'd limped into casualty at around eight that morning, flinching with every step she took, she'd made sure everyone understood she was a woman in a hurry.

Wednesday 3 June 2009 was, for Deborah, Day 222 of a year-long adventure in which she was attempting a world-record-breaking run around Australia. The seasoned ultra-marathon runner wasn't just trying to set a new world record for the longest continuous run by a female by running around this vast continent – running the entire 365 days without a single day off – she was on another equally important mission.

'I'm running for a cure,' she'd explained to the triage nurse, gesturing towards her bright pink t-shirt, shorts and cap bearing the logo of Running Pink, the breast cancer charity she'd founded more than two years earlier after mounting her own battle against the disease. Now in remission, Deborah was running around Australia to raise funds for breast cancer research.

Yet, in the past seven months since the mammoth challenge began on 25 October 2008, not even Deborah could have envisaged the rousing welcome that lay waiting for her along the road.

Everywhere she went, from crowded city centre shopping malls, to suburban parks, to remote outback cattle stations and isolated indigenous communities, she'd been mobbed by crowds of pink. Breast cancer survivors and battlers – supported by their husbands, children, parents and friends – had turned out in their fluffy pink droves, their imaginations sparked by this inspirational crazy pink lady running around the country with her dog. Deborah wasn't just running for herself, she realised, she was running for anyone whose life had been touched by breast cancer.

The Australian public had responded to her cause with such generosity that money was pouring into Deborah's charity from the collections she made at the countless community rallies and awareness meetings she'd addressed along the way. All the money Deborah's adventure raised would, she promised her supporters, go towards vital medical research that she hoped might one day eradicate a disease known to strike more than 1.3 million women around the world every year. In Australia, every day more than

30 women discover they have breast cancer – about 11,500 people every year.

It was a cause close to Deborah's heart. When breast cancer first sneaked up on her in March 2006, she'd been utterly devastated. But in her typical stubborn way, she'd simply refused to let the disease slow her down. Long before doctors confirmed she was in remission, Deborah had already beaten the cancer in her head, vowing to herself that she would tackle the disease the only way she knew how – by outrunning the bloody thing!

Now, over 10,000 kilometres into a run Deborah estimated would exceed 18,000 kilometres, she had shuffled past the halfway mark of Darwin with a new appreciation that she wasn't only on the run of her life, Deborah DeWilliams was running *for* life. Or at least she had been, until an unfortunate mishap almost four weeks ago that now threatened to put the brakes on her world-breaking attempt.

'I can't just sit here,' she'd told her husband Glyn, checking the hospital clock and limping back to the triage desk to ask the nurse again: 'How long now until these bone scans?'

In truth, Deborah appreciated that this busy hospital had pulled out all the stops to help her. When news of the pink philanthropist and her astonishing charity run spread through the emergency waiting area, Dr Johnson had rushed her through to a private room in the busy casualty department where he'd ordered urgent X-rays. Then he arranged for the impatient patient to be immediately assessed by the hospital's physiotherapist.

'She's got a huge following,' a young nurse whispered to the physio who had been paged by casualty. The nurse's curiosity was piqued by this gutsy 39-year-old artist-turned-entrepreneur. Only a few days earlier, she'd turned on the ABC radio news to hear Deborah De Williams' interview as she ran into Darwin on two badly injured feet she'd hurt almost a month earlier in an accidental fall.

'She's running with her dog,' continued the nurse. 'Wherever she goes, people turn out to cheer her on. She's really amazing.' Deborah's run had certainly fuelled the imagination of a nation, her name regularly popping up in newspapers along the way, her voice now familiar to ABC listeners in each of the states she'd already travelled through.

Yet now it was Deborah's imagination that ran riot as she lay in casualty, checking the clock again, and wondering how long it would take to organise those bone scans.

'To keep the record alive, I have to run a minimum of 20 kilometres every single day non-stop,' Deborah explained to the physio who studied the X-rays that offered no explanation for the excruciating pain in both feet. 'That means no days off – including today!'

The physio didn't reply, focussing his attention instead on Deborah's locked and painful thigh muscles, which were showing signs of deep bruising.

'This bruising and pain is a direct result of your awkward gait,' he said, after observing her limp up and down casualty. Deborah's body was definitely compensating for the injuries in her feet. Her hip and back were now hurting too as she adopted a clumsy shuffle favouring her right foot and protecting the more injured left one.

She winced as the physio pressed on the more badly swollen left foot, asking her to elaborate on the fall that had knocked her off her feet 23 days earlier as she'd headed through the Northern Territory towards her halfway goal.

'It was unbelievably dumb . . .' began Deborah.

Monday 11 May 2009 was the start of Week 29 in an adventure that had begun in Deborah's hometown of Hobart. The morning had begun typically early for Deborah as she climbed out of bed and peered from the caravan window over the Stuart Highway across the sunburned outback where there wasn't a person or truck in sight.

While Glyn, Deborah's artist husband, was still sleeping when she woke at five a.m., Maggie, her adorable pure-bred Border collie, was already wide awake.

Deborah opened the caravan door to find her seven-year-old 'baby' panting in anticipation, circling impatiently at the annexe door and wagging her tail, ready to join her owner on their usual early morning run. Maggie's soft brown eyes searched Deborah's face as she opened a bottle of cool water and gulped it down. Any minute now, she'd slip into her Saucony runners for the first run of the day, which they always did together before breakfast.

A canny dog, Maggie knew the drill. As soon as her owner had strapped her GPS onto her wrist — the device which recorded the number of kilometres she ran each day — she'd open the door and they'd be off.

During her run Deborah had become fanatical about keeping accurate records. It was important that she provide evidence of every single kilometre she ran if she was to beat the current record.

Each morning Deborah carefully logged her starting point location, the time and GPS coordinates, repeating the exercise again at the end of every day when she arrived at a new overnight stop. This information was also recorded on a GPS in the car and in a separate log book, as well as a witness book, which was witnessed by strangers encountered along the way, who were more than happy to sign their names alongside the times and locations as testimony that this runner was adhering to the rules.

So far, her witnesses had included an assortment of people — police officers, truck drivers, caravan site owners, roadhouse workers, schoolteachers and community leaders — all inspired by Deborah's purpose and her steely determination to make a difference.

'C'mon girl,' whispered Deborah, closing the caravan door and setting off into the early morning sun with Maggie.

The long dusty highway stretched ahead like a ribbon, undulating as it cut a bumpy line through the red dirt of the outback until it disappeared somewhere in the distant heat haze like a shimmering mirage.

The early morning was Deborah's favourite time of the day and she constantly found herself pausing to marvel at brilliant sunrises, the warm hues of a new day casting a shimmering kaleidoscope of colour across the stark landscape where flame-coloured flowers scattered like confetti in the humidity.

'Come on Maggie, not far today,' encouraged Deborah, watching her faithful running buddy's silky ears prick up, her paws settling into an even pace as she trotted along the road, a black wet nose ahead of her owner.

For Maggie, Deborah's year-long adventure around the sprawling continent was more of an extended fun run and she was in her element padding along the dusty highway beside her mum. But for Deborah, an ultra-marathoner, this was serious business. By nightfall Deborah's goal was to have completed a gruelling 65 kilometres that would take her one step closer to her dream of setting a new world record. But her incredible feat was not just about setting records or achieving personal goals. And it wasn't entirely about raising money either.

Deborah was also on a quest to raise awareness and to educate people wherever she went. Women, including younger women with no family history of breast cancer, needed to be alert to the importance of checking out suspicious lumps that might be the early indicators of this shattering disease.

'The prognosis is so much better if you catch the disease early,' she emphasised to the women she met along the way. 'I'm proof of that.'

The first stop on Deborah's route on this beautiful Monday morning was the tiny Northern Territory township of Elliott, an isolated, largely indigenous community of around 400 people. In Elliott, as in many other communities, towns and cities she'd passed through, Deborah's support crew – consisting of Glyn and her retired parents, Owen and Karin – would 'bunny hop' ahead, their bright pink caravans designed and wrapped by Think Big Printing trailing behind their 4WDs.

In each new town, they had the task of setting up the pink information stall bearing literature about breast cancer, and an assortment of merchandise from pink ribbons and pens to brooches and t-shirts that bore Deborah's Running Pink logo. So far supporters had been digging deep, slipping their donations into collection tins whose proceeds were already mounting.

Elliott lay about 24 kilometres up the highway, but because Deborah had an 11.30 a.m. reception scheduled with the town's Chief Executive Officer and councillors – and a meeting organised with the local Aboriginal women's group – the night before, her support crew had parked their matching pink caravans on the side of the highway 67 kilometres north of Renner Springs. Deborah had completed her run at this point the previous evening, within easy running distance of Elliot.

The day before had been Mother's Day, and Deborah had spent 14 hours running along the road. That evening she'd presented her mother with a hand-made card. With no chance of finding a shop out here in the middle of nowhere, she'd decided to make her mum's card a few days ahead so she'd have something to hand to her on her special day.

She'd given the card to Karin as she rustled up a roast in the small oven of their cramped caravan on the side of the road. Then they'd all celebrated what was left of this special day for mums, sitting wearily around the table and toasting Karin with a glass of wine.

The next day Deborah planned to run through Elliott and on towards the bigger town of Katherine. She'd estimated she'd spend the next couple of weeks running north towards Darwin. Now, just knowing that the 'halfway mark' was only a little over 700 kilometres away gave Deborah a boost as she ran with Maggie on this beautiful sunny morning, her sights firmly focussed on a dream that, for the first time in weeks, actually felt within her grasp. While in terms of distance Darwin wasn't strictly the journey's halfway mark, for Deborah her run north ended here, where she would begin the long trek south.

Deborah glanced down at Maggie, already pricking up her ears for the familiar purring of Glyn's and Owen's engines on the road behind them. They didn't have long to wait. About half an hour later, Glyn and her parents flashed past; two continuous streaks of pink, trailblazing their way up the highway on the first bunny hop of the day, looking for a suitable spot to pull over for breakfast.

The peculiar pink convoy always brought a smile to Deborah's face as they waved and shouted words of encouragement out of the windows – the lairy road show attracting beeping horns from good-humoured truckies, all familiar with the sight of this pink lady running with her dog to God knew where.

'Nice arse,' shouted some of the cheekier larrikins, zooming past. The gush of wind from the wheels of these monster road trains knocked Deborah sideways as they went.

The Greyhound bus drivers who followed the regular route up and down the country showed more decorum. 'Hey Pink Lady,' they'd shout, giving her and Maggie a friendly wave before telling their curious passengers what the comical pink road show was all about.

On a route where the scenery remained unchanged for days, the sight of two pink caravans with an equally pink woman and her dog in hot pursuit provided a welcome interruption and regularly drew applause and whistles from appreciative sightseers.

Today, Glyn headed the cavalry, slowing down only to hand his wife some cold bottled water. 'I'll put the kettle on,' he promised, pulling away.

'Come on Maggie, we're running for our breakfast again,' said Deborah 30 minutes later, as the smell of bacon, eggs and tomatoes wafted down the road towards them.

Karin was already dishing up breakfast when Deborah arrived, pulling off her sweaty socks and changing her runners before joining the others around the table for the first meal of the day.

'You're a culinary genius, Mum,' she said, munching on the delicious oaties her mother had baked on Mother's Day in the small caravan. The oat cookies were made to a secret traditional family recipe and were Deborah's favourites; the treats went down well with a high-protein breakfast, and provided her with a much-needed energy boost in the form of snacks during the day, when Deborah thought nothing of running for 14 hours.

'How far is it from Elliott to Darwin?' queried Deborah, sipping on hot black coffee infused with honey.

'735 kilometres,' replied Owen, studying the map again.

'Back to business then,' said Deborah, heading back to the road.

Maggie, on cue, wagged her tail and trotted to the passenger side of Glyn's 4WD. After her usual early morning romp before breakfast, she'd done her bit for Team D and was content to spend the next leg of the run putting her paws up in the passenger seat of the air-conditioned vehicle. When Glyn passed by 10 minutes later, Deborah could see Maggie's ears flapping in the breeze, barking her instructions through the open window, her big brown eyes staring back at her owner in sympathy, while she enjoyed her hard-earned ride.

By the time Deborah arrived in Elliott, she hoped the formal letter of introduction which she'd sent on ahead had opened official doors that a solo runner shuffling around the country would never have managed alone. The letter, thoughtfully penned by the Lord Mayor of Hobart, Rod Valentine, before she'd left Tasmania, had so far proved a Godsend. It not only prepared the ground by introducing the plucky Tasmanian to the mayors and senior council officials of every town along her route, it also encouraged them to urge their communities to support the pink ultra-marathoner, who already had the full backing of her entire home state.

As well as the letter Mayor Valentine had kindly written, Deborah had also set up a link on the National Breast Cancer Foundation website which directed readers to her own Running Pink website. Here, she explained all about her attempt at a new world record, and how her own brush with the disease had inspired this run to raise money for vital research.

The highly imaginative Deborah had also taken the step of setting up a 'dog blog' for Maggie, her newly appointed Director of Greetings – D.O.G. for short. Maggie's humorous postings, ghosted of course by her fun-loving owner, had attracted thousands of fans. Animal lovers by the score were addicted to the comical blog – generously sponsored by the run's only financial sponsor, VIP Pet Foods – keen to hear the daily updates on Maggie's adventures.

'You've done better than me Maggie Moo,' said Deborah, thrilled with the $10,000 sponsorship she'd managed to secure for her dog.

In the end she'd decided to fund the run herself by bumping up her Visa card and adding the escalating debt to her now expandable mortgage with the help of the friendly manager at her local Westpac Bank, who'd become her new best friend. Still, with hundreds of women sending her messages of encouragement, and even more turning out to cheer her on, the adventure so far had been worth every cent.

Until Deborah set out on her run she hadn't really considered how far-reaching the shockwaves generated by a cancer diagnosis could be. After her diagnosis, she'd only told Glyn, her parents, and her business partner and good friend, Alistair Cameron.

'I told you not to tell *anyone*,' fumed Deborah, when she discovered Karin had shared her fears over her daughter's diagnosis with her sister, Monika.

Now, after shuffling up Australia's eastern seaboard, away from populated cities, through the bush and on to the isolated outback towns where cancer survivors and patients emerged with their own support crews, Deborah realised how wrong she'd been. Breast cancer – any cancer – was never *just a*bout the patient.

'It's like throwing a pebble into a pond – the impact sends ripples far and wide, far beyond where the eye can see,' she told Glyn with a new humility. She was sorry she'd told her mum off.

Wherever she went, pink, the internationally recognised colour that symbolises the ongoing fight against breast cancer, just kept popping up like a giant marshmallow beacon to guide her on her way. Deborah felt constantly humbled as cheer squads of smiling women gathered around her, ready to open their arms and their hearts to a woman on a mission.

Almost overnight, Deborah De Williams had become public property. She was mobbed by mums – many of them still bald from treatment – and grandmothers sporting the coarse wiry regrowth of hair that was their legacy from months of chemotherapy. They came together by roadsides and linked arms at rallies where men still grieving partners who'd lost their own valiant battles against breast cancer joined them to cheer this crusader on her way.

So far, not a single day had passed when someone hadn't stopped to give her a donation or share a story of their own cancer experience. This meant Deborah was late wherever she went, but her supporters waited patiently and nobody seemed to mind. Deborah remained amazed that anyone could find a woman simply running along the road with her dog inspirational. Over the past months she'd met so many incredible women whose own personal tales of courage had humbled her that it was her privilege to pause to honour their experiences.

For her, these women were the real inspiration, their stories bringing tears to her eyes and giving her the will to keep going when the challenge became so confronting she considered calling it quits. It was because of these women that Deborah now felt such a huge obligation. Fuelled by this new responsibility, she'd outrun both injury and tough times, finding the strength to climb out of bed day after day to keep moving onwards to the next town.

So on 11 May she shuffled on towards Elliott, aware that she'd need to step up her pace of 8.5 kilometres an hour if she wanted to be there for her 11.30 a.m. meeting.

'Where *are* you?' Karin asked, calling from Elliott on her satellite mobile. It was 10.45 a.m. and Deborah wasn't sure. 'Well, hurry up,' replied Karin.

If Deborah had expected her usual pink support crowd to be the first thing to greet her in Elliott that morning, she couldn't have been more wrong. In the distance she became aware of flashing blue lights moving in her direction down the Stuart Highway. Deborah was already running half an hour late and, as the enthusiastic gathering in Elliott had been getting restless, the local police had dispatched two patrol cars to check on the location of their much-anticipated guest. Now the police patrol, spying their visitor, did a U-turn and slowly cruised alongside her.

'Only another three kilometres,' shouted one of the police drivers, vanishing back up the highway with an update for the waiting crowd.

Five minutes later, Glyn's car appeared with Maggie yapping instructions through the passenger's window.

'Go girl,' said Glyn, letting Maggie out to join her running buddy for the final leg into town.

Deborah clipped Maggie on her leash. 'Don't want you getting mobbed, Maggie,' she said, glimpsing the sign for Elliott and the returning police patrol.

'We're giving you an official escort into town,' announced the friendly police drivers as Glyn pulled back and trailed slowly behind his wife.

'C'mon, Maggie,' said Deborah, running on adrenalin as she spotted a pink-clad crowd of Aboriginal women making their way towards the roadside, 50 metres ahead of her.

Maggie trotted obediently ahead, her leash firmly clipped to the belt around her mum's waist, head up, tongue down, ready to make another celebrity guest appearance for her fans. Lately, Maggie had been taking her role very seriously. When they arrived in new places and her owner collapsed, exhausted, under the shade of the nearest tree, Maggie, the real star of the show, could be found rolling on her back in the dust, her new fans tickling her tummy and patting her. She was lapping up all the fabulous attention that this newfound celebrity had brought her, thought Deborah.

Already, the caravan's cramped cupboards brimmed with the piles of doggie treats and chewies showered on the star attraction. Deborah had even been forced to empty the toilet area where she'd been storing other things, so she could accommodate the growing treasure trove of dog bones and biscuits.

As Deborah plodded on towards the group of women, her police escort suddenly turned their sirens on and flashed their lights, alerting the town to the guest's arrival.

But the sudden howling of the sirens startled Maggie, who became so spooked by the sudden noise and flashing blue lights that she bolted directly into Deborah's path, doing one of her crazy 'ratty runs'. Darting wildly from side to side, Maggie tugged hard at the leash on her owner's waist, tripping Deborah into a clumsy stumble.

As her feet buckled sideways, she fell with her weight on to her ankles, desperately trying to steady herself to regain her balance. In freefall, Deborah's feet screamed, waves of pain searing through them like electrical shockwaves pulsing from her ankles to the tips of her toes.

Deborah bit her lip and tried not to yelp, limping in pain towards the community park where the town's entire population now congregated around their council officials, cheering and clapping.

Behind them, Karin and Owen peeked out from their stall, wondering what the commotion was about and why their daughter, who seemed fine this morning, was now limping badly.

Glyn's CB radio was turned on and he heard a policeman's deep voice over the transmitter: 'Oops – I shouldn't have done that.'

Probably wasn't a good idea, thought Glyn to himself, appreciating that the poor guy only wanted to give Deborah a hero's welcome.

The ensuing 100-metre run towards the park, where the smell of a sizzling barbecue awaited, was a killer and Deborah collapsed on the ground, rubbing both ankles which now throbbed.

But with so many excited people waiting patiently to talk to her, Deborah put on a brave face and tried to focus on the job in hand. These people had taken time out of their busy days to meet her and she now had an obligation to fulfil.

As an ultra-marathon runner, pain was something Deborah had long learned to conquer. The early part of her journey had been dogged by an agonising pain that had crept up both her shins, and which persisted for more than 3000 kilometres.

'You've done it once, you'll do it again,' Deborah told herself as she hobbled out of Elliott.

She felt like Forrest Gump, that loveable hero of the Tom Hanks' movie, who just got up one day and decided to run around a country.

'Run Deborah run,' she silently chanted, the mantra going around her head as she waved to the kindly town officials and moved off on feet that were now absolutely killing her.

'I've probably sprained my ankles,' she moaned, catching up with the convoy as they stopped for a break just 2.5 kilometres the other side of Elliott. She'd anticipated being further along the road by now, but her injured feet were so painful they were really slowing her down.

Glyn slipped a stretchy elastic bandage over each of Deborah's feet. 'This will give you some support,' he said, unconvinced.

But the ensuing 25 kilometres up the highway towards Katherine proved more painful than Deborah ever imagined possible. She could barely manage a shuffle as she limped that night towards the pink caravans at the turnoff to Newcastle Waters.

'I've fallen short of my goal for the day,' she said, recording just 50 kilometres in her log book, 15 kilometres below her target.

Deborah's mum watched anxiously as her daughter lay on the bed in her van, her feet elevated and iced.

'This is bad,' Karin whispered to Owen, who looked worried too.

Glyn was convinced Deborah had sprained her ankles. But even a sprain was a great concern since it could throw a spanner in the works on a record-breaking run that required a minimum of 20 kilometres to be covered every day.

That night, Maggie slunk into her bed looking guilty.

'Hey . . . it's not your fault, Maggie,' Deborah said, giving her a reassuring pat.

It wasn't Maggie's fault any more than it had been Glyn's fault the day before, when he'd driven off without Maggie. Glyn had been focussed on collecting up his pencils and sketch pad after an hour quietly working, while Maggie had snoozed outside in the shade. The dog's ears pricked up at the sound of the 4WD engine suddenly jerking into action, and she watched forlornly as her owner slowly disappeared down the highway. Owen and Karin had already hopped on ahead, so Maggie cut a solitary figure as she contemplated her options. Thankfully the canny canine was smart enough to figure out that if she galloped up the Stuart Highway, she might catch up with her mum. Deborah had been astonished to hear Maggie's paws clicking along the road behind her, all alone in the heat of the day in the middle of nowhere.

The poor dog was so exhausted and thirsty she could run no further, and with no water to give her a drink, Deborah sat beside Maggie on the road patting her gently, and apologising for Uncle Glyn's forgetfulness.

They'd sat there until a passing motorist pulled over and offered them a drink, finally shuffling on until Glyn appeared in front of them in the darkness. After parking the vans, he'd realised his mistake and decided to jog back down the road, hoping to find Maggie with Deborah. He ran the final stretch with his wife and her dog in the dark.

'Only nine kilometres,' he'd told Deborah. But even though she couldn't see her GPS, she soon realised they'd already jogged much further than that.

'Not far now,' said Glyn, when she asked again. But after 14 hours of running, the last leg home felt like a marathon and Deborah, through tears of frustration, cursed her dad, and Glyn, for driving so far ahead.

'Shussh,' said Glyn, his usually laid-back expression crinkling with annoyance. 'Your dad couldn't find a camping spot off the side of the road that would fit two vans.'

With no caravan park out in the middle of nowhere, Owen had to drive another 14 kilometres before finding anywhere suitable where Karin could rustle up her Mother's Day roast.

Owen and Karin had sacrificed a whole year of their retirement to support Deborah on her adventure, chided Glyn. 'So stop making a fuss.'

In the end the three of them arrived, worn out and dirty, under a rising moon resembling a big beautiful orange ball which lit up the entire landscape.

Maggie's blog that night claimed the moon 'made me feel peaceful after such a stressful day'.

Now, after today's unfortunate accident, the guilty dog blogger's ghost writer penned a more unsettling footnote:

It's all my fault . . . All I can say in my defence is that all these early morning starts coupled with the full moon must have made me feel a bit moonstruck. Ya know what they say happens on a full moon. I was so excited by all the attention and already being moonstruck I went into my ratty run trick. Don't ask me why I did it, and oh how I wish now that I hadn't.

I really didn't feel comforted by the sad expression on D's face, so I thought it was best to make myself scarce and go to bed.

I am now crossing my paws that my silliness hasn't caused too much damage. I think it will be the last time I ever use my ratty run trick again.

Now, 23 agonising days later, after Deborah had run a staggering 820 kilometres on feet that had worsened with every step, Maggie wasn't the only one crossing her paws.

Broken Feet, Shattered Dreams

The physiotherapist listened to Deborah's account of the accident and studied her feet again.

'They stop hurting as soon as I take my weight off them,' explained Deborah, trying to sound optimistic. Even after the accident, there'd been no swelling or redness to indicate anything too serious, which belied the excruciating pain that had worsened as she'd reached Katherine. The lack of any outward sign of an injury was a mystery.

Deborah didn't tell the physio, or the doctor who now joined him to inspect the damage, that a nurse she'd met on the road in Katherine had told her about an old-fashioned remedy which was successful in healing sprains: electric soda crystals. Glyn found the supposed cure in the laundry section of the nearest supermarket in Katherine. The salts were normally used to soften water. The nurse had instructed them to place the salts in a stocking which should be soaked in water and placed like a poultice on the sprain. Glyn dutifully carried out the nurse's instructions, placing the soggy socks on Deborah's painful ankles. It hadn't made a scrap of difference, and sounded too silly to mention now, so Deborah kept the supposed cure to herself.

'Can't you just strap them up or something and I'll be on my way?' Deborah now asked the physio, looking hopeful. But the therapist shook his head.

'I suspect you might have broken your feet,' he ventured.

The patient didn't want to hear this. The thought of two sprained ankles was awful enough without considering something far worse.

An Aboriginal man walked past Deborah's cubicle. 'Hey, remember me?' he asked brightly, peering at her from the gap in the curtains and sporting a sling. Deborah recognised the young man.

'Hi Peter ... What are you doing here?' she asked, amazed at the coincidence.

A couple of weeks before, Deborah had come across Peter, his mate and their two families, sitting beside the highway 200 kilometres south of Katherine, wondering what to do about their broken-down car.

'Got a phone mate?' Peter had asked as Glyn pulled over with the pink caravan to wait for his wife, still several kilometres behind him. 'I need to call a cab.'

'To where?' asked Glyn, astonished that anyone would consider calling a taxi to the middle of nowhere.

'To Katherine,' replied the poor guy, looking miserably at his mate, their wives and their children, all sitting glumly in the heat.

The two men explained that even if they had been in possession of a phone, no cab driver would be coaxed into making the 200-kilometre drive down from Katherine. 'Not for us indigenous folks, mate,' he said, downcast. When Deborah finally appeared on the horizon, she was surprised to find Glyn chatting with the two Aboriginal dads, their partners sitting on the roadside trying their hardest to entertain two lots of bored, worried children.

'They'll come if you call,' Peter pressed, as Glyn explained the situation to Deborah. She studied the men's concerned faces. This must be a very important appointment if these poor guys were considering the expense of a round-trip cab ride of more than 400 kilometres.

She dug out her satellite mobile and made the call.

'We need a cab for two indigenous families whose car has broken down,' she explained, giving the operator directions to their location. 'They need to go to Katherine.'

A couple of hours later, a yellow cab pulled up in the dust and steamed away from the pink convoy, its now smiling passengers waving back at her from the open windows as they trailed up the highway towards Katherine.

'Who calls a cab for a 200-kilometre trip?' Glyn asked, scratching his head in disbelief. Only a year before, he and Deborah had become partners in a joint taxi venture of their own in Launceston. They laughed as they wondered what their mate and business partner Alistair Cameron would say if he found himself with a fare that would take him from one end of Tassie to the other.

Now, Peter and Deborah smiled as they crossed paths again. 'What are the chances of meeting you guys here?' chuckled Peter.

'What did you do?' asked Deborah, sitting up on the bed.

'Did it in a footie game, mate,' he replied sheepishly. And despite her predicament, Deborah smiled too. So *that* was the pressing appointment, she thought, as the injured footie player headed out of casualty, waving back at his good Samaritan.

'We've got you booked in for a CT scan tomorrow morning,' explained Dr Johnson, finally returning to his patient. Deborah checked her watch.

'Well there's no point wasting any more time here then,' she said, turning to Glyn and hobbling to her feet. Gritting her teeth, she limped through casualty, out of the main entrance of the hospital and across the car park, refusing the crutches the nurse offered her.

It was clear to the doctor that this stubborn patient's mind was made up; two badly injured – possibly broken feet – were not going to stop this obsessed woman from the run that would keep her record alive. She'd already run almost 1000 kilometres battling these painful injuries – so a mere 20 kilometres, while daunting to anyone else, wasn't likely to deter her.

'Don't worry . . . I'll be back tomorrow,' the patient shouted over her shoulder – and vanished.

It was 2.30 p.m. when Deborah and Glyn arrived back at the caravan site where Owen, Karin and Maggie waited anxiously for news.

'Shouldn't you get your weight off those feet?' suggested Karin.

Deborah shrugged and strapped her feet again. Then she put on her runners.

'*After* my 21 kilometres,' she said.

Aware his wife was now in a great deal of pain, Glyn joined Deborah on her run, shuffling slowly beside her as she limped along the dusty road. Owen drove slowly ahead of them with Maggie watching nervously from the window. The support crew was on hand . . . just in case.

Deborah's friend Ken Nash, an army man and runner from Darwin who had first encountered the pink runner just north of Pine Creek shortly after her accident two weeks earlier, now appeared on the highway again. Ken had been concerned to learn from their regular phone chats that Deborah was battling serious injury, most likely sprained ankles. The previous day, in a show of support, he'd organised a lift down so he could run the final eight kilometres with Deborah into Darwin's CBD to her meeting with the city's Lord Mayor. Now that he'd learned she'd been to the hospital, he turned up again, ready to help Deborah as she ran out of Darwin back towards Katherine. Ken's generous display of moral support and his valuable words of encouragement quickly helped Deborah to re-focus as they again battled the pain barrier, together.

When the minimum-21-kilometres run was finally over, Glyn marked the dusty roadside with a pink paint marker.

'I'll drive you out here tomorrow to pick the run up,' said Owen, as Ken witnessed Deborah's log as evidence of the completed run.

'Here's to another day of keeping the goal alive,' said Ken later as they gathered in the cool shade of the caravan park drinking cold beer.

The following morning, Deborah returned to Darwin Hospital as she'd promised she would, lying in silence as the doctor gave her the radiation injection that would be highlighted in the scans and hopefully explain the cause of her pain.

'No running now – this dye has to travel around your body,' Dr Johnson warned. During the scan, the dye would illuminate areas of damage where blood would have collected.

With three hours to kill until the results were ready, Deborah managed a gentle hobble around a nearby shopping mall where she bought a pair of gold earrings. Not far away, in the centre of Darwin, Owen and Karin continued the fundraising drive, their pink stall now attracting more donations to the cause. 'The show must go on,' Deborah instructed before leaving for her scans.

'So . . . what's the verdict?' asked Deborah later that afternoon, her heart sinking as the doctor pinned her scans on the lightboard where a dark area of damage was now clearly visible on both feet.

'This is where the blood has collected,' explained the doctor, pointing to a shaded area around the bone. The damage centred around a small but crucial bone in each foot.

'This navicular bone is the keystone that holds the entire foot together,' he said, pointing. 'And if you look there, it's split down the middle.'

Deborah groaned as he continued: 'When racehorses get broken naviculars, they're shot.'

This patient had just run more than 820 kilometres on two broken feet. And while she didn't want to think about it, the damaged bones, now glaringly obvious, were not the only things that had been shattered. Deborah's dreams to achieve a world record run and hand over a $300,000 cheque for breast cancer research had just been shattered too.

The Never Say Never Girl

When Deborah De Williams was five years old, her Estonian-Mongolian father moved his young wife and their two Australian-born children to Adelaide – only to vanish.

On the day he left, Deborah and her older brother Adam had returned from school to their old house in an inner city suburb, where they found their devastated mother sobbing in distress in her bedroom – a row of empty coat hangers jangling on the rail in the half-empty wardrobe. Dad's clothes had disappeared, and so had Dad.

Six months earlier, their dad had persuaded Karin to uproot their young family and leave their home in Perth for greener pastures in South Australia, where his wife's German-born parents ran a bedding business.

That afternoon, as Karin wept, Deborah's father's real motive for wanting his family to be closer to his in-laws suddenly became very transparent. He'd left her with two kids and a mortgage on an old house with a leaky roof.

'You've been very bad,' rebuked Karin's father in his thick German accent. He frowned as he scolded the bewildered children, closing the door to the back room where he regularly marched his grandchildren to berate them for some perceived misdemeanour.

'That's why your father has left you . . . and if you don't be good, your mother will leave you as well.'

The thought of being abandoned by *two* parents and left in the sole care of this stern old man and poor, gentle Oma, who was too afraid to argue with him, struck terror into the highly imaginative

Deborah's young heart. She couldn't imagine anything worse. She would try her hardest to be better, she promised, shuddering at the idea of returning from school to a home devoid of a mother.

But while her brother Adam was a compliant boy who wisely held his tongue, this feisty younger sister with wild black pigtails had apparently inherited the same wilful nature that drove her grandfather, and his bull-headed stubborn streak.

As she grew up, Deborah grew to resent her grandfather's rigid control over his family. She was especially resentful of the domineering way he treated her acquiescent grandmother – Oma Erika – and her mum, Karin and aunt, Monika. It seemed mad to Deborah that all the women in this family invested so much energy accommodating the unreasonable demands of a damaged old man for whom nothing was ever right. Even Karin – a tiny munchkin of a woman whose tough, no-nonsense nature belied her outward appearance – went to extraordinary lengths to avoid confrontation with her overbearing father.

In all other areas of her life, Karin was a capable, gutsy woman who worked like a trouper – firstly taking a job as a telephonist to keep the family afloat, and later joining her father's growing bedding business. She worked tirelessly, returning home after long hours to single-handedly deal with the demands of two energetic children. Karin was not afraid to tackle anything, yet when it came to Opa, she did everything in her power to keep him happy.

The same could not be said for Deborah, who grew up a free-spirited little Aussie girl, happily riding her bike in the afternoon sunshine of California Street and escaping the black cloud cast by Opa by walking for hours with her two beloved dogs, Lady and Jolline. To everyone who knew her, Deborah was an outdoors tomboy, in her element amongst the new generation of 'Aussie-wog' kids whose heritages hailed from a colourful mixture of Greek, Italian, Polish, Russian, German and Middle Eastern parents. She ran barefoot in the sun, her long tanned legs dangling out of shorts like strings of knotted cotton, outracing her brother and her cousin, Gary. It greatly irritated Opa to see his granddaughter racing around without shoes. Deborah, knowing this, made a point of deliberately kicking her thongs off whenever she spotted him coming up the footpath of their home. It was her own personal act of stubborn defiance and she enjoyed that it irritated the hell out of Opa.

If Opa had an issue with this new generation of disrespectful children, Deborah couldn't care less. She embraced every second of life as a first-generation Aussie.

'Your brother and your cousin will be the achievers in the family,' pronounced her old-fashioned grandfather, dismissively.

'Why?' asked Deborah, her green eyes challenging him.

'Because they're boys!' responded Opa, frowning and shaking his head at her stupidity.

Deborah eyeballed him defiantly. The old man hailed from a culture and a generation where women were nothing more than unpaid staff, their sole purpose in life to ensure that meals were cooked, homes were cleaned and children were cared for.

Opa's constant put-downs left Deborah bristling. But it also made her determined to prove the old man wrong. 'That's what you think,' she'd tell herself, through gritted teeth. She was a survivor and an adventurer; she could be anything she wanted. Just wait and see, she vowed.

'Quiet Deborah . . . please,' chided Karin, 'Do it for poor Oma!' Karin and Aunty Monika knew full well that their long-suffering mum – who they both loved dearly – would pay the price for Deborah's defiance. They had no doubt that signs of rebellion would spark one of Opa's dark, smouldering moods where nothing would be right.

So Deborah would grudgingly hold her tongue, not caring to listen to the conciliatory soothing tones of Oma Erika as she endeavoured to diffuse another of her husband's outbursts.

The little girl didn't want to hear her mum's explanations about the trauma of her grandfather's experiences in the war in Europe which had left him so damaged. All Deborah knew was that her life was ruled by this miserable old tyrant and his constant complaints about this carefree new generation of half-dressed Aussie kids who spent their time outside playing cricket when they should be doing chores. Like this wilful granddaughter of his, they showed no respect for their elders and betters and would amount to nothing!

But if Deborah and her troubled grandfather locked horns over her supposedly wild ways, there was little doubt in Karin's mind that Deborah had inherited the same defiant fighting spirit that had helped save Gerhard Haufe's life and that of his young family in the final days of World War Two.

'Your Opa comes from tough stock,' Karin would tell her children, explaining how Gerhard – conscripted by Hitler – had abandoned the Russian front in the winter of 1944 as the tide of war turned and the empire of the Reich began to fall. Starving, and battling bitterly cold conditions, the young conscript could see the writing on the wall long before the German surrender.

Watching close friends and colleagues dying of starvation, injury and bitter cold, Gerhard made his mind up to survive the madness. He deserted at Stalingrad and decided he would walk thousands of miles across war-ravaged Europe back to his home and family in devastated Berlin.

It was just a matter of time, he reasoned as he tramped through Poland, one step ahead of the advancing Russian forces who would soon overrun the beautiful historic city that had been his family's home for generations. He had to move fast if he was to beat the Red Army to Berlin and save his young wife and two small daughters – Karin, then six, and Monika, four.

While Berlin burned – the target of relentless Allied air attacks – Gerhard, his wife and children fled to the safety of the smaller German city of Bremen. After the war the family were thankful they had escaped Berlin, their hearts with their native countrymen whose families were confined to the eastern zone of the once-beautiful city when it came under strict Soviet occupation. By the early 1950s, the erection of the Berlin Wall provided few choices for those Germans remaining on the eastern side of the Iron Curtain.

As the Cold War and the spread of communism in Eastern Europe left the western world uneasy, the Haufes began to make plans. In

1952 Gerhard Haufe decided to leave Europe behind, and with his family boarded the Dutch ship *Fair Sea* in Amsterdam to sail halfway around the world to a new country and a whole new life.

The Haufes and their daughters were part of the wave of post-war European immigrants seeking to build new lives in the Australian sunshine. It was rumoured amongst the many non-English-speaking families on their giant liner that kangaroos hopped down the streets in broad daylight and crocodiles snoozed in suburban backyards.

In the 1950s Australia welcomed migrants in their boatloads, as they arrived to populate the growing cities scattered around the country's coastline. They laboured on the land and in the factories; many more lent their muscle to the construction of the Snowy Mountains Hydro-Electric Scheme, or the new power stations springing up in Victoria's La Trobe Valley. Everyone pitched in together to provide the vital infrastructure for this new country.

The family began their new lives in the sparse conditions of a South Australian migrant hostel, where they were fortunate not to be separated — as was the fate of migrants elsewhere. To thousands of families, the primitive living conditions of the countless hostels were nothing compared with the deprivation and hardship they'd experienced in Europe after the war.

Within months, Gerhard found a job as a farm hand, later securing accommodation for his family in a growing Adelaide suburb where he established the family business.

The Haufes could not afford to allow their oldest daughter to continue her education, so at 15, Karin left school and joined the family's bedding business which soon began to flourish. The Australian dream was already taking shape for this determined, though damaged man.

Decades later, amidst the new cosmopolitan generation of young Aussies growing like sunflowers in the heat of South Australia listening to rock bands and watching pop music shows on their parents' new colour TVs, Gerhard Haufe's granddaughter, Deborah, was a girl with dreams of her own.

Now those dreams appeared to be very shaky, as Deborah arrived home from hospital after her scans that afternoon. Karin watched her daughter, strapping her feet again for her minimum run, reflecting on Deborah's determination and stubbornness. Without a doubt, pondered Karin, she'd inherited it from this feisty line of German battlers. Ever since Karin could remember, Deborah had been a little girl with big dreams and an unshakeable belief that, despite what Opa claimed, anything was possible if you believed in it enough. Perhaps she'd even inherited this drive to walk and run incredible distances from Opa, who had walked for his own life so many years before. They were both stubborn survivors.

While to Karin Deborah's innate stubbornness was often an irritating characteristic, to her husband, Glyn, Deborah's steadfast refusal to give up was more of a gift. She was, without a doubt, the 'never say never' girl and a force to be reckoned with.

Yet tonight, as they'd driven back from Darwin Hospital, Deborah's own adventure had certainly lost some of its lustre. They'd exchanged few words as they sat quietly in the car, each lost in their own thoughts, mulling over the doctor's words and the appointment he'd organised for Deborah the following morning with a prominent sports physician in Darwin.

But while the future of this run now seemed very uncertain, Glyn was certain about one thing. It was going to take far more than two broken bones to destroy his wife's dreams!

Dr Johnson had warned Deborah as she'd left casualty that her badly injured feet could have imploded at any time during the last month as she'd run towards her halfway destination.

He'd also posed a question that took them both by surprise. 'Have you had any pain in your legs?' he asked. 'I mean before the accident?'

Deborah nodded, recalling the agonising pain in her shins that had dogged her from Mallacoota all the way to Rockhampton. 'I had shin splints,' she said, the common curse of long distance runners.

She'd experienced shin splints for the first time in 2004 when she was taking part in the Colac Six Day Race in Victoria. The pain was so intense she'd spent the final three days of the run sitting with her legs in buckets of ice, trying to ease the agony. But even that hadn't stopped her breaking the Australian record for the longest distance walked in six days for the Under 35 age group.

So when the same painful ache crept up her legs in Mallacoota over Christmas 2008, she thought it was the same problem again. Deborah had only been on the road eight weeks when the pain first struck as she'd completed her first 4000 kilometres. It was Christmas and she'd limped into the scenic coastal town of Mallacoota close to the Victorian border with New South Wales, battling the pain barrier by distracting herself with the music and audio books on her iPod.

Despite her escalating pain, she ran on, completing the loop inland to run into Canberra. Then, with her legs strapped up, she continued on to Sydney and north to Brisbane, where the gnawing pain ultimately slowed her down. She'd lost important kilometres but promised herself she'd make it up later in her run, once this pain went away.

The surge of relief that finally washed over Deborah as she ran into the Northern Queensland town of Rockhampton had been overwhelming. Deborah had run 3000 kilometres before shattering this pain barrier.

'No, it wasn't shin splints,' said the doctor, now pointing at the scans. 'These scans show stress fractures in both legs,' explained Dr Johnson. 'You would have been in a lot of pain – but luckily they've healed on their own.'

Now, sitting forlornly in Glyn's 4WD and staring blankly at the dusty road ahead, she wondered if it were possible for two broken feet to heal on their own, too.

'This is not going to stop me,' she said, almost reading Glyn's unspoken thoughts.

'Nope,' he said, resigned.

At 4.30 p.m. Deborah's parents swallowed their dismay as they watched her strap her injured feet up and squeeze them gently into her Saucony runners. She still had a few hours in which to complete her minimum 20 kilometres to keep her record going – broken feet or no broken feet.

'I've got an appointment at 6.45 a.m. tomorrow with a really good sports specialist called Dr Geoffrey Thompson,' Deborah told Owen and Karin, as she set off. 'He's here in Darwin and he's treated Australian Olympians so he's one of the best.'

Dr Thompson was also the doctor for the Paralympic Team and had a wealth of experience in the field of sports injuries. Karin and Owen wondered what the doctor would say if he knew his new patient was now on her way down the highway towards the pink road marker, 78 kilometres south of Darwin, where the previous day's run had ended. But there was no point in discouraging Deborah, so nobody tried. Just like her Opa, thought Karin.

Over the next three to four hours, Deborah shuffled along the road, trying not to think about bones imploding in her feet, focussing only on completing the day's run. All the time, Glyn drove 500 metres ahead, crawling along in the car, anxiously keeping his concerns to himself.

When darkness fell, he handed his wife a torch and she continued her painful run on her broken feet, by torchlight.

At eight p.m., he pulled over and marked the road again. Deborah had just run 21.7 kilometres and, despite her agony, she smiled all the way back to the caravan park, her record beating attempt still intact.

The following morning, Deborah and Glyn arrived at the Territory Sports Clinic, where Dr Thompson sat across the desk studying the X-rays, CT scans and MRIs in front of him.

'You've run how far on two broken feet?' he asked, staring at the patient in disbelief.

'800 kilometres if you don't include the minimum runs of the past couple of days,' she said, matter of fact.

And Dr Thompson thought he'd seen it all!

'The navicular bone is one of only two bones in the entire body that gets its blood supply from one source,' he said, studying the scans again. 'It's the worst place you can get a fracture in your foot, and left unattended, as this has been, the bone can shatter and die and then you'd never be able to run again.'

He went on to tell Deborah about Glynis Nunn, who won a Gold Medal at the 1984 Olympics. 'She had broken naviculars,' he said. 'Unfortunately her navicular bones did shatter and today she has plastic replacements and can't run any more.'

Deborah's heart sank. 'I plan to be running a mile a day when I'm 90,' she said stubborn as ever. The doctor studied the hospital reports. 'Yes I know,' she said, pre-empting his next statement. 'Racehorses with broken naviculars are shot!' She paused: 'So . . . what's the treatment?' she asked slowly.

'I'm going to ring a few experts . . . I have a few mates who are surgeons in Melbourne.'

The patient's face fell; she'd been dreading the thought of an operation.

'Even after surgery, an athlete can start training again within three months, and compete again within seven months,' he said, throwing Deborah a lifeline.

But three months felt like a lifetime from where Deborah now sat. Her face brightened as she posed another question.

'Do you think I could run in moonboots?'

The doctor laughed, imagining this pink woman trudging along the road in the giant boots she'd have to wear after surgery.

'Let me talk to a few other experts first,' he said, chuckling, and asked what the world record run was about.

Deborah explained her dream. 'I had breast cancer,' she said, matter of fact.

'I had prostate cancer,' said Dr Thompson, looking her in the eye. 'I'm a survivor too.'

So you understand then, thought Deborah to herself, her spirits suddenly lifting. She hoped he might understand the drive that goes beyond a simple desire to set a world record. She was desperate for hope, and knowing a survivor was dealing with her was a positive sign. The show wasn't over . . . well, not yet.

Deborah explained the importance of her minimum daily run to keep her record alive.

The doctor nodded: 'OK, go and run your 21 kilometres and I will ring you this afternoon.'

But even as she completed her run that afternoon in a fog of painkillers, Deborah's own niggling doubts were already creeping in.

'Will I really be able to do this?' she silently asked herself. Of course, she responded in her head. *I'm the never say never girl.*

That hot afternoon, as she'd done the previous two nights, Deborah slipped into the caravan park pool, where she would paddle around in the cool water, relieved to take her weight off her agonising feet.

Earlier she'd sat on her bed, staring at the board on her caravan wall where she'd scribbled the words; 'I will be the first woman to run around Australia and will reach my charity target of $300,000.'

Even before leaving Tasmania, Deborah had written out the cheque from Running Pink, and signed it. On days when the pain had been too bad to handle, she'd closed her eyes and pictured herself running across the finishing line back in Hobart where it all began. She'd try to imagine the feeling of elation that would rush over her as she ran into the arms of her last pink cheer squad, high on life. This image had sustained her greatly over the past weeks since her accident.

'I think I can, I know I can,' she told herself, hauling her feet out of bed and into her runners, ready to battle through another day of excruciating pain.

Deborah had spent days blocking out the pain, distracting herself with the audio book by Rhonda Byrne called *The Secret* on her iPod. The positive self-affirming messages in the bestseller inspired her to stay focussed.

Now, as she floated in the pool awaiting the doctor's call, she had begun to dread that her dream, like her $300,000 cheque, might be slowly drifting away.

Stage Zero Cancer

When Deborah was diagnosed with cancer on 15 March 2006, it had felt like a dream of the worst kind – a nightmare. At just 36, her diagnosis had come as a complete shock.

'I've always had lumpy breasts,' she told the GP in her new hometown of Hobart. Deborah rarely went to the doctor and was never sick. She hadn't time, she told herself.

In Melbourne, where she'd fallen in love with Glyn, she'd only been to the doctor a couple of times. Her first attendance was in 1992, when she'd found a lump which a biopsy later proved was a harmless cyst. Since then she'd been back to her doctor on two other occasions, each time after finding lumps during self-examinations. Again, by good fortune, the small hard lumps had turned out to be benign growths.

So when Deborah discovered another tiny lump in her right breast just after her move to Tasmania in January 2006, she was unconcerned. It would probably be just another one of those harmless cysts.

In late 2005, Deborah and Glyn had decided they needed a life change. With the axe falling at the Monash University's Faculty of Art and Design, where Deborah had majored in tapestry weaving and where Glyn, himself a talented painter, had taught for 18 years, they had decided to follow their good friend Alistair Cameron to the nation's smallest state, Tasmania.

'Property's cheaper here than elsewhere in Australia,' said Alistair, 'and you can get a good bargain for a renovation project in Hobart or Launceston.'

Alistair had grown up in Tasmania where his Scottish-born family had been farmers. Now he'd decided to settle in the picturesque town of Launceston where he had been eying up the property market. He was aware his artist friends had already made a tidy sum renovating a number of run-down properties in Melbourne. Alistair also knew from his regular phone calls to Deborah that Glyn's job was likely to go in the next wave of staff cuts.

Just before Christmas 2005, Glyn quit his job and the couple decided to start the New Year by joining Alistair in Tassie, where they'd already bought a new investment project. After spending time together on the road, the couple had been operating on faith and instinct. Now they also decided to join their new friend in a joint taxicab enterprise, awaiting the necessary cab licences which they hoped would arrive by the time Glyn and Deborah made the move to Tasmania in 2006. It was both a tree-change and a sea-change rolled into one, and life was looking up.

With Glyn working out his notice and finalising things at their home in the Melbourne suburb of Altona, Deborah arrived in Tasmania ahead of him, splitting her time between the run-down investment property they'd bought in Launceston and their home in Victoria.

On St Valentine's Day 2006, Deborah found a house to rent in Hobart, in the sleepy suburb of Lindisfarne. Aware of the city's flourishing local art scene and its plans for a new museum, the two struggling artists found Hobart more appealing than Launceston as a home base. Instead, Alistair their friend moved in to the investment property in Launceston where he would help his mates with the renovation.

Amidst the whirlwind of the move and Glyn's impending arrival, Deborah was rushed off her feet. She was a woman with big plans, and breast cancer was certainly not one of them. In early March the discovery of a new lump sent Deborah to the nearest doctor's.

'I think we'd better get an ultrasound of the lump,' said her female GP. 'Best to be sure with these things.' Even with Deborah's history of harmless lumps, and the absence of breast cancer in her family, the doctor thought it prudent to be thorough.

A few days later, Deborah lay on a bed in the private room of the local clinic where the ultrasound technician rubbed gel on her breast and ran the device over the tiny, hard lump. The technician was ominously silent as she studied the image on the screen in front of her.

'It'll just be another cyst,' said Deborah flippantly. The woman said nothing, her eyes trained on the screen.

'That's for your doctor to decide,' she answered, after a long pause.

Only a year before, Deborah had spent 12 months walking around Australia raising funds for Kids Helpline. By the end of the walk, Deborah had broken five world records – including the record for the longest continuous walk by anyone on the planet. She was young, fit, didn't smoke, and lived a very healthy lifestyle. So when she returned to the doctor's surgery a couple of days later in March 2006, for the results of her scan, she was completely unprepared for the news that lay waiting.

'This lump doesn't look quite normal,' said the GP, looking concerned.

Deborah's stomach lurched. Not *quite* normal, she thought. What did that mean?

The doctor compared the ultrasound with Deborah's previous breast scans. 'I think we need to do a biopsy on the lump.'

And so Deborah watched in silence as the doctor inserted a fine needle into the solid mass in her breast, her mind flooding with serious niggling doubts as the small sample of fluid was drawn off and placed into a test tube.

'This will be sent to the pathology laboratories for further testing,' said the doctor as Deborah buttoned her shirt.

The doctor's face gave nothing away when Deborah filed back into the surgery a few days later.

'The aspirate was inconclusive,' she said, non-committal.

That's good, right? thought Deborah. But the more cautious GP wanted to repeat the procedure.

'There are active cells in the sample,' the doctor explained. 'I want to run another test. Just to be sure.'

Confusingly, the new test was also inconclusive. And Deborah felt even more confused when a third test came back negative.

Still unsure, the doctor arranged for her patient to attend the Peter MacCallum Cancer Centre in Melbourne. The Centre is renowned for world-class research into a wide range of cancers, and for treating patients with the disease.

The aspirate was performed again, and this time, Deborah felt anxious.

'You have a ductal carcinoma in situ,' explained the specialist who studied her results. Deborah was stunned, a sick sinking feeling gripping her stomach. It was 15 March 2006 and her world suddenly stood still.

The doctor wanted to see her again to discuss treatment and surgery. 'But I have to be somewhere,' she explained, feeling wobbly. Her record-breaking walk the previous year had earned her such recognition within the community that Alistair had nominated her to be a baton runner for the opening of the Commonwealth Games.

The Queen was due to open the Games in Melbourne that day, and the honour of running through the city's streets carrying the baton had been bestowed on only a handful of Australians who had made significant contributions. Deborah had been thrilled when she'd received the call in January to say she'd been chosen.

Now, unable to comprehend the shattering news she'd just received, or what the diagnosis actually meant, Deborah put the phone down and headed off in deep shock to join the bus which would ferry her and the other proud runners to their positions. The bus would stop at points along the road where runners would pass on the baton to new runners, relay-style, travelling across the city towards the Melbourne Cricket Ground where the main athletic events would be broadcast to world-wide audience.

Deborah found herself sitting silently on the bus, surrounded by proud, smiling people yet feeling totally alone. In her trauma she watched people moving around her, their mouths opening and closing, not hearing anything they said.

It was like being in an awful movie, she thought, where she was watching a woman who resembled her, going through the motions of socialising, chatting and smiling. Participants happily hopped out of their seats to pose in groups for photographs they'd cherish. Amidst all the excitement, Deborah's shock went unnoticed. She found herself robotically leaving her seat and preparing for the next drop-off. She could hear herself talking, though she wasn't really registering what she was saying or to whom. In her shock, she moved unsteadily on her feet, unsure of where she was going or what she was going to do.

Inside she was screaming, 'Today I have been told I have breast cancer.' Even thinking about it felt unreal; like a horrible mistake. As the bus pulled over, and more baton runners hopped off, their faces excited as they prepared for their turn in the historic run, a policeman stared at Deborah's blank face.

'Smile,' he said, as cameras flashed. 'Smile – this is a happy day to remember.' She stared back at him with empty eyes.

It was certainly a day she'd remember, Deborah thought to herself. But happy? If only the well-meaning police officer knew.

'Are you OK?' asked a tall, handsome-looking guy as they stood together on the now-empty bus. The man put his arm on her shoulder. 'You all right there?' he said, now looking concerned.

Around them people chatted, sharing stories about why they'd been chosen to take part. But there was something about this runner's stunned face that said something was seriously amiss. She looked shell shocked. Deborah stared into the man's kindly eyes, a flicker of recognition sweeping over her. He was the popular Melbourne footballer, Jim Stynes. The Irish-born footballer had migrated to Australia, where he'd swapped his talent for Gaelic football to become an Australian Rules player. He was with two Somalian children and had been nominated for his work with his new charity, Reach, set up to help disadvantaged youth.

'Everything OK?' she heard him ask again.

'I've just been diagnosed with breast cancer,' blurted Deborah, choked.

Jim, who was also running with the baton that day, put a comforting arm on her shoulder. 'You'll be fine, to be sure,' he said. 'They do great things these days.'

Deborah nodded, feeling bleak inside. She hadn't even had time to ring her family, yet here she was, sharing this dark secret with a complete stranger. On shaking legs, she ran through the streets of Melbourne holding the treasured baton. It would remain a fog.

She never noticed Glyn and Alistair, her mum and dad, waving to her from the footpath along her route happily snapping photographs. In fact, she noticed nothing about this faceless crowd. It was a day that would disappear into a haze of shock, the cheering faces lost in the blur of a run she'd later struggle to remember. She just put one foot in front of the other, wondering as she ran where her life was now taking her. Deborah knew nothing about breast cancer except that women died of it.

Later, Deborah would look back at photographs Karin snapped that day, depicting her smiling with her baton gripped firmly in her hand. But they were moments lost in a time she couldn't recall. Her mouth smiled but her eyes were empty. This was one run she just wanted to be over.

An hour after completing her run, Deborah sat with Glyn, Karin, Owen and Alistair in Melbourne's Highpoint Shopping Centre sipping coffee.

'I've been diagnosed with breast cancer,' said Deborah, taking a deep breath.

The table fell silent. Deborah continued matter-of-factly, explaining what the doctor had said. The last thing she wanted was pity. That would only have made this surreal experience even more frightening and real. Karin's face paled as she processed the news, and she started to weep softly.

Telling people made it suddenly very real. 'I just want it over,' she said.

Glyn finally broke the silence. 'Bullshit,' he said, refusing to believe a word of it. 'You've just walked around bloody Australia . . . doing 48 kilometres a day, you're fit as a horse . . . take some vitamins, you'll be right.'

Deborah felt wounded by her husband's denial. Still, somewhere in her mind she also felt herself relegating this shattering diagnosis to a deep, dark place where she was carefully blanking it out with her own denial.

'What needs to be done?' asked Alistair, his practical common-sense Scottish attitude kicking in. They listened as Deborah explained how the specialist had mentioned surgery to remove the lump. She hadn't really processed the rest of what he'd said – only that he needed to see her again. 'You can do this,' said Alistair, his voice reassuring her.

This diagnosis wasn't *so* serious, she told herself later. This cancer scare was just a hiccup. She'd get the bloody lump out and beat this thing. In Deborah's mind she was already over it.

'You won't be under long,' said the theatre nurse at Peter MacCallum a few days later. Deborah lay on the bed lost in her thoughts. She just wanted the lump gone.

'Fortunately we've caught it in its very early stages,' advised her breast surgeon. 'Because it was a ducted carcinoma, it was contained so you won't have to lose your breast,' he said. 'It will be a simple lumpectomy and we'll make sure it hasn't spread anywhere else.'

Thankfully, the doctor was correct. In Deborah's mind it was a 'Stage Zero' cancer. And though she would require chemotherapy and radiotherapy to ensure no rogue cancer cells remained, the treatments were more a preventative measure.

On the day Australian marathon runner Kerryn McCann won a Gold Medal in the Commonwealth Games, Deborah De Williams was in the hospital's recovery room – her cancerous tumour gone. In an incredible irony, the talented gold medallist would herself be diagnosed with breast cancer within months, while she was pregnant with her third child.

'This is for you, dear,' smiled two elderly women, appearing beside Deborah's hospital bed next morning. The women told her they were long-term survivors of the disease and handed her a cancer 'show bag'. It contained an empty journal where, they helpfully suggested, she might like to record her cancer journey, and a soft pillow for her to rest her arm on while the tube that had been inserted into her breast during the op drained away excess fluid and blood.

Deborah inwardly groaned. 'Er thanks,' she smiled weakly. She wouldn't be needing either of these things, she thought silently. This bloody cancer journey ended right here! There was no way she could imagine herself wanting to record her darkest hours in some journal of misery let alone wanting to pore over it in years to come. Not only did she never wish to look back on this time in her life, she was already looking forward.

'This cancer support group thing just isn't me,' she told Glyn. She understood the comfort many other women found in sharing their experiences, but she didn't even want to think about breast cancer let alone talk about it. She just wanted to move on.

She'd read the show bag's literature and was well aware that more than half of all new cases of breast cancer diagnosed in Australia were in women between 50 and 69.

At only 36, Deborah was among the 24 per cent of Australian women under the age of 50 to be diagnosed with breast cancer – a disease which remains one of the leading causes of cancer-related deaths in women after lung disease.

But she couldn't imagine how a support group would help a young childless woman in her prime, whose issues would be very different to those facing older patients like mothers with teenagers, or retired grandmothers. She'd have nothing in common with these women *except* for this disease.

So she dumped the contents of her cancer show bag, and on her first day of chemo back in Tasmania had one of her Deborah moments, stopping off at a local newsagent's in Launceston where she bought herself a map of Australia.

In a flash she'd made her mind up she would beat this disease by focussing on something positive in her future. As far as Deborah was concerned she still *had* a future and needed to know something truly amazing lay waiting for her on the road ahead. She decided in that moment that another adventure around the country would be her new positive goal. Buying that map was the first step towards her dream.

In another Deborah moment she'd also decided she was not going to have anyone fussing over her at the hospital. There was no need, she told herself. It wasn't *that* serious and now her Stage Zero cancer was gone, it was just a question of getting through the treatment.

So she sat alone at the hospital, refusing to even look at the intravenous drip pumping toxic chemotherapy drugs into her arm, and spent the half hour of treatment poring over the map of Australia and planning the route for a round-Australia run. She would beat this disease by running it out of her. A round-Australia run would be a great focus because it would provide her with a distraction that would help banish the negative thoughts she'd been keeping at bay since her surgery.

She would turn the worst experience of her life into the best thing that ever happened to her! Cancer would be a turning point in her life's journey, directing her up a new highway where an exciting new challenge now waited.

But while Deborah was feeling suddenly very positive, Glyn was so concerned about her first trip to hospital that he'd driven up from Hobart to Launceston to wait for her.

'What are you doing here?' asked Deborah, surprised to see him.

'It's your first chemo,' he said, worried.

'Oh that's all done,' she said, dismissively, and she went off to look at houses. She simply refused to talk about her treatment and instructed her family to do the same.

'God, you've let yourself go,' commented a friend a few weeks later, unaware that Deborah's sudden weight gain was due to her ongoing treatment. The comment cut her deeply, but she remained silent, not wishing to share the real reason she now appeared so out of shape.

Her oncologist was surprised by the patient's apparent flippancy.

'But Deborah, Stage Zero or no Stage Zero, this lump was a cancerous tumour all the same,' he said. 'True, it was only very early stage cancer, but everything starts somewhere and if we hadn't found it so soon, it would certainly have spread and then you'd have been facing a very different prognosis.'

But Deborah didn't care about what ifs as she studied her map and pictured herself running along open roads, free as a bird in her shorts and sunnies.

Chemo Brain

Deborah was already familiar with the route around Australia thanks to the 12 months she'd spent walking around the country on her previous fundraising walk. Now, with another world record in her sights, she began nutting out her training schedule for a 365-day continuous non-stop run. It would be a world record attempt and Deborah De Williams would be the first woman to achieve this goal in over 20 years. With her new dream taking shape, Deborah also made her mind up she'd run throughout her treatment, so that once this breast cancer thing was behind her, she'd be fit enough to tackle a more intensive training program. By training three times a week she'd hopefully have the stamina for a practice run to prepare for the task ahead.

The morning after her first chemo, Deborah scrawled on the whiteboard of her home office in giant letters: 'Deborah De Williams will be the first female to run continuously around Australia.'

Then she slipped into her runners and headed out for a run, picking up speed and enthusiasm for her project as she pounded the streets of Hobart.

Even when preventative chemotherapy on her breast left Deborah so exhausted that all she wanted to do was sleep, she still managed a quick jog around the block, grateful for the time and space to unwind and think. Deborah was convinced the fresh Tassie air was the best medicine in the world, since it cleared away any remaining dregs of negativity still floating around her 'chemo brain'.

But if chemo left her foggy, Deborah's runs brought her a newfound clarity and it was during one of those runs a few months later that she had another lightbulb moment. 'This run won't be just about me,' she said aloud.

The hyperactive, enthusiastic woman who as a little girl dreamed of being an elite athlete wasn't about to run all the way around Australia just for herself. This new adventure had to mean something more than achieving personal goals, however amazing they might be. Deborah's run would benefit a worthy cause. A year earlier the Kids Helpline charity had benefitted from her record-breaking walk, but this time she wasn't sure which national charity would be the 'wind under her feet'.

In April, as Deborah braced herself for another round of chemotherapy, an unexpected call set her off on a new mission.

'The landlord wants us to do an inspection,' said the agent who had rented her the house in Lindisfarne. Deborah was taken aback.

'But we've only been here a matter of weeks,' she replied, aware that the property in Melbourne they rented out to tenants only warranted an inspection once a year. 'What's the sudden rush about?' she asked, dismayed.

But the agent was persistent.

'Well, does it *have* to be today?' Deborah asked, explaining that she'd been diagnosed with breast cancer and had to leave right now for chemotherapy. 'I haven't even had a chance to clean up,' she said.

There was no time to argue, and the agent insisted that this inspection had to take place today. Later, hooked to her IVF drip, she mulled over the conversation and left hospital feeling very aggravated. Life already felt out of her control, but this latest move felt positively intrusive.

'The landlord can go to hell,' she said to Glyn that night. 'We'll buy somewhere of our own.' The following day they bought a small house in the sleepy Hobart suburb of Midway Point. 'We're terminating our 12-month lease,' she informed the agent, unimpressed.

'You're not really supposed to do things like buy houses or make other life-changing decisions when you're going through a crisis,' said Glyn gently. This was their second move in a matter of months, and though buying a new home tops the list of life stressors after death, serious illness and divorce, Deborah's mind was made up. If the new property was an impulse buy, it was perfect. It had a studio for Glyn, a room that would make a home office, and there was plenty of room for their two spoiled-rotten cats, Pig and Squish.

After grappling with an unexpected diagnosis, and dealing with chemo and radiotherapy, Deborah felt like the rug had been pulled from underneath her. All she wanted now was some certainty restored to her shaken life – and that included being in control of where she lived. She organised a month-long settlement and began to pack. It felt good being back in control again.

Maggie

Deborah first glimpsed her beloved dog Maggie, heavily pregnant and tethered to a tree in a dirty Tasmanian backyard. The neglected state of the young dog, and the deep circular trail her paws had created in the earth around the tree where she was chained, suggested that the two-year-old border collie had spent every day of her life tied up.

But as Deborah approached the dog, crouching down and speaking to her in a gentle, soothing voice, she saw a spark appear in those big sad eyes. Deborah knew in that instant she'd just found her new running buddy and that she'd just given this young animal the glimpse of hope she'd been waiting for. It was October 2005 and it was a case of love at first sight.

At the time, Glyn was still finalising things in Altona, and Deborah wasn't sure that he shared her desire to own a dog, preferring the company of their cats, Squish and Pig, who ruled the roost in Melbourne.

But for Deborah, who had grown up with dogs and had adored her childhood bitzer, Lady, that Owen had bought her, and her beloved German shepherd, Jolline, having a canine companion to join her on her training runs for the distance racing circuit was a must.

'Anyway, having a dog will be compensation for giving up all my mates in Victoria,' she told Alistair, not even bothering to discuss her intentions with Glyn.

Deborah was poring over the local Launceston newspaper when she came across an advertisement that caught her attention.

'What are border collies like?' she asked, handing Alistair the paper to read the ad.

'They're beautiful dogs that love to run,' he responded, mixing them up with Staffordshire terriers or the border collie bitzers he'd owned while growing up on the farm his Scottish father managed near Launceston.

Deborah's interest was piqued and she immediately rang the breeder who was selling the puppies. 'They're not quite ready yet,' he'd informed her, vaguely giving them directions to check out his two expectant bitches who would soon deliver litters of the adorable black and white pups. But it was his last throwaway comment in the conversation that sent shivers down Deborah's spine.

'I'm moving to the mainland so if they don't sell I'm putting 'em down,' he said, callously. Deborah put the phone down horrified; 'I've got to rescue those dogs,' she said to Alistair.

The road out to the breeder's property was a treacherous one, but Deborah was intent on making the journey convinced she was now on a mercy mission. Her suspicion that she was dealing with some unscrupulous backyard dealer was confirmed by the dreadful condition of the two miserable young dogs who stood tethered to two trees in a scruffy backyard.

'Which is your sookiest dog?' asked Deborah, deliberately avoiding the breeder's eyes, and desperately wanting to rescue both dogs and save their puppies.

'That one there,' said the man, gesturing towards Maggie.

Deborah saw the faint glimmer of hope surfacing in the dog's soft brown eyes. 'I'll take her,' she said. Desperate to be rid of his dogs, the man didn't even ask for money.

Maggie had obviously never been in a car before, but she sat in the front passenger seat beside Alistair looking relieved to escape. Deborah, sitting behind, stroked her head and whispered to her in a soothing voice.

'Good girl, Maggie, beautiful girl,' she said gently. Maggie's ears went up and down. 'She's a smart dog,' commented Deborah.

Arriving home, Alistair disappeared into the shed and made a warm bed for Maggie, now inside the house, wagging her tail and enjoying the cuddles of her new owner. Deborah ran a warm bath for the poor dog, who she noticed had cringed at the sight of the hose pipe lying in the garden. 'Bet he put the hose on her instead of bathing her,' she remarked. Privately she wondered if Maggie's owner had done worse with the hose than spray her with water. She'd already observed the dog flinching as she'd sat beside her in the chair and raised her feet.

'Has somebody kicked you, girl?' she wondered, gently lifting Maggie into the warm bath. A very happy, glossy little dog emerged from her bath, enjoying the comfort of the towel and sitting quietly as her new owner dried her fur.

Now, Maggie snuggled down beside the heater on the blanket Deborah had found.

'She's sleeping outside,' said Alistair, whose rural upbringing with working dogs meant a dog's place was definitely outside. Deborah watched Maggie snuggling down on her new bed in the shed. 'She's much cosier here than she was at her old house,' said Alistair. 'She'll be fine.'

But next morning Maggie was wagging her tail from her blanket beside the heater, which within weeks would be her permanent home.

A week or so after Maggie's arrival, she began scratching at the back door. So far she'd been very clean and had always alerted her new owners whenever she needed to go out to do her business. Despite the lack of fences, this beautiful dog had made no attempt to wander off, apparently content with the doting woman who gave her biscuits and milk for her breakfast and spoiled her with delicious kangaroo mince for dinner. And with so many cuddles at her disposal, her life couldn't have been happier.

But on this day, Deborah watched with interest as Maggie wandered off to the pile of cardboard they'd been stacking up in the garden for recycling.

'What's she doing?' asked Deborah, as Alistair watched her sniffing and scratching beneath the cardboard. He had his suspicions.

Next morning, Alistair called Deborah outside. 'Come and see

Running Pink

what Maggie's been doing!' he shouted. Maggie lay proudly under the cardboard, with eight adorable pups snuggled underneath her. 'She's lost one,' observed Alistair, picking up a small cold black and white bundle.

'Good girl, clever girl,' whispered Deborah, inspecting the other pups which snuffled and snorted up to their proud mother, their tiny eyes tightly closed.

Maggie was a beautiful mother, who later removed her pups, one by one, into the warmth of the shed where she proved a loving mum to the growing litter.

'Had enough of them, Maggie?' said Deborah one day, noticing that Maggie was very unimpressed at having to share the attention with eight lively, yapping though very adorable pure-bred puppies. Maggie had only enjoyed a brief few days of being the sole star of the show, and was certainly ready to offload her babies at the soonest possible moment.

'Would you be interested in taking eight gorgeous pure-bred Border collie pups off my hands?' she asked a reputable pet dealer. The man said he would and so Deborah scooped the puppies up, allowing a last goodbye with their now exhausted mum, and drove them to the pet dealer. He later contacted Deborah saying these in-demand puppies had each gone to good homes where they would enjoy the kind of attention she now lavished on their mum.

Princess Maggie was certainly happy to be centre of attention again, thought Deborah, as Maggie wagged her tail and snuggled on her blanket by the heater, lapping up every pat and stroke and gnawing on the delicious treat of a juicy bone.

Not once had there been any need for her to raise her voice to this beautiful well-behaved dog. Maggie responded perfectly to gentle instruction and Deborah figured praise was the best reward in the world for a dog who'd been seriously neglected.

The first time Deborah took Maggie for a walk, the poor confused dog had no idea what was happening. After being tied to a tree for two years, a prisoner, she was understandably anxious when confronted by the great outdoors.

Maggie

'She looked lost and wouldn't walk,' Deborah later told Alistair. 'The whole concept of going for a walk after being a prisoner doesn't sit well with her.'

Maggie had spent the entire walk running around her owner, tripping her over and winding the leash around Deborah's legs. Convinced the frightened dog was likely to trip her up badly, or cause her to break something, Deborah eventually took Maggie off her leash and instead of leading her around the block on a lead, she simply coaxed the dog into following her. Within a week, Maggie had gained enough confidence to trot alongside.

Soon the dog's delight at the sight of Deborah putting on her runners saw Maggie gaining the confidence to lead the way, trotting further and further ahead and casting a careful eye backwards to ensure her owner was following *her*. When Deborah ran, Maggie would run a few feet ahead, though a gentle word would always coax her back whenever Deborah wanted her.

'You're on a linguistic leash, Maggie,' laughed Deborah.

Maggie was also well-behaved around other dogs, though she wasn't too keen to share her newfound attention with them and soon tired of their company.

When Glyn finally arrived in Hobart the following February, Deborah was not a bit surprised that 'Uncle Glyn' fell in love with Maggie too. As a result, his wife's new running buddy quickly became her driving companion too as Deborah drove up and down Tasmania, splitting her time between the renovation project in Launceston and the rental in Lindisfarne where Maggie's arrival made little impact on the lives of two spoiled cats. Two cats were not significant enough, in Maggie's eyes, to warrant any of the attention befitting the real star of the show.

After Deborah's shock diagnosis in March that year, Maggie's delight as her hyperactive owner implemented her new training regime was unmistakeable. She wagged her tail, happy to join Deborah on her regular training runs. But chemotherapy and radiotherapy took its toll on Deborah and there were days during her treatment when she could just manage a jog to the post box and back.

Food didn't taste the same with the metallic taste she had developed since treatment began – even her favourite cups of coffee were now no longer palatable to a nauseated Deborah. There were times after her chemo when she just couldn't sleep. Yet she refused to stay home on the couch. 'If I lie down then I *will* feel sick,' she protested, stubbornly. So Alistair came up with a plan, taking Deborah out after treatment, with a blanket over her, and driving her to various locations around Tasmania for a spot of sightseeing. They called these regular jaunts their 'cancer rides' and just the glimpse of new places distracted Deborah from focussing on feeling sick.

But on the days when she felt well enough, Deborah tried to maintain her three-days-a-week training regime, telling everyone that her running was a tool that helped her to feel normal in a world that at times felt out of control because of her disease.

When the treatment finally ended and the patient's training runs became more intensive, Maggie had become a familiar face around town, trotting obediently alongside Deborah, her ears flapping wildly in the fresh Tasmanian air. Now Deborah could step up her pace, relieved to be well enough to run off the additional kilos she'd piled on as a side effect of the combined medication and radiotherapy on her now fluctuating hormone levels.

Deborah had been her slimmest after completing her walk around Australia two years earlier, when she'd begun entering a number of long-distance running events that had helped her keep her fitness levels up.

But after her diagnosis and subsequent treatment she tipped the scales at a hefty 93 kilos. Now in serious training, she was confident she'd soon shed this weight and pick up speed.

But Deborah was still feeling unwell since her radiotherapy and chemotherapy and had begun suffering the hot flushes, mood swings and exhaustion she recognised as the signs of early menopause brought on by her medication.

Amazingly, during her treatment, Deborah had only spent one day in bed feeling ill. Back then, in May 2006, the treatment specifically designed to kill-off all rogue cancer cells and halt their spread to other organs had by default attacked the healthy cells whose role was to safeguard her body's immune system. With Deborah's weakened immune system compromised from weeks of treatment, the utterly exhausted former live-wire decided one day to take some time out from the renovations to spend the day in bed in Launceston.

She'd been mortified when she emerged to discover that Alistair had left the house because he was unable to handle the outward evidence of an illness Deborah had never acknowledged.

'I'll never stay in bed ever again,' she vowed. 'I just *can't* be sick!'

Follow-up blood tests after Deborah's treatment finished soon revealed that her white T cells — her immune system's 'defence soldiers' — were falling dramatically. This prompted fears amongst her doctors that the cancer might be spreading. Worried, they organised urgent tests to ensure the cancer had not travelled to Deborah's bones. She was greatly relieved when the tests revealed nothing.

Deborah was feeling better when, a few weeks later, she crossed paths again with one of her old ultra-marathon friends, Vlastik Skvaril. The generous spirited Czech-born runner lived in Burnie and had completed a number of charity runs in his life, raising thousands of dollars for many different causes.

'I didn't take up distance running until I was 56!' the former bush walker once told Deborah.

She had first encountered Vlastik in late 2004, a month after returning from her world record walk around the country. Deborah had been invited to join a race where Vlastik, a very well-known face, was also competing. This race was also where she had her first taste of the long distance runner's curse — shin splints.

Now, at 70, the superfit Czech runner was planning a new charity run around Tasmania for Camp Quality, an organisation that supports children with cancer. And he had a proposition for his young friend.

'Why don't you come with me?' he suggested, aware from a private chat with Deborah that she'd just completed treatment for breast cancer and was planning a run of her own around Australia.

'It would be a great practice run,' she responded. 'I'll do it.'

The Bosom Buddies

Deborah's mum looked doubtful when she visited her daughter's home in Tassie and heard her intention to join her old running mate on his charity run around Tasmania.

'It will be a great practice run for my new world record attempt,' she told her parents cheerfully.

'Don't you think it's a bit too soon?' ventured her mum, worried that her daughter was pushing herself a bit hard, but suspecting her mind was already made up. Karin's instinct was right, and since she knew there was no point trying to dissuade Deborah, she had a back-up plan.

'We'll come too,' she said.

This time Deborah would be taking her new four-legged running buddy for her first taste of life on the open road, so Glyn decided he might as well tag along as the support crew.

'I'll help too,' offered Alistair, who had already had his fair share of practice as Deborah's support crew on her world-record-breaking walk in 2004. The crew would rotate on the road, taking it in turns, so Deborah had all the support she needed.

Since the Britz she had used previously had only been on loan for the duration of her 12-month walk and had been returned to the generous Melbourne dealership, Deborah's thoughts turned to accommodation.

'You can borrow my parents' caravan,' suggested Alistair.

Just seven weeks after finishing treatment, in March 2007, Deborah set off with her good friend Vlastik – her parents driving ahead in the Spartan ancient caravan that a very frugal Betty and Angus Cameron were glad they'd kept for the past few decades. Glyn followed in hot pursuit and Maggie took turns trotting beside her owner on the roadside on her verbal leash and hopping into the car where she lounged on the passenger seat beside Uncle Glyn when she'd had enough.

'Go gently,' advised Vlastik, aware of his young running companion's recent treatment. 'Don't push yourself too hard.' When Deborah felt too tired, the thoughtful elderly runner would slow down to a walking pace, speeding up again when she perked up. Vlastik was kind and considerate, observed Deborah. But his traditional European background and his age meant that, in spite of his generosity, his view of the world was very different to Deborah's — especially when it came to his views on the roles of women.

'I used to be in Rotary,' said the benevolent spirit.

'That's a great organisation,' agreed Deborah brightly.

'Yes . . . well it was . . .' he said cagily. 'I left when they started letting women in.'

Deborah gritted her teeth and ran on, making no comment. After her solo walk around Australia, running with a partner took a little getting used to. If Deborah had hoped the run would bring her some thinking time, she was wrong. Vlastik's incessant chatter drove Deborah crazy and she found herself wondering if he'd ever stop talking.

Running through the densely forested hilly terrain up the west coast of Tasmania, she began to wonder if this old runner ever paused for breath. After witnessing him knocking back beers and singing and talking at the same time, she doubted it. But Vlastik's generosity and gentleness greatly outweighed his endless chatter. He was a lovely, charismatic, funny old guy and Deborah couldn't have asked for a more kindly running buddy, even though she thought it would be helpful if he occasionally engaged his brain before he opened his mouth.

Generous donations poured into Vlastik's fundraiser as they ran from town to town.

But Deborah had still not decided which worthy cause she would choose to support when she began her own charity run around Australia on her new world record attempt. Privately, she doubted the cause would be related to breast cancer because then she'd be forced to talk about her own experience, and she wasn't yet ready for that. She couldn't imagine anything worse than reliving her cancer journey with people up and down the country. Deborah was running as fast as she could to leave that unfortunate chapter in her life behind. 'This disease will never come back,' she told herself. 'I am running it out of me!'

But during her practice run, she and Vlastik encountered a group of women on the side of the road who soon helped Deborah change her mind.

'What are you doing here?' asked a larger-than-life woman as they jogged from Burnie towards the northern Tasmanian town of Smithton and through the tiny township of Stanley. The gregarious older woman had approached them near the old cemetery on the side of the road where her group of friends observed the unlikely running buddies.

'Hi, I'm Judy King,' said the no-nonsense woman, introducing herself. Deborah smiled.

'I'm Deborah De Williams and this is my friend Vlastik. We are running around Tasmania to raise money for Camp Quality,' she explained. 'What about you?'

The group gathered around, explaining they were all friends who shared a common experience and a worthy cause of their own.

'We've all survived breast cancer,' revealed Judy, pointing to the gathering of 22 women. Deborah surveyed the group, some of them still sporting the classic tell-tale regrowth of chemo hair. What this lively grandmother lacked in height she made up for in energy as she chatted on. 'We're called the Bosom Buddies and we're on a practice jaunt too,' she said, introducing her friends. 'We're planning to walk across Tasmania to raise money for breast cancer research.'

Reluctantly, Deborah explained that this was a great cause and one she completely understood because she'd only seven weeks earlier finished treatment for breast cancer. The women's ears pricked up.

'I'm on a practice run for a bigger adventure,' she explained. 'I've already walked all around Australia, but now I intend to become the first woman to run around Australia. I walked last time for Kids Helpline, but I haven't decided yet who I'm going to run for this time around.' The women looked amazed.

'What do you mean? Do it for breast cancer research, of course,' they chorused, greeting her adventure with great enthusiasm.

Deborah shook her head. She'd spent her entire treatment trying not to even think about breast cancer, how could she manage a fundraiser without being able to talk about it?

'I'd have to talk about it though,' she said softly. 'I don't know if I'm ready to do that.' But the women were persistent.

'Of course you can,' said Judy, explaining that she was now in remission from the disease. 'Your story is really important because you can tell women that finding something positive to focus on helped you survive . . . trust me . . . women like us need to hear that.'

Deborah studied the women's enthusiastic faces. Their passion was infectious.

'There's so much negativity surrounding this illness,' added another of the pink-clad walkers, stepping forward. 'It's great to hear something positive and inspirational, which you are.'

Judy agreed. 'Go on your run and give people hope – it would mean so much to us if you did.'

And so the deal was done. Deborah returned home having helped Vlastik to raise $10,000, as well as completing 1250 kilometres – with Vlastik talking non-stop for their entire 23 days on the road – and with her new cause.

'I reckon if I train really hard I should be ready to tackle this new world record in October 2008,' she said. During her run the side effects of the Tamoxifen had lingered in her system, and Deborah had been plagued with what felt like period pains and irrational moods that left her wanting to snap. Perhaps it hadn't been

Vlastik's endless chatter at all, she thought. But if she was going to throw herself into rigorous training she needed to be in tiptop condition.

'I'm going to check myself into a health retreat,' she said, Googling a health retreat called Living Valley Springs run by the Seventh Day Adventist Church in the picturesque Queensland hinterland. The resort was in the tiny secluded town of Kin Kin in the beautiful Noosa hinterland. 'It offers a month-long detoxification program,' Deborah told Glyn. 'They offer to cleanse your body and your soul.' It all sounded very appealing to Deborah.

In July 2007, Deborah checked herself into the exclusive resort, though her introduction to the four-week detox program saw her consuming gallons of her most hated food. 'Oh no . . . not celery,' she groaned, as one of the therapists handed her a glass filled with the green, antioxidant-rich drink. Of all the things Deborah detested, she hated celery the most. But for the next three days she drank nothing but celery, which the therapist explained was a great auto-immune booster and a natural healthy cleanser.

'It gets rid of everything,' another guest told her, as they checked out the meditation classes, relaxation therapy and feasted on a diet of fresh fruit, vegetables and healthy vitamins.

Deborah spent hours relaxing in her favourite fever bath, which acts by bringing your core body temperature up so you sweat and rid your system of toxins. And there were endless massages and hours of meditation – even colonic irrigation for those who wanted to clean their systems right out. Before every treatment the therapist would ask: 'Can we pray for you?' And after a year walking around the country when her prayers at her lowest moments had yielded miracles and angels, Deborah had no problems with everyone and anyone praying for her.

She whiled away the hours on beautiful long walks around the property, enjoying the tranquil environment.

'I come here every year,' said another visitor, introducing himself. As a musician and nightly consumer of alcohol at his regular gigs, the man had become accustomed to escaping his working life at this peaceful health retreat where he used the month away from the world to dry out.

A month later an invigorated Deborah checked out of the health retreat feeling like a new woman. Re-energised, she accepted an invitation in August to take part in a 48-hour run on Queensland's Gold Coast. She won the race by default because she was the only female to finish.

Back home in Hobart, Deborah began the 12-month countdown to her new adventure feeling fitter and healthier than she'd done since her treatment, and she upped her training program from three days a week to five days intense training, much to Maggie's delight.

When she had told Glyn that she intended to circumnavigate the country on foot for a second time he hadn't batted an eyelid. 'Are you coming?' Glyn paused and looked up from the abstract painting he was working on. 'I suppose so,' he said.

Glyn understood Deborah's experience with breast cancer had been a wake-up call. Now as she threw herself into project mode, it was clear she was going to use that experience to make a difference to other women's lives.

'With enough money, perhaps one day breast cancer will be just another treatable, pain-in-the-bum illness,' she continued. She liked to picture a future where women being diagnosed with the disease would face treatment knowing this was no longer a possible death sentence.

Deborah knew first-hand the trauma that a diagnosis of breast cancer could create in the life of a healthy young woman. Like others diagnosed with the disease, she'd found herself confronting her own fragile mortality. Her diagnosis had also brought a new awareness and vulnerability.

'But I'm one of the lucky ones,' she constantly reminded herself. She hadn't lost her breast and her cancer had been detected in time to avoid the need for the prolonged aggressive chemotherapy that many other patients were subjected to. It was a treatment that left women bald, sick, missing breasts and in many ways robbed of their former identities.

Fortunately, Deborah's diagnosis at such an early stage meant her radiotherapy was less aggressive and over more quickly than it was for many of her peers. Her chemotherapy had been a preventative measure only, and she'd even managed to keep her long dark hair.

Deborah spread the map out on the table. 'I reckon I could run 18,250-odd kilometres in a year if I run non-stop every day,' she estimated.

'Guess I'll be the support crew then,' said Glyn. That's what she most loved about Glyn; he never told her *not* to do anything.

The next morning Deborah rang her accountant, Evan Lowenstein.

'How do I go about setting up my own charity?' she asked, explaining her plans.

'I'll do it for you,' offered Evan. 'And since it's a good cause I'll do it for free.'

Deborah chose the name Running Pink because it sounded catchy and immediately informed people what she was about. The money her charity raised would go towards breast cancer research.

After Evan's first act of kindness, Deborah was even more convinced that the true blue Aussie spirit of a fair go would be waiting on the road ahead of her.

In October 2008 Deborah and Glyn rented their home out for a year and, leaving the taxicab business in Alistair's capable hands, the Running Pink Crew braced themselves for Deborah's attempt to become the first woman to run continuously around Australia.

'Go for it,' said Judy King, who rang to say that the Bosom Buddies who had inspired Deborah's cause had just raised an astonishing $137,000 for breast cancer research. They had walked from Smithton to Hobart down the middle of Tasmania in just 11 days, raising this amount from their tiny community.

'Remember, you are doing this for women like us,' said Judy. And so Deborah sat down and wrote out a cheque for $300,000 from Running Pink which she'd hand over in a year from now for vital research into finding a cure for breast cancer.

'Come on Maggie,' she said. She had a whole year ahead of her and her biggest challenge yet.

One Journey Ends

Now, seven and a half months after setting out from Hobart, slipping into the pool on a Darwin caravan site waiting for the sports specialist's call, Deborah was secretly worrying that this might be the end of the road.

Today was Day 224 of her adventure and despite her injured feet, she'd succeeded in running 10,825 kilometres to reach her halfway destination. Even between scans and hospital appointments, she'd managed to keep her record-breaking attempt alive. And she'd raised $100,000 for breast cancer research.

Surely this *can't* be the end of the journey, she told herself, as her ringing mobile interrupted her thoughts.

Glyn, Karin and Owen fell silent as Deborah listened intently to the doctor on the other end of the line. Her face began to crumple, and tears began to fall. This truly was bad news.

'I'm sorry Deborah,' said Dr Thompson. 'You just can't run any more.' Deborah stood in the pool, water lapping around her chest, silent. The doctor continued, and Deborah's stomach lurched with every unwelcome word.

Dr Thompson had spent the afternoon chatting with some surgeon friends in Melbourne, and they had told him to warn his patient that if she ignored their advice, she risked completely destroying her navicular bones.

'If you destroy your naviculars you may never run again,' he warned.

But amidst the misery, there was a glimmer of hope as the doctor began to detail the surgery she would need to undergo back in Melbourne.

'When can I do it again?' she interrupted. 'When will I be ready for my second attempt at this run?'

The doctor wasn't sure. 'The prognosis after this surgery is very good,' he said, his voice sounding encouraging. With intensive physiotherapy, she could be back on the road again in perhaps a year. But after running halfway around the country every single day for months, a whole year felt like a lifetime. Deborah wiped away the salty tears of bitter disappointment streaming down her face.

'Come and see me in the morning,' he urged.

'OK,' she said, in a quivering voice.

'At least there's hope,' she told Glyn and her parents, hobbling out of the pool. The specialist knew just how much this run meant to his patient. He had taken care to ensure her hopes were not shattered even if her feet were. She climbed out of the pool, clinging to the lifeline he'd thrown her. With a heavy heart, Deborah willed herself to remain positive, focussing on what she had achieved so far and what she might achieve again in the future.

She and Maggie had just become the first female runner and her dog to run from Hobart to Darwin via the east coast of Australia. It was hardly the world record Deborah had dreamed of, but quite incredible for a crazy pink woman who had captured the imagination of an entire nation and who had run the last 862 kilometres on two broken feet! The adventure was far from over.

That night, Maggie's ghost writer penned a final posting in her dog blog:

> So even though this journey ends today, a new one will begin in the not too distant future . . . and I say to you all, keep watching and reading this space, as I will keep you all posted on D's recovery and journey back to the road.

Chasing Hope

When Deborah was first diagnosed with breast cancer, a sinking feeling gripped her unlike anything she'd ever experienced before. The ache was a physical pain, which dragged her heart down towards her toes, wrenching her soul as it descended. The world as she'd known it was slipping away beneath her, and Deborah felt as if she were being swallowed up by her own worst fears.

She felt a similar sensation in Darwin as she'd paddled in the cool water of the caravan park's pool, surrounded by people but feeling utterly alone. Life had sneaked up on her from left field, bringing uncertainty and worry into a world where plans and dreams were now on hold.

Just hours after Dr Thompson's phone call, Deborah somehow managed to set her own bitter tears aside, aware that this was Owen's 61st birthday. In the same blur that had overshadowed her Commonwealth baton run in 2006, Deborah found herself sitting in a Darwin restaurant, chatting and trying her hardest to smile while joining in a chorus of 'happy birthday' with Karin and Glyn.

Back in Dr Thompson's rooms the following morning, the sinking dread started to subside. She listened carefully to the specialist's instructions as he detailed the prominent surgeon he'd spoken to in Melbourne.

'He will see you in four weeks' time and assess you for the operation that will put you back on your feet,' said Dr Thompson. 'You can be fixed up so you can do it again,' he added, his positive expression coaxing her out of her gloom.

As she left the clinic, Deborah determined she would approach this in the same way she'd approached her cancer diagnosis more than two years earlier. She'd do whatever she needed to do to get through it, and she'd focus her thoughts on the road ahead.

'You're sure I'll be able to do this run again?' she asked one last time.

'Yes,' said Dr Thompson, looking her squarely in the eye.

And so Deborah returned to the campsite clinging to this ray of hope. She always believed that no matter how tough things became, and no matter what challenges life threw at you, if you had faith and hope, you would survive. Even if that hope was only as big as a grain of rice, she could look past the negatives and believe she could triumph.

The morning after her appointment with the specialist, Deborah climbed out of bed and ate her breakfast in silence. With no more early starts, and after expending so much energy on the last leg of her run, she'd exhausted her mental and physical reserves. After breakfast, she crawled back into bed where she slept soundly for hours.

'We'll drive down to Berry Springs,' said Glyn, packing up the next day. There was no point staying on. Aside from the cost, the owners of the Darwin caravan park hadn't treated the star of the show, Maggie, very nicely at all. The next place, he vowed, really would have to be more dog friendly.

The owners of the new caravan site at Berry Springs were astonished to see the strange convoy parked outside their office. They were lovely people, and when they heard about Deborah's abandoned run and how she'd run more than 800 kilometres on two broken feet, they bent over backwards to help her.

'No, we really don't want payment – this is on us,' they insisted, waiving all site costs. 'Stay as long as you like.'

And so this wonderful act of generosity saw the Running Pink crew kicking back for a few days. After bunny hopping more than 10,000 kilometres, they spent five days straight lazing around the caravan park while Deborah floated in the pool reflecting and planning.

'I reckon I could be back on the road in January,' said Deborah, looking ahead. 'Geoff Thompson reckons six months should be long enough.' Deborah was now latching onto that hope like a life raft.

Incredibly, now Deborah was no longer pushing her body onwards, the pain really kicked in. And when it did, it was excruciating.

'Now you've stopped focussing on your goal, your body is telling you how much damage you've done,' said Karin wisely.

Loaded on painkillers, Deborah slipped back into the pool, determined not to lose muscle tone. She needed to maintain her fitness for the new adventure next year, and since Dr Thompson had said it was OK for her to swim, she could at least keep her upper body in tiptop shape.

'Just don't go kicking off the side of the pool with those feet,' he warned.

The pink convoy hit the road again, this time heading south towards Katherine, where Glyn had found the soda crystals in the laundry section of the supermarket. It might have been a good water softener, but it was never going to cure two badly broken feet, Deborah thought wryly.

This morning, instead of picturing herself heading west from Katherine towards the Kimberleys for the second leg of her run towards Western Australia, Deborah found herself looking in an entirely different direction. There was no point looking backwards, she reasoned, so instead, she would try to keep her eyes firmly on the future – beyond her surgery and convalescence to a new run on the road.

With no vacant appointments in the Melbourne surgeon's busy schedule until at least the end of June, Deborah had lots of time now to think. She was no longer a woman in a hurry – something that would take some adjusting to.

'We might as well take our time,' she said, announcing her desire to visit Katherine Gorge and hopefully Ayers Rock, the sacred place the Aboriginals call Uluru, which stands imposingly in the red landscape. But for Deborah there'd be no trudging up the rock on these injured feet.

She certainly wasn't going to risk further damage to her feet before her surgery now this new dream was taking shape in her head. After much discussion, the Running Pink support team agreed they'd enjoy the spectacular scenery of the Northern Territory and take the long road home at a leisurely pace.

But glimpsing some of the tiny Northern Territory towns she'd only recently run through, it all looked surreal and very different from her new vantage point in the passenger seat of the 4WD.

'I can't believe that only a week ago I was actually running through this place,' she said, as another town disappeared in the dust behind them.

She'd shuffled through so many of these towns feeling emotionally and physically numb, seeing them again made her feel such a failure.

'I've let so many people down,' she said, turning to Glyn. The first sympathetic phone calls she received from the supporters in her breast cancer network had been excruciatingly painful.

'I'm so sorry, Deborah,' sympathised Sue Murray from the National Breast Cancer Foundation when she heard about the aborted run. But it was Deborah who couldn't stop apologising as she telephoned her friend Janelle Larkin, who worked for the breast cancer support network back in Hobart.

'I'm sorry,' she'd said, feeling hopeless. So many people had followed her adventure and supported her, it was hard not to feel like a very public failure. But like Sue, Janelle wouldn't hear a word of it.

'Don't be so silly,' she soothed. 'Just look after yourself.'

'I will,' she promised, the events of the past seven and a half months replaying in her mind.

It had been a cool spring day when she'd set off on her world record attempt, and Deborah had been suffering a bad case of the flu. She'd set off loaded on hot lemon and honey drinks which she hoped would shake her cold off, leaving Hobart's Parliament House Gardens where representatives of the Breast Cancer Network congregated, together with the Kingston Rotary Club, Breast Screen Tasmania, the National Breast Cancer Foundation and Tasmania's Dragons Abreast paddlers.

Her friend Keona, from Anaconda, the outdoor adventure specialists, ran the first 15 kilometres with her, the first leg ending with the team camping on the roadside before dark.

Unfortunately, the hot honey and lemon drinks did little to relieve Deborah's flu symptoms, leaving her family fearing that if she pushed herself too hard too soon, she'd only get worse. Amongst the rules of the run was that after marking her finishing spot for the day, the runner was permitted to ride in a car to travel to evening engagements. But she must return to the exact spot to pick up the run the following morning. The marking of the spot would be achieved through a GPS system in the car, which would be paired with the GPS Deborah wore on her arm.

Because of her worsening flu, she'd been forced to reduce the number of kilometres she ran for the first few days. Deborah felt so sick that even she, who never succumbed to sickness, would have liked to stay in bed. But since she had to stick to the rules, and that meant running every day, she struggled on. She tried not to worry, knowing she had a whole year to gain the kilometres back again.

The third day of the run was Pink Ribbon Day, the national day to remember women lost to breast cancer, those lucky enough to have survived, and the patients still fighting the disease. There were many tears that day as women stopped Deborah to share their own breast cancer journeys.

That same day, Deborah's running buddy Vlastik completed his own trek across Australia raising thousands of dollars for CanTeen, the cancer support organisation which helps young Australians with the disease. Vlastik had told Deborah all about this fundraising trek during his non-stop chatter on their practice run around Tasmania the previous year.

By the end of the first week of running, Deborah's flu symptoms had left her battling a severe chesty cough, aggravated by the mountainous terrain of the Tasmanian wilderness. She'd barely shaken it off when the Running Pink convoy boarded the ferry at Devonport for the eight-hour crossing to mainland Australia.

Because Deborah was required to log every step of her journey, including every stop and start point, she ran onto the ferry in Devonport where the ship's captain signed his name in the witness book as evidence of the location where the runner had joined his ship. He detailed the nautical miles to the destination where Deborah would switch her GPS back on and the run would begin again.

Deborah had to wait until all other passengers had disembarked, before turning on the GPS and running off the boat. She was filmed jogging down the gangplank at Port Melbourne by a Channel Nine TV crew who had been patiently awaiting her arrival. The image of the pink runner, on a mission to become the first woman in the world to run continuously around Australia, was later viewed by thousands on the evening news.

Along the road Deborah and her Running Pink crew encountered a beautiful family from the Great Lakes in New South Wales who had travelled down the coast to Victoria. Over drinks and a meal at a coastal campsite, they related a story that would haunt Deborah for weeks to come.

'We have a young family friend who was diagnosed with breast cancer following a needle biopsy,' they revealed, eager to spend some time with the pink convoy and the woman who was running for people like their friend.

The middle-aged couple explained how their young friend's doctor had, without further medical investigations or scans, told his young patient that her cancer had most likely already spread into her lungs and brain and warned her she did not have long to live.

But following a double mastectomy – yet with no radiotherapy or chemotherapy – a subsequent test revealed no sign of any secondary cancer. And with the support of her loving family, the patient, who had believed she was dying, suddenly realised she now had a very real chance of recovering and living a full healthy life.

Deborah was horrified by the sobering story. What gnawed at her most was that this patient's doctor had, in one sweeping statement and without fully investigating her situation, robbed the young woman of any hope. He was like so many doctors she'd already heard about from people on her run who flatly gave patients terrible news or focussed only on negative statistics. Some doctors, she thought, could steal hope away as easily as they wrote a prescription.

Deborah always wondered how anyone could ever be arrogant enough to think they could confidently say how much time another person had left to live. As far as she was concerned, hope – like faith, love and a good attitude – was vital in the fight for survival. Every time she thought of this story she couldn't help remembering the loving wife she'd met on her walk in 2004 who'd been told to put her husband in a nursing home because he'd never speak or walk again. Instead she'd given him his dream of owning a cattle station where he'd defied the doctors to live an even more fulfilling life. To Deborah they were living proof of the power of hope.

Christmas Eve 2008 was Day 61 of Deborah's run, and she'd shuffled more than 44.7 kilometres into the pretty Victorian coastal town of Mallacoota with what she now knew had been shin fractures, straight into a cheering group of pink supporters and an official police escort.

The group had been waiting excitedly to join Deborah on the last leg of her run before she crossed the border into New South Wales. Some were on foot, others waited on bikes ready to join the sole pink lady moving towards them with her black and white dog.

As they surrounded her and ran or cycled alongside, Deborah noticed a woman beside the road, fighting back tears. She wore a headscarf, alerting Deborah immediately to the fact that she was enduring chemotherapy, and she appeared so touched by the sight of the procession that Deborah ran towards her and held her tightly in her arms. The woman shared her story about her battle with breast cancer, and Deborah hugged her again.

'Be brave and have hope,' Deborah told her. Through her tears, the woman thanked her.

'Thank you so much for making a difference,' she said, and Deborah fought tears of her own as she continued on towards the town where the local community health organisation had put on a sausage sizzle at the Men's Shed for their guest.

While the star of the show willingly succumbed to the pats and praise of her new fans and graciously obliged them by gobbling a few welcome sausages, Deborah headed out along the hilly, curvy road towards the highway and on to the town of Genoa. Her Christmas gift to herself that afternoon would be to mark the road at Genoa with a line of pink – tomorrow's starting point.

But for now she joined Glyn in the 4WD on the return journey back to Mallacoota for a Christmas Eve shower and hard-earned rest. As is the European custom, Karin celebrated Christmas on 24 December, and did so with traditional German fare, putting on a special effort to arrange a spread of Abendbrot, a selection of salamis, cheese and salads and wurst, a type of ham. With a big day ahead of them they exchanged Christmas gifts beside their small blow-up Christmas tree early in the evening.

While the rest of Australia was watching Carols by Candlelight and putting gifts under their Christmas trees, Deborah crawled into bed, knowing she'd be up long before Santa had finished filling the stockings of children around the globe.

Very early on Christmas morning, Deborah slipped into her running shoes and headed back to her road marker to begin her daily run. With Deborah on the road all day completing her 47.2 kilometres run, the Running Pink support crew postponed their Christmas lunch plans until dinner time. The decision to delay dinner was just as well given the trouble they'd had finding a dog friendly caravan site that would accept Maggie.

'I've tried three campsites already,' said Glyn, when Deborah finally joined them late on Christmas Day. In the past few weeks, even those sites with a strict 'no dogs' policy, had weakened when they heard about the reason behind Deborah's run, many of them waiving the campsite fees as their own contribution to her worthy cause. But not even the sight of beautiful Maggie on this most significant day in the Christian calendar had been enough to persuade anyone in Eden to let the pink convoy or their Director of Greetings in.

'Sorry Maggie,' said Deborah, patting her dog. 'There's just no room at the inn.' It seemed ironic that on this important day of giving and kindness not a single campsite in Eden had enough Christmas spirit to let the nomads in. It was getting late when Glyn had a better idea.

'Bugger it,' he said, pitching the caravan on the grass area right outside one of the caravan parks on the side of the road. And so Deborah and her crew enjoyed their Christmas dinners right under the Scrooge campsite owners' nose.

'Bah Humbug to them, Maggie,' she laughed.

Even in her small caravan oven, Karin managed to put on a traditional European spread consisting of roast duck and roast veggies with all the trimmings, all topped off with a brandy pudding which the hungry family crowded around the caravan table to gratefully devour.

'This is one gift I could have done without,' complained Deborah, rubbing her painful right leg that night. Santa had not so thoughtfully brought Deborah a gnawing pain which would dog her for the next 3000 kilometres. 'Thanks for the shin splint, Santa,' she grumbled, climbing into bed. Still, Christmas was a time for counting blessings, she mused, telling herself it could have been worse. She could have had shin splints in both her legs.

The pain was worse by Boxing Day but she had a record to consider, and so she spent it on the road again, running 53 kilometres, unaware that she actually did have injuries to both legs — and they were not shin splints at all, but fractures.

'Deborah is working and hobbling through the pain and trying to keep up with her kilometres,' blogged Maggie that night. 'She is keeping her spirits up and saying that the shin splints usually last about a week. I am praying for an early recovery.'

Ironic, thought Deborah. The pain was far more persistent than she'd ever imagined. It would be another 7000 kilometres before she discovered the true cause of her pain – and by then her run would be over.

The last day of 2008 ended on New Year's Eve with the biggest run so far. In a single day Deborah covered nearly 70 kilometres in mountainous terrain over gravel roads towards the Snowy Mountains and the tiny town of Cooma. On this final day of the old year, Deborah passed her 3000 kilometres mark, climbing into bed very early that night and sleeping her way into 2009 dreaming of a new world record.

The first day of 2009 began at four a.m. for Deborah and her crew as they welcomed the new year watching a spectacular sunrise over the peaks of the Snowy Mountains, the pink light washing warmly over their faces. Deborah began her morning jog thinking of all the people she loved, imbued with a new gratitude. Maggie wrote that night:

> Dawn is such a special time. If you listen the earth whispers its secrets to you. I love to watch the start of a new day with all its hopes and promises and today D and I ran along together in silence, contemplating our own thoughts about the coming of the new year and the blessings of the old one.
>
> We can also say that last year we raised over $50,000 for the NBCF but this year we intend to raise over $250,000 for the charity.

Deborah clung to her positive affirmations for the rest of the day as she ran into 30-kilometre-per-hour winds which lasted for a whole nine hours. There were periods when it was a battle to simply stay upright, the winds were so powerful. But by nightfall, she finally limped into Cooma, windswept and dirty, to be greeted by the town's Mayor and his wife, who donated money to the worthy cause. Deborah ended the first day of her New Year sitting with her right leg in a bucket of freezing ice and bracing herself for an extra-hot shower that might help rid her of this supposed shin splint.

Over the coming days Deborah tried everything to combat her painful legs, including an old comfrey poultice – a remedy dating back to the Middle Ages consisting of different herbs and oils which have been used for centuries to treat inflammation and circulation problems. Santa's unwelcome gift left Deborah with post-Christmas blues, her legs aggravated by the mountainous terrain that would take her into Canberra.

On Saturday 3 January at 8.30 a.m., Deborah crossed the border into the Australian Capital Territory. Maggie posed happily with her mum outside Parliament House in Canberra – the proudest Aussie dog on the planet. Deborah was thrilled to be personally welcomed into the city by ultra-marathon friend Neil and his daughter, Jemma, who had been following her itinerary on Facebook. And there was just time for a quick catch up with another ultra-marathoner, Phil Essam, who somehow tracked the pink convoy down especially to cheer them out of Canberra.

Twelve hours later, Deborah and Maggie crossed the border back into New South Wales, where Glyn and Owen had set up camp for the evening.

'How many dogs can say they've covered a state in just one day?' she said, patting Maggie.

But by now the pain in Deborah's right leg was slowing her down and she was achieving her daily minimum using a combination of three minutes running and two minutes walking. As the pain escalated she found herself having to rest every six kilometres, elevating her sore legs or plunging them into buckets of ice for up to 15 minutes at a time.

Deborah managed to hobble into the tiny town of Yass to be greeted by a sole local called Lyn, who had waited especially to escort

Deborah and Maggie, jogging slowly beside them along the road until they caught up with the pink convoy which had driven ahead.

'Adam is going to be at McDonald's on the Hume Highway at 9.30 p.m.,' revealed Karin, excited at the prospect of seeing her son, a long-distance truck driver, for the first time in 2009. It always amused Deborah to think that both she and her big brother had inherited a wanderlust that saw each of them on the road in solitary pursuit of some of the peace that had eluded them in childhood. But while her journeys were on foot, Adam was surveying the landscape from the seat of a double B truck. In spite of her pain and exhaustion, Deborah was thrilled to discover her brother was in the area, and it spurred her on over the next four kilometres to the nearest Maccas where she knew he'd be waiting.

Adam smiled broadly as he watched the strange pink convoy converge on the car park, and Karin couldn't have been happier to see her son for the first time in this new year.

'I'm going to make potato salad,' she told Deborah, springing to her feet to chop up spuds in her cramped caravan kitchen. 'It's his favourite.' After months on the road indulging her daughter's crazy dream, it was the least she could do for her boy.

After lots of chatting and catching up on family gossip, the pink convoy set up camp for the night in the car park, parking the vans beside the rows of giant trucks which do the long-haul runs up and down Australia's major highways. Deborah closed her eyes, feeling she was sleeping in one of those dinky toys that Adam had liked so much as a boy.

The tiny community of Boorowa, between Yass and Cowra, welcomed the Running Pink team with open arms, raising $2000 which they donated at a town reception where a group of barber shop singers from Sydney called the Silver Foxes serenaded the pink runner. It was the highlight of the New Year so far and Deborah was feeling more positive in spite of her pain.

Deborah ran into the industrial city of Wollongong, south of Sydney, where the Illawarra Dragons Abreast team turned out in force to welcome her. These dragons were all breast cancer survivors who now banded together to paddle dragon boats in various competitions. When they took to the waters of Sydney's Darling Harbour during the Chinese New Year celebrations, they always raised a resounding cheer from the crowd.

Now it was the paddlers who turned out to support this pink crusader, lending their voices to a cause they understood first-hand.

'I beat breast cancer 35 years ago,' one of the older members told Deborah.

'That's amazing,' she said, in awe. 'That's practically the whole of my lifetime.'

She left the group inspired by this incredible long-term survivor's story which, she had no doubt, filled many of her peers with great hope for their own futures. Treatment had certainly come a long way in the decades since this woman was diagnosed.

Deborah's original send-off in Tasmania had attracted its own dragon boaters and it appeared to Deborah that the dragon boat network was working overtime, informing their fellow battlers across the country to welcome this Tassie runner and give her encouragement as she ran through their towns for women like them.

A Black Day

A sweltering sunny Saturday greeted Deborah on 7 February when a much-needed boost of inspiration from her meeting with the dragon boaters, and her reunion with Adam, had given her a new burst of energy. Despite the intense heat that day, and the ongoing pain of battling shin splints, Deborah's renewed zeal for her cause left her on target to achieve her 60 kilometre goal for the day. But while Deborah ran in sweltering temperatures through Coffs Harbour to Corindi, a tragedy was unfolding near Adam's home in Victoria that would go down in Australian history. That morning Victorians had climbed out of bed to sweltering temperatures. With the mercury predicted to hit a sizzling record of 47 degrees, the Country Fire Authority's volunteers were already on high alert, manning the tiny fire stations which by afternoon would be battling bush fires of epic proportions.

By lunchtime, a number of spot fires had broken out around the state and, fanned by northerly 100-kilometre-per-hour winds, a number of fire walls were soon building across Victoria.

In the densely forested areas north-east of Melbourne, the hot winds sent those fire fronts racing from Kilmore in Central Victoria towards the heavily forested mountainous townships of Kinglake and Pheasant Creek, and towards the pretty tourist town of Marysville. The tiny township of Kinglake sits on the edge of the Kinglake National Park, a short drive from Healesville where Karin and Owen had sold the family home the previous year in preparation for the leisurely retirement trip they'd put on hold to become the Running Pink support crew.

When Deborah caught up with her convoy for snacks and a cool drink, her mother's worried face told her something was badly wrong.

'Listen to this,' said Karin, turning up the ABC radio news, where updates on the fires revealed a dire situation. Panicking, Karin's immediate thoughts were for Adam, his wife and their four children living in the heavily forested region of Woori Yallock close to the fires now speeding down the state from Marysville towards Narbethong and Healesville.

'We're OK for now,' Adam had said, explaining that more fires had broken out in the La Trobe Valley. 'But it's looking pretty serious.'

Karin was panic-stricken. 'Just pack up and get the kids out of there,' she advised. But her son was as stubborn as his sister.

'No way,' he said. 'We're going to stay and fight.'

Owen called their former neighbours and some of their friends. 'They're on high fire alert in Don Valley too,' he said, clearly anxious.

By late afternoon, the situation in Victoria was escalating and more hurried phone calls between the convoy and home revealed the severity of an intense fire storm, which only a matter of hours earlier had torn across Victoria, razing Marysville, Narbethong and the Toolangi State Forest to thick, smouldering ash. Firefighters from all over Victoria were now battling a fire wall that was threatening the small logging town of Healesville, where Karin and Owen's former home would soon burn to the ground. And while the new owners would be safe, casualties in the devastated region would continue to mount overnight as the true extent of the worst fires in Australian history were revealed.

By now Owen and Karin had lost phone contact with Adam and his family, and were very worried. 'The phone lines are probably out,' said Owen, trying to calm his wife. But they remained glued to the radio for more news and it was a sleepless night for everyone.

The morning brought good news and shattering news.

'We're fine,' said Adam, ringing his mum. 'We're among the lucky ones.' Adam confirmed what the media were already reporting

A Black Day

around the country that Sunday morning: more than 4000 individual fires had burned in Victoria that terrible day, where the biggest bush fires ever seen had caused the highest number of fatalities Australians had ever known. In Kinglake alone, the fire wall that ripped over the ridge and down the face of the mountain towards the vineyards of the Yarra Valley where grapes now clung black and shrivelled to the vines, accounted for 120 of the 173 deaths recorded.

The cool change that hit Victoria in the early evening, far from bringing relief, brought with it gale force winds of up to 120 kilometres which suddenly changed direction. These powerful winds whipped up the flames of the out of control fires, which travelled at such incredible speeds and with such ferocity that many of the tiny townships that had earlier escaped now found themselves engulfed in the fire storm.

The fires that had raged across the state had, until late in the day, burned some distance away from Adam at Woori Yallock. But when the late wind change sent the flames heading towards his home, he packed the car and the family fled. Fortunately, his home was still standing when he returned, though many other Victorians had not been so lucky.

For the pink convoy, sitting thousands of miles away in Coffs Harbour, New South Wales, listening in horror to the ABC's regular news updates between hurried calls home to check on family and friends, it defied imagination. It was impossible to imagine that 78 individual townships had already perished and that more than 7500 people were now without homes.

The Victorian bush fires were without a doubt, the worst natural disaster ever seen by Australians with the highest ever loss of life. Over 170 people had died and hundreds more were seriously injured. The day became known as Black Saturday.

Deborah was stunned as she contemplated the thought of losing her parents or her brother, and a heavy sadness hung in the air that night as the Running Pink crew tried to imagine the plight of the thousands of Victorians now mourning loved ones, family homes and memories they'd never replace.

When Deborah began her run that Sunday morning in the wake of the disaster, her heavy heart was back in Victoria. 'How can I possibly complain about my legs hurting when so many have lost so much more?' she told Glyn at her morning break. From that moment she vowed not to grizzle again.

The day after Black Saturday, Deborah managed 46.4 kilometres, blocking out her pain to reach the Grafton Bridge and the 5000-kilometre mark. She had planned to celebrate the milestone by cracking open the bottle of Jansz Tasmania Sparkling Cuvée she'd been given a few days earlier in Forster by a wonderful family called the Hognos.

John Hogno was a larger-than-life man who had turned up in the town of Maitland, New South Wales, to cheer Deborah on, making the 290-kilometre trip along winding roads to join her again in Forster near the Great Lakes just to say hello and spend some time with her.

Deborah's legs had been so painful at the time that she'd limped into Forster and spent the night floating in the moonlight in a salt-water pool. Though her support crew had said nothing, they were all privately worried about Deborah's physical ability to survive the next 265 days of the run. The pain was taking its toll on her mental and physical strength.

In Forster, John Hogno's face had grinned broadly as he handed Deborah the bottle of Tasmanian bubbles.

'You can do this,' he said. 'This is for you to drink when you celebrate your 5000-kilometre mark!'

But in the wake of the Black Saturday fires, the Running Pink crew somehow hadn't felt much like celebrating anything.

'We'll save the bubbly until I reach the 6000-kilometre mark,' said Deborah. And she put John's bottle away for a happier occasion.

It was now just four months since that 6000-kilometre milestone, though for Deborah, sitting glumly in the 4WD nursing two broken feet, it seemed as far away as the Black Saturday fires. And though the Running Pink crew hadn't been expecting to be returning home after only seven and a half months on the road, the entire family's thoughts were very much on home now as they pondered the fate and progress of the many Victorian casualties of that tragic day.

'It'll be really cold there now,' said Deborah, aware that many of the hundreds of homeless would be braving cold wintery conditions in the fire-ravaged mountainous areas, probably living in transit accommodation as they contemplated rebuilding their homes, their towns and their lives.

'Many of the people whose homes were burned down will rebuild in the very same places,' predicted Owen. Aussies are a resilient lot and it would take more than bush fires to drive them away from homes and communities they loved. And he was right. The worst fires ever had sparked an even more powerful sense of community as bonds were forged between strangers who had battled through a shared experience too painful to be understood by outsiders.

Deborah stared aimlessly out of the car window lost in her own thoughts. Only a week had passed since her long-held dreams had bitten the dust in Darwin. Now, cold reality had begun to set in.

She'd found herself stifling a sob that morning as she'd clipped on her seatbelt, trying her hardest not to look in the side mirror where, at intervals, she glimpsed the bright pink caravan trailing behind her. It looked as useless as she felt.

For almost eight months this had been her mobile home. Now it was an empty reminder of all the lost hopes she'd harboured when she'd set out on her record-breaking attempt.

Glyn sat beside her, concentrating on the dusty highway ahead and leaving another town behind them while Deborah closed her eyes and quietly relived the highlights of the trip, wondering how such a simple stumble could have caused such calamity.

'I met some really amazing women,' she said, turning to Glyn. Deborah recalled her arrival in the New South Wales town of Lismore, shortly after the induction of its new mayor, Jenny Dowell. Jenny had just completed her treatment for breast cancer and had run her entire election campaign while battling the disease. When she received Rod Valentine's letter of introduction, she was so inspired by Deborah and her charity run that she decided to pull out all the stops to ensure this philanthropist received a welcome she wouldn't forget.

'We've got to get behind her,' she instructed her town councillors and officials. By the time Deborah arrived in Lismore, Jenny had organised a sausage sizzle in her guest's honour, personally greeting her in style. The 50-something dynamo waited with the warmest welcome, sporting a bright pink wig with dangling plaits and a snazzy cowboy hat, and gave Deborah the biggest hug before sharing her own inspirational story and encouraging her entire town to donate to the pink runner's fundraiser.

Some of these women were so courageous it brought a lump to her throat. Many bore their illnesses with such quiet dignity, thought Deborah, remembering the bravery of Queensland farmer, Ann Stewart-Moore. 'You must stay at Ann's place,' said the mayor of Hughenden, which lies off the Barkly Highway about 700 kilometres from Townsville in North Queensland.

The mayor had attended the fundraising BBQ organised by the owner of the town's supermarket, where he offered to call Ann, who he felt sure would put the Running Pink crew up for the night. 'She's a breast cancer survivor and she has a beautiful place up the road,' he said, picking up the phone.

Deborah ran the 32 kilometres to Ann's cattle station which had been in the family for over 100 years. The station owner welcomed the runner and her crew, allowing them to plug their vans into her power supply and enjoy a hot shower.

Over dinner that night Ann shared a sobering story that Deborah would never forget.

'My kids were only young when I was diagnosed with breast cancer,' explained Ann. 'But with a cattle station to run and two children to home school, I couldn't possibly travel to and from Townsville hospital for chemo and radiotherapy so I just told the doctor "Take 'em off and I'll see you later."' A week after her double mastectomy, Ann returned home and simply carried on working.

A Black Day

It seemed that people felt more comfortable sharing their stories with a complete stranger who they sensed, might understand something of their pain.

Men seemed to find it so much harder to share pain, thought Deborah. While women chatted more easily about the disease with fellow patients, their girlfriends and their families, men seemed to close down. She remembered how annoyed she'd felt with Glyn when he'd unknowingly interrupted a grief-stricken father's attempt to share an experience she suspected he'd never found the courage to discuss with anyone before. She had been running out of the North Queensland town of Gladstone when a man in a car pulled over. He had spotted the pink convoy and wanted to hand Deborah a $50 donation. He also seemed to want to talk to someone.

'It's my daughter,' he faltered. 'She's just been diagnosed with breast cancer . . . she's only 15!' Deborah felt her heart sink.

'That's so young,' she said. 'I'm so sorry.'

The man stared uncomfortably at his feet, and took a deep breath as if he was poised to say something more. But just then Glyn arrived, not realising his bad timing, and the moment was lost.

'I have to go now,' said the father, shyly shuffling towards his car, his words caught in his throat. He looked close to tears as he drove away and a frustrated Deborah was cross with her unsuspecting husband.

'That man had something important he needed to say and you just spoiled it,' she snapped. Glyn shuffled his feet in the dust.

'Sorry . . .' he said. 'I didn't realise.'

There were many poignant moments like that, but men certainly struggled when it came to opening up about their feelings. Many husbands whose partners had battled breast cancer found it much easier to talk to a total stranger about the journey. Perhaps it was less uncomfortable sharing a black part of your life with a woman who, two minutes later, would head up the road and never see you again.

But mostly, men simply handed over generous donations, saying little and driving off, their sadness intact. Deborah recalled arriving in one town and calling into a local milk bar to find an unexpected gift waiting for her.

'This $50 note is for you,' said the smiling woman behind the counter. Deborah looked shocked.

'For me?' she said puzzled. 'I don't know anyone here!'

'I know,' continued the shop assistant. 'But a guy came in saying he'd driven past you on the road. He told me I had to give you this when you arrived.' She handed Deborah the money. 'He said it was for a good cause,' added the woman.

'It certainly is,' smiled Deborah.

Each of these inspirational stories now replayed in Deborah's mind. They had been the memorable highlights in her journey. There had been some low points, too, that she wouldn't forget in a hurry. The worst, apart from her broken feet, had been the family's panic the previous February when Owen became so sick with pneumonia that he had to be rushed to hospital in the middle of the night.

Deborah had just arrived in the pretty town of Woodburn, 35 kilometres from the coastal town of Ballina in northern New South Wales when disaster struck. Owen, who had been unwell for days, had gone to bed with what Karin assumed was a bad dose of the flu. But when he woke at three a.m. with a raging fever, his wife became so concerned she'd woken Deborah and Glyn, saying he needed to be taken to hospital immediately. With Owen still in bed in the caravan, the pink convoy rushed him to the nearest hospital where he was admitted suffering severe pneumonia.

For the next five days, Karin was forced to leave the caravan in Ballina, driving ahead in the car to take care of Deborah's fundraising and appointment schedule. At the end of each day she would drive back to Ballina to visit her sick husband who would spend 10 whole days in a hospital bed.

But because Deborah had to run every day, she continued up the highway towards the Queensland border. The further north she ran, the further the distance that Karin had to drive each night as she raced back to the hospital and rejoined the convoy again later. Karin, aware her daughter couldn't possibly continue to fundraise on her own and run, was afraid of towing the caravan herself into Queensland where Deborah had a pressing appointment with Brisbane's Lady Mayoress, Lisa Newman.

'What are we going to do?' wailed Deborah down the phone to Alistair in Tasmania. 'Mum hasn't been able to see dad for the past five days at all, and he's so sick!' Alistair didn't need to be asked.

'I'll fly up,' he offered. And he was as good as his word, arriving in Brisbane the following day and driving down to Ballina to collect the caravan and drive it up the coast to help with the fundraising effort until Owen was back on his feet.

But as the convoy moved towards Brisbane, Karin's desire to be with her sick husband became more desperate. For weeks Deborah felt distressed as she recalled her poor mum's worried face as they'd patiently awaited the overdue arrival of a community figure who they'd been informed would greet them. By the time Karin received the phone call saying the meeting was cancelled, visiting hours at the hospital had almost ended and she was beside herself. She fled to the hospital, desperate to make the most of the little time that was left, upset she'd wasted precious moments. Thankfully let-downs like this were few and far between.

Karin had made no secret of the fact that she had not wanted to join her daughter on her round-Australia run. In 2008, she and Owen had just sold their family home in Healesville, their heads brimming with dreams of a leisurely retirement trip around the country, and had purchased a caravan from Regency Caravans in Melbourne in preparation for their adventure. But before they'd even had a chance to christen their new van, their retirement plans had been put on the backburner as they succumbed to the lure of Deborah's latest project.

Karin had already been Deborah's support crew in 2003–2004 when she drove a small Britz van around Australia while her daughter walked and raised money for the Kids Helpline charity. At 64 the plucky pensioner had driven through deserts and cyclones and across the most isolated roads in the land. She'd finally arrived back in the Yarra Valley, vowing never to do it again.

'No way,' she snapped, when Deborah first announced her intention to run around Australia to raise money for breast cancer research.

'But I'll be the first woman to walk and run around the country,' cajoled Deborah.

While Karin was adamant she wasn't going, Owen's eyes sparkled with interest. This gentle, pragmatic man who had married Karin when Deborah and Adam were still very young, was up for an adventure.

'If my daughter is going then so am I,' he announced. Owen had never considered himself anything less than a father to his stepchildren, and they felt the same way about the only dad they'd ever known.

Unlike Deborah's real dad, who had walked out on his family in Adelaide and meant nothing to her, Owen meant everything. Her biological father had left when they needed him most and now Deborah's only clear memory of him was the day he walked out. Even that had been overshadowed by the memory of what Opa had threatened.

'He's just a sperm donor,' Deborah snapped when Adam renewed contact with their father. She wasn't even surprised when, after being told about his daughter's breast cancer, the 'sperm donor' didn't even take the time to pick up the phone and call her.

Now, as far as Deborah was concerned, Owen was her dad, and she adored him as much as he loved her. Wild horses wouldn't stop him joining this adventure and Deborah was confident it was just a matter of time before she wore her mother down.

By the time the hunt began for a caravan for the new trip around Australia – this time running towards a new record – Karin had resigned herself to the fact that her retirement trip would have to wait a while.

'Why don't you go to the caravan dealership where we got our van?' she suggested, pointing her daughter to the mainland and the friendly family owned business where the owner would be bound to remember the two pensioners and their recent purchase.

Within days, Deborah had tracked the dealer down and appeared on his forecourt in Melbourne to remind him who her parents were.

'How is the retirement trip?' he'd inquired. Deborah grinned.

'They're not retiring just yet,' she explained brightly. 'They're going to be my support crew.' And she detailed her adventure and the reason she needed a mobile home for a whole year.

The man's interest was piqued as he quizzed Deborah more closely about the trip she was planning, and listened to her story about her own brief battle with breast cancer.

'So, let's get this straight, you're going to run all around Australia to raise money for breast cancer?'

'Yep, that's the plan,' Deborah replied enthusiastically.

Aware the plucky pensioners were part of this ambitious trip, the older man wanted to make a contribution of his own. It was a second taste of the generous Australian spirit already shown to her by her accountant, which she hoped lay ahead of her on her journey.

'My father died of cancer,' he said. 'That's why I'm in the business now. I'll do you a good deal.'

It turned out that one of his co-workers organising the chassis also had a relative who had battled cancer and wanted to help too.

'He's donating the chassis free,' Deborah said, thrilled. 'And all the suppliers who provide things for the fit out, like the cooker, fridge, oven and shower, are doing it for free because it's for a good cause.'

With lots of goodwill, Deborah's caravan was soon ready for collection and Glyn, who had never towed a caravan in his life, suddenly found himself driving off the forecourt towing away a massively discounted mobile home for well below retail price. It was a great start to a great adventure – an omen, thought Deborah, optimistically.

Now, driving south through the desert landscape of the Northern Territory towards home, Deborah recalled this wonderful act of generosity which had kicked-started her doomed fundraising run.

Days of sitting still had left Deborah feeling so downcast that even the picture that had inspired her to keep going during that last month of painful running, now eluded her completely. Try as she might, that vision of herself running in her pink t-shirt, hat and sunglasses through the Kimberleys had been erased from her mind and a less appealing image was emerging of her lying bedridden in hospital with two feet in plaster —grounded and going nowhere.

As another town vanished behind them in the dust, Glyn interrupted her silent brooding. 'Your run is on temporary hold, that's all,' he reminded her again, as if reading her thoughts. 'It's not over yet.'

'Hold that thought,' she reminded herself as she climbed into bed that night. When this surgery was out of the way she'd be off all over again.

Outback Angels

The last 300 kilometres of Deborah's journey from Katherine to Darwin on two injured feet had been so agonising that it was undoubtedly the worst pain she'd ever experienced in her entire life. While she struggled to admit it, even to herself, there had been many days after her accident when she'd felt like giving up.

Loaded on anti-inflammatories and painkillers, she had cried herself to sleep most evenings during that last month, only to wake again in the morning with an overwhelming sense of dread as she wondered how she'd manage another day on her feet. Privately she feared her dreams were already running away and leaving her far behind.

All her life, Deborah had firmly believed that people attract the energy they put out into the universe. So when the pain became too hard to bear, she'd fallen asleep silently praying for a miracle. To her amazement, in her darkest moments her prayers were always answered and angels would appear on her journey, as if from thin air, lighting the road ahead and giving her the strength she needed to keep going.

If this journey meant anything, it was that miracles really can happen if you believe in them enough.

Deborah had been in the grip of the worst pain on her hobble from Katherine when her first angel appeared before her in the unlikely guise of a quirky but kindly South African national called Crusty.

In his forties, Crusty was a member of the Darwin Hash House Harriers, a social running group which met for weekly 'hashing' sessions. 'Hashing', Deborah soon discovered, was first introduced in Malaysia in 1938 by a group of British ex-pats who used to gather together to eat at a place they named a 'hash house'. While hashers congregate in many countries around the globe, the Darwin group boasted between 20 and 53 members who met for weekly jogs following trails laid by an appointed 'hare' who trots ahead.

Crusty was particularly good at following tracks and trails. He'd somehow found his way across the world from his homeland to a new life in New Zealand – his trail leading him on to Australia where, between his work as a tour operator, he'd discovered the motley crew of Darwin hashers. Now a seasoned hasher, he'd taken part in several Australian and overseas runs and, like Deborah, loved the thrill of the chase.

So when he noticed the lone pink runner shuffling across the Northern Territory in April with her dog, he'd been curious enough to pull his bus full of tourists over to ask her what she was up to. Crusty was a benevolent man, a warm-hearted spirit who for weeks had been hearing stories about this crazy pink lady and her black and white dog, who were taking part in some sort of solo charity run. He wasn't about to pass up the chance of introducing himself to this fellow distance runner, and seemed oblivious to the sightseers impatiently peering out of the bus windows as he chatted by the roadside.

Deborah was sipping water from a bottle when the bus driver approached her with a smile. 'My husband,' she explained. 'He leaves cool drinks for me at strategic points along the road, like this.'

She'd listened with interest as Crusty detailed his own hashing runs around the world and asked her what her run was all about. In the weeks that followed this brief encounter, he'd made sure to keep updated on Deborah's progress, and had been alarmed at talk amongst the other bus drivers and truckies who stopped at the roadhouses and service stations along the route that she was now battling some sort of injury.

Whatever it was that suddenly inspired Crusty to pack his bags and head off from Darwin into the early morning sunshine on a quest to track down the pink entourage again in early June, Deborah would never know. But while she'd been crying in pain and wondering how she could possibly continue towards her halfway destination, Crusty had been gripped by an urge to persuade his girlfriend to drive him down towards Adelaide River.

Like a hasher chasing a trail laid by an imaginary hare, he eventually found the pink convoy bunny hopping along the highway, and had his hare in his sights as she sat beside the caravans on the side of the road, nursing her sore ankles in abject despair.

It was lunchtime, and Deborah had risen early that morning, desperate to complete 35 kilometres of the most excruciating run so far, before the afternoon heat set in.

She had rashes in places most girls didn't want to even think about, and was so sticky from the draining humidity and the searing pain in her feet, that when Crusty saw her it was clear to him that this runner was mentally and physically exhausted.

Unknown to Crusty, Deborah had stopped on the Katherine side of Adelaide River ready to call it a day. She was amazed at the sight of this friendly face now hopping out of a car which had slowed down on the road ahead, and which just as quickly motored off again, leaving him standing in a cloud of red dust.

'That's my girlfriend,' said Crusty, walking towards Deborah, as casually as if he'd bumped into someone he knew at his local milk bar. 'She's going to wait for me at Adelaide River in a camping site there, while I run with you.'

He studied the miserable looking figure rubbing her ankles with some concern.

'It's not easy to hide two pink caravans on a highway is it?' said Deborah, wryly, her smile belying the agony searing through her feet.

He nodded. This looks bad, he thought.

'I can't go on any more,' she suddenly sniffed to her mother, as Karin emerged from the van. Her mum looked concerned. Even when Deborah had battled shin splints her mum hadn't seen her this despairing, or in this much pain.

It was still another 35 kilometres to Adelaide River and Crusty, explaining that he'd heard from other drivers that her dream was in trouble, was desperate to help keep it alive. He knew well what the threat of injury meant to a long distance runner. He strongly suspected, looking at Deborah now, that her injuries might be threatening to put the brakes on her incredible dream. He even sensed she might be ready to give up.

'It's *only* another 35 kilometres to Adelaide River,' he ventured, brightly, sitting beside her. 'You can do it . . . we'll run it together.'

Glyn shook his head, staring hard at his obviously badly injured wife. 'Don't be ridiculous, Deborah,' he said cautiously. 'You can't possibly run all that way like this.'

But Deborah's eyes were on this kindly stranger's face. If her dream was important enough for this guy, a virtual stranger, to hitch a lift all the way from Darwin, just to run with her for a while, then she felt an obligation to at least honour his generosity and try.

Encouraged, she swallowed two more Nurofen. 'Come on then,' she said, getting awkwardly to her feet. She settled into a slow lopsided limp alongside her new running buddy.

Maggie turned her nose up, rejected, and hopped behind Glyn into the van. As the car passed Deborah and this new running buddy, Maggie peered back at them from the window with soft brown eyes.

As the kilometres slowly passed, Crusty's words of encouragement spurred Deborah onwards. Without her noticing, he slowly upped the pace, pushing her on until darkness finally fell. Together, they hobbled side by side into Adelaide River and the campsite – a dirty limping runner and her dusty guardian angel.

'Those feet really *are* sore,' he said, watching her pulling off her runners in the blinking lights of the caravan. Deborah nodded, her earlier tears leaving dry red streaks down her cheeks. She really had been ready to give up today, and owed this 35 kilometres to a lovely, gregarious man whose generous gift she had no words for.

Another day, another town, she thought, barely able to stand under the warmth of the campsite shower. She watched the grime of her labours swirling downwards into the plug hole and wondered how she'd do this again tomorrow.

'Good luck – keep running,' Crusty told her next day, as he left with his girlfriend for Darwin and home. 'I'll see you in Darwin. You can do this,' he said, as the car pulled away and vanished in another cloud of dust like an outback angel.

Deborah spent the ensuing day on the road alone, trying to distract herself from her pain with her motivational tapes and another instalment of the audio book *The Secret*.

But the relentless pain that now dogged her every step soon saw her spiralling back into another hopeless low and praying for another miracle. She guessed later some higher power must have taken pity and answered her prayers because another outback angel was soon winging his way towards her.

'It's Ken Nash,' said Glyn, as the army man they'd met in full military uniform some weeks earlier at Pine Creek emerged unexpectedly in the haze of the morning sun.

Ken, a former sprinter, originally hailed from Adelaide and had been travelling to his home in Darwin after a military exercise in the Kimberleys when he first ran into the Running Pink support crew at the Pine Creek service station in May.

At the time, his attention had been drawn to Karin and Owen's pink caravan and the small merchandise and information stall they'd set up in the car park where they were busy collecting donations from passing travellers for Deborah's cause.

The soldier's first wife had died some years earlier after losing her own battle with cancer, and Ken wanted to donate to the fundraiser. His interest was piqued when he learned from Deborah's proud parents that their daughter was attempting to break a world record while raising money for breast cancer.

He was even more intrigued when he learned that this plucky young woman was a survivor herself. When he pulled away from the forecourt and set off in the direction of Darwin he was on the lookout for the woman everyone was talking about.

Not long afterwards, he spotted Deborah running ahead of him along the side of the highway. He pulled over and introduced himself and offered words of support.

Deborah thought the stranger cut an imposing figure in his army gear and felt an instant connection with this likeable, bubbly character who detailed his days as a sprinter.

'After my wife died, I tackled a charity run of my own,' he revealed. He had wanted to do something positive, so he'd sprinted 100 kilometres a day for 10 days in a run which raised money for a cancer charity. Later, he'd decided to become an ultra-marathon runner, explaining that a trainer had refused to coach him because he ran too fast.

'I ended up training myself in the end,' he said. 'I just had to teach myself how to slow my pace right down.'

With lots of practice he soon slowed down to 10 kilometres an hour, later adopting the more typical eight- to nine-kilometre shuffle managed by most successful ultra-marathoners.

'I do around nine kilometres an hour,' panted Deborah. 'Any faster than that, day after day, and you'd simply burn your body out. That's the pace you can manage to sustain yourself over a 12-hour run.'

He nodded. Ultra-marathons were not about speed; not when you want to keep going day after day. But while Deborah had been managing eight kilometres an hour *before* her accident, her pace had certainly slowed down by the time Ken called her on her mobile to check her progress.

When she'd waved goodbye to Ken on the highway, he'd urged her to look him up when she made it to Darwin. Now, it was 1 June, and aware her arrival was imminent, he'd decided to call for an update.

'How are you doing, buddy?' Ken asked, worried. He'd learned from her website and updates on ABC radio that the run was in trouble.

'I'm struggling, Ken,' confessed Deborah in tears. 'I think I've sprained my ankles.'

Ken was silent. He understood what it was like to have a mission, as he'd had his own after his wife died. And like Crusty, he also understood what damage a serious injury could do to long-held dreams. He put the phone down, worried as he told his new wife he intended to join this plucky woman on the last stretch of her run.

'She's going to need all the help she can get if she's to reach Darwin on two sprained ankles,' he said.

A pink runner and two caravans would not be too hard to find, he reasoned. So his wife, Ros, drove him down the same highway where Crusty had travelled a few days before, on a similar mission.

Unknown to Ken, after his call the previous night, Deborah had hung up only to collapse on her bottom next to the traffic lights leading to the outback town of Humpty Doo. Her support crew, who had parked their caravans at a camping site in the town, had become worried enough about her deteriorating mood that they'd driven back down the highway to find her. That day Deborah had been uncharacteristically silent. She was in so much pain, it took every bit of energy she had just to stay upright. Words now eluded her.

'I can't do it, I can't run,' she told her mother that night, dissolving in floods of anguished tears. 'I'm a failure . . . I can't go on.'

'Just come off the road,' advised Karin, barely able to conceal her own distress at her daughter's deep despair. With some persistence, she managed to coax Deborah into the car, while Owen marked her finishing point on the road, and Glyn turned the GPS off.

'Deborah, come to the park for a shower,' urged Glyn. 'At least get some sleep and some rest. You can pick up the run again tomorrow.'

But Deborah was panicking. She had to make the last leg to Darwin by 11 a.m. the next day to meet the Lord Mayor. 'How can I manage that when I'm in this much pain?' she yelped.

Still, the bed in the caravan was calling and after a shower, and few hours rest, she was back on her feet again. At two a.m. Deborah limped to the pink road marker with her GPS and began the slow hobble towards Darwin and her elusive halfway goal.

This was where Ken found her at six the next morning, slowly limping along the road, a solitary figure pushing herself beyond the limit through a pain barrier that would have seen many runners abandoning their dreams long before now.

Ken fell in beside her at an excruciatingly slow pace. Soon just his presence and his positive chatter boosted her flagging spirits. He slowed the pace to allow Deborah enough breath to give ABC

Radio Darwin an interview on her phone for their early breakfast show. Then he pushed the pace back up, encouraging her along the approach road into Darwin.

Just after 11 a.m., Deborah shuffled into a city shopping mall in a blur, where the Mayor of Darwin waited amidst another cheering crowd of pink supporters.

The local dragon boaters, who had no doubt heard along their grapevine that Deborah was on her way, turned out to give her the most rousing welcome yet.

'Why don't you join us?' they teased, as Deborah numbly celebrated her achievement.

'Because I get seasick in the bath tub,' she said, trying to smile. It was true, Deborah needed to feel the ground under her feet.

Ironically, the ground today could barely hold her. But as her legs buckled a familiar face appeared in the crowd, smiling broadly.

'You did it!' said Crusty, patting her on the shoulder. Deborah nodded, fighting back her tears of relief and gratitude. She stared from Ken to Crusty. Two guardian angels – one on each shoulder, she mused.

After the reception, Deborah's outback good Samaritans joined her on the 7.5 kilometre run to the caravan park where Owen and Glyn had parked the vans.

Amazingly, Deborah struggled out of bed again the next morning, to limp the minimum 21 kilometres out of Darwin and into another dog friendly caravan park, where she lowered herself into the cool waters of the park's pool.

But the searing pain in her feet still showed no sign of easing up, and when Maggie opened her eyes to peer at her mistress the following morning from under her blankie, in her usual sleeping spot beneath the caravan table, the wag quickly fell out of her tail. Her mum was sobbing in pain.

'I've given everything,' Deborah wept, patting her dog and cringing with every step she took towards her parents' van. 'I really need to go to hospital.'

And nobody argued with her.

Ten long miserable days after Dr Thompson's phone call advising Deborah to abort her run, the Running Pink crew sat at a campsite in Tennant Creek on their homeward journey. They exchanged glances but said nothing as Deborah suddenly announced her intention to ring the surgeon in Melbourne.

'Perhaps I can hurry things along,' she said hopefully. She'd been told he was such a prominent, in-demand doctor that his first appointment was three whole weeks away. But that felt like a lifetime and Deborah was feeling impatient.

She returned to the group animated, the phone dangling in her hand.

'Guess what,' she said, barely able to contain her excitement. 'I've got an appointment . . . in five days' time!' Glyn was as stunned by the news as Deborah's parents. Nobody had expected this but perhaps Deborah was right, mused Glyn. Perhaps you really did get back whatever it was you put out into the universe.

News of the pressing appointment meant the plans for a leisurely return trip and a visit to Uluru were now off. But Deborah, brimming with enthusiasm and adrenalin, didn't care. She had a new dream to chase and no time to waste. Deborah was a woman in a hurry again.

Deborah and Glyn left Owen and Karin in Adelaide. 'We're going to see my mum,' Owen had informed Deborah the night before. With his mum now in her nineties and the 12-month road trip prematurely over, for now anyway, Owen wanted to spend some quality time with his elderly mother. He kissed Deborah goodbye. 'Take care,' he said. 'And do what the doctor orders.'

Driving into Adelaide, Deborah had a stop she really needed to make.

'Make sure you come and stay with us,' her friend, charity marathon runner Colin Ricketts had insisted. He had turned up on the road during Deborah's walk for Kids Helpline and walked her out of Mount Barker. He'd also been one of her first callers when he discovered her attempt at a new world record had ended in tears in Darwin.

'What are you going to do?' he asked. And Deborah told him all about the surgery waiting for her back in Melbourne. 'You'll have to pass through Adelaide,' he said. 'Make sure you call.'

Deborah recalled with a smile how Colin had eventually headed off in 2005 on what was to have been a round Australia run for the McGuinness McDermott Foundation, which supports children with cancer. His own son, Luke, had battled a brain tumour as a child, and this was a cause close to Colin's heart. But unable to raise any sponsorship for his run, he decided to walk instead, pushing a small cart that he nicknamed Wilson after the volleyball belonging to Tom Hanks in the movie *Castaway*.

Ken Nash, who had run with Deborah into Darwin, also hailed from Adelaide and was a friend of Colin's, too. He had turned up on the road to offer Colin support on his walk, which appears to be a common habit amongst the close-knit long-distance-running fraternity.

'Let's see how fast we can push Wilson,' Ken had joked. And they ran ahead as fast as they could, pushing Wilson at speeds of 20 kilometres an hour over a bridge, laughing loudly like a pair of schoolboys. Colin became a familiar, if not comical, sight as he plodded along the same roads that Deborah had walked a year earlier, with his good 'mate' Wilson, bearing all his worldly goods. He finally arrived in Melbourne – where his friend Deborah provided him with a bed and a free feed. The camaraderie amongst ultra-marathoners was as powerful and unbreakable as the bond they forged on the open roads. Colin was one of the few people Deborah called after her breast cancer diagnosis. And he was one of the first to offer his support when he discovered she'd broken her feet. Now he was there for her again, as she braced herself for surgery.

'It's ruined my dreams,' she said, finally breaking down in tears as she and Colin chatted late into the night, when she visited him in Adelaide. 'What if they can't fix me?' Her friend put his arm around her.

'They will,' he soothed. For the first time since her bad news in Darwin, Deborah's tears were unstoppable.

'I feel like such a failure,' she continued. Colin looked visibly shocked.

'No way, Deb,' he said. 'You are an amazing person . . . an angel . . . you will get back out there and you *will* do it!'

Instilled with Colin's strong belief that her dream was still within her grasp, Deborah got back in the car the next day for the eight-hour drive to Melbourne. That night Glyn parked the pink caravan in the historic goldfields town of Ballarat in Central Victoria in readiness for the 90-minute drive down to Melbourne to the specialist's rooms the following morning.

Mark Blackney, a prominent surgeon who had operated on the feet of many AFL stars and other leading Australian athletes, came highly recommended. But first the patient had to be assessed by another sports doctor.

'I've broken my feet . . . Will I be able to run again?' asked Deborah, eying him up. The doctor stared hard at this persistent new patient.

'I know of a young sprinter, a girl who had stress fractures in both naviculars,' he began. 'She was put in double plaster, but she didn't have to have surgery. After three months she ripped the plaster off and after spending time in a wheelchair, she went on to be a sprinter again.' Deborah wanted to kiss him. This story made her feel very optimistic indeed.

But her optimism was short-lived when she returned two days later to meet Dr Blackney. This eminent surgeon, in his late forties, exuded a clinical and more cautious air as he studied the patient fidgeting in front of him.

'Can I have both feet done at the same time?' pressed Deborah, eager to hurry the process along.

The doctor held her gaze. 'No, you can't have double surgery and live your life, that's impossible,' he said matter of factly. Deborah felt her stomach sink; this was not sounding very positive at all.

'But you *can* have one foot done, then the other,' he ventured, examining her notes and studying the medical reports from Darwin.

'But can you guarantee I'll run again?' Deborah persisted, holding her breath. His murmured response was inaudible. 'Well, you'd better do a bloody good job,' she suddenly blurted out. 'Because I'm going to run again.' The surgeon carried on scribbling in his notes.

'I'll do my best of course,' he said, guardedly, as the patient hobbled to her feet.

Deborah limped into his reception area, to make an appointment for her first surgery. The nurse pencilled her in for 23 July.

'You have to give up on your dream,' she advised, not looking up. 'You'll never run 1000 kilometres again.' For the first time since Darwin, Deborah burst into tears. The nurse continued. 'Perhaps you'd like me to make an appointment for you to see a sports psychologist,' she offered. 'He could help you come to terms with losing this dream.'

Deborah finally lost it. 'Don't you tell me what I can't achieve,' she yelled angrily. 'I've already beaten breast cancer, I'm a survivor – I'll show you. I'm a fantastic healer!' Her voice echoed around the room. The nurse was visibly taken aback by the sudden outburst. In silence she handed Deborah her appointment card for her surgery.

Deborah limped angrily away. If her feet weren't so injured she'd have stormed out. Watch this space, she thought to herself. This is the never say never girl you're dealing with.

Freedom

As soon as she was old enough, Deborah left her home in Adelaide, keen to put as much distance as she could between herself and Opa, who continued to wreak havoc on his long-suffering family with his criticism and put-downs.

'I've been accepted into an architecture course at RMIT in Melbourne,' explained Deborah, taking a breath for the lie that was about to pour out. 'They don't have the course I want to study in Adelaide.'

Studying was Deborah's ticket to freedom – an escape from a family that had become stuck together like ingredients in a tired old stew that had simmered too long on the stove. Now the water had boiled away it was hard to distinguish the different ingredients which had become fused together into one solid, inedible lump that stuck in Deborah's throat.

The freedom Deborah badly wanted would continue to elude her forever in Adelaide, she reasoned. Especially with Opa, now more demanding than ever, still obsessively controlling everyone around him and clouding everyone's happiness with his dark moods.

As a child, Deborah came to dread her mum's regular Sunday visits to her grandparents' house, where Opa's rants at his grandchildren in the back room left Deborah mute with fear. She knew better than to answer Opa back, afraid her mum might be right and that timid Oma would suffer for her rebellion.

Yet, ironically, Opa's rigid insistence on his family's regular weekend visits had already sparked a subtle rebellion in his own daughters.

Deborah, as a child, often observed Karin sneaking off to visit her younger sister, Monika, both desperate for some sisterly time together away from their father. Deborah knew better than to break the secret, knowing full well how Opa would react if he discovered his daughters enjoying themselves without him. It would have meant he was no longer in control and she couldn't begin to imagine how he'd handle that. To Deborah, it seemed the entire family spent all its time treading on eggshells around the old tyrant, always worrying about upsetting him.

'Don't mention the war,' Oma Erika constantly reminded her grandchildren. They knew better than to ask about Opa's wartime experiences or inquire about the memories that often caused him to disappear to some dark place in his head, when he'd appear absent for minutes at a time.

Deborah would wait, knowing that when the haunted faraway look on Opa's face finally vanished, his brow would furrow and he'd be back to reality with his misery and complaints, bringing a gloom that determined the mood of his family. Being around Opa was like living on quicksand, thought Deborah. And try as they might, nothing was ever right.

'You need to change,' Opa snapped at Deborah. Yet she spent an entire childhood trying her hardest to change, not quite sure what it was she needed to change into, or what she was doing wrong in the first place.

To Deborah, Opa was unfathomable, and she never understood why he behaved so badly around those he supposedly loved.

Because of Opa, Deborah had grown up to hate card games. She'd appeared visibly shocked when she'd first met Glyn, to discover poker was supposedly fun.

'You're kidding,' she'd said. 'Not in my family!' Glyn struggled to understand why anyone would cringe at the suggestion of a quiet game of cards with friends.

Even as an adult the very mention of playing cards gave Deborah the same gnawing anxious feeling she'd felt as a child when Opa insisted his family sit down on Sunday evenings and indulge him in a favourite card game. Opa was such a dreadful sport that a highly anxious Deborah would peer anxiously at him from behind her cards, watching for the frown which inevitably crept over his face before he tossed his cards in the air and exploded into a tirade of abuse.

'You're all cheating,' he'd rage in his heavy accent. 'You did this on purpose . . . I should have won.' Because Opa was such a terrible sport, when Deborah was dealt a hand of aces, she would slip them under the table to her brother, not wishing to risk winning a game where there were never any winners. It always ended badly no matter what, with her mum in tears and Opa raging.

For Glyn, who had experienced a reserved middle-class upbringing in a leafy Melbourne suburb where his father was a respected dentist, cards had always been an enjoyable pastime which his entire family, usually played on hot summer evenings during their stays at their holiday home in Lorne. There would be gentle banter as people lost, and others won. But never any ranting or tears. 'It is great fun,' he insisted, bemused.

But not for Deborah, who had been conditioned for years, to approach this game with abject dread.

If Opa was a strict disciplinarian, Owen was the very opposite. When Karin introduced the new man in her life to her children, a couple of years after their father's vanishing act, Deborah and Adam were thrilled. But Owen was a pragmatic man, and though he carefully avoided any comment on Opa's bizarre controlling nature, he brought subtle relief to his new family.

'If you can spell my last name, Drogemuller, correctly, I'll give you five squares of chocolate,' said this softly spoken man, his eyes twinkling as the kids grabbed a pen and began scribbling. Deborah loved Owen's Friday night visits to the house and it wasn't long before the children could spell the German name proficiently, which was a good thing as they later chose to adopt it as their own.

Ironically, after Deborah married Glyn, one of the first things the newlyweds did was to change their names by deed poll to something simpler. 'I can't write Deborah Drogemuller Williams on a cheque,' laughed Deborah, trying to squeeze the now double-barrelled name into her smallest handwriting to fit along the dotted line of the bank cheque she was signing.

A month later, they laughed all the way into Melbourne where they officially became Deborah and Glyn De Williams – a mixture of Glyn's Welsh family name and Owen's surname which in German translated into 'pharmacist'.

The couple waited their turn in the queue at the city office, laughing even louder at the notice on the wall that warned people they could only change their name once in a 12-month period. 'Who on earth would want to do that?' giggled Deborah.

But as a child Deborah had *wanted* to adopt her new stepfather's name, warming instantly to the new younger man in her mum's life. She had squealed in delight the day Owen arrived home from work and produced a tiny scrawny bitzer puppy from his work overalls and presented it to his little stepdaughter.

'I'm calling her Lady . . . like the dog from Lady and the Tramp,' trilled Deborah, gently stroking this precious new bundle of life. The pair soon became inseparable walking buddies, Deborah relishing her new chore of walking her new pet that never felt like a chore at all.

While Owen couldn't have failed to notice Opa's moody behaviour and the demands he made of his wife and daughters, he hailed from a German background himself and came from a generation where outsiders never questioned the head of the family. A fifth-generation Aussie, Owen was a quiet laid-back man who disappeared into his garden shed after work with a beer in his hand. Deborah thought that was his thinking time, where he devised his own ways of managing the problem of a tricky father-in-law.

Owen had married Karin aware that difficulties after Deborah's birth meant she'd never be able to give him children of his own. But he embraced Karin's young children as his own, loving them and caring for them in a way their real father never had, and ensuring his new family found respite from the intense dynamic at home.

It was no coincidence, Deborah thought later, that Owen drove them all away to far-flung places on adventurous camping holidays that were totally unsuited to the needs of elderly grumbling pensioner grandparents.

'I love camping,' Deborah announced after Owen introduced his family to the great outdoors. They'd spent their Christmas holidays that year camping and exploring the many bush trails in the Grampian Ranges on the South Australian border of Victoria.

'You can't take a six-year-old girl on a long bush walk,' Oma had told her daughter, worried.

'Yes I can,' Karin replied, much to Deborah's great relief.

And Deborah had the best holiday ever tramping around the bush and breathing in the scents of the flowers and the mountain air. It was on this first holiday that Deborah's love of walking first blossomed. For an invigorated Deborah, being far away from people and traffic, from houses and towns, lying under the stars in her sleeping bag, gazing up at the sky was the most exhilarating feeling she'd ever known.

The following Easter, Owen took the family to a farm north of Tailem Bend in South Australia where they went rabbit shooting and trapping – and again the highlight was the sleep-outs where they curled up in sleeping bags under the stars.

It was Owen who gave Deborah a first taste of freedom and adventure that lay waiting for her in the world outside. There was an understanding between Owen and Deborah that she could find freedom, and peace, walking along the lonely tracks in the fresh air. 'It's good for the soul,' he told her. Owen's own sense of adventure had grown from his time in the Australian Army Reserves, and now it positively blossomed in this free spirited little girl.

If Opa was rigid, unreasonable and inflexible, Owen's parents were the very opposite. Deborah loved her days at Nana and Papa's house. Owen's mother had been a nurse and his dad a policeman who had supported their young dyslexic son at a time when there was little awareness of this disability. They taught him to read by cutting a paper rectangle and making him fold it into quarters, each bearing different words. As he learned, his mother constructed sentences until he read as proficiently as his peers. Deborah adored Owen's mum, who fulfilled her notions of what a real grandmother should be. In turn Nana loved Deborah and Adam, spoiling them with raspberry cordial and their favourite cheese snacks.

After such breath-taking bursts of freedom, Deborah always returned to Adelaide with a heavy heart. Yet Owen had given her a glint of hope that a brighter world lay beyond Opa's back room and that one day she would find it.

Perhaps the shared experience of shaking in their shoes together behind the closed door of the dreaded back room, being berated for being two incorrigible children, formed the basis of the bond Deborah came to share with her brother Adam. Perhaps it underpinned the wanderlust that they both developed as adults as they travelled great distances around the countryside.

But even that close relationship between the two siblings didn't stop Adam thoroughly embracing his rightful role as his little sister's tormentor. Adam's constant brotherly teasing drove fiery Deborah crazy with rage, and it gave him great delight when she finally snapped and chased him down the street, intent on getting even.

'He sold my bike,' she howled when she returned home one afternoon from school to discover that her 13-year-old big brother had sold her bike to some mate up the road. Their mother, tired from her working day with Opa, didn't want to hear about it. She was too busy with her evening meal.

'Get on with your chores,' she warned, and Deborah slinked off to peel potatoes and help with the dinner.

Deborah and Adam were typical of other first-generation Aussies whose migrant parents worked long hours to achieve the Australian dream. Like their peers in their multicultural street, they had their chores to do and homework came ahead of friendships.

But Deborah relished the melting pot of 1970s Adelaide and the street filled with sunburned kids in thongs and shorts, who played cricket in their backyards and where the smell of simmering spaghetti Bolognese floated across the heat of early evening, mixing with the delicious aroma of other foreign dishes like schnitzel and goulash. The Italians next door introduced Deborah to schnitzel Milanese, which would remain her all-time favourite food, and her kindly Greek neighbours handed dolmades over the fence. Meals that were too big were shared around other families in the street.

There were many nights where Adam and Deborah enjoyed two evening meals as the street's stay-at-home mums dished up dinners to those kids whose mothers worked, then the children would eat dinner again when Karin arrived home. It was an era when nobody had much, and everyone shared what they had — and when everyone turned a blind eye to the Greek guys across the street who enthusiastically made their own ouzo and drank it with gusto.

Despite Opa's rigid insistence that girls could never amount to anything, the influence of a young female teacher at Nailsworth Primary School told Deborah otherwise. At a time when members of the women's lib movement were burning their bras and challenging the place of women in the world, this outspoken young teacher was the first person to instil in an impressionable young Deborah the firm belief that anything was possible.

'You are amazing,' she told the 11-year-old. 'You are a girl, which means that you can do anything with your life . . . anything!' The teacher's wonderful encouragement sparked a rebellion in Deborah, who walked tall all the way home that afternoon, and soon began enlightening her conservative family with her militant views on women's lib. Owen and Karin weren't sure about all this women's lib stuff and didn't like the sound of the teacher at all, brainwashing their daughter with notions they found confronting.

But Deborah's burst of confidence was brief. By high school, years of Opa's continual put-downs had undermined her self-esteem and she headed towards adolescence, a quiet, introspective girl unsure of her place in the world.

A growth spurt soon changed everything, and Deborah's height and athletic build quickly saw her developing a talent for basketball which buoyed her flagging confidence to a new level. On the school basketball court Deborah's long legs quickly earned her a reputation as a rising star, her skills as a centre making her one of the most in-demand players in the local team.

Because both Owen and Karin worked, Deborah would catch lifts with her friends' parents to games on match day, or to regular training sessions. When their cars were full, she was independent and resourceful enough to hop on buses or to jog or walk to the various venues. In sport she found a release for her bursting energy and competitive nature. And found herself daring to dream that one day she might carve out a career in professional sport.

'I want to be an Olympic athlete,' she told Karin and Owen, returning from Port Adelaide and another successful win. At 12 years old Deborah had dreams of being a professional basketballer. 'I wouldn't mind representing Australia,' she'd said optimistically.

Perhaps then Opa would see he'd been wrong about her all along, though she doubted the stubborn old man would ever admit it.

Sadly, an accident on court at 12 left the almost-teenager with a serious knee injury. 'You've done your kneecap cartilage,' advised her GP, inspecting the badly swollen knee. And in a heartbeat, Deborah's Olympic dreams fluttered away.

As her knee healed, Deborah found a new contentment in the long walks she took with Lady and her German shepherd, Jolline. The lingering walks in the fresh air around the winding footpaths and walking trails of Adelaide gave Deborah time to ponder on a future far away from the bickering phone calls her mother endured from Opa.

So at 19, in one of her Deborah moments, she found herself making the snap decision to leave Adelaide behind and make her own way in the big wide world.

Though she told her family she was going to study architecture at RMIT because the course wasn't offered in Adelaide, it wasn't true, and neither architecture nor RMIT really featured in Deborah's dreams. They were, however, her ticket to freedom and a handy excuse to get away and start a new life.

Melbourne was only an eight-hour drive to the east, but the distance gave Deborah space to think. At 20, suddenly gripped with a new wanderlust, having seen many of her peers heading off to

Europe, she dropped out of architecture and decided to go off on her own adventure.

'I'm going to India,' Deborah told her mum on the phone. Karin sounded cautious, but it was too late. Deborah had her passport and her plane tickets and a week later she was gone.

India was magical for a young enthusiastic traveller and opened up a whole new world for Deborah away from the fast-food, quick-fix ways of the West. Deborah quickly fell in love with its rich culture and its people and her encounters with new friends opened her eyes to a bigger world.

Her holiday also gave Deborah time to reflect on who she really was. In many ways, it became a journey of self-discovery, and Deborah, now enthralled by the new wave of self-help books and with an opportunity for introspection, found herself contemplating the positive aspects of herself and her life. She didn't need to change, there was absolutely nothing wrong with her. 'I'm a nice person,' she realised. 'People like me for who I am.' Whatever damage had been done to Opa was his to deal with and she would no longer allow his negative view of the world and everyone in it to destroy her any more. She also realised that she no longer hated him any more than she hated her 'sperm donor'. How could you grow as a person if you were filled with bitterness?

Deborah finally returned to Australia in 1993, convinced that travelling was the best way of opening the mind to new possibilities. With her wanderlust now satisfied, Deborah returned to Melbourne, where she enrolled at Monash University's Faculty of Art and Design as a mature-age student. She studied Fine Arts, majoring in tapestry weaving and joined the College's painting classes as a sub-major.

It was here in 1994 that Deborah first met Glyn, a laid back artist and painter whose long-term marriage was already on a downward spiral. Glyn taught the painting class, and from the moment he met Deborah, her energy, enthusiasm and passion for life set her apart from the other students. This effervescent, highly creative student simply lit up the room and before he knew it, Glyn found himself looking forward to seeing Deborah's smiling face in class. He quickly realised that what he recognised in her eyes was the same passion he'd once felt as a young art student, when life was one big adventure stretching ahead of him.

The connection between them was instant, though Deborah steadfastly refused to consider dating a married man and only accepted Glyn's offer of a date after his crumbling marriage finally ended.

When it did collapse Deborah had been on holiday, and Glyn surprised himself by missing her badly. When she returned he was so delighted he asked her out for lunch.

'And then,' he would later recall, 'the soup just got thicker.'

The fledgling relationship between the 40-something art teacher and the vivacious student 20 years his junior, quickly set tongues wagging around the arty campus community.

'He's too old for you. You should find somebody else,' people told Deborah.

Deborah was still studying when they finally married on 20 September 1996. Thankfully the gathering of carefully selected chosen guests at the hard-up artists' low-budget nuptials consisted of a number of equally artistic friends who were more than willing to help with the arrangements. The couple had just purchased an 1876 factory with a beautiful chimney stack in Geelong, an hour's drive west of Melbourne's Westgate Bridge. It would be a great place for a home and studio where two struggling artists could eke out a living. With this major renovation project underway, Glyn and Deborah needed all the help they could get to fund their shoestring wedding. And thanks to the creative efforts of their artistic congregation, they got it.

Deborah's best friend and bridesmaid, Ruth, created her rich Botticelli-style bridal gown using crimson embossed upholstery fabric. And with lots of helping hands, the empty factory which had been strewn with loose bricks, was transformed into a lavish reception venue, with Glyn's paintings adorning the walls.

The decorations included jasmine, irises and an assortment of colourful flowers illicitly acquired during a night-time raid by the bride and her girlfriends. After identifying the best gardens around during daylight hours, the bridal party hit the streets after dark, stifling their laughter as they targeted the flowers that would turn the factory into a splendid arbour.

The food was provided by the guests themselves, who each arrived bearing a plate of something delicious, instead of the usual swag of useless wedding presents. The only thing Deborah splurged on was a bouquet of her favourite scented red roses, which she thought was worth every cent.

The groom cut a dashing figure in his black suit as he exchanged vows with his bride. And artist friends stepped over bricks to pick their way towards the Baroque-style feast arranged on giant platters amid giant pumpkins and eggplants, resembling a scene from a colourful painting.

The centrepiece of the entire spread was a home-made wedding cake. As the radiant bride and groom cut the cake, their guests toasted them with champagne.

Walk Before You Run

In 1993 Deborah de Williams had been settling into her new course at Monash when she turned on the television one night and saw a news report that captured her imagination.

On the screen in front of her was a short little balding guy with sticky-out ears and tufts of wiry grey hair who bore an uncanny resemblance to ET. Deborah, intrigued to know what he was talking about so enthusiastically, rushed to turn up the volume.

It was ultra-marathon walker Nobby Young, who had just become the first person to walk all the way around Australia. Nobby revealed in excitable tones that he was a postman by trade, but had gone on to set a new world record. His excitement was so infectious that long after his image had disappeared from the screen, Deborah found herself imagining what it must feel like to just take off into the blue in pursuit of a dream.

Although she didn't realise it then, the seeds had already been sown for a dream of her own, though it would be another nine years before it pricked at her consciousness and blossomed into a real possibility.

After gaining her Fine Arts degree, Deborah felt that an arty career no longer held any appeal for her. Instead she wound up taking a 'real' job, securing a safe position in the finance industry where she felt like an animal sprung in a trap. Deborah detested the mundane nine-to-five routine of an unfulfilling role and the sense of being tied to her desk for every long second of her working day. Even worse, she found the end result unrewarding.

As the months passed, Deborah's growing disillusionment began to stifle her hyperactive, creative nature which lacked a positive outlet. 'I hate it,' she told Glyn miserably one night. To her dismay she felt she was drowning in her own misery and knew something had to change.

'How would I feel, if on my deathbed, I looked back with sadness and regret over things I'd wished I'd done?' she asked Glyn. He wasn't sure where this was leading.

'Dunno,' he answered truthfully. Deborah wasn't even sure herself.

What she was sure about, was that she needed to get away. She paced around the house, pondering her options.

'Can't we just go somewhere?' she asked, yearning for some of the space and freedom she'd once enjoyed as a little girl when she'd felt suffocated by Opa's moods. She recalled all those holidays when Owen had thoughtfully whisked the family away when she'd felt overburdened by her life. Deborah now hungered for that fresh air and some of the perspective that Owen's wonderful respite had brought her.

'Let's go camping,' she said, brightening up. As a child she'd shared Owen's love for the Coorong, revelling in the camping trips he'd organised along that spectacular stretch of the South Australian coastline, now one of the country's most valuable conservation areas.

The scenic region is as well-known amongst nature lovers as it is amongst movie fans, its miles of beaches and wetlands and abundance of wildlife providing a scenic backdrop to the famous movie *Storm Boy*. Deborah remembered it as a picturesque breeding ground for the families of giant-billed pelicans who scrutinised her family every Easter on their camping breaks, where the sea air chased away all negative thoughts and fuelled her dreams of adventure.

Glyn didn't take a lot of persuading, keen to experience some of the exhilarating freedom his wife often chatted about as she relived those happy highlights in her life.

'Let's do it then,' replied Glyn, and he set about arranging holiday leave from the university. The following week they were heading off for their very first camping trip as a married couple, pitching their small tent close to the shoreline along the Coorong.

But while the great outdoors certainly appealed to Glyn, being confined in a tiny tent when you're a self-confessed claustrophobic wasn't exactly conducive to a good night's sleep.

'Open the flap,' he demanded, gasping for breath as Deborah wriggled out of her cosy sleeping bag and tried to untie the canvas tent door.

'The mozzies will eat us alive,' protested Deborah. But a suffocating Glyn was already hyperventilating and desperately needed to glimpse the outside world, even if it was only through the slit in the tiny door flaps.

Given the choice of mosquito bites or a glimpse of the sky, Glyn would settle for the sky every time. As a result, they woke each morning, rubbing red, itchy welts from the midnight mozzie feast. For the next two weeks, Deborah found herself dreading bedtime as much as her claustrophobic husband, whose link with the outside world soon became her worst nightmare.

'Will you shut up?' Deborah complained, snuggling down in her sleeping bag, trying to block out the sound of his rapid, breathless, breathing and the buzzing of mosquitoes around her head.

For Glyn, after years of holidays revelling in the familiar comfort of the family's spacious holiday house in Lorne, walking and exploring the countryside was every bit as inspiring as Deborah had promised it would be. And apart from the prospect of spending every night in a confined space, Glyn had to admit he thoroughly enjoyed himself and began the long drive home agreeing that his very first camping trip would not be his last.

For Deborah, sitting thoughtfully in the car, it had also reignited her hunger for future adventures, just as it had all those years ago. She returned to Melbourne with a heavy heart, back to a job where the clock was already ticking.

Deborah had been in her first year at university when Opa finally passed away, and she, like her brother, had struggled to shed a tear. At the funeral she and Adam incurred the ire of their grieving family by recalling a private childhood joke that sparked off a fit of the giggles.

As a boy, Adam would regularly survey the morose faces of his German grandparents and their equally serious daughters, and whisper to Deborah with mischief written all over his face: 'Do you reckon they'd have comedy clubs in Germany?' Neither of them could recall an occasion growing up when their family had laughed out loud at anything, and Adam's black observation would inevitably set Deborah off the minute he caught her eye, a smirk curling across his top lip.

'Nah . . .' she'd choke, trying not to look too hard at the flat expressions of their totally humourless family and dissolving into hysterics. Life was certainly no joke in this serious household.

Now Adam's twinkling eyes held Deborah's gaze across their grandfather's grave, trying not to laugh as his sister recalled their little joke. Trying to quell the laughter rising in her throat, she tried her best *not* to look at the sombre faces all around her – aware the occasion deserved some degree of solemnity.

But Adam's eye caught hers again as the mourners began to lower Opa's coffin into the ground. It seemed to take an eternity, the coffin dropping lower, and lower . . . and lower.

'For fuck sake!' blurted Adam. 'How deep does it have to go?'

And the laughter that Deborah had been choking on, erupted. 'Thank God he's gone!' whispered Adam. It was the only comment her brother ever made about their childhoods. And to Deborah it spoke volumes.

Their mum's hot scowl flashed at her disrespectful children, and other mourners tut-tutted and shook their heads in general disapproval. The two mischievous siblings left the graveside feeling the disapproval of their family burning holes in the backs of their heads. Do Germans even laugh? wondered Deborah. She promised herself that one day she'd make a pilgrimage to Berlin to see if comedy clubs really did exist there.

'How could you do that?' said their mum, in tears after the mourners had left. Adam's comments and Deborah's outrageous laughter had caused a family scandal and poor Karin had been left bearing the brunt of her children's antics.

'Sorry, Mum,' said Deborah, trying her hardest to look suitably remorseful.

When poor beleaguered Oma Erika died a year later, both Karin and Aunty Monika, who'd been extremely close to their stoic, loving mum, were grief-stricken. They knew that Oma's life with Opa had not been an easy one, but she rarely complained and loved her children very much.

The passing of her parents left both Karin and her sister embracing a newfound freedom. Some years before Oma and Opa passed away, Karin and Owen had followed their two children to Victoria. In 1993, just after Deborah started her university course, Opa and Oma had followed.

Owen and Karin initially settled in the green belt area of Melbourne's eastern suburbs in the pretty bush suburb of Eltham where they quickly befriended their new next-door neighbours, Fran and Ian Henke, who forged an instant connection with Deborah.

'You can be our honorary daughter, Deborah,' said Fran, who adored this gregarious young artist as much as Ian did. Fran, a talented journalist, had once been a theatre critic in London, and her husband, a writer, who researches the law and stands up for ordinary people adversely affected by government departments. Ian and Fran later became great friends with Glyn and were flattered when the couple decided to marry on their wedding anniversary. Deborah had deliberately chosen this date to honour the honorary parents who laughingly offered to adopt her.

Long after Owen and Karin moved further east away from the city to the picturesque township of Healesville — a small logging town overlooking the rolling green vineyards of Victoria's prestigious wine growing area, the Yarra Valley — their daughter's friendship with the Henkes continued, Glyn becoming an honorary son-in-law.

The move from South Australia and the passage of time had only served to strengthen Deborah's relationship with her mum, whose years of gutsy hard work had been one of her most enduring memories of a childhood overshadowed by a damaged Opa. What Karin lacked in size, she certainly made up for in strength and character, thought Deborah who, as an adult, gained a whole new appreciation for her mum.

Out of her father's shadow, Karin now had options, and amongst those choices came the freedom to do the two-hour drive each week to visit Deborah and Glyn, now living in the western suburb of Altona.

In late 2002, Deborah scooted her two spoiled cats out of the way and opened the door to her parents, barely able to contain a plan she'd been mulling over for many weeks. For years now she'd felt like running away from her miserable job. *Well, what's stopping me?* she pondered, driving home from work. Her thoughts kept drifting back to the funny little bald runner she'd seen on telly nine years before, talking so animatedly about his record-breaking walk.

At work, Deborah often dreamed of following in Nobby Young's footsteps and walking around Australia. Perhaps she might even break his world record. Now, after weeks of mulling it over, the idea had really taken root in Deborah's imagination.

'I've got this crazy plan, Mum,' said Deborah, looking pleased with herself. Owen and Karin glanced at one another, while Glyn looked up in surprise. 'I'm quitting this finance business,' she announced. Her mum smiled, very aware that the job had been making her daughter hopelessly miserable.

'Thank God,' she said, patting Deborah's hand.

But Glyn already suspected from the eager look on Deborah's face that there was more to this life-changing decision than a simple change of job.

'What?' asked Karin, as if reading her son-in-law's mind.

Deborah sat down brightly beside her mum.

'Do you remember that little old guy Nobby who walked around Australia nine years ago?' Karin nodded. 'Well, I'm going to do it, too – I'm going to be the first female to walk around Australia, only I'm going to beat his record!'

Glyn stared at Deborah without batting an eyelid. Life was never boring with Deborah, and though this was the first he'd heard of it, it was hard to surprise this laid-back artist. 'Uh – OK,' he said, as if she'd just announced she was off to the milk bar for a loaf of bread.

To Deborah's astonishment, Karin's surprise turned to excitement and she put her cuppa down and began mapping out a route around the country.

'Do it,' she said, leaving with a spark in her eye.

On her visit the following week, Karin had something she wanted to show her daughter.

'I've worked out an itinerary for you,' she said, handing her a piece of paper with names, times, dates and places. Deborah studied Karin's itinerary.

'Well, if we're leaving in October I'd better start training and figuring out how I'm going to do this,' she said.

Apart from her lengthy walks, Deborah had to admit she hadn't got a clue how to walk really long distances. If she was going to walk around this vast country she'd better learn how to do it – and quick!

In March 2002 Deborah entered the Coburg 24-Hour Race, keen to learn the tricks of the trade from experienced ultra-marathoners. There had to be some sort of training involved, she reasoned, though she wasn't sure, as she looked across the faces of mostly elderly men, what that might involve.

Still, with her new idea growing in her imagination, she was already running on adrenalin and dreams and, being Deborah, she simply dived in.

'Let's just see what happens,' she told her family, stretching her long legs and preparing for her first competitive event. Deborah's enthusiasm was infectious as she joined other walkers and runners at the starting line, ready to take on the world.

But she'd only been walking for eight hours when disaster struck. Deborah had been struggling to maintain a slow, steady shuffle, but now she held her stomach, gripped with excruciating cramps that made her double up in pain. What's wrong with me? she thought, hobbling on. She didn't want to abandon this race before it had begun, but she felt terrible.

Deborah struggled on for another two hours feeling positively nauseous. By now she was stopping to throw up and had begun develop severe diarrhoea – her nagging headache warning her she was also likely to be suffering from dehydration.

Her legs felt wobbly and the cramps were worsening with every step. Exactly halfway through the race, Deborah finally pulled out, limping away towards the nearest toilets.

'What did you eat?' asked one of the more seasoned runners at the close of the event.

'Lots of fruit!' groaned Deborah, holding her sore tummy and listing the orange and three bananas she'd devoured, believing they would be good for her. The man raised his eyebrows.

'Do you normally eat three bananas in a single go?' he asked.

'No,' she replied miserably.

The runner rolled his eyes. 'Don't eat things you wouldn't ordinarily eat,' he advised. 'Stick to your regular diet and don't go eating three bananas at once and you'll do fine.' The runner had another piece of sage advice: 'Next time, pace yourself,' he said. 'To survive in this business you have to learn not to quit even if you do get diarrhoea. The worst thing you did was to stop. You have to keep going if you want to succeed.'

'But I was so sick,' complained Deborah. The man narrowed his eyes.

'The only time you really fail is when you stop!' he repeated.

He's so right, thought Deborah, returning home in the car, weak but not defeated. That would be the last event where she'd ever stop. Ever.

By the next race Deborah had begun to perfect the skill of walking long distances. She watched carefully, learning from the older ultra-marathon runners who taught her how to keep exercising, even on a full stomach, and how to run or walk for eight hours at a time, eating as you went.

But most of all Deborah took the advice of sticking to her usual diet of healthy wraps and sandwiches. By the time she tackled her next race she succeeded by lasting the distance, crossing the finishing line in triumph.

Because she was walking so much, she decided to make it work for her, taking a job delivering pamphlets door-to-door, which gave her walks a new purpose and kept her in training. Glyn would join her as she pushed a trolley filled with pamphlets, power-walking up and down driveways and footpaths around the western suburbs where they lived. By the time she quit six months later in readiness for her walk around the country, the pamphlet people made her an offer she could easily refuse.

'They want me to organise the whole pamphlet round because I'm so reliable,' she laughed. At least there was always work for her when she came back.

'See, look at Cliff Young,' she said, pointing to the TV where she was now studying re-runs of this old solitary runner that Australia had nicknamed Gumboot Cliff. Cliff Young had captured the Aussie imagination with his extraordinary habit of shuffling around his Victorian farm, training in his gumboots, before taking off along the isolated roads of Australia on charity runs. To many, Gumboot Cliffy was Australia's very own Forest Gump and when a local woman called Mary, young enough to be his granddaughter, joined him on the road and married him, the media fell in love with the unlikely celebrity too.

Deborah had observed Cliff with his slow shuffle in the Colac Six Day Race along Victoria's spectacular Great Ocean Road, taking careful note of the way the elderly man barely lifted his feet from the ground as he shimmied along.

'It conserves energy if you move like that,' explained another seasoned runner. 'Which is good if you want to run long distances.'

Deborah's passion soon opened the door to other events, where she continued to compete with great success, still grateful for the advice and experience of the old guys on the ultra-marathon circuit who were only too happy to share their tips on how she might improve her training regime and walking technique.

Word soon got out around the traps that Deborah was planning to challenge Nobby Young's world record. Nobby was a hero amongst the other ultra-marathon runners who offered her some sound advice.

'If you want to break Nobby's record, you have to walk every single day — no days off,' said one old guy.

At home Karin looked worried. 'That means I'll have to change the itinerary,' she said, unimpressed. Karin had estimated it would take longer than a year but she hadn't realised her daughter would have to walk every day to beat the current record.

'But that's the rules, Mum,' said Deborah, not in the least fazed. 'I have to follow the rules.'

There was another change to the itinerary that Deborah had hoped might be a possibility.

'I'll come too,' said Karin, to her daughter's great relief.

While Glyn could certainly organise some long service leave from his job at the university, they couldn't afford for him to take an entire year off and Deborah had no idea how this adventure could happen without some sort of support on the road. Now her 64-year-old mum, a pensioner, was planning to leave her comfort zone to lend a helping hand.

'I can get Owen to drive me or fly out to places to meet with you along the road when Glyn's holiday leave runs out,' said Karin. It was a perfect solution.

Like her daughter, Karin's mind was made up, and nobody could change it.

These Feet are Made for Walking

Before Deborah set out she decided that if she was going to walk around the continent, then she ought to be doing it for something bigger than her own whim.

In March 2003, shortly after her disastrous first race event, Deborah was invited to a women's business breakfast hosted by the Melbourne Business Chicks at the city's swanky Windsor Hotel, where they were promoting the national charity Kids Helpline.

Deborah had discovered the charity's website after Googling a number of different causes which might benefit from her walk. At the breakfast she was introduced to Lyndley, a representative of the organisation. Lyndley chatted at length about Kids Helpline and the support and counselling it provided to needy youngsters, as well as its 24-hour hotline manned by volunteers that had been set up to support children and young people dealing with crisis or abuse within their families.

After their marriage, Deborah had briefly worked as a volunteer for Lifeline in Geelong, a counselling and referral service for adults in crisis. It was 1996 and Deborah had found the work a rewarding change from her arts degree. But by 1997, after the death of Glyn's brother, Rhys, from suicide, she'd found the role too painful and had to leave. Glyn had been so distraught over his brother's alcohol-related death that it had fallen on Deborah, then only 27, to identify Rhys's body. Glyn had become so distressed at the sight of the coroner and police at his brother's home – his body had not been discovered for several days – that the police had asked Deborah if she would identify him. The discovery of eight empty bottles of Southern Comfort suggested that Rhys's final drinking binge had caused his pancreas to burst with fatal consequences. The final image and the bleak scene left a haunting impression on Deborah's mind for many months to come.

As time passed, Deborah had managed to replace that vision of Rhys with a more amusing memory she had of him in one of his more comical moments. She recalled him hopping onto a tram in one of his more ebullient states, where he proceeded to produce a giant cabana sausage from his jacket with the same sort of flourish that a magician might pull a rabbit from a hat. To the bewilderment of the crowd on the tram, now pulling away, Rhys waved the cabana enthusiastically at his brother and bemused wife, slurring: 'Do you want some cabana?' While the other passengers pretended not to notice the bizarre antics of this larger-than-life man, Deborah laughed out loud. That enduring memory now brought a smile to Glyn and Deborah's faces whenever they thought of Rhys.

It was crazy memories like this – along with recollections of Opa's bizarre card games, and the cheerless Christmases Deborah spent with a dour Opa who insisted his Aussie grandchildren should sing all Christmas carols in his native tongue in between scolding them, that made her question her suitability for a position as a Lifeline counsellor. But Deborah always loved helping people and reasoned that coming from a dysfunctional background was actually a bonus when it came to understanding people in crisis. She certainly related to children from difficult homes, and in talking to Lyndley from Kids Helpline she soon found herself warming to the idea of helping an organisation that helped and supported children who needed someone independent to talk to. There was nothing like that when she was a kid.

Deborah discovered from her breakfast discussions that a number of celebrities already supported the organisation and that Australia's most popular songbird, Kylie Minogue, was the charity's leading light.

'If it's good enough for Kylie, it's good enough for me,' she told her family later.

With a long road trip ahead, Deborah also wanted to be sure her mum enjoyed at least some basic comforts on the journey. While Deborah had a number of product sponsorships, supplying goods for her journey, including the donation of a number of pairs of Saucony runners which the company agreed to let Deborah road test, she was funding the day-to-day costs of her dream by herself.

Luckily, the Gschwenter family, who owned Britz Australia, offered her the free use of a small second-hand Britz motor home for the duration of her trip, impressed by her challenge and her worthy cause.

'That would be wonderful,' said Deborah, who was organising her adventure on a shoestring budget. While the motor home had only enough room to sleep two people, Deborah decided to buy a trailer, which could be attached to the Britz and towed along behind. The trailer's pull-up top housed a fold-out bed that would provide sleeping accommodation for an exhausted distance walker.

The cost of the trailer came from Deborah's already dwindling savings account which was bolstered from time to time by the sale of properties the couple had bought and renovated – long before the TV networks recognised such enterprises made good viewing.

On 11 September 2003, after a mere six months of distance training, Deborah set off for Melbourne airport and the short flight to Hobart. The walk around Tasmania was only a trial walk, so she would not be required to walk non-stop every day until she reached the mainland on 17 October.

The trip got off to a bad start when Deborah missed her flight. But she and her mum shrugged it off, saying extended goodbyes to their husbands and finally arrived in Hobart where they made their way to Britz Australia to collect the van that would be their home for the next year.

Their first stop of the day was the nearest supermarket where they stocked up on supplies. Then Deborah enjoyed a brief introductory meeting with the Lord Mayor of Hobart, Rod Valentine, who waved her off.

By late afternoon Deborah was on the road chasing a dream, her plucky little mum cautiously driving the Britz and towing the trailer behind her. Deborah wrote in her diary that night:

> Lao Tzu wrote: 'A journey of a thousand miles begins with a single step.' Today was the beginning of an exciting journey and I am pleased that I chose to start my walk in the small and wonderful state of Tasmania.

She had no idea then that five years later the tiny state would be her new home.

By day six, Deborah had walked the length of Tasmania, arriving in the northern town of Launceston on a typical Tassie spring day. It was freezing, and due to continuous rain and strong head winds, Deborah already had a severe pain in her ankle and was feeling positively miserable.

But as her mood began to sink, an angel appeared by the roadside. Ellis Shaw was a 69-year-old local man who had turned up especially to walk the gutsy world record contender out of his hometown, where they headed straight into blustery winds.

As they walked, they chatted about the important things in life, about good relationships with those you love and the fortune of enjoying good health. Ellis's company boosted Deborah's flagging spirits and after he disappeared, she continued with a new spring in her step. Half an hour later, her angel was back again, this time bringing an assortment of jelly beans, which she ate with a smile on her face, thanking the universe for the gift of this generous old soul. Ellis would be the first of a veritable host of angels that would appear as if from nowhere on her journey along the road.

Eight days after landing in Hobart, Deborah and her mum boarded the ferry at Devonport bound for Melbourne where the official send-off and start of the world record attempt awaited. Gazing out of the ferry window at the choppy waters of Bass Strait, Deborah was already feeling encouraged; one state down and only five to go – plus the two territories.

One month later, on 17 October 2003, the official start of the walking record began in Melbourne. Glyn took over as the support crew, cautiously driving into the city centre and negotiating the Britz through the traffic with the trailer Deborah fondly referred to as the Deluxe Penthouse Suite. So far the sleeping accommodation in the trailer had proved surprisingly comfortable. She'd found her fold-out bed more than welcoming as she snuggled under her doona at night, placing two hot water bottles onto her already painful legs. On a budget that did not stretch to masseurs or even a session of physiotherapy, hot water bottles were the best she could manage to ease the pain now gnawing away at the shins of a novice shuffler.

While Deborah had been unable to raise any financial sponsorship for her trip, she was determined she would do better when it came to raising money for Kids Helpline. It was her intention to talk to youngsters at schools and youth centres around the country about the importance of having dreams. Wherever she went she would be rallying the public to donate to the support services that might make those dreams a reality for youngsters facing domestic violence, abuse and major family crises.

It was also agreed that she would be an ambassador for Kids Helpline and would promote the work of this wonderful welfare agency that works so tirelessly to help kids in need.

In Melbourne, the charity organised a fundraiser and send-off for their new ambassador and world record contender. Deborah duly arrived in the city centre with Karin and Owen and was astonished to find a turn-out of celebrity faces and crowds of children ready to give her a big 'hurrah'.

Singer Vanessa Amorosi, who had been a huge success at the

opening of the Sydney Olympics three years earlier, belted out her now famous number 'Shine' to a gathering of 50 schoolchildren, while Olympic pole vaulter and silver medallist Tatiana Grigorieva signed autographs and introduced herself to Deborah.

'Here's something to get you started,' said Lyndley, handing Deborah her first donation. To her amazement it was a personal cheque for $500 from Kylie herself.

Mid-morning, after the singing, the speeches, some photo opportunities for the media and the ceremonial cutting of the starting ribbon, Deborah headed off with a throng of children. They walked with her all the way through the city to La Trobe Street, where the rest of her family waited to farewell her out of town.

Then, with all the hype over, Deborah put her best foot forward and headed away from the small group of supporters, suddenly feeling mixed emotions about the next stage of an adventure she'd spent half the year planning. After all the adrenalin of the past few weeks, the organisation of the van, and the razzle-dazzle of the send-off, a now very anxious Deborah walked along the Princes Highway towards Geelong – and slap bang into reality.

Suddenly the journey she'd been hanging out for seemed positively terrifying. The challenge ahead in the cool light of this spring morning felt more overwhelming than she'd countenanced and she was startled as she faced the realisation she'd be doing this every single day for the next year, on her own. The thought left Deborah panic stricken.

'What have I *done*?' she sniffed. Glyn raised his eyebrows at his wife's alarm and, looking worried, sipped on his afternoon cuppa in silence. Deborah stared anxiously towards the signpost to Werribee, knowing that half an hour's drive behind them lay the suburb of Altona and their home. How on earth would she cope, being away from home for a whole year?

Deborah's legs felt like jelly as she finally arrived in Werribee, still pondering what she'd do without the security and comfort of her home. She checked the old-fashioned GPS calculator, recorded her walk of 40 kilometres, and promptly burst into tears.

'Take me home,' she sobbed, much to Glyn's amazement. 'I can't do this!'

Her stomach lurched with butterflies as she watched him marking the road where she'd begin her walk next day. In silence Glyn drove back towards their home, where he unlocked the door and put the kettle on.

'It's so daunting,' sobbed Deborah, over her steaming coffee. 'Can I really do this?' Glyn didn't know what to say.

Deborah lay in bed early the following morning. It was a cool spring October day outside, and she already felt a knot in her stomach. She had 42 kilometres to walk today, and all she felt like doing was crawling under her doona and hiding. But after announcing to the world that she was going to set a new record and raise funds for Kids Helpline, abandoning the walk when she'd barely begun proved an even bigger dilemma than continuing on.

So, with this new sense of obligation already growing inside her, Deborah crawled out of bed and put on her runners.

'Ready?' asked Glyn, eyeing his wife as he washed up the breakfast things. He'd expected to be eating this breakfast in the Britz van and now he wasn't sure what the plan was. But Deborah cautiously nodded and they were off again.

The Grey Nomad

It had been agreed that Glyn would accompany his wife for the first couple of weeks on the mainland and that her mum would take over for the drive across South Australia towards the Nullarbor.

Around Christmas Glyn would take his annual leave and when he returned to work in time for the new university term, Karin would fly out to become Deborah's support crew, driving across some of the most remote and isolated roads in Western Australia and the Northern Territory. Glyn would then take long service leave and join his wife for four and a half months.

On 19 October Deborah walked into Colac, the home of celebrity shuffler Gumboot Cliffy – and into the path of another ageing runner. At the age of 83, Drew Kettle was a seasoned ultra-marathon legend who had raised more than $270,000 in his lifetime for various charities. Not even the terminal lung cancer he was now battling, was worrying him enough to miss this chance of offering some moral support to a fellow distance walker.

His weathered face was well-known around the ultra-marathon traps where Deborah had seen him in a number of events. Meeting him again lifted Deborah's spirits and when they finally parted ways, she left promising she'd say a prayer for him under a full moon as she walked across the expanse of the Nullarbor Plain to Western Australia.

'Don't forget,' he said, pleased that this new young walker was following in his footsteps.

Battling heavy rain, Deborah trudged on, aware that her all-too-brief time with Glyn was coming to an end.

On the day that is said to stop the entire nation, Deborah was in Policeman's Point in South Australia. It was Tuesday 4 November, Melbourne Cup Day, and she'd spent the morning talking to the 15 students of tiny Salt Creek Primary School, telling them all about Kids Helpline. But she still managed to stop at Policeman's Point to take part in a sweep that Glyn and her best friend KT McLorinan had organised. While Deborah had no luck with any of the eight horses she picked, her friend picked first and second, and Glyn picked third place.

Emotions were running high the day Glyn headed back to his work in Melbourne. In the eight years they'd been married, they'd only been apart for 10 days and this adventure would certainly prove a challenge as it meant months apart. Deborah watched her husband driving away in Karin's car, as her mum took the wheel of the Britz again. Knowing that Glyn would be back in time for the weekend lifted her spirits as she headed along the road towards Adelaide and the family's former home.

Deborah's fundraiser was certainly attracting attention, with numerous media interviews and a generous public keen to donate to her cause. At the Henty Bay Caravan Park in South Australia the owners, David and Wendy, were so impressed by Deborah's mission that they offered to cook her dinner and spent the evening entertaining the two travellers, offering words of encouragement for the trip ahead. Wherever she went, Deborah walked into new acts of random kindness as people, aware of her charity fundraiser, shouted her free meals or waived camping or other accommodation fees. It was a generosity she would discover in abundance on the long road ahead.

By now, Deborah was feeling much more positive than she'd been that first night in Victoria when she'd instructed Glyn to take her home. And having your mum as the support crew also had its advantages, thought Deborah, as Karin pulled over that evening to serve up her usual Sunday roast. She'd even done roast vegetables, all creatively cooked in a giant electric frying pan in astonishingly pokey conditions. Nothing was going to stop Karin dishing up her traditional hearty Sunday meal – even without an oven. Conditions were so cramped in the van that there wasn't even room for a big fridge, so they had been managing with a small bar fridge, adding a second smaller fridge that plugged into a cigarette lighter in the van.

When Lyndley from Kids Helpline first spied Deborah's accommodation at her send-off, she'd been amazed. 'Where will you hang all your clothes?' she'd asked innocently, unable to see a cupboard. What clothes? laughed Deborah to herself, picturing the sparse wardrobe she'd packed of shorts, undies, runners and t-shirts bearing a handful of sponsor's names.

But with Karin on board, the limited space they had in the caravan was more useful for storing food for the hearty meals she somehow managed to create, despite the spartan conditions.

On 10 November Deborah walked into Adelaide where she was due to speak to students at her old high school, Concordia College. Later she would be a guest speaker at nearby Nailsworth Primary School and she had an evening engagement at the local Lions Club. Chatting to schoolchildren was among her medium-term goals – her journey having been broken down into short, medium and long-term goals.

The overall long-term goal was completing her walk and setting a new world record. The medium-term goals involved promoting the work of Kids Helpline every day, and the short-term goals were the kilometres she set herself to cover by nightfall every day.

She found other small goals to keep her focussed as she walked. She'd started to break the monotony by giving herself little rewards at the completion of these sub-goals. When she reached the 20-kilometre mark each morning, she'd treat herself to a Chupa Chup; lunch would be her reward for completing 30 kilometres; and when her feet ached or her legs hurt, she'd turn on the radio and listen to her favourite music or some motivational tapes as special pick-me-ups. Best of all, at the end of each day she looked forward to her favourite cup of chai tea, sweetened with honey and splashed with soya milk as a special reward for her hard work. She would make herself wait for this, first rewarding herself for achieving her daily kilometre goal by stretching out on her yoga mat beside the van, stretching her sore muscles and aching limbs, and meditating for 15 minutes.

Then there were the unexpected treats, like the surprise arrival of her friend, ultra-marathon runner Colin Ricketts, who turned up on the roadside at six a.m. and walked with her until well past the pretty town of Mount Barker. Colin had himself run from Melbourne to Adelaide the year before, raising $25,000 for children with cancer, and was also in the process of planning a charity walk around Australia. His arrival bought much-needed support to Deborah, who was thrilled to chat to someone who understood the thoughts now swirling around her head and the tests her body was enduring.

In Adelaide she'd also been thrilled to have a little time out to enjoy a relaxing massage with the masseur recommended by Tatiana Grigorieva, the Olympian who had waved her out of Melbourne and who waited for her again in Adelaide, ready to cheer her on.

A few days later, Deborah was resting from the heat of the morning in a tiny township called Lochiel, over 100 kilometres north of Adelaide, licking a lemon icy pole, when a truck driver pulled over.

'Are you the woman walking around Australia?' he inquired, poking his head out of the window.

'That's me,' smiled Deborah.

'Well, there's a guy who has been on the UHF radio service asking all the truckies if they know where you are.'

Deborah stopped licking her icy pole in surprise. She couldn't imagine who might be looking for her in this remote neck of the woods. She was only a stone's throw from the infamous South Australian town of Snowtown, which had made headlines in 1999 when 11 bodies were discovered in barrels in a disused bank in the tiny township. The case made news around the globe and put Snowtown on the map for all the wrong reasons. The headlines had been very much in Deborah's mind as she walked towards the unfortunate town. But now, pondering the news that someone was trying to find her, all gory thoughts of bodies in barrels quickly disappeared.

'Who is looking for me?' she queried, confused.

'Dunno . . . I'll see if I can contact him again on the radio,' said the equally puzzled truckie, turning on the CB radio in his cab. 'I've found the woman who is walking around Australia,' he announced on the CB. 'Who's lookin' for her?'

A few minutes later he stuck his head out of the window. 'Heard of Nobby Young?' he shouted as Deborah almost choked on her melting icy pole.

'Yes, I most certainly have,' she said, amazed.

'Well . . . he's the guy who's looking for you!' said the truckie, starting up the engine and pulling away.

A few kilometres out of Snowtown, a familiar little balding guy with sticky-out ears climbed out of his van and began walking back down the road towards the lone walker now shuffling in the heat haze towards him.

'I heard you talking about me on ABC radio,' explained Nobby, who looked even more like ET in the flesh than he'd done on TV.

Nobby had been so amazed to learn that his world record walk had inspired another long-distance novice to set off on the road with the dream of beating him, that he'd decided he wanted to meet this person for himself.

'I was in the area,' he said vaguely, walking beside Deborah into one of the most notorious towns in Australia. 'I got onto your website after hearing you on the radio, and figured you'd have to be somewhere around here.' Deborah nodded. It seemed that everyone knew everything that was happening on the highways and byways of this sprawling country.

'You weren't too hard to find,' he laughed. Nobby explained that he'd figured the fastest way to find Deborah would be to put out a call to the truckies on the CB, asking them to look out for a woman walking along the road. His hard work had finally paid dividends.

Just out of Snowtown the pair stopped at a nearby pub where they chatted over a cool drink. Nobby explained all about his own world record walk and offered the new contender his words of advice and encouragement.

'The fact that you've got this far already is a very good sign,' observed the elderly distance guru, who now spent his days roaming around the country, walking everywhere. Over a few beers, he expressed surprise that nobody in the past nine years had succeeded in breaking his world record walk. 'You have to be mentally and physically tough because it's hard out here,' he added. Deborah smiled.

'Certainly is,' she replied.

Deborah was amazed at the generosity of this kindly spirit as he now gave her his best advice: 'Don't look at the big picture, it's too daunting. Just focus on every day and getting through that.'

The old record-holder gave Deborah a hug before he left.

'I'll follow your progress,' he promised. 'Keep going and set that new record.'

Deborah watched the balding nomad walking off in the direction of his van, still pinching herself that the man who had inspired her journey had taken the trouble to find her and offer his personal support. Just recalling this special meeting left Deborah feeling both honoured and humbled – his flying visit would become the wings under her feet for many weeks to come.

The Australian summer was setting in as Deborah's adventure took her into outback South Australia. 'Boy, do I know I'm here,' she wrote in her journal entry on 19 November. It was Day 34 of her walk and while it was a 'cool' 36 degrees in the shade, it was at least 42 degrees on the road by lunchtime.

Deborah had decided to tackle the problem of flies and heat by rising at three a.m. each day and walking as fast as she could before the draining temperatures of the day set in – and before she'd swallowed or inhaled enough bugs to convince her they were now a part of her diet.

In Port Augusta Deborah spoke to a group of Year Five, Six and Seven students at Flinders View Primary School and the South Australian School of the Air. In the past 34 days Deborah had addressed countless schools, always leaving with a lump in her throat after an encounter with yet another solitary student who had hung around afterwards to share a secret story of pain that had wrung her heart.

Some admitted they'd already called Kids Helpline anonymously to chat with someone who understood their lives and could offer help; others were more cagey as they asked questions or hinted at subjects too painful to discuss with a stranger. But Deborah always left glad she'd chosen this charity as her cause and hoping she could encourage a generous-spirited public to donate so volunteers could continue to answer these cries for help.

These days it wasn't just donations of money that were helping Deborah on her way. Saucony's representatives tracked her down along the road to deliver new runners for her to wear on her walk to Perth. And Deborah's water sponsor, Moores Water, who delivered water to her en route, drove 70 kilometres down the highway to catch up with her after realising their delivery to Port Augusta had missed the charity ambassador.

Another family had even offered Deborah and her support crew a night's free accommodation in Port Pirie, giving her a welcome break from her fold-out bed and a chance for a hot soothing bath.

Now on target for her world record, Deborah decided she would complete the walk in the same amount of time it had taken her hero Nobby Young nine years before. But her original plan had been to exceed Nobby's distance by adding 500 extra kilometres to the journey and doing it in the same number of days. As she'd walked, she'd changed her mind. Now she planned to walk the extra kilometres in even less time than Nobby's 365 days – her new goal giving her an added incentive to pick up her pace as she tramped along the lonely highways west of Adelaide.

If all went to plan, Deborah wanted the extra kilometres up her sleeve in time for Christmas, so she would only have to walk 20 kilometres on the special day of the year, instead of her scheduled 45. Time off was to be her Christmas present to herself, even if she couldn't have the whole day off.

At Ceduna, the place where Owen had been born and the last big

South Australian town before the vast Nullarbor Desert, Deborah and Karin spent a night at the local caravan park. The campsite owners, keen to support Deborah's cause, put on a celebratory barbecue for their celebrity guest and other campers crowded around in a show of support.

But not everyone was enamoured by Deborah's adventure. 'What gives you the right to do this?' demanded an angry retired camper, as Deborah stood with a cool drink in her hand, waiting for her food.

'I spent 45 years working in the same office at the same desk, and have only just retired and got my gold watch,' he said crossly. 'I've had to work all my life to earn the right to travel around Australia and I want to know what gives you the right at your age to just go off and do this!'

Deborah was shocked. But the angry camper was unstoppable, as he pointed to the brand new 4WD and caravan he'd just invested his retirement money into for the three-month trip he'd worked a lifetime for.

'Young people today have no idea of responsibility,' he vented. 'This is insane . . . you should be at work being productive not jaunting around the country because you feel like it!'

Deborah drew a deep breath. 'No,' she responded evenly. 'What's really insane is spending 45 whole years of your life in the same office, at the same desk doing a job you can't stand!'

The man was so furious he stomped off and slammed the door of his brand new mobile home, which she imagined three months from now would be advertised for sale – still in pristine condition – in the *Trading Post*. She couldn't help feeling sorry for people and the angry outburst made her sad for many days to come.

Before she left Ceduna, Deborah went wild on her food shopping, stocking up on supplies of water and the extra food she would need. The tiny toilet was now unusable as Deborah filled it to the ceiling with cartons of water. Every spare inch of the campervan was used as storage and since cupboard space was limited, every available shelf and closet was brimming with supplies of food and drinks. There would be no more supermarkets until Norseman on the other side of the Nullarbor which, for a self-confessed suburbanite like Deborah who lived just 10 minutes from her nearest supermarket, was an eternity.

Since Norseman was still a good month's walk away, Deborah's supply of fresh fruit and vegetables would not last long, so she ate what she could now and stocked what she could manage into the two small fridges.

To make things worse, in 10 days' time when she arrived at the border of Western Australia, all fresh fruit, vegetables and honey would be confiscated due to strict Australian quarantine laws that prohibit travellers from transporting fresh foods from one state into another.

Deborah had no idea where she and Glyn would spend Christmas once he arrived to take over from Karin for the final leg into Western Australia, but she estimated that at her current pace, they might spend Christmas Day in Balladonia in the middle of nowhere. She was keeping her fingers crossed that they might find a roadhouse where they would be lucky enough to find turkey sandwiches and tinned vegetables – though she wasn't holding her breath!

Deborah's mum, who had taken the wheel at Port Augusta, was now poised to drive across the larger part of the Nullarbor Plain. For an elderly woman who was usually a worrywart, driving ahead of her daughter into the middle of nowhere was something she appeared to be taking in her stride. Perhaps the freedom of the outback had left her feeling calmer and more in control, thought Deborah.

The two women spent their last two nights before the Nullarbor in Ceduna washing away the red dust of South Australia, standing under the cool showers at the Shelly Beach Caravan Park and watching the ruddy streaks disappearing between their toes.

The following day Deborah began the slow trudge towards the eastern edge of the Nullarbor and scenery that took her completely by surprise. She walked in wonder up and down slow inclines and declines, taking in the gentle undulating hills where eucalypts grew, sending vapours wafting across the heat of the day. It was nothing like she'd imagined. But she'd been told that from Yalata the gums would slowly disappear as the landscape changed dramatically into the flat vista of shrubby blue bush that marked the start of the Nullarbor Plain.

In November, Deborah approached this enormous expanse of desert with great anticipation, convinced there was something mystical about walking over such a barren landscape where there'd be only herself and the lonely road ahead. Somewhere in the distant heat, her mum would be waiting in the solitude with cool drinks and refreshments.

Despite the isolation, Deborah felt strangely connected to the sunburned earth beneath her feet, and the infinite universe above her head. It was a contented feeling deep within her soul that had eluded her in the city. Now it brought the deepest sense of peace she'd ever known. Slowly, the gum trees disappeared into the distance behind her, the wind ahead blowing strongly in her face, almost knocking her off her feet. Deborah had prayed that Mother Nature might be kind enough to supply her with a gentle east wind as she walked across the flat landscape to Norseman on the other side of the Nullarbor. But when a strong west wind began to pick up speed, she wondered if this was perhaps the universe's way of testing her mental strength.

A Silent Prayer under a Desert Moon

A full moon greeted Deborah's arrival into Western Australia, where she would spend at least the next four months of her walk.

As she crossed the border from South Australia it occurred to Deborah that the next time she crossed a state line, she'd be well over halfway into her journey and on her way home.

The first four days of her walk across the eastern end of the Nullarbor Plain was as magnificent as she'd anticipated. The universe, she mused, had been very kind to her and had even granted her wish of an easterly gentle wind that had blown her way. But on 9 December, Mother Nature's gift of a gale force wind served to remind her who was in charge. A strong wind wasn't the only thing Mother Nature sent Deborah's way. She'd paused in wonder at a spectacular thunderstorm and accompanying lightning show that lit up the sky for hours. Walking through such a storm was probably not the most sensible thing to do, she thought later, especially when you happen to be the tallest object on the landscape for miles. But the risk was worth it for the incredible 360-degree view of wild weather at its most fierce and dramatic. She couldn't wait to see the breath-taking views Drew Kettle had told her about at the end of the Nullarbor where the Great Australian Bight can be viewed from the peaks of amazing cliffs that fall perpendicular into the sea.

But right now, on the eastern edge of the Nullarbor, Deborah paused thoughtfully beneath a brilliant canopy of stars, planets, spacecraft trails and, perhaps, even some distant meteorite. Closing her eyes, Deborah kept her promise and said silent prayers for

Drew, the generous spirit who had saluted her on her walk through Victoria.

'God bless you, Drew,' she whispered to the heavens, 'for all that you have done for others.' And she wished him a safe journey from this life to the next, when his battle against cancer finally came to an end. Drew was certainly with her in spirit as she watched the moon emerging in its full glory, sending shafts of soft moonlight across the landscape in its own salute to an old runner who had travelled this path before.

That night Deborah collapsed, exhausted, into the Deluxe Penthouse Suite, remembering Ken Keyes' words in his *Handbook to Higher Consciousness*: 'Everyone and everything around you is your teacher.'

The hot sultry weather leading into Christmas continued to yield surprise after surprise. When an outback downpour suddenly sprinkled the landscape with much needed rain, Deborah found herself marvelling at its beauty for hours afterwards. The warm rain breathed new life across the carpet of pink, gold and flame-coloured flowers, which scattered as far as the eye could see. The vision was so inspiring and smelled so sweet it took her breath away.

Another deluge which poured from heavy skies that had been threatening rain for days, made Deborah feel so alive and invigorated that she spent an entire day walking the highway singing loudly to the music on her portable CD player. She felt certain that the curious long-haul truckies passing her as she trudged across the middle of nowhere must have thought her insane.

'Earth is really heaven if you just stop and look,' she wrote in her journal.

> I wish you were all here with me to smell the woodlands after the rain. There is a type of wattle bush around Yalata that has a very subtle green flower but the smell they produce is like liquid honey.

Her stay in the tiny township of Yalata had been altogether sweet, she thought. She and Karin had the honour of being guests at the Yalata community school's Christmas celebrations where the children and their parents welcomed them with kindness like a pair of old friends.

Curiously, she'd felt very at home when, on the last night at the local caravan park, the owners' cat crept into her tent and purred on the bed beside her until dawn.

'We are not here just to survive and live long,' she wrote in her journal that night, quoting Bhagwan Shree Rajneesh from *The Sacred Yes*, which summed up her last few days before the Nullarbor:

> 'We are here to live and know life in its multi-dimensions, to know life in its richness, in all its variety. And when one lives multi-dimensionally, explores all possibilities available, never shrinks back from any challenge, goes, rushes to it, welcomes it, rises to the occasions, then life became a flame. Life blooms.'

Life was certainly blooming for Deborah, as her mum continued the long-haul drive across the remote landscape towards the Great Australian Bight. Two unlikely adventurers . . . an elderly woman and her daughter travelling the loneliest stretch of road in Australia; the ultimate in girl power, thought Deborah.

The long hours of driving, which often started before sunrise and lasted until well after dark, gave Deborah a new respect for her mother. She'd always marvelled at her pint-sized mother's enormous stamina, but never more than she had on this journey. While other pensioners were enjoying leisurely retirements, playing bowls or visiting friends, this little munchkin of a woman – barely able to peer over the steering wheel – was driving single-handed around Australia. If Deborah came from tough German stock, she wasn't the only one. Karin, who as a little girl had survived bombing and starvation in Berlin, was as tough as they came.

Each day since the changeover with Glyn at Port Augusta, Karin had been in the habit of rising long before her daughter's usual four a.m. start. She would prepare breakfast and juggle the morning chores before climbing behind the wheel of the Britz for another long day on the road.

Once on the road, she would watch Deborah's back, fearlessly overtaking the giant road trains, to park the Britz somewhere in the distance where she'd prepare meals and supervise the constant changes of sweaty socks and runners. She turned a blind eye to Deborah's changeable moods when she arrived at the van each night, dirty and exhausted, and busied herself preparing an evening meal in her cramped cooking facilities.

All those years handling Opa had certainly generated a resilience in Karin that defied description. But Deborah, alone in the middle of nowhere with her mum, recognised for the first time in her adult life what a true survivor Karin really was. If Opa was a gutsy survivor, then the same could certainly be said about his eldest daughter.

Long after Deborah had debunked to the Deluxe Suite, her support crew of one would still be washing, cooking or cleaning to ensure everything was in order for the following day.

Deborah wondered how on earth she'd have persuaded anyone else to consider a job like this. The role was certainly a labour of love. Deborah amused herself by writing an advert for the position in her head:

> Wanted: person to work 16–18 hours a day for entire year for cranky, difficult boss. Location: nature's finest settings. Qualifications: an aptitude for driving at six kilometres per hour, chef's qualifications preferred, background in servitude desirable. No payment – and no days off for 365 days. No overtime payments or holidays. Would best suit crazy person.

Deborah laughed again as she wondered how many applicants would have vied for the position.

She'd watched Karin's tired face at the Mundrabilla Roadhouse where the hosts who put them up had been so welcoming. Karin had been so pleased when a woman at Eucla a few days earlier had handed them some fresh apples for free. Coming from a frugal generation where waste was frowned upon, the hardship of Karin's childhood had left its scars and even the smallest gestures of kindness were treasured.

On Saturday 13 December, Karin finally waved goodbye to her daughter and headed home to Owen, grateful for a few months off with her husband, who had been missing her. Glyn, now taking the annual leave he'd promised, took over the driver's role, arriving in the middle of nowhere ready to be his wife's new support crew for at least the next six weeks.

Deborah would certainly miss her mum, she thought, hugging Karin goodbye and wishing her a happy Christmas. But the thought of spending Christmas in the arse end of the world with Glyn put a bounce back in her step and a smile on her face.

Six days before Christmas, Deborah and Glyn found themselves nearing the end of the Nullarbor, the world's largest single lump of limestone covering 250,000 square kilometres – about the size of the state of Victoria.

'If you stop, be silent and listen, the landscape here is not quiet,' she told Glyn, as they sipped on their drinks in collapsible chairs beside the camper van.

They paused and listened; absorbing the richness of nature all around them, pitying the travellers speeding by in their cars across this amazing stretch of land. At 110-plus kilometres an hour, these motorists saw nothing and missed everything. For them there was no chance to smell the incredible tiny flowers that spread in abundance across the red earth, or to hear above the roaring tyres the myriad birdcalls. Their car wheels generated clouds of red dust that rose from the road denying them the simple pleasure of glimpsing the soft hues of nature's palette at dusk. From the comfort of their air-conditioned seats they'd never know how good it was to feel the warm wind brushing – sometimes battering – against your skin. Deborah felt sad for these people who hurried through life so fast they missed it.

On the Nullarbor, Deborah's soul felt a sense of stillness. But after four weeks, the western edge of the Plain was beckoning and

Deborah felt a new calm and contentment during her final days there as she marvelled at her surroundings. To Deborah, the Nullarbor was a place where time simply stood still and where freedom felt strangely exhilarating. There were days when she stared into the sky amazed by the giant hawks hovering high above her as they shadowed her journey.

'I'd never have witnessed that spectacle if we'd been driving,' she told Glyn.

Crossing the Nullarbor on foot was a special pilgrimage that would stay with Deborah long after the desert sun had set on her adventure. She would never forget the majestic sight of the huge red kangaroos that leapt on sprung feet across the desert at dusk, or the lingering smell of constant road-kill as progress steamed its way across the ancient landscape leaving casualties in its wake.

Christmas was now days away and some of the truckies, waving as they passed, had decorated their giant windows and bull bars with tinsel that glinted in the sun as they raced up the long straight highway. One morning a giant road train pulled over ahead of them. 'How's it goin'?' asked the driver, a burly New Zealander. He'd spotted the couple, chatting as they strolled up the highway in the middle of nowhere towards the waiting campervan. To their amazement, he presented them with a Christmas gift.

'Guylian chocolates,' beamed Deborah, accepting the gift graciously. These were her favourite chocolates and she was touched by the wonderful thoughtful gesture of this kindly stranger.

'No worries,' he said. 'Merry Christmas – enjoy them.' And with that, he was gone, waving from the window as his giant truck pulled away again.

For a while Glyn and Deborah sat in the warm rain, absorbing the beauty of their surroundings and another wonderful act of random kindness. Glyn certainly didn't feel claustrophobic out here, and he was too tired each night when he climbed into bed in the Britz to feel the panic he'd felt on their first camping holiday. At morning tea that day, Deborah opened the lavish box of designer chocolates and rewarded Glyn with a delicious praline which tasted even better with the black filtered Melbourne coffee she'd sweetened with honey.

The spirit of Christmas seemed to be everywhere during December as the changing landscape yielded the scenic granite hills of the Fraser Ranges and Deborah made her way through a eucalyptus forest where gum trees stood to orderly attention, their trunks a colourful blend of salmon pink and olive.

In her quest to reach Norseman by Christmas Eve, Deborah had now upped her pace to 47 kilometres a day, achieving 50 kilometres a day the past few days which had put her five days ahead of schedule and on target for her world record.

The festive spirit welcomed them as they arrived at the Cocklebiddy Roadhouse, where friendly faces and free drinks gave them another taste of true blue Aussie hospitality and made another long day on the road worthwhile.

On the last few days of the journey across the Nullarbor, Deborah walked what is commonly known as the 90 Mile Straight – the longest stretch of straight highway in Australia. It seemed endless and Deborah felt a flutter of excitement in her chest as she neared the end of it and spied in the distance the first crossroads in over a month.

Glyn, swept up in the moment, joined his wife in a little celebration dance on the road, though they were certain the passing motorists staring from their windows, bemused, would have thought it more a 'silly buggers jig'.

'It is great having my Glyn here,' Deborah's journal read that night. 'The blanket of calm that his soul gives to mine always makes me thank the universe for letting us find each other.'

Christmas Crackers

As the signposts for Norseman appeared, so did a small host of Deborah's own heavenly herald angels. Two benevolent Aussies called Bruce and Tim stopped along the road to hand Deborah freshly caught and cooked crayfish – an even bigger luxury in the middle of the desert. And a Dutch couple, Rob and Marijke, who had left their homeland to set up home in Adelaide where they had met Deborah a few weeks earlier, now greeted her again.

'We're on our way home from WA for Christmas,' said the good-natured pair, as they hopped out of their car to hug Deborah like an old friend. They presented her with a Christmas card and left her with their gift of friendship.

Deborah and Glyn spent Christmas Day in Norseman, agreeing ahead that as reward for her trek across the expansive desert region they would blow their budget on a motel room for a few nights.

'We're going to push out the boat,' promised Glyn, pulling up outside the Railway Motel on Christmas Eve. The owner was a friendly guy who explained he'd just taken over the pub and happily took a three night booking from the dirty strangers at his reception desk.

'We're doing Christmas lunch if you're interested,' continued the man, elaborating on the banquet they'd organised for some locals which included crayfish, seafood and an assortment of salads.

'Sounds good,' said Deborah, thrilled at the prospect of her second seafood feast in a matter of days.

But the Christmas Day pub spectacular proved to be more of a spectacle for a highly amused Deborah and Glyn, who turned up to find the casual waiting staff the enthusiastic new owner had just employed, glassy-eyed and strangely disconnected from Christmas.

'They're bloody stoned,' chuckled Glyn, amazed, as two of the waiters vanished behind the door with vacant expressions.

For another hour, the feast on the buffet table remained untouched under mosquito nets, while the bar filled with hungry locals knocking back drinks, waiting and wondering what on earth had happened to Santa's little helpers. People were getting hungry and restless and the Christmas spirit, in spite of the booze, was definitely flagging. For Deborah, who had already done her minimum walk and who would be walking again the following morning, her Christmas cheer consisted of a couple of soft drinks. But with everyone around her definitely well and truly loaded with Christmas spirit, she and Glyn were sober enough to see the funny side of things. After more than an hour of waiting patiently amidst the escalating chaos, one sloshed diner finally decided enough was enough.

If this buffet was supposed to be self service, then he was more than ready to serve himself.

'Bugger it,' he announced, staggering to his feet. 'I'm starving — who's for dinner?' And 30 hungry revellers joined the dash to the table to tuck in.

'It's chaos,' laughed Deborah, joining the stampede. It was like a scene from *Fawlty Towers* as people jostled for food, tucking in like pigs around the trough. It was even more chaotic than her family's own Christmases back in California Street when, as children, she and Adam would be dragged off to church and in true European style, would return home to open their presents late on Christmas Eve. But Opa insisted everyone should first wait for the appearance of the Holy Star which once shone so brightly on the birth of Jesus. This posed an obvious problem for Christians living in the Southern Hemisphere where that elusive Holy Star — if it ever managed to find its way to Adelaide — didn't put in an appearance until almost midnight. Then Opa would demand a chorus of a traditional German Christmas Carols, forcing his overtired grandchildren to sing for their presents.

But this true-blue Aussie outback Christmas took the cake, thought Deborah. She ran next day wondering whatever happened to the stoned staff at the hungry gathering. Her last sighting of them had been fleeting, as they vanished behind the 'staff only' door, more glazed than the ham on the buffet table.

It was, without a doubt, one of the most memorable Christmas Days Deborah and Glyn had ever had. And though there had been no spare room in the tiny Britz van for Christmas presents, the numerous phone calls and emails from family, friends and strangers wishing Deborah well on her travels meant more than anything.

Boxing Day morning opened to sunny skies and Deborah, by now out on the road, was still chuckling over her hilarious Christmas Day. Life didn't get much better than this.

The Flying Fossil

After the mammoth walk across the Nullarbor, Deborah swore she was suffering a rare psychological condition she christened 'Nullarbor walkatitis'. It was a syndrome, she told Glyn, which only afflicted those people crazy enough to tackle the journey on foot.

Symptoms included an acute onset phobia of curved roads and hills; a compulsion to collect tacky memorabilia including fridge magnets and stickers proclaiming 'I crossed the Nullarbor'; grand delusions of camels dancing in your head; and hearing Skippy the Kangaroo's voice in your dreams.

In reality, the post-Nullarbor blues were no joke. After weeks of being focussed on making it to Norseman in time for Christmas, Deborah had used up so much adrenalin she now wondered if it had drained her emotional reserves. Whatever it was, the high that had buoyed her on her way to Norseman had evaporated and Deborah felt horribly flat.

Thankfully, those low reserves received a boost thanks to the repeated toots from the grain truck drivers beeping their Claxton horns as they passed from Norseman to Esperance. Their waves, and the words of encouragement that they yelled from open windows, along with their handsome donations when they stopped, soon sent her spirits soaring.

Deborah and Glyn spent New Year's Day 2004 in Esperance on Western Australia's southern coast, where a chance encounter with a former Sydney businessman fuelled her belief that anything was possible.

Mark Reid had been a pillar of the community, a coach with a Sydney rugby club who enjoyed a happy marriage to his wife Lee and had grown-up children. But his life changed overnight when Mark was diagnosed with a brain tumour. An operation left him unable to walk, talk or do anything independently, and the doctors told his wife that Mark would never walk or talk again. She should find a nursing home, as he would require full-time care. But Lee refused, and while Mark couldn't talk, she knew in her heart he didn't want this.

Over the years Mark had talked often of wanting to own a cattle station, so Lee decided that to help her husband's recovery, they would sell up their home in Sydney and invest in a cattle station near Goulburn in New South Wales. Now, here he was – a man that medical professionals had written off as a vegetable – living a happy life on a cattle station where he had regained his speech and mobility.

'He even rounds up the cattle on his four-wheel motorbike,' Lee revealed proudly.

'I often think what life we would choose if we had a choice, Mark with full health again and back in Sydney, or would we choose the life we have now,' pondered Lee.

Mark answered for her: 'This life now, as I am happier.'

The Reids' story showed Deborah the power of the human spirit to adapt to challenges.

'It's not what happens to you, it's what you do about it that makes a difference in your life,' she told Glyn that night.

And with that inspirational story flooding her mind, Deborah found the strength to keep on going.

A number of West Australian radio stations had been receiving calls about Deborah's fundraiser and now sought her out along the road for interviews. 747 Radio West alerted listeners to Deborah's walk for Kids Helpline and encouraged locals to donate if they spotted her in their area. Then there was another interview with a local station in Ravensthorpe.

Now Deborah had spent days craving raisin toast, and the delicious idea of raisin toast invaded her thoughts as she was interviewed on her mobile phone as she walked into the small town of Ravensthorpe.

So when the announcer asked her to tell listeners where she was, a Freudian slip prompted Deborah to blurt out 'Raisintoast', instead of 'Ravensthorpe'. Deborah's on-air error must have made an impact on her listeners because when she arrived at the Ravensthorpe Hotel, she was approached by several cheeky punters asking her if she'd had her raisin toast yet. She left the pub in a shower of cold rain, reminding her of the cold miserable Victorian weather. And for the first time on her trip, Deborah felt homesick.

In Ravensthorpe Deborah ventured into a supermarket, splashing out on treats like macadamia nuts and some excellent marinades before heading off again, Glyn in the Britz van hopping ahead.

Glyn wasn't the only one hopping around the countryside on this stage of Deborah's trip. She was amazed at the number of children in Western Australia who appeared to have baby kangaroos as pets. At many of the isolated farms and cattle stations she passed she spotted children with joeys.

At the tiny town of Jerramungup, which the locals fondly call Jerry, Deborah was offered an orphaned joey to hold. Its mother had been killed on the road between Ravensthorpe and Jerry, explained Sherryle, who ran the local caravan park.

Deborah left recalling a conversation she'd had when she travelled in India in her single days. She'd been chatting to a non-English-speaking Spanish man who had asked her where she hailed from. When Deborah told him she was from Australia, he'd said, 'Austria yes?' and she'd tried to explain that she was referring to the great southern land of *Australia*. The Spaniard's blank face stared back at her. 'Kang-a-roo,' she said, adopting a hopping pose like Skippy the TV star. A smile of what she thought was recognition fluttered across his face. He understands, thought Deborah, nodding. But the guy suddenly said. 'Yes . . . yes . . . Kang-a-roo-hoo – you from Kang-a-roo-hoo!' To this day it amused her to think there was a Spanish man somewhere who believed Australia was called Kang-a-roo-hoo. In her wanderlust travels, she'd also met an American who was convinced everyone in Australia had kangaroos as pets in their backyards. Deborah didn't want to wreck the illusion, fuelling the guy's fantasy by informing him that children down-under rode kangaroos to school. In Jerry that seemed almost possible.

Whether January was the silly season for news, Deborah wasn't sure, but by Albany the requests from media for interviews about her walk and fundraiser were flowing in. She was interviewed on her mobile by a number of radio stations, even appearing briefly on GNW TV talking about Kids Helpline and her walk. She was also photographed and interviewed for the *Albany Advertiser*.

Deborah understood the media was an important tool in getting her message across, but she was intensely uncomfortable in the spotlight and in front of the cameras. Worse still, the intense flurry of media attention left her behind schedule and she was relieved to finally leave Albany behind, hobbling with sore shins to the next town and caravan park where she was amazed to find herself the centre of attention all over again. With so much publicity she'd become an overnight celebrity and people wanted to talk to this woman they'd heard on the news or glimpsed on TV. With all this fame, Deborah found herself wishing she was back on the Nullarbor where not even the passing wildlife turned a hair at the sight of a lone walker.

Towns came and went and donations for Kids Helpline continued to grow. On the road from Denmark to Boat Harbour Deborah was joined by ultra-marathoner George Audley, more commonly known in distance walking and running circles as the Flying Fossil. At the age of 65 he'd also crossed the Nullarbor and he now joined Deborah on the road to offer her moral support.

In Pemberton a childhood dream of Deborah's finally came true. Since she was 12 and had enjoyed a holiday in the Southern Forests region of Western Australia with her family, she'd harboured a dream that one day she'd return and climb a famous tree called the Gloucester Tree.

Deborah had been goal-orientated even then, and while her brother revealed it was his cherished dream to visit a movie lot, Deborah's was to one day climb the tree that is said to be the highest fire lookout tree in the world. She had attempted the climb at 12, shouting to her family as she climbed 'See you at the top!' But her mother, terrified of heights, screamed at her to stop immediately. And Deborah had climbed back down feeling cheated.

Now, 22 years later, she couldn't resist climbing the 153 rungs to a height of more than 60 metres. The steel rungs, set 30 to 40 centimetres apart, spiralled around the trunk and challenged Deborah's sore shins. The spikes bent with her body weight and she felt the tree swaying as she climbed towards the sky. It was definitely not a venture for the faint hearted, but gazing from the lookout at the top, Deborah congratulated herself on achieving her childhood goal.

January 21 was the tenth anniversary of the day Glyn and Deborah got together and she wanted to do something special and romantic to mark the occasion, appreciating that most of her days were spent walking along the road alone, while Glyn was by himself in the van.

But she knew she'd be so exhausted by nightfall that all they'd manage would be a light dinner around the not-so-romantic light of an insect repellent candle. Worse still, because Deborah had a speaking engagement that evening in Balingup, the anniversary feast would more than likely be the previous day's leftover pasta.

But the local community, learning this was a special day for the couple, stepped in. After Deborah's speaking engagement, Glyn and Deborah were driven to a romantic hilltop cabin, where a well-wisher had donated the night's accommodation. When the speechless couple arrived, the table had been set with a delicious vegetarian meal complete with red wine. A good night's sleep in a real bed was the finishing touch to a wonderful night.

Next day a strong contingent of supportive locals gathered to walk Deborah through the Balingup-Donnybrook Shire, where Deborah's donation tin was now brimming with public generosity.

Deborah celebrated Australia Day on 26 January as the special guest of the Bunbury Running Club's Australia Day Fun Run, which she was invited to open. She was thrilled when the organisers later donated the proceeds of the Fun Run to Kids Helpline. The following day she would achieve another medium-term goal as she completed the walk from Adelaide into Perth, arriving in the city to spectacular views of the Swan River and a rousing welcome from the Mayor and the crowd which had gathered to support her.

After another round of media interviews, Deborah was off again, leaving the city to a beautiful sunrise. But they didn't get too far along the road before an unexpected event put the brakes on their plans.

'It won't start,' sighed Glyn, sitting in the lifeless Britz. Deborah panicked. They'd already had a few problems with the Britz in Bunbury that had slowed down her walk. But while the last hiccup wasn't too much of a problem, as Glyn was just 20 kilometres from Bunbury and a mechanic to help get the Britz started, this time the nearest town was 150 kilometres away.

'I'll be back,' promised Glyn, finally getting the spluttering engine going. Deborah watched him disappear up the dusty road towards Geraldton, suddenly feeling very alone and vulnerable. With no support crew or van, she had to carry her daily supply of water in a backpack and still make 42.2 kilometres.

It was a sultry 34 degrees and carrying eight litres of additional water weighed her down considerably. Luckily Glyn had been struck with the idea of planting bottles of water along the way, painting marks on the road that indicated the hiding place he'd found near local landmarks like signposts, that would direct her to the stash of water. Deborah wondered how many people could walk a marathon while carrying an additional eight to 10 kilograms on their back.

The walk this day was by far the hardest and for the first time since leaving Melbourne, she found herself wondering what she was doing. When the water supplies finally ran out, she was forced to flag down coaches or buses and ask the drivers – who were shocked to see a solitary woman walking along the roadside – for a bottle of water. She now had an acute pain in one of her feet and was feeling very sorry for herself.

Darkness fell and there was still no sign of Glyn, leaving Deborah feeling anxious and vulnerable. Usually, just the knowledge that the support crew was parked up ahead and could drive down to check on her, was reassuring. But with that comfort temporarily gone, she felt totally alone. Her sense of relief at the sight of the blinking headlights of the Britz in the distance was indescribable.

'They've fixed it for now,' explained Glyn, pulling over. The mechanic, like the serviceman in Bunbury, fixed the engine for free. 'It's only temporary though. We're going to have to get more work done on it in Geraldton – I don't want your mum driving off into the middle of nowhere with a dodgy engine.'

With Karin's arrival in Western Australia now only days away, Deborah knew Glyn was right. There'd be no handy garages or service stations as they made the drive north to more remote areas, and Deborah wanted to be sure the Britz was rock solid to avoid any panics.

They celebrated Glyn's departure a few days later with a last supper, feasting on the local Geraldton speciality of rock lobster, also known as crayfish. Glyn had decided that because they would be apart for the next four and half months, it was worth the expense, though only a really special occasion like a wedding anniversary would warrant such an extravagance back home.

In Melbourne they'd expect to spend $54 a kilo for a crayfish and were amazed when a woman at a local shop pointed out a giant rock lobster and asked for just $13.

'Is that $13 a kilo?' asked Deborah innocently.

'No, the lot,' said the woman. She asked the astonished visitors to wait a while, since the boats had only just bought the day's catch in and they were still cooking.

'No worries,' said Glyn, delighted at his bargain. 'We'll take two!'

Glyn's subsequent departure from Geraldton Airport was a sad affair, and Deborah kissed him goodbye with a heavy heart. Her mum had arrived the previous evening, ready to sacrifice the next four months of her time with Owen for Deborah's adventure. She was bracing herself to drive across some of the most remote expanses of the country and Deborah was grateful for that. Still, she would miss Glyn all the same.

Cyclones and Detours

By the time Karin took over the Britz, Deborah was days behind schedule because of the breakdown and the mechanical repairs.

'The next few days are going to be big ones,' Deborah warned her mum that night. If Deborah was to make up for lost time, she'd have to walk 50 kilometres plus every day for a while.

On 13 February Deborah gave herself the goal of 57 kilometres, arriving at the van to hear her mum say: 'You've done 56.8 kilometres.'

Deborah decided she'd push it to 57 kilometres anyway and watched Karin drive up ahead, expecting that in a couple of hundred metres, she'd pull over. But Karin had misunderstood. Believing Deborah aimed to complete 60 kilometres that day, she continued driving. Deborah watched in dismay, knowing she had no choice but to catch up. When she finally arrived, she felt exhilarated, knowing she'd set a new daily record.

Karin and Deborah were emotional over dinner that night – Deborah missing Glyn who had just departed for many months, and her mum missing Owen and worrying how she'd cope driving across such remote territory.

They distracted themselves from their gloom with a highlight they'd promised themselves, and the next day they stopped off at Monkey Mia, slipping into the Indian Ocean where they fed the dolphins who leapt from the warm turquoise waters in a spectacular show that exceeded their expectations.

But the thrill of watching the dolphins was short lived. As they prepared to leave, they discovered they'd run out of diesel. 'Muuum!' groaned Deborah, aware that running out of diesel was not as straightforward as filling the tank again – an empty diesel tank meant some kind of technical repair was needed, and that meant calling a mechanic.

Fortunately, the night before Deborah had been a guest of the Denham Shire, and so she rang the person who had welcomed her, asking for help. The idea of leaving her mum sitting alone in a Britz van on the side of the road certainly did not appeal after her own stint of solitary walking outside Geraldton. For the first time since leaving home she felt the weight of a responsibility she had not considered before.

There had been times on her walk, especially in solitary places, where motorists had been so shocked to see a woman walking on her own that they'd pulled over to inquire if she needed help. 'Oh I'm just walking around Australia,' she'd say, as casually as if she were hunting down the nearest milk bar. But this was different – this was her mum. In the end, the Denham Shire sent out a mechanic to fix the problem and fill the tank.

'From now on we're going to carry jerry cans with extra diesel,' Deborah told her mum. She couldn't believe they hadn't thought about this before.

Back on the road again, Deborah headed up-country where she was aiming for her next medium-term goal, the town of Port Hedland. From there she would walk on to Broome, and Darwin would be in her sights. It was now late February and the soaring temperatures of the hot Australian summer had become so draining that Deborah decided to begin her walks each day even earlier.

So when the temperatures suddenly dropped on 28 February, Deborah arrived at the Britz smiling from ear to ear, optimistic that if this unexpected cool change lasted for another four days, she'd arrive at Karratha a day ahead of schedule. But her delight at the changing weather was short-lived when she realised the reason for the dramatic change in temperature.

'You need to get off the road,' urged a passing motorcyclist, slowing down to talk to Deborah. 'Haven't you heard? There's a cyclone warning and you're walking directly into it!' Deborah was visibly shocked. With no radio reception in the Britz van due to the lack of an antenna, Deborah hadn't heard the news. Because she'd also failed to keep in contact with the local weather bureau, she had no idea that most of the West Australian coast was already battening down for a lashing from Tropical Cyclone Monty.

But with the weather bureau predicting that the cyclone would strike Karratha, the very town that Deborah was heading for, she knew she was in trouble.

'There's a cyclone warning,' she said, arriving at the Britz at the Onslow turnoff. Karin was horrified, remembering the devastation caused by Cyclone Tracy when it struck Darwin on Christmas Day, 1974. 'Just stay calm,' warned Deborah, sensing her mother's panic.

Cyclones, like hurricanes, are categorised according to their severity and Cyclone Monty was predicted to be a Category Three based on its potential for destruction.

'That's not too bad then,' said Deborah, trying to sound optimistic. 'If the worst category of cyclone is five then Monty is only a half Monty not a full Monty.' Deborah's cheeriness belied her own concern, which was more about the damage this cyclone would do to her world record attempt. If it held her up, she might not be able to catch up and could ultimately fail to beat Nobby's record.

She was also concerned about how her mum would cope driving a motor home towing a trailer through the predicted powerful winds and rain when it was likely visibility would be very poor. Karin's face clouded with worry. Deborah too, was uneasy about the idea of being exposed on the road on the rim of a cyclone.

Karin had already spent an anxious day, aware her daughter was out in heavy rain. But she never dreamed a cyclone warning was already circulating in the region.

Deborah hurriedly called the weather bureau and the police in the nearest town of Onslow to ask what her options were.

'Get the hell out of there,' ordered a worried policeman. 'Head south – for Nanutarra Roadhouse – and do it quick!'

Karin turned the van around and headed cautiously back towards Nanutarra, 40 kilometres away – her bag packed just in case they had to abandon it. Deborah set off behind the van in the pouring rain. The walk meant backtracking, but Deborah finally caught up with her mum at the Nanutarra Roadhouse about six hours later, windswept and soaking wet.

'I could hardly see a hand in front of me,' said Karin, relieved to see her daughter.

However, at Nanutarra the owners of the roadhouse were concerned they didn't have anything to tie down the van with in the high winds and urged Deborah and Karin to head further south, to Minilya, 217 kilometres away. With no other option, mother and daughter drove on to Manilya, where the roadhouse welcomed them.

While Karin enjoyed a sleepless night in the van, her daughter spent an even more restless night in the De Luxe Penthouse Suite, rocking and swaying in the gale force winds and worrying what the morning might bring.

She wrote in her journal that night:

My ignorance of the cyclone was a big mistake, a huge learning curve and a scary experience. In this case ignorance was not bliss but rather risky and stupid. We were lucky to be safe and escape with only some car damage. Some of my ignorance was due to my stubborn nature and the fact that I have a little rule that I don't want to know about the weather . . . lack of information is really stupid and I vow from here on in to get the weather information for the area I am walking in. I have also learned that the stubborn side of my nature is a dual thing. On one hand it makes me determined to succeed in my quest, but on the other it can put my life at risk.

The following morning, Tropical Cyclone Monty crossed the coast 500 kilometres away, bringing hazardous weather conditions which made the prospect of walking along the open roads extremely dangerous. Confined to the roadhouse, Deborah made an urgent call to her long distance guru Nobby Young, who conferred with the records committee and offered a temporary solution to the problem of keeping her record attempt alive.

'If you can't go out on the open roads, you could walk the distance in circles,' he'd suggested. 'That means you're keeping within the rules.' On his advice, Deborah spent the next four days walking 5.5 kilometres north of the roadhouse – then returning to walk 5.5 kilometres south before doing a 180-degree turn and walking back to where she began.

'When I did my world record 10 years ago, I spent 13 days walking around Mount Isa after my van broke down,' he said sympathetically. 'But at least I had a pub to go to for a beer at the end of it!'

Deborah laughed. Better than me, she thought. But at least Nobby understood her concerns. People who had gathered at the roadhouse due to roadblocks and flooding, watched her with curiosity as she walked up and down in driving rain, looping the loop.

'I'll come with you,' offered a guy called Rod. And so for the next 10 kilometres two crazy travellers trudged up and down and around the roadhouse in loops, their clothes sopping wet and clinging to their bodies, their shoes squirting with water.

Deborah climbed into bed that night hoping that the following morning would bring more information on the road situation. She'd been concerned to hear from some of the locals that many roads along her route where now underwater or entirely blocked off. The road authorities were unsure whether the bridge near Karratha which Deborah had planned to cross was even still there.

The next day brought news Deborah didn't want to hear. The cyclone had taken out the bridge at Karratha and the main highway on her route would be closed for at least the next two to three weeks. Worse still, the weather bureau was predicting that a second cyclone, Tropical Cyclone Evan, was forming in the East Kimberleys, which meant more bad weather and more delays.

For this reason the authorities recommended that Deborah take an alternative route to Port Hedland, turning off at the Nanutarra-Wittenoom Road and walking inland towards Tom Price. From there she could walk up the Great Northern Highway towards her destination. Deborah groaned when locals explained this route would take her through the hottest part of Australia.

'It will also add an additional 400 kilometres to my journey. This means I'll be eight days behind my record by the time we get to Port Hedland.' She had many long hard days of walking in front of her if she was to catch up. The inland route into the Pilbara at the hottest time of year struck dread into Deborah. Suddenly all her positivity drained away and her mind was flooded with negative thoughts, as if the cyclone had swept away her goal.

Walking in temperatures of 47 degrees was a very unappealing thought. But she had two options – take the detour, or quit.

'To me there was no choice. I couldn't live with the knowledge that I had quit,' she wrote on 9 March in her journal. 'Deborah De Williams is no quitter!'

The detour would take two weeks of solid walking, but if she quit now she'd have to live with that decision forever. Instead, Karin packed the van and she and Deborah drove back to the Nanutarra-Wittenoom Road, where Deborah had finished before the cyclone. From the Nanutarra-Wittenoom Road, Deborah walked up the highway to start her detour in the pouring rain.

Surprisingly, Deborah's gloomy mood brightened with the changing scenery. To her amazement the road from Nanutarra to Paraburdoo turned out to be one of the most beautiful outback roads she'd seen yet. For the next five days she walked for hours at a time without once being overtaken by a single car, coach, road train or caravan.

'It's heaven out here,' she wrote in her journal. 'I love the solitude and I spend my days strolling in the middle of the road surrounded by the rich Pilbara colours of fiery reds, golds and brilliant blue skies.'

Tropical Cyclone Monty had brought so much rain that the country was green again and the wildflowers had begun to blossom everywhere. The heavy rain also meant that the rivers and waterways were flowing – the wind blowing across the water creating cool moments of relief from the sweltering heat of the day.

Deborah's detour also gave her the opportunity to witness the most spectacular night skies as they lit magnificent views across a rugged landscape two million years in the making. 'I am thinking about Monty and I am grateful because if Monty had never crossed my path I would never have witnessed such incredible beauty,' she wrote in her diary that night.

If she now thanked Monty for her gift, she was even more thankful for the patience of Ernie Reynolds at Main Roads Carnarvon for putting up with her pestering phone calls and constant questions about road conditions in the wake of the cyclone. In the end she congratulated herself on being a serial pest after Ernie got so sick of his new stalker that he finally allowed her to walk along one stretch of road before it was officially re-opened! He understood the urgency for her to resume her journey, he said. But Deborah, laughing as she headed off, thought it more likely he was just worn out by her.

Deborah's detour yielded another blessing; a glimpse of the Karijini National Park, the second largest in Western Australia, where millions of years of erosion have created a startling landscape of rugged scenery and spectacular gorges where sheer rock faces, waterfalls and rock pools appear against the many colours of the Pilbara.

Karijini is the ancient land of the Banyjima, Kurrama and Yinhawangka peoples, the park recognising the contribution of the inhabitants whose occupation of the land dates back at least 30,000 years. The indigenous ranger told Deborah that this is the land of giant serpents called the Thurra, which emerged from the sunburned ground when the earth was soft and travelled through the country creating gorges and waterholes. He said his people still believe the thurra lives in these waterholes, and visitors should take care not to offend them. After Deborah's recent run of bad luck, she had no intention of offending anyone!

Even though she was now several days behind her record, the scenery proved so breathtaking that Deborah couldn't resist taking a few short walks through the national park to view some of the highlights and enjoy a cool swim in the Fortescue Falls.

'Turn the lights off, Mum,' whispered Deborah one night. She grabbed her mother's hand in excitement and they stepped together out of the van into the darkness, where the sky greeted them with the most spectacular display of stars and planets. The women stared in wonder; the stars were so close, they could almost reach up and touch them.

For all the cursing she'd done about Cyclone Monty, Deborah now thanked the universe for sending him into her path and giving her such life enriching experiences. More were to come.

As Deborah made her way up the Great Northern Highway, about 260 kilometres out of Port Hedland she had the gift of seeing an incredible sunrise at Munjina Gorge. As the sun slowly rose it cast an intense red glow over the great shafts of rocks dotted with the silhouettes of spinifex balls, and for Deborah it was a sacred and moving experience.

On 20 March, after a staggering 400-kilometre detour, Deborah finally arrived in Port Hedland just three days behind her world record. She'd made up for lost time by walking 50 kilometres most days, all the time praying the weather would remain stable enough for her to keep going.

She began her walk out of Port Hedland at three a.m., heading onto the 610 kilometres of highway to Broome, and what is considered Australia's most boring stretch of road. But she was fortunate enough to be joined by some early morning visitors whose knowledge of the Pilbara offered her a new insight to ponder over the coming 13-day walk.

At four a.m., while the rest of the world slept, visitors Andriena Ciric and Neil Owen took turns walking and chatting to Deborah about the Pilbara and the Kimberley. The two regions are separated by the western edge of the Great Sandy Desert which extends all the way from the Northern Territory to the Indian Ocean. The area was once an ice landscape before a meteor hit the earth and spun the planet out of its orbit into its current position. Sweating in the intense heat, Deborah rubbed her hand across her dusty face, struggling to imagine ice around here on a 45-degree day.

She'd been told there'd be nothing much to look at until she reached Broome except for the proliferation of spinifex, the long grass which grows abundantly in this region and which the Aborigines once used for fire kindling as well as utilising the seeds for food. Deborah made sure she kept a safe distance from the towering grass, which she'd also discovered was home to an even bigger abundance of snakes.

As well as snakes, the region is the home of a small lizard called the Ta Ta. The Ta Ta is grey in colour and has two white stripes on either side of its body, and is often observed sitting on the roadside in the hot Pilbara sun. It is said that the lizard appears to wave to passing motorists as it lifts one leg at a time and waves like a child waving goodbye. For this reason locals have called it the 'Ta Ta'.

It was late afternoon when Deborah walked past the Marble Bar turnoff, a tiny township which lived up to its reputation of being the hottest town in Australia. Its 47-degree temperature sizzled down on the road, making the tarmac surface so sticky that it now melted the rubber soles of Deborah's runners. She reminded herself to tell Saucony that walking or running at Marble Bar in the height of summer was not a good idea.

In the 1920s, temperatures in Marble Bar are said to have topped 37 degrees for 160 consecutive days. Deborah wasn't surprised to hear the locals saying that the best time to visit Marble Bar was between May and September and that she was in the region during the hottest month of the year. She walked on, questioning her own sanity for such bad timing and appreciating why the locals leave their air-conditioned homes, for air-conditioned cars, which they drive to air-conditioned workplaces and schools.

While Tropical Cyclone Evan failed to amount to anything, hovering precariously over the Indian Ocean and eventually petering out, the weather bureau was now warning about the pending arrival of a third cyclone. Tropical Cyclone Fay was already moving south towards Port Hedland at a speed of seven kilometres an hour. The news left Deborah panicking again, aware she had eight bridges and river crossings to cover between Port Hedland and the town of Pardoo in the coming days.

'If these bridges get washed away there's no detour route to

Broome,' Deborah told Karin, studying the map. 'I'm going to have to hurry because if there's more flooding I'm going to be held up again.'

As a precaution, she decided to walk faster and put more kilometres behind her before Cyclone Fay hit. Secretly, Deborah's growing paranoia about cyclones and bridges were now causing her some sleepless nights.

The days that followed were a game of cat and mouse as the warnings about Cyclone Fay grew. Thankfully the cyclone still hadn't struck by the time she reached the Pardoo Roadhouse and she'd been able to cross all the river and bridge crossings on the route so far, one step ahead of the cyclone.

When the weather bureau announced they were downgrading the cyclone from a Category Five to a Category Two, Deborah and Karin were greatly relieved, not wishing to repeat the earlier experience they'd had with Cyclone Monty.

Having learned her lesson from Monty, Deborah was now closely monitoring Fay's progress via her mobile satellite phone, calling the Bureau of Meteorology at Port Hedland for continual updates. On 25 March the predictions from the bureau were for rain and winds of 20 to 30 knots and Deborah, aware that this was a downgrading, felt confident enough to continue her walk.

But within hours Cyclone Fay was being reclassified from Category Two to Category Three and was heading Deborah's way.

'It might be wise to return to Port Hedland,' advised the experts at the weather bureau when growing winds caused Deborah to phone in for another update. Her stomach sank. There was no way she was going to backtrack and risk crossing all those bridges again until this cyclone threat had passed. Worse still, even if she made it and this unpredictable cyclone took out those bridges as Cyclone Monty had done at Karratha, she'd be stuck all over again.

But Deborah worried about continuing on and being caught without shelter in the middle of nowhere when this new cyclone hit. So she decided to get in the Britz with her mum and drive forward to Willare Bridge, 160 kilometres east of Broome. From there she could walk backwards in an anti-clockwise direction for seven days to rejoin her mark. Then she would drive forward to Roebuck Plains Roadhouse, which sits on a T-Junction between Willare Bridge and Broome.

'That's probably your safest option,' agreed the guy at the weather bureau.

But Deborah wasn't sure if the rules governing the walk allowed for this. She rang Nobby to find out.

'Is it OK to drive forward then walk in the opposite direction for a time, based on the rules of the walk?'

Nobby confirmed it was completely within the rules. And so Karin began the 500-kilometre drive to Willare Bridge with her daughter safely in the passenger seat beside her.

The wind was certainly picking up and rain now thundered down on the Britz which rocked in the gale force conditions, the trailer behind it lurching violently from side to side. Karin looked terrified as her hands shook on the steering wheel.

'Don't worry, Mum, I won't put us in danger,' promised Deborah.

The deteriorating conditions prompted the authorities to issue a Code Red Alert for the area, instructing locals to stay inside and keep off the roads until the cyclone had passed. Observing Karin's trembling hands on the steering wheel, Deborah suddenly felt very responsible for her mum's safety.

'We'll be all right, Mum,' she said, taking over the shaking steering wheel, the windscreen wipers working overtime in such poor visibility. They were now 150 kilometres from Broome and the wild weather now made the earlier cyclone look like a windy shower. Over the next 50 kilometres, the visibility deteriorated further and the high winds were escalating. Deborah's ringing mobile interrupted the silence of the two very nervous travellers.

'Deborah, where are you?' It was Andriena, who had walked her out of Port Hedland with Neil Owen. Now her voice sounded anxiously down the crackling phone line. 'Cyclone Fay has changed her mind, she's moving towards Broome which is now on Red Alert. You must find shelter somewhere.' Karin looked panic-stricken. 'That's a bit hard,' Deborah said, trying to stay calm and not worry her mum further. 'I'm on the edge of the Great Sandy Desert! There are no trees, no mountains, and definitely no shelter.'

Andriena took a deep breath. 'The nearest shelter is the Roebuck Plains Roadhouse,' she advised. 'That's 70 kilometres away.' The wind then knocked out the satellite mobile's connection.

When Andriena got through again some time later, her voice sounded very worried. She urged Deborah to hurry to the roadhouse as fast as she could. Karin was now becoming hysterical as Deborah gripped the wheel of the Britz and put the accelerator flat to the floor. Panic was rising in Deborah's throat and she felt more afraid for her poor mum than she did about maintaining her record.

With Deborah now out of range, Andriena was so worried she'd contacted the area's police patrols who were busy blocking off the roads where conditions were now treacherous.

Back in Melbourne, Glyn had been keeping an eye on the cyclone warning and had been on and off the phone to Deborah with updates, and was worried too. He called the authorities to alert them that his wife had now lost telephone reception and was somewhere out on the open road in possible danger.

Everyone was now concerned for the women, and Alistair Cameron, the co-owner of the Roebuck Plains Roadhouse received several phone calls from different individuals asking if they'd arrived yet.

'Not yet,' he said each time, observing the wind and rain through the restaurant window. 'I'll let you know as soon as she gets here.'

Both Deborah and her mum couldn't have been more relieved at the sight of the blue signpost alerting them to the roadhouse up ahead. They drove into the car park, swaying as they passed the police patrol now blocking off the three roads out of Roebuck Plains.

'Get out of this crazy weather,' said a police officer, approaching the van in the driving rain. 'This is a code red cyclone and you're putting yourself in danger.' Deborah parked the Britz and ushered Karin inside; with her mother now safe, her only concern was how she would keep her record alive.

In spite of the chaos there was a party mood building inside the roadhouse where locals and travellers now gathered to shelter from the pelting rain and howling winds. Everywhere people settled down with drinks and meals, happily chatting and grateful for a few unexpected days off work. Since nobody was going anywhere, they might as well make the most of it, they agreed.

'It's a bit of a party up here when there's a cyclone,' explained Alistair Cameron, relieved to see the two women he'd been receiving all these inquiries about. Even the State Emergency Services had been on the lookout for this crazy walker.

But while nobody else appeared to be too bothered about being grounded for a few days, Deborah was very worried indeed.

To Alistair's astonishment and her mother's dismay, Deborah disappeared from the restaurant and she was now negotiating with police in the car park about whether she could continue her walk.

'No,' said the officer, shaking his head. 'We've closed off some of the roads, you have to come inside.' They were not going to allow this woman to put herself in any more danger, or risk the lives of anyone else if they had to come looking for her because she was in trouble. 'Nobody goes walking in a Code Red Cyclone,' he said, aghast.

With floodwater now causing river levels to rise, and flooding everywhere, many roads were already impassable. Deborah had no idea what she was going to do about her record, and in desperation she rang Nobby Young again.

'Nobby, it's me. How can I complete this minimum record in a Code Red Cyclone?' she asked down the crackling phone line. Nobby suggested she paint a marker 100 metres out of the car park, and simply walk up and down in full sight of the police.

'Don't walk beyond the road blocks then or we'll arrest you,' warned the police officer now stationed at the roadhouse for the duration of the alert. 'We want you in our sights at all times, do you understand?' Deborah agreed, cautiously bracing herself for a few hours in this terrifying weather, scared by the prospect, and terrified of not keeping her record alive.

'I'll help,' said a motorcyclist from Victoria, sensing her nervousness. He drove up and down, his cycle wavering in the howling wind and rain, measuring and spraying markings on signposts beside the road 100 metres in front of the roadhouse as Deborah instructed.

Deborah then began the first of 210 laps up and back as she battled on to complete her minimum 21 kilometres. The weather conditions were appalling outside and the watching travellers and locals in the roadhouse had become so curious they were now moving their chairs towards the windows. Soon a whole row of faces lined the windows, front-row seats for a birds-eye view of this unexpected free entertainment.

The cyclone party, which was well and truly underway in the tavern where drinks now flowed freely, kicked up a gear as word spread that Deborah was walking in 120-knot gales for charity. Impressed, customers cheered her on as she struggled to stand upright and walk against the ferocious winds now battering her about. The cheering grew louder as she completed every arduous lap, now accompanied by Roebuck, the roadhouse's resident dog whose paws sloshed along in the rain beside her, his pink tongue dangling, enjoying the fun.

Inside, Alistair Cameron began a collection for the woman he was now convinced was a lunatic. If this cause was so worthy that this woman was crazy enough to walk for hours on a day like this, then Kids Helpline must be worth public support. As the drinks continued to flow, the donations poured in.

'Feel the fear and do it anyway,' Deborah chanted to herself. She had to admit, she was scared stiff; but she had to complete this daily goal, cyclone or no cyclone. Hours later, the water gushing from her sodden runners and dripping off her clothes, Deborah trudged back into the roadhouse to a resounding cheer.

'What about a drink?' suggested Alistair. Neither of them realised it then, but the seeds of a very important new friendship were being sown in the middle of nowhere. As they chatted, Alistair told Deborah he hailed from Tasmania where only months earlier she'd completed the first leg of her mammoth journey. She discovered that his Scottish-born father, a former shepherd, managed a farm near Launceston and that he had a stake in the roadhouse. In turn, he heard all about her adventure so far, and about the generous

Australian spirit that had spurned her on. He was inspired by this incredible woman's guts.

'You won't get the van through the floods tomorrow,' warned the police. They were not prepared to allow her back onto the road to return to her last marker, or to begin the walk back towards the roadhouse in stages in a Britz. 'You'd be putting yourself at risk,' they said.

'They won't let me go,' groaned Deborah, sitting back at the bar where Alistair put in long hours. But this hard-working guy, who managed everything from the tavern, the petrol station and the associated caravan park where Deborah and Karin were now staying, had a solution.

'You'd better take my 4WD,' he offered. Deborah smiled to herself. Another outback angel right when she needed one, she thought gratefully.

For the next few days the Roebuck Plains Roadhouse became Deborah's base as she backtracked in Alistair's 4WD to her last marker on the road where she'd first heard about Cyclone Fay. Each day, she trudged through flooded roads, up to her shins in water and her runners sloshing as she went; each day she ended it by spraying a white painted mark on a signpost along the road so she'd know where to begin again the following morning. Slowly, the white marker crept nearer and nearer to the roadhouse until she finally completed the walk in the wildest of weather in shorter stages of 21 kilometres.

But things weren't *so* bad, she reasoned, as she chatted to her new friend, Alistair, who seemed to work 24/7 and who was considering relinquishing his stake in the roadhouse partnership. The connection between the pair had been instant, and he'd been so helpful to her. Now he offered her the words of encouragement that she needed to hear. Watching him work, Deborah felt as though she'd known Alistair from another life. It was as if they'd had an entire lifetime together before they'd even met – and both of them sensed it.

As the days passed, the friendship bond between them grew and her unexpected delay turned out to be a gift. It was an added bonus that the restaurant served up the best roadhouse food in Australia, particularly their Sunday roasts which were almost as good as her mum's.

Deborah had really forged a connection with this sensible big-hearted Tasmanian who she was now convinced was her 'guardian angel'. When she finally waved goodbye, she promised she'd keep in touch with her new friend.

By the time Deborah reached her halfway mark of Fitzroy Crossing in mid-April, she felt as though she'd climbed a mountain and was on the downward descent. With more days behind her than ahead of her, she was encouraged to know she was on her way home. But the challenges of battling two cyclones had left her emotionally as well as physically battered and she spent a day after her departure from Roebuck sitting by the road in tears.

'I want to quit,' she sniffed as Alistair, her guardian angel, appeared in his 4WD.

He'd been wondering how the two women were travelling, given the destruction and flooding from Cyclone Fay. When his day off came, he had decided to drive up the road to find them. Now he sat with Deborah in the shade of a boab tree, listening in silence as Deborah poured her heart out. Afterwards they swam in the cooling waters of a crocodile-free billabong. Alistair's sensible words of encouragement restored calmness in Deborah and helped her focus again.

Deborah thought of Glyn back home in Victoria, where he was about to do his first long-distance run in the Coburg race, where runners compete by running for six, 12 and 24 hours. She couldn't help smiling as she recalled her own experience in that same race just a year earlier, when she'd eaten three bananas and made herself so sick she'd been forced to quit. She hoped Glyn had learned from her mistakes as she sent her best wishes towards him.

The Break-in

But if Deborah had considered quitting in the wake of the cyclones, another unexpected event a few days later made that option more appealing than ever.

At 1.30 in the morning, Deborah was woken by her crying mum, who told her they'd just been burgled. They had parked the van at Halls Creek in Western Australia, where Karin had decided to leave the door open to allow some cool air to circulate. Like her daughter sleeping in the Deluxe Penthouse Suite, she had been so soundly asleep when thieves broke into the van that she had not heard them rifling through their belongings. They were long gone when she suddenly woke and discovered that their pursues, jewellery, all Deborah's CDs and tapes, her digital camera and memory sticks recording her walk of a lifetime, their mobile phones and seven pairs of the Saucony runners Deborah had been road testing, had vanished with them.

Worse still, the donation bins complete with the thousands of dollars that Deborah had so keenly collected for Kids Helpline had gone too.

Acting Sergeant Hank Wiltschut arrived on the scene to find the women distraught for two very different reasons. Karin was alarmed and upset that they'd been robbed and were in possible danger; Deborah, now left with a single Saucony runner, was concerned about how she could continue to walk without credit cards, money or her shoes. By the time the sergeant left them, still lamenting the extent of their losses, it was three a.m. and Deborah, dejected and unable to sleep, decided to begin her walk of the day, leaving her mum afraid and alone.

'It felt good to walk under the stars,' wrote Deborah that night. 'It is a magical time on the earth to be walking out there as the sun starts to rise and the earth gives off a cool breath that revitalises your soul.'

She told her mum later that she knew if she hadn't gone walking, she would have fallen into bed in tears and called the whole thing off.

In the cold light of day, Deborah was distraught about the donation money and the loss of her precious memory sticks recording all the places she'd been and the angels she'd met. But most of all her heart ached as she blamed herself for letting Kids Helpline down. The burglary had denied all those needy youngsters the vital funds Kids Helpline needed to keep its welfare lines manned. Without the help of support workers, who was going to help these deprived kids escape terrible lives and realise their dreams? After all her efforts Deborah would be returning practically empty handed.

The locals at the Kimberley Hotel in Halls Creek were so horrified when they heard about the break-in and the theft of the money Deborah had collected for the charity that they promptly organised a raffle to try to replace some of the lost funds. The winner of the raffle even donated the money he'd won back to Kids Helpline.

'You're having two nights here, free on us,' insisted the man who owned the Kimberley Hotel chain in Halls Creek, aware that Deborah's mother was very shaken by the burglary and was now afraid of sleeping in the van at night.

The local radio also put out an appeal for the return of Deborah's camera and memory sticks, explaining the purpose of her walk. For the next three days Deborah was forced to walk in her Birkenstocks, avoiding inevitable blisters by rotating her shoes every 15 kilometres.

She was staggered to discover that Sergeant Wiltschut had apprehended the culprits – seven local youngsters, all of them still wearing the brand new Saucony runners Deborah had been given. The snazzy footwear quickly attracted the attention of a very suspicious Sergeant

The Break-in

Wiltschut, who confronted them, demanding: 'Where did you get those shoes?' The youngsters eyed each other up, feigning innocence. 'Bought 'em boss,' replied one, avoiding the officer's disbelieving gaze. The policeman knew full well from his discussions with the victims of this crime that these particular runners were being road tested and were not available for sale anywhere in Australia yet. The offenders were forced to hand over the sought-after items to the unimpressed officer who promptly returned them to their rightful owner.

'You mean the burglars were kids?' said Deborah, incredulous when the sergeant returned with her stolen runners. The realisation reduced her to tears. Somehow, being burgled by children when you're walking around Australia, through breakdowns and cyclones, just to raise money for needy children exactly like these, made her heart sink lower.

But she felt even more dismayed when the officer detailed the young offenders' family backgrounds, and later learned from various community members how widespread crime was in the region as a result of domestic violence and alcohol abuse.

'For some kids it's too unsafe to even consider going home at night,' said the owner of the hotel chain whose wife was a local police officer.

'There is often nothing in the cupboards to eat and they will steal from strangers for the money to get something to eat.'

The hotelier who had offered the two distraught women free accommodation told the story of another local burglary that, in spite of the seriousness of their situation, managed to put a smile on Deborah's face.

'Some local kids did a series of raids on hotels in the Kimberleys including the local bottle shop,' explained the owner. 'They took a wheelie bin into the bottle shop and filled it with grog, but decided to sample some of the bottles before they left,' he said. 'They wound up drinking so much they were still there next day, all passed out from their binge, with all the empties and the wheelie bin of remaining grog all around them.'

It was such a sad and desperate state of affairs that alcohol and need fuelled such crime in these remote areas, thought Deborah. When she told Glyn about the burglary he was more philosophical.

'Just think of it like this,' he soothed. 'The money you raised actually did go to kids who needed it . . . it just went directly there, instead of through the charity you are walking for!'

Thankfully the appeal on local radio for the return of her precious memory sticks resulted in one of the sticks later being found and posted on to Darwin, where it awaited her arrival.

Alistair, who had been in regular contact, was concerned when he learned about the burglary. 'My mum doesn't want to go any further – she's had enough and wants to go home,' confided Deborah, not blaming Karin at all. Since the burglary her mum now felt very vulnerable during the long hours on the road and she was also no longer sleeping. The burglary had also shaken Owen, who shared his wife's distress when she rang from Halls Creek. He too felt very uneasy about the prospect of the women being alone on the road.

'I'm coming to help,' said Alistair, and he drove 400 kilometres from Broome to Halls Creek, spending the following two days with Deborah and her mum, hoping his company would be moral support and a reassuring presence for Karin at night. He really was a guardian angel, thought Deborah. It seemed more than just coincidence that these 'outback angels' always seemed to appear when she was at her lowest.

News of the charity walk and the burglary had by now reached the ears of a famous Australian sporting legend. The local community at Halls Creek had discovered that the famous sportsman Herb Elliott was in the area and, feeling the philanthropic Deborah was in need of some inspiration, asked if she had time and would like to meet him.

'Would I ever!' she said, though she couldn't imagine this significant Australian middle-distance runner taking time out of his schedule to meet with *her*. Herb had won a gold medal in the 1960 Rome Olympics in the 1500 metres, and two Commonwealth gold

The new generation of migrant 'Aussies' in 1971, building a new life in the South Australian sunshine. From left to right: (back row) family friend, Dieter Langner; Deborah's Aunt Monika; Deborah's Oma, Erika Haufe; family friend, Inge Langner; Deborah's mum, Karin; Monika's husband Ray holding Deborah's cousin Garry. From left to right: (front row) family friend, Purzel Langner holding Deborah's brother, Adam, aged four; Deborah's Opa, Gerhard Haufe holding Deborah, aged two.

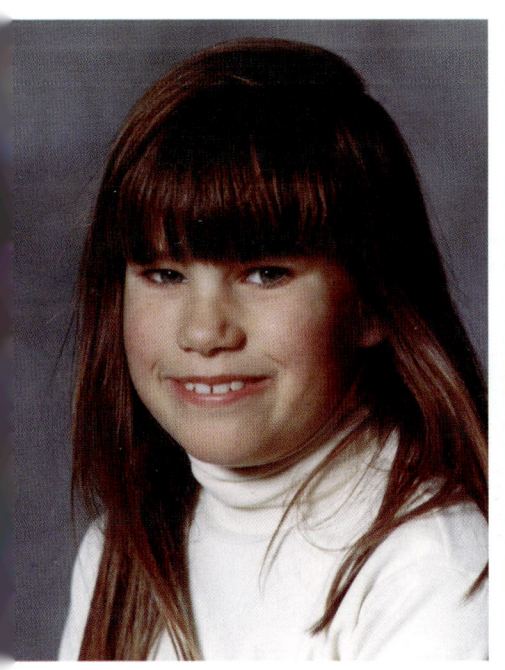

Even at six years old, Deborah was a little girl with big dreams

Deborah's inspirational meeting in November 2003 with her mentor, running guru Nobby Young, who tracked her down to Lochiel in the South Australian outback, to support her as she attempted to break his own world record walk around Australia

A 'pep' talk from former Olympic Running Legend, Herb Elliot, in Turkey Creek, Western Australia in April 2004, boosted Deborah's flagging spirits after outback burglars raided the Britz, stealing seven pairs of Deborah's runners – and all the donations she'd collected during her round-Australia walk

The small Britz van that Karin drove through hurricanes and deserts pulling the pop-up trailer Deborah nicknamed the 'Deluxe Penthouse Suite' that became home for 365 days during her world record walk around Australia

Crikey – Who's Crazy? Crocodile Hunter, Steve Irwin, welcomes Deborah to Australia Zoo in August 2004, later signing her witness book and agreeing that adventurers should follow their dreams – no matter how crazy they sound

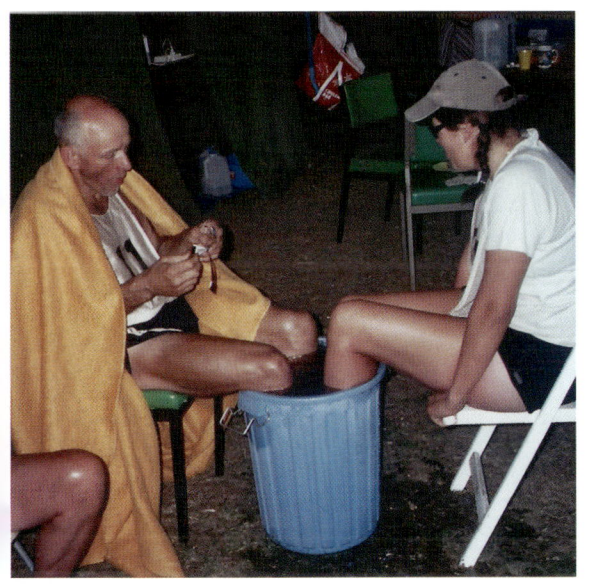

November 2004: On ice... Deborah shares a bucket of ice with fellow ultra-marathoner, Graeme Watts during the 2004 Colac six-day race as she battles the pain of shin splints. But her injury didn't stop her from breaking the Australian record for the longest distance walked in six days for the Under-35 age group.

A historic moment lost in time for Deborah, whose shock breast cancer diagnosis – just hours before this photo was taken – left her unable to recall a second of her run with the Queen's Baton on 15 March 2006 at the Opening of the Commonwealth Games in Melbourne

Deborah's chance encounter with inspirational Tassie breast cancer survivors, the Bosom Buddies, during her charity run around Tasmania with mate, Vlastik Skvaril, convinced her to set up Running Pink and run around Australia for breast cancer research

Deborah crosses the 9000-kilometre mark outside Mount Isa in April 2009, blissfully unaware that by the time she reaches her halfway mark 1000-kilometres up the highway, she'd be battling two broken feet and her dream run would soon be over

Above: Deborah and Maggie head into Elliott on 11 May 2009, just seconds before the police sirens spook the terrified dog and trigger the unfortunate fall which breaks both Deborah's feet

Right: When Deborah marked the end of the road on 5 June 2009, after running the last 864 kilometres of her 10,825-kilometre dream run on two broken feet, the journey was far from over! The pink marker she left on the corner of Crater Lake Road and the Stuart Highway, 99 kilometres south of Darwin, was still there the following year as she ran past again on her second world record attempt.

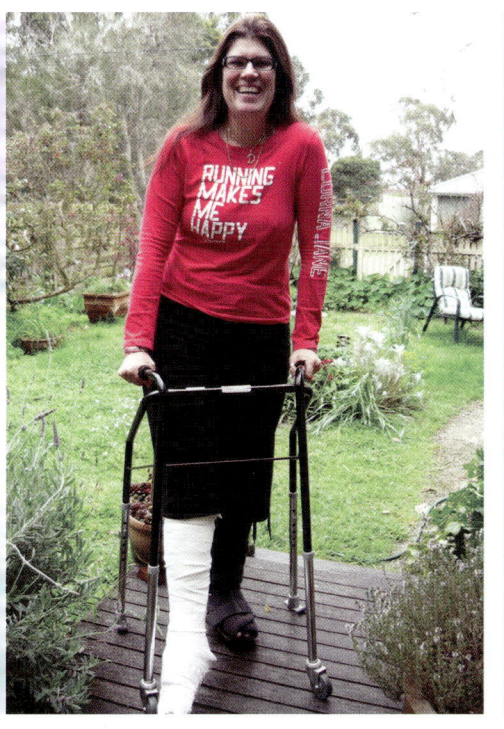

'Running Makes Me Happy', announces Deborah's bright pink t-shirt, as she recovers from her second surgery in September 2009. An email from another breast cancer survivor soon inspires Deborah to resume her run for a cure.

Back on her feet with no time to waste, Deborah attends this breast cancer fundraiser in October 2009 to encourage other breast cancer battlers and survivors to get behind Running Pink and her new world record attempt

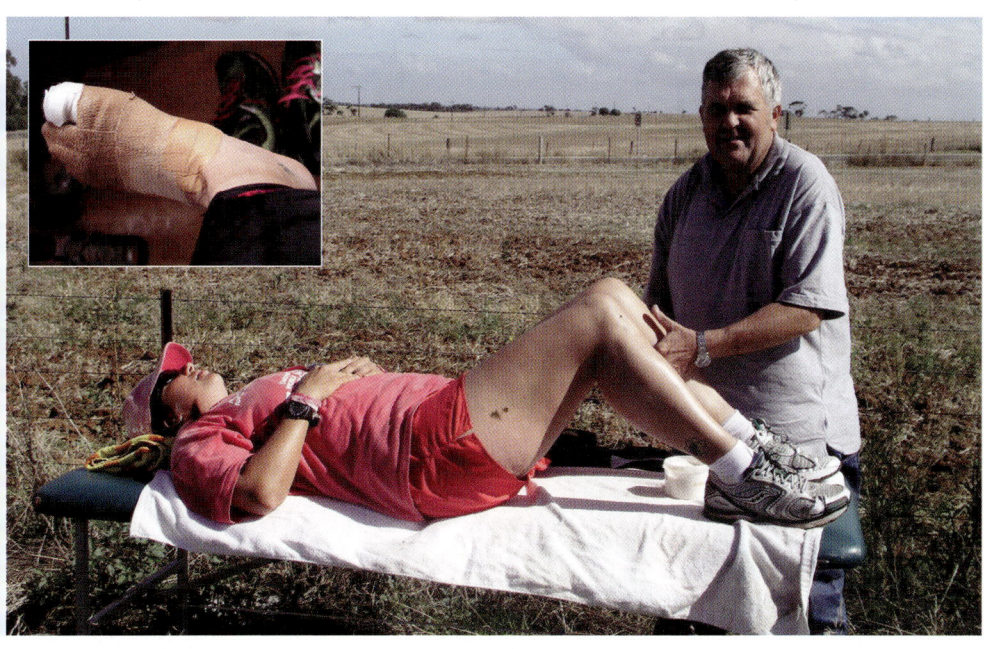

A second run and the appearance of Deborah's first highway 'angel' as good friend, Malcolm Matthews, arrives on the roadside to give Deborah a much needed massage and tend to the giant blisters that threatened to end her new dream. By April 2010, Deborah's blisters were so painful that Malcolm flew to Adelaide to change the taped dressings on her feet – and found love!

Back at the marker south of Darwin where her doomed first run had ended 15 months earlier, Deborah poses for a photo with 'outback angel' and important support crew member, Alistair Cameron. This photo, taken on 4 October 2010, marks the moment Deborah completed the loop to become the first female to run around Australia (non-continuously).

Above: A family with wanderlust in their genes! Deborah, who is running around Australia for the second time, is reunited with her truck driver brother, Adam at the Nundroo Roadhouse. This photo, taken on 19 May 2010, shows them having brief family time on the road with parents, Karin and Owen.

Left: Pink PJs and highway hi-jinx are a highlight for Deborah and relief crew member Merienne Shortridge, whose cheeky antics captured the imaginations of bemused truckies on the road north of Carnarvon, Western Australia on 25 July 2010.

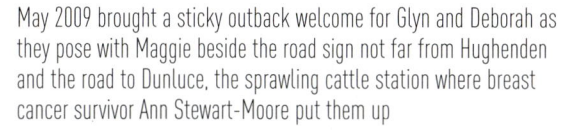

On 13 March 2011 Deborah finally catches up with breast cancer battler Donna Crebbin and her mum, Ruby, in Sydney. This photograph was taken after Donna joined Deborah on the road and ran her very first half marathon — just four weeks after finishing her treatment!

May 2009 brought a sticky outback welcome for Glyn and Deborah as they pose with Maggie beside the road sign not far from Hughenden and the road to Dunluce, the sprawling cattle station where breast cancer survivor Ann Stewart-Moore put them up

Pink Pigtails and a cowboy gal's welcome from breast cancer survivor, Lismore Mayor, Jenny Dowell, when Deborah arrived in her town on 17 February 2011. On both of Deborah's runs, Jenny — who had run her mayoral campaign while battling treatment — turned out to welcome the pink crusader in her bright pink wig and glitzy cowboy hat.

An 'oarsome' guard of honour as breast cancer survivors from Hobart's Dragon-Abreast group welcome Deborah back into their home town at the culmination of her world record run in May 2011

Left: Deborah being 'pinked' by the Canberra Bosom Buddies as she arrives in the nation's political capital on 15 January 2009 during her first run

Right: On 15 March 2011, on the anniversary of her own breast cancer diagnosis, Deborah places flowers on the memorial stone of former Olympian and fellow breast cancer battler, Kerryn McCann at Sharkey's Beach, New South Wales. Kerryn's run for gold gave Deborah the inspiration and hope she needed as she watched the historic event on the hospital TV after having her cancerous tumour removed. Shattered at Kerryn's death during her first run, Deborah's took a detour on her second run, passing Kerryn's hometown to pay tribute to a true Aussie champion.

Larger-than-life 'angel' John Hogno from Maitland, New South Wales – who turned out on the road to cheer Deborah on during her first run – presented her with a breast cancer flag second time around. This photo was taken on 2 March 2011 as he cheered her on her homeward-bound journey through New South Wales.

Deborah and Maggie 'paws' for a photo with flamboyant breast cancer fundraisers, the X-Men who had tracked Deborah down to the Northern Territory outback town of Larrimah on her second run in October 2010. They'd heard about this crazy pink woman's run for a cure from Deborah's doctor at the Master's Games in Adelaide, and drove out onto the road to applaud her efforts.

Clouds of pink tulle and some very unlikely hairy fairies give Deborah and their tiny Western Australian town of Jerramungup a chuckle on 18 June 2010. Their hilarious antics raised thousands of dollars for Running Pink.

Even the tinest, most remote communities turned out in their pink hoards to welcome Deborah and Maggie with donations and a good-old Aussie barbecue. This sausage sizzle held by the Childer's Professionals in Queensland in January 2011 was one of many community events in support of Running Pink.

Up before Santa had finished filling his stockings, Deborah ended Christmas Day 2010 feeling worn out after running all day in the wake of Cyclone Tasha

Running Pink's Director of Greetings was the star of the show on both runs, and Maggie took her duties so seriously that in August 2010 she happily obliged ABC Radio Kimberley with a quick phone interview south of Broome before her morning roll in the dirt

It's a dog's life but somebody's got to do it. Maggie strikes a pose for yet another flash light during warm up aerobics with her mum at the May 2011 Mother's Day Classic in Hobart. When this photo was taken, Deborah was just an hour away from completing her record-breaking run around Australia.

The ultimate in outback girl power as Deborah poses with her mum, Karin, at the Tropic of Capricorn landmark road-sign on 28 July 2010 during her second attempt

Food on the go . . . as Karin's creative culinary skills see her cooking up a hearty breakfast of pancakes in her pink caravan in the middle of the Nullabor during Deborah's second run in May 2010. Karin's spectacular roasts became her speciality on both runs.

Deborah runs in the dark in a desperate bid to make it to Bundaberg Airport in time to catch the plane to Canberra for the 2011 Australia Day awards the next day

Deborah's peculiar appearance as she ran with a mask drenched in eucalyptus oil to combat a debilitating cold, prompted one larrikin driver in Western Australia in June 2010, to nickname her 'Michael Jackson!' But not even sickness could put the brakes on this road show.

Santa gets snow in December but his Christmas present to Deborah on Christmas Day 2010 was Cyclone Tasha. This photo shows Deborah outrunning the floods due to strike Giru in Queensland for higher ground. By the end of January 2011, the devastating floods that destroyed homes and caused countless fatalities, saw the state declared a national disaster zone.

Before the rains, in August 2010, Deborah had battled intense temperatures through the Kimberley region – though the generosity of road crew workers donating to her collection tins meant her efforts were well rewarded

The rains that brought devastation to Queensland earned Deborah the nickname 'the rain genie' and prompted many detours and delays for the pink crusader, pictured here in January 2011 running up to her shins in water with Maggie sloshing alongside her

With the floods finally behind her, Deborah is joined by ultra-marathon legend Gary Parsons on her run near Caloundra, Queensland

On the last leg home through Victoria on 16 April 2011, outback angels and fellow ultra-marathoners, Colin Ricketts and Ken Nash, turn up for a group hug and keep their good friend's spirits up on the road

Many breast cancer battlers and survivors were so inspired by Deborah's adventure that they turned out on the roadside to join her run and share their stories. In this photo, taken on 18 April 2011, cancer patient, Kirrily (on Deb's left) runs five kilometres before heading off for chemo!

Friends in high places as Karin organises a VIP meeting between Deborah and Australia's PM, Julia Gillard, and Health Minister Nicola Roxon. This photo was taken on 24 March 2011 – just weeks after the PM met Deborah at the Australia Day Awards. The PM signed Deborah's witness book and later appeared on Question Time wearing the silver breast cancer brooch the runner had given her.

'Only the runner and only the cook!' Deborah's meeting with celebrity chef Maggie Beer was a highlight of the Australia Day Awards, where the culinary queen was not surprised to learn that the true-blue Aussie fare awaiting Deborah on the road was good old snags and tomato sauce!

The 'never say never' girl arrives back in the 'never never' a second time, again marking the corner of Crater Lake Road and Stuart Highway where two broken feet had caused her to abandon her dream run first time around. This photo, taken on 4 October 2010, captured the historic occasion when Deborah became the first female to run the entire loop of Australia. But she kept on running – to become the first female to run around Australia continuously without a day off.

Not even a bottle of flat passion pop was enough to burst Deborah's bubble on 6 May 2011 when she finally broke the 21-year-old record held by American Sarah Fulcher to become the female title holder of the longest continuous run in the world. When Deborah popped the cork to celebrate her milestone five kilometres from New Norfolk in Tasmania, it wouldn't even fizz.

Above: Deborah's 'mission impossible' finally ended on 8 May 2011 back where it had begun – on the steps of Parliament House, Hobart, surrounded by the crew who had helped her achieve her dream

Left; Right royal bragging rights for Karin on 21 October 2011 when she accompanied Deborah on her historic meeting with the Queen who learned all about the astonishing record run from the PM, who introduced the philanthropic runner as 'a very special Australian'. Deborah and Karin later posed for this photograph with another special Aussie, running legend Robert De Castella.

Putting their best feet forward on a new fundraising mission, Deborah's new Running Pink recruits for the 2012 London Marathon meet with Tasmanian Liberal Opposition Leader Will Hodgman in November 2011, at the launch of their new adventure. Pictured from left to right are breast cancer survivors, Deb Watkins and Teresa Mitchell; Paul Taranto whose mother survived the disease; Will Hodgman who lost his own mother to breast cancer; Commonwealth runner and breast cancer survivor, Mandy Giblin; Deborah; and team mascot, Maggie.

The Break-in

medals in 1958 at Cardiff in the 88 yards and one-mile races. In his heyday he also set a new world record for the mile in 1958. If anyone knew about world records, Herb did!

The chief executive officer of the local council, who had heard about the burglary, joined forces with Tom Stevens, the Minister for the Kimberley, and made contact with Herb. They told him all about this worthy walk around the country and about the burglary and loss of the charity funds for Kids Helpline. Herb said he definitely wanted to meet Deborah.

A couple of days later, Deborah and her mum were introduced to Herb over dinner at the local roadhouse in Turkey Creek.

'You must be the woman I've been hearing all about,' he said, shaking Deborah's hand.

She sat in front of this famous sportsman in awe, unable to believe he'd been willing to find time for this incredible meeting. After the misery of the past days, meeting this legend was a thrilling and unexpected distraction and Deborah just kept pinching herself. Herb was as fascinating in person as she'd imagined he'd be, and chatted easily to the two women over the usual roadhouse fare of fish and chips. Deborah had heard him on radio once talking about doubt sabotaging dreams. Now, in person he gave her a similar inspirational Olympic-style pep talk.

'You must not let this get to you,' he said, referring to the break-in. 'And don't start doubting yourself – doubt destroys dreams and ruins goals.' He told Deborah, one of his biggest fans, to stay focussed and not to quit. 'You have come so far now that you couldn't possibly think of giving up . . . you *can* achieve this dream.'

The meeting was another highlight in her journey, and an encounter she would never forget. She shook hands with this amazing Australian and left the roadhouse feeling very blessed. Angels really did appear on the road when she needed them most.

On 27 April Deborah crossed the border into the Northern Territory, smiling at the news that her camera had been retrieved and filled with the hope that her remaining missing memory sticks might also turn up.

She had spent the previous night battling frogs which leapt into her bed and even onto her pizza, contemplating all the amazing people she had met on this incredible journey. Earlier that day, she'd had a chance encounter with a former journalist called Bruce, who told her how he'd once ran away to join a circus. He'd achieved his dream of becoming a lion tamer, he told her, and though he was now working as a journalist again, he'd never regretted pursuing that dream.

He had turned out along the road to cheer Deborah on, keen to give his support to another Aussie with a dream to chase.

The Never Never

Deborah's first few days in the Northern Territory were dogged by jetlag. After nearly five months in Western Australia she'd become used to waking at four a.m. and watching the sunrise at 5.30 a.m. But the time difference meant the Northern Territory was 90 minutes ahead, and this left Deborah's body clock struggling to adjust to waking in darkness and waiting an extra hour until 6.30 a.m. for the sun to put in an appearance. Walking longer hours in the dark had left her feeling as if she had jetlag.

As Deborah ran along the Barkly Highway in the Northern Territory, she found herself smiling at the rather appropriately named town of Marathon. She'd been heading into the town and had reached the intersection on the highway when she saw a woman wearing large sunnies, crossing the intersection to talk to her.

'I didn't have breast cancer,' said the woman, checking out Deborah's t-shirt. 'But I did have brucellosis, a very rare disease . . . there are only 18 cases of it ever recorded in Australian medical history.' The disease, apparently contracted from cattle, initially robbed the woman of her memory. 'Later it cost me my eye,' she said, sadly. She removed her sunglasses.

Deborah was visibly shocked to see the woman had an empty eye socket.

'That's not so bad,' said the woman, openly. 'Not remembering my family was far worse.'

Walking in crocodile territory was a new experience for a wary Deborah who spotted her first wild crocodile from a distance, worrying that he might see a lone walker as some sort of fast food. Another phone call from Nobby Young, who was still monitoring his apprentice's progress, had left Deborah feeling very encouraged. But sadly her mum was not.

After outracing cyclones and the recent burglary she was missing Owen and feeling worn out from long, lonely days behind the wheel. Since Alistair's departure, Karin was feeling even more vulnerable. Her heightened state of anxiety since the burglary escalated when she couldn't get hold of Owen on the phone.

'It's not like Owen,' said Karin, looking worried as she hung up the satellite mobile that night. She'd tried several times over the past couple of days, wondering in her state of hyper-vigilance if something had happened. The following day all was explained when Owen pulled up beside them on the road outside Timber Creek. Karin's face lit up with relief when she saw her husband emerging from their car. Owen had been so upset by Karin's distress on the phone that he'd organised annual leave and made the long drive from Melbourne to accompany her for the next two weeks.

'Glyn is flying to Darwin for the last part of Deborah's walk home,' he said. 'You're coming home with me – I don't want you doing this any more.'

Glyn was due to arrive in Darwin in a fortnight to begin his long service leave, and with her husband beside her, Karin's spirits lifted considerably and Deborah's private concerns that her walk would be over if her support crew bailed on her, were greatly alleviated.

By early May Deborah had crossed the spectacular Victoria River Crossing, which passes over the river that sits among sandstone gorges and high cliffs and where the flat top range provides an impressive sight. Deborah walked down the descent towards the river at sunset, enjoying the spectacle of the gorges which glowed red in the early dusk making it look like something from a sci-fi movie.

When she reached Katherine, 190 kilometres away, Stephen Gschwenter, the son of the owners of Britz in Australia appeared on the road ready to walk the visitor into town. A group of schoolchildren waited to welcome her, along with the town's Mayor, James

Forscutt. Deborah and her parents spent an enjoyable night with Stephen who proved as generous as his parents, and took them all out to dinner, promising he'd see her again very soon.

Stephen was as true as his word, arriving in Darwin a few days later to walk Deborah into the city. Afterwards he kindly drove Deborah and a newly arrived Glyn around town, taking them out to dinner again and providing them with an evening of interesting conversation.

The walk down-country towards what Australians call the Red Centre, was uneventful until Deborah suddenly contracted a bad case of food poisoning. Suffering vomiting and diarrhoea in such intense heat caused her to become very dehydrated and so weak she struggled to even manage her minimum daily distance.

As if the sickness wasn't enough, the battery then failed in the Britz and she had to walk on in the heat carrying litres of water on her back while Glyn returned to Katherine to get the battery fixed. She felt as though she was dying as she trudged on and by the time he returned, she'd completely run out of water and was sitting on the side of the road looking very sick.

The last few days in the Northern Territory was dogged by cold temperatures and a strong head wind that left Deborah struggling to complete 33 kilometres.

'The weather will clear soon, then you'll be warmer,' said Alistair, worried by the flat tone down the phone line. Alistair had another observation. 'Your diary entries sound like you're doing a walk in the park,' he said. Deborah burst into tears.

'It's no picnic out here,' she sobbed, recalling the many challenges and the low points when she could so easily have called it quits.

'So . . .' said Alistair, drawing his breath, 'tell people about the struggles then. Be honest . . . it will allow people to understand more of what this journey is really all about.'

Alistair was right, thought Deborah. From that moment she vowed to ensure her journal was more frank and reflected the trials and tribulations of a walk that would soon be over.

Crossing the state border into Queensland brought a rush of

relief. Now she was in the eastern states she felt even more strongly that she was homeward bound and on her way towards her world record. To save time, Glyn had begun parking alongside the road instead of seeking out campsites, so that his wife, now walking longer days, could get going first thing every morning.

In Queensland, Deborah had her first close encounter with a snake. With the van's toilet being used for storage, she had tentatively made her way into the bush near Mount Isa and was cautiously squatting as she went about her business, when she spied a giant black snake slithering towards her. Frozen with fright, she held her breath as the highly poisonous snake slithered silently over her feet.

'Good job I'd already been,' she later told Glyn. The sight of that snake was enough to make anyone pee their pants.

But if Australia is a vast country, this was still a small world, thought Deborah as she ran into a familiar face again in the tiny Queensland township of Prairie.

'I was just in the area,' said the grey nomad who pulled up ahead of Deborah in his van and was now walking towards his protégé, still apparently keen to monitor her progress at close quarters.

Again, it hadn't been a difficult feat to find Deborah and everyone definitely seemed to know everyone else's business, even up here in the middle of nowhere thousands of kilometres from where she had first encountered Nobby in the South Australian outback.

Deborah was glad of Nobby's companionship as he walked beside her in the humidity from Prairie to Charters Towers.

'You're doing great,' said her mentor, looking particularly impressed with her efforts, his generous spirit shining through as he encouraged her to keep going. While other record-holders might have been precious or overly protective of their own great achievement, this big-hearted little man actually seemed to want this young woman to break his record and set a new one of her own.

'A few have already tried, but nobody's beaten it yet,' he said, amazed himself. 'I guess nobody realises how tough it is out here unless they've tried it. It's hard yakka on the body and the mind!'

Nobby also had a word of advice for Deborah. 'Girl . . . you are running a bit behind because of all those cyclones,' he said, thoughtfully. 'You've got to up the ante if you want to beat my record . . . which I know you can do!'

Nobby left Deborah walking on towards Cairns and Townsville which sit on the coastline overlooking the sparkling waters of the Pacific Ocean and the Great Barrier Reef.

When Deborah arrived in Townsville, her guru was there again, just 'happening' to be in the area. He greeted her warmly and escorted her into the northern Queensland town with great pride, aware he'd been in the inspiration of this new world contender. Nobby's kindness amazed Deborah; she believed he had given her a beautiful gift. His selflessness had taught her that this walk was not about records, it was about giving yourself to others and being gracious. Nobby's innate kindness had already seen him giving his home to his former wife, seeing no sense in keeping a home base when he preferred to live a nomadic life wandering around the highways and byways of the country that he loved.

'Keep it up, girl,' said Nobby, as he waved goodbye and vanished as quickly as he'd arrived. 'You're going to make it!'

Deborah had taken Nobby's advice on board and had now ramped up her walking pace from 49 kilometres a day to 56 kilometres, in days that began even earlier and finished much later.

Deborah's reward for her hard work came as she walked out of Townsville and lifted her gaze to glimpse a magnificent rainbow arcing its way across the sky in the afternoon heat.

Crikey – Who's Crazy?

When Deborah arrived in Rockhampton she realised that in order to beat Nobby's record she still needed to add some extra kilometres to her journey. She decided she would do this by walking a loop inland through Emerald and back into Rockhampton.

On the road from Rockhampton to Emerald, a local police officer had a request: 'Would you mind speaking to the kids at the school here? They could do with some sound advice and a few dreams to follow.'

Later that day, Deborah addressed the tiny gathering at the indigenous community school and talked about her journey so far, showing the interested youngsters maps of where she had been and where her dream would take her next.

'It's important to have goals, to have a dream,' she told them. Then it was down to more serious business as she spoke about the work of Kids Helpline and how the charity could help kids with problems at home. A teenage girl with a solemn face was observing Deborah closely, and after the meeting sidled shyly up to her.

'So I can tell them about my dad?' she whispered, looking nervously around. 'I can tell them what he's doing to me?'

Deborah's heart went out to the youngster, who was about 13. 'You can tell them anything and they can help,' she advised gently.

But Deborah left that day battling the urge to rush back and drag that poor girl out of there and take her home. She'd heard similar stories at so many schools, but this girl's anguished face would be etched in her mind forever.

'There was nothing I could do,' she told Glyn, feeling helpless.

'Yes, there was,' he said. 'And you did it! You told her about the Helpline and what the charity could do to help.'

Deborah knew that in cases where the phone-line counsellors suspected serious abuse, they had an obligation to alert the appropriate authorities. But she couldn't help thinking about this girl and other children like her.

At the same little town, the policeman also asked Deborah if she would talk about the work of Kids Helpline to his colleagues. It was reassuring even for the police to understand exactly what they were dealing with, and to understand the work of an organisation that was there to help youngsters in remote communities where alcohol abuse, domestic violence and other forms of abuse are rife.

Deborah completed her loop and was on her way into Rockhampton when an unexpected injury looked like threatening her world record again.

'Owwwwwh,' yelped Glyn as Deborah rushed outside to see what the commotion was about. She was shocked to find Glyn writhing on the ground, his face clouded with pain. 'I fell,' he explained, pointing to the ladder leading to the top of the pop-up trailer. He had been fixing something when he'd lost his footing and fallen, landing heavily on his hip.

No amount of painkillers that day seemed to ease Glyn's pain, and he was clearly in agony as he tried to climb back into the driver's seat of the Britz. At the end of the day, he was in so much pain Deborah suggested he should make the time to see a doctor in Rockhampton.

'You've bruised your hip,' said the doctor at a local medical centre the following morning. But Glyn, unable to get around without crutches or even to lie comfortably in bed, wasn't so sure. Since he was now Deborah's only support crew and was obviously in too much pain to even sit behind the wheel, let alone drive, Deborah flew into a panic, aware that without a support crew, her walk was over.

'Is there any chance you could come back?' she asked her mum. But in her heart she already knew the answer was 'no'. Owen had only just arrived back home in Melbourne with his exhausted wife and there was no way Karin wanted to assume the role again.

'What am I going to do?' she wailed down the phone to her friend Alistair.

Since she'd left Roebuck Plains, Alistair had relinquished his share in the roadhouse and had returned home to Tasmania, where he was pondering on his future. But with his friend's final homeward bound journey hanging in the balance, he didn't hesitate.

'I'll fly to Rockhampton,' he offered.

Deborah continued her walk the next day, heartened to know that Alistair was already on his way. Glyn, loaded on painkillers, managed the short drive to the small regional airport to wait for him, leaving his wife walking along the road to the town of Gladstone further down the coast.

Glyn anticipated that with Alistair behind the wheel they would catch up with Deborah within a couple of hours. But a flight delay saw Alistair's plane arriving five hours later than expected and Deborah, with her water and food on her back, trudged on wondering what had happened.

By the time the men found Deborah she'd already walked into Gladstone, the gateway to Heron Island, one of the many pretty islands scattered around the Great Barrier Reef. With no sign of her support crew by dusk, she had trudged into Gladstone without any food or water left, and without any money.

'Would you mind giving me a glass of water?' she asked the owner of a local hotel, after sitting outside for ages wondering where the Britz was and what she would do that night without any money. The hotelier, observing the thirsty dusty woman, had a better idea.

'Come upstairs with me,' he said, leading Deborah to the upper floor of the hotel where he made her a roast beef sandwich and handed her a cold drink.

She was greatly relieved to see Glyn and Alistair arrive at the hotel that night, as she'd begun to worry something bad had happened to them on the road. The pain in Glyn's hip would see him struggling all the way back to Melbourne where X-rays would later reveal he'd been suffering from a fractured hip.

Deborah continued down the east coast, the anticipation of beating the world record building by the day. By August 2004 she was walking down the picturesque Sunshine Coast, an hour and a half's drive from Brisbane, when she realised she needed someone to sign her witness log for the day. She'd spotted the signposts for Australia Zoo, the home of celebrity wildlife ambassador and global TV personality, Steve Irwin.

'I should go and get Steve to sign my book,' laughed Deborah after breakfast that morning. But as she trudged off, Alistair and Glyn decided that they would drive ahead and make a stop-off at the country's best-known wildlife park where they'd find someone to sign the log. Who knows – perhaps the celebrity himself might be around to do the honours, they agreed mischievously. Then they would be able to turn Deborah's throwaway joke into a reality that would knock her off her feet.

'Where are you?' asked Alistair down the phone, a couple of hours later.

'Not far,' said Deborah, checking her GPS. The boys were at Beerwah, close to Australia Zoo, when they rang again.

'Where are you now?' they asked.

Deborah was a bit taken aback. They were unusually persistent today and she wasn't sure why they appeared to be pushing her along. Alistair instructed her to follow the signs for Australia Zoo and she assumed he'd found someone on the gate to witness her log.

About half an hour later, Deborah made her way up the long winding road towards the world famous zoo, where a crowd of staff were gathered around the turnstiles at the front entrance. They made a huge fuss of the world record contender, handing her Australia Zoo t-shirts, a hat and other memorabilia.

'Would you like a drink?' offered one of the khaki-clad staff members.

'Thanks,' said Deborah, gratefully. She sipped her juice and checked her watch.

'Would you like a seat?' offered a friendly faced woman. But Deborah never sat down during a long day of walking.

'I'd just get stiff and I'd never get up again,' she joked. She checked her watch again, knowing she needed to get going if she was to keep her kilometres up and make Brisbane the following day, where she had a reception with the Lady Mayoress of Brisbane and had organised to visit the Kids Helpline Call Centre.

Deborah was so focussed on the time she barely noticed the exchange of knowing looks between Glyn, Alistair and the staff still thronging around the gates.

Deborah was stunned to see the familiar faces of Steve Irwin and his American-born wife, Terri, suddenly appear at the gates. When the staff had heard the purpose of Deborah's walk from Glyn and Alistair, they'd telephoned their celebrity bosses who instantly wanted to meet the woman behind this terrific cause.

'Welcome,' said the Crocodile Hunter. Deborah stretched her hand out to shake his, and was surprised to find that this friendly guy suddenly pulled away. 'Sorry,' he said. 'But I have to be careful, I've just come back from the Northern Territory where I've been tagging crocs for the university,' he explained. 'Broke two of me fingers wrestlin' crocs!'

This famous Australian was so passionate about his work that he'd volunteered to work with the croc tagging team.

'Sounds like a very dangerous job to me,' laughed Deborah.

Steve studied his hand and nodded. 'Crikey . . . it certainly was!'

But if Deborah was interested in Steve's work, he was far more curious about her adventures.

'Heard you've outraced a couple of cyclones,' he said, amazed to learn about Deborah's two a.m. starts and how she was now walking up to 60 kilometres a day to beat Nobby Young's 10-year world record walk. 'You must be crazy,' laughed Steve.

Now it was Deborah who shook her head: 'You think I'm crazy ... from where I'm standing you're insane – you wrestle crocs for a living!'

The pair of adventurers laughed as they posed together for photographs.

'We're both doing what we love,' said Steve. 'And we're both following our dreams!' Deborah smiled.

'And we both think each other's dreams are crazy – now *that's* crazy!' There was a story in that, she thought, as Steve and Terri signed her book and waved her on her way.

At her next school in Brisbane, Deborah made a point of relating the story of her special meeting with Steve Irwin, the 'Crikey' man.

'People might tell you you're crazy when you follow your dreams,' Deborah told the schoolchildren. 'But you should do it anyway, because here were two people doing crazy things they absolutely love, and each of them think the other one is totally nuts! But it won't stop us doing it because that's what we are most passionate about.'

On 23 September at exactly 4.40 a.m. Deborah finally achieved her dream – arriving in Sydney in darkness to break Nobby Young's world walk time and distance record.

'We thought we'd walk you past your finish line,' beamed Glen and Heath from Saucony, whose runners she had well and truly road tested. They had arrived on the outskirts of Sydney at three a.m. eager to join Deborah on the last lap of her walk as witnesses to the momentous occasion. Deborah achieved her world record with the biggest smile on her face, hurrying towards the city's Central Business District and the studios of Channel Seven where she had been invited to celebrate her amazing achievement on its popular breakfast show, *Sunrise*.

The show's producers had organised for a gang of children to welcome Deborah outside Brekky Central when she arrived for her interview, in which she talked about Kids Helpline and her astonishing new world record. An exhilarated Deborah explained that she'd walked 70 kilometres through the night to get into Sydney that morning and break the 10-year record and make her TV appearance on time.

She was still running on adrenalin when she headed out of the city with a crowd of well-wishers and Kids Helpline people.

'How do you feel?' strangers asked, crowding around the new world record holder. Deborah wasn't sure. She didn't really feel much different. Deborah knew the 1000-kilometres walk back to Melbourne would see her setting a new benchmark for the new world record walk.

Her answer was simple: 'I feel like I'm walking against myself now,' she said.

Deborah felt strangely flat the next morning on the long walk home to Melbourne, just as she had when she'd left Norseman after using up all her emotional and physical reserves to get there in time for Christmas. But Norseman had been a smaller, medium-term goal and this was the real thing: the ultimate goal she'd been picturing for a whole year. Now continuing the arduous walk with the record already safely under her belt, felt lacklustre.

'Well, you've got to get home somehow,' she told herself. 'So just keep walking.' Her spirits were lifted when Nobby, hearing that his world record of 10 years had finally been broken, made contact by letter, congratulating her on the great achievement. It touched Deborah's heart that this generous spirited man, who had joined her on the road to offer his support, was so thrilled that someone else had finally over taken his success.

'Others have tried over the years,' said the guru of the long distance walk. 'But only you have succeeded!'

In mid-October 2004 Deborah finally arrived home in Melbourne, where Kids Helpline had organised a welcome committee of local schoolchildren and celebrities at Federation Square, next to the small square where her walk had originally begun a year earlier.

'Well done, what an achievement,' said the Victorian Minister for Sport, Justin Madden. World title winner and Olympic skier Kristie Marshall gave Deborah a congratulatory hug.

'What a challenge,' she said.

You're not kidding, thought Deborah, who posed for a few photographs and short interviews with a variety of news channels.

Then she wandered off towards the square where her walk had begun, finishing her adventure right back where it started.

Her incredible journey was at an end, but the lessons she'd learned, the amazing people she'd met, and the memories would last a lifetime. This world record walk had taught her who Deborah De Williams really was. It was a challenge that had reaffirmed who she was, what she stood for, what was important to her, what her ethics were and what mattered most in her life.

Deborah's incredible walk broke five world records, including the record for the longest continuous walk by anyone on the planet. She had walked 16,684 kilometres in 365 days without a single day off and had raised over $150,000 for Kids Helpline. It was an achievement that would later prompt Alistair to nominate her as an inspirational Australian – a woman worthy of being a baton runner in the 2006 Commonwealth Games.

Deborah De Williams had survived last-minute nerves and breakdowns, cyclones, crocodiles, snakes and burglary to achieve her dream.

Bedridden

The new attempt to achieve Deborah's dream to become the first woman to run continuously around Australia was the only thing she could think about the afternoon she hobbled away from the specialist's rooms in East Melbourne — the nurse's dismissive words still ringing in her ears.

Deborah hadn't known a single thing about ultra-marathon walking when she'd set off to walk all around the country back in 2003. She'd simply told her family: 'If ET can do it, then I can do it!' But she now told herself that if she could run more than 800 kilometres on two broken feet that could have imploded at any moment, then anything was possible!

Better still, she had an added incentive to complete this new goal, knowing that *when* she finally succeeded she'd be the first woman to continuously walk *and* run around the country non-stop.

Deborah also knew, from all her amazing encounters with inspirational strangers and from the many stories of hope she'd been told on her walk, and again on her doomed run, that anything really is possible if you want it enough.

So many of the wonderful Australians who had crossed her path on her two big adventures had now heard about the unfortunate injuries that had brought her world record attempt to a premature end. They shared Deborah's disappointment in their many emails, phone calls, cards and letters which somehow found their way to her in Melbourne.

She'd lost count of the number of people who had urged her

not to give up hope. The new Facebook page she'd set up since her injury to keep her growing fan following up to date on her progress – along with Maggie's ongoing Dog Blog – was, to her amazement, now attracting thousands of hits every week.

Every time Deborah logged onto her Facebook page there would be dozens of new friends and postings from around Australia as breast cancer survivors and battlers wished the pink runner a speedy recovery, and encouraged her to get back on her feet so she could chase her dream all over again.

Now, just the knowledge that so many people believed in her dream, left Deborah feeling that she couldn't possibly consider giving up.

'Don't even think about quitting,' urged larger-than-life John Hogno in yet another email. This lovely, generous man who had brought her the best champagne to celebrate her 5000 kilometres milestone as she'd run up-country through Maitland and Forster, remained as encouraging as ever. 'Never give up on your dreams, Deborah,' he said.

Colin had kept in touch, too, wanting to know what the verdict from the surgeon was. 'You can do it, Deb,' he said, confidently. Her mentor Nobby Young had written, and Ken had called regularly for updates. Crusty from Darwin was keeping in contact via Facebook, as were many of her other ultra-marathon friends whose positive words of encouragement had kept her going during the challenges before her first run came to an abrupt end.

Ian and Fran Henke also rang offering their support after learning that their honorary daughter's dreams were now in apparent tatters. They were horrified to learn that Deborah and Glyn were still cruising around Melbourne in their pink caravan.

'We can't really go back to Hobart, there's no point,' Deborah had told Glyn. With the house at Midway Point still rented out for a whole year, the only home they had *was* their pink caravan. Glyn agreed.

'We might as well just have a bit of a holiday until July when the doctor can do your first operation.'

But the Henkes were more practical. 'What will you do after your surgery?' asked Fran, from the property she and Ian had bought in Hastings on the choppy waters of Westernport Bay.

'Put my feet up in my caravan!' said Deborah, dismissively. Secretly, she was still a little worried about the recovery process. But with a new adventure already beckoning and nowhere to live, staying in Melbourne was only a temporary arrangement and seemed a better option than going home to Tasmania.

Since Owen and Karin were still in South Australia visiting Owen's mum, Deborah had spent the past couple of weeks since her initial specialist consultation on the road on another mission.

She had been trying to decide where to locate the pink caravan, sussing out camping sites which might provide an invalid with a suitable place to convalesce after two operations.

'At least I can park the van next to the disabled toilet,' said Glyn, inspecting the toilet and shower block of a caravan park in Werribee South, a short drive from Geelong and close to their previous home in Altona which they had rented out when they moved to Tasmania. It might just meet the needs of a reluctant invalid.

But Fran and Ian wouldn't hear of it, unable to imagine a campsite being conducive to the post-operative convalescence of their adopted daughter.

'You must come and stay with us,' Fran insisted. And reluctantly Deborah conceded, agreeing that she wasn't going to get a wheelchair into a cramped caravan.

On 2 June Deborah turned on the television to some shocking news. Jim Stynes, the kindly Irish footballer and philanthropist who had offered her such words of comfort on the day of the Commonwealth baton run had himself been diagnosed with cancer. He had called a media conference to announce that the tumour doctors had found on his back was malignant and that he would require treatment.

'I will beat this,' he said, positively. Deborah felt so sad.

'He is young and fit and healthy too,' she said. This disease was just so random.

On 23 July Deborah was admitted to hospital for her first operation. The surgeon operated on her left foot first, opening it up and pinning the navicular bone to repair the fracture. He took a graft from bone in her ankle, which he grafted onto the injured bone.

Luckily, his very impatient patient went to theatre first thing in the morning, waking up afterwards to find a back-strap of plaster and a bandage around her foot. After an overnight stay, Deborah was breaking her neck to get home and begin the recovery process that was holding up the next operation.

'Luckily I don't have to go to work,' she said brightly, arriving on the Henkes' doorstep, promising she'd do everything the doctor ordered to get back on her feet.

'If you do exactly what I say, this should heal quickly,' Dr Blackney warned. 'The longer you keep your foot elevated, the quicker it will heal.'

If Deborah had been working, as other patients would certainly have been, she'd have struggled to keep her injured foot elevated for even three days. But with nowhere to go and nothing else to do, Deborah kept her foot up for 10 whole days. Then she crossed her fingers.

On Day 10, and counting, Deborah returned to the hospital to have her stiches out. The same nurse who a few weeks earlier had told her to forget her dreams, now carefully avoided the patient's stare as she deftly removed the dressings and the stitches. Deborah was relieved to see a clean healing scar running along the top of her foot.

'Gee that looks fantastic,' said the nurse, also happy to see how well the scar had healed.

'See,' said Deborah pointedly. 'I told you I was a fantastic healer.'

Privately, she'd become so desperate to recover that she'd resorted to giving her feet a talking-to; her inspirational words to them, becoming a new mantra: 'I'm a fantastic healer and you are strong beautiful feet. You will run again!' She still believed that what you put out into the universe was what you attracted back. She decided to share this with the nurse, who didn't appear to be listening. 'She probably thinks I'm a lunatic,' she told Fran later.

By the time Deborah celebrated her fortieth birthday on 10 September, she'd spent six weeks in plaster and was now sufficiently healed to be wearing one of the heavy moon boots she'd once contemplated wearing to complete her run. Dr Thompson, the Darwin specialist, had looked highly bemused when she'd suggested it. Now, plodding around in the clumsy boot, she could see why.

Four days after turning 40, Deborah had her second operation. 'I hate sitting still,' she grizzled, arriving home in plaster again. For a runner who had just shuffled halfway around Australia and had already walked all around the country setting world records, sitting on her bum definitely did not come naturally.

'Come on, Maggie,' said Glyn, leaving Ian and Fran's house with his invalid wife, now sitting glumly in plaster in her wheelchair, her faithful running companion jogging happily alongside on her leash.

There wasn't much use being Director of Greetings when there was no crowd to greet these days.

'I'll bet Maggie wonders what the heck is going on,' said Deborah, studying her poor dog's confused face, her brown eyes watching the patient who was spending hours on her back watching movies and reading. There was no doubt that after all the attention from her fans, Maggie was not settling into mainstream life any better than her bored, hyperactive owner.

Since July Deborah had been sleeping on the sofa bed in the spare room at Fran and Ian's while Glyn and Maggie lived in their driveway in the pink caravan. For a while, when both feet were in plaster, Deborah had struggled even to get out of bed to go to the bathroom alone. For a free spirit like Deborah this predicament was both physical and mental torture.

By the time the plaster came off her second foot, it was almost November and Christmas was looming. Deborah felt a rush of adrenalin. But her excitement didn't last long.

'I don't even know if you *can* run again,' said Dr Blackney. 'But if you are going to do it, we need to make sure you are safe.' Deborah looked forlorn. Even the never say never girl felt nervous.

'You're insane,' her podiatrist told her, examining her feet at her next appointment. 'Twenty years of medical history shows it's impossible for you to do this again,' he added. According to the podiatrist, this patient was nothing short of a walking miracle. Deborah, dressed in her pink 'Running Makes Me Happy' t-shirt, wasn't so sure.

Deborah and Glyn were so grateful for Fran and Ian's generosity and having the run of their home that Glyn was happily lending a hand in the kitchen, cooking up delicious meals, allowing Fran time to study for her final exams for her degree.

And despite the Henkes' protests, Deborah and Glyn insisted on sharing the bills, desperate to contribute something towards the cost of their stay. But in truth, nothing could reward this couple's amazing generosity at a time when they were truly stuck.

By now, Owen and Karin had returned to Victoria where they were living in their caravan on a friend's property in the pretty Don Valley, a short drive from Melbourne's winery region in the famous Yarra Valley.

The now 70-year-old Karin wasn't sure that after the hard slog of the past seven and a half months she was ready to face another long-haul journey on the road. At a time when her peers were playing bowls or babysitting grandchildren, Karin had been rising at 4.30 a.m. and driving astonishing distances; there'd been the endless cooking, washing and fundraising not to mention the organising – between housekeeping duties she performed the role of Deborah's PA, ringing ahead and arranging rallies and events at each town on the route.

All Karin really fancied now was the chance to be a regular old-age pensioner, enjoying the peace and quiet of a relaxing retirement.

It had taken great persuasion to coax Karin onto the doomed run in the first place, especially after she'd already sacrificed an entire year of her life on her daughter's record-breaking walk.

If Karin's instinct had been to flatly refuse being part of Deborah's breast cancer fundraiser the first time around, doing it all over again less than a year later was even more unappealing. Deborah recalled asking the Running Pink Crew in Darwin, after just being told she had two broken feet, if they'd be prepared to do it all again when she was better.

'Yes, definitely,' said Owen. Glyn, being Glyn, had nodded in his usual laid-back way, and Karin had cautiously said 'yes'.

But Deborah now suspected that after a lengthy rest period, her mum's heart was no longer in it. She didn't blame her mum; she just hoped she'd change her mind.

Everyone's lives are on hold, thought Deborah miserably. She and Glyn had already spent $40,000 funding this doomed dream run, adding the mounting bills to their ever-expanding mortgage. And since her mum and dad had sold their own home in Healesville, investing their hard earned funds into superannuation before the Black Saturday Fires of 2009, nobody really had the cash to spare to fund another dream.

What am I thinking of? thought Deborah, looking more forlorn than ever. Even the *Spirit of Tasmania*, who had given her $5000 worth of free passage when she'd started her run last October, now rejected the suggestion of yet another donation for the new run.

In the cold light of day it wasn't only Karin who was finding the prospect of a new run daunting. Anyway, there had still been no indication from the surgeon that the patient was even *able* to run yet.

'When can I go in the pool then?' pestered Deborah at her next appointment.

The surgeon inspected her healing scar. With two lots of plaster, pool therapy had been out of the question. But now, with her feet healing nicely, he changed his mind.

'OK, but take it gently,' he warned, shaking his head as Deborah limped out of his rooms on her walking frame. He knew how important it was for this athlete to recover her physical fitness. Now, with the go-ahead, Deborah was back in the pool, working her upper body and running in the water to build her muscles up again. The next step would be to get herself to the nearest gym, where she could sit on her backside using hand-weights to give her upper body a more intensive workout.

But Deborah was growing impatient. 'When can I run?' Whenever things had been bad in the past, running was the one thing that lifted her spirits. Yet this time, running had been the one thing she couldn't do.

It had been several months since her injury. And for Deborah, who had run every single day for seven months before that – out on open roads, free as a bird in her sunnies, the sun beating down on her face – spending an equivalent amount of time lying in bed watching TV, doing nothing and going nowhere, was hell.

'Can't I even try a short run?' she asked the surgeon again, looking very depressed and sorry for herself. He shook his head.

'Not yet.'

Deborah wept as she put the phone down.

Feeling as though she was surrounded by negativity, Deborah's mood began spiralling downwards into a big black hole of hopelessness and despair. During her convalescence, she'd kept her spirits up by continuing Maggie's dog blog. Deborah remained amazed by the amount of fan mail her beloved dog was attracting on an almost daily basis as people praised their efforts and asked when their next adventure would begin.

Her Director of Greetings had even found herself a four-legged stalker called Brookie, who contacted Maggie repeatedly wanting to know the ins and outs of her celebrity lifestyle and when she'd be back on the road. Brookie revealed he was a Labrador who strongly resembled his new doggy sweetheart. It was a clear-cut case of stalker fusion, thought Deborah. That's what happened to John Lennon, whose stalker copied the former Beatles star's appearance and even found a Japanese wife resembling Yoko Ono.

Deborah laughed as she struggled to imagine how a Labrador could possibly imagine he looked like her black and white Border collie. The cheek of some people! But the persistent fan continued to dog Maggie's paw-prints by bombarding her with adoring emails. But watching her dejected dog lounging idly on the carpet of Fran and Ian's house, with nowhere to go and no fans to greet, Deborah doubted the four-legged stalker would want such a dog's life.

But what neither Deborah, nor Maggie, were able to confirm at this stage on either of their respective Facebook sites, was when the dream would be resumed.

Deborah was feeling particularly despondent when she logged onto Facebook one day to find another new email from a stranger. The email came from a Melbourne woman called Jan, who revealed that at 34 years of age, she was battling breast cancer. Worse than that, she'd just been told by her doctor she was terminal; her Stage Four cancer diagnosis meant the disease had already travelled to her bones. Jan had been given three months to live.

It was Deborah's worst nightmare, and the poignant email touched her very soul. 'I found your Facebook page and the Running Pink website through the link on the National Breast Cancer website,' Jan wrote. 'I have been following your journey around Australia and think what you have been doing is inspirational.'

Jan was just two years younger than Deborah had been when she'd received her own breast cancer diagnosis. But her heart broke for this young woman who had already fought the disease for around two years. Originally she'd had the cancer in one breast and thought she'd beaten it. But a second tumour had then been discovered in her other breast. She'd since had a double mastectomy but the disease had travelled to other major organs, and to her bones. Jan's email showed a strong fighting spirit: 'I intend to beat this,' she wrote.

Deborah noted that at no time in the email did the sender refer to herself as a breast cancer 'victim' – which Deborah herself had also refused to accept as a definition. Jan simply described herself as a 'breast cancer *patient*' and Deborah – who actually didn't like being called a patient – or even a survivor as that implied she'd been a victim in the first place – instantly connected with this courageous young woman.

'I am so sorry to hear you have broken your feet,' Jan went on. 'It must be a very long journey for you to get back on your feet again, but don't forget you have survived breast cancer – so you must get better and do this again. Do it for me.'

Deborah felt a lump rise in her throat. She wanted to give this woman a big hug – to run all the way to her home wherever it was – and hold her hand tightly. This was such a brave young woman. At a time when most people, faced with a scenario like Jan's, would have been crawling into bed and staying there, this woman was generous enough to be sending her best wishes to someone else. If Deborah could have run to her side, she would have. But in her present predicament she couldn't even walk a step without her walking frame.

What she could do, though, was to stop feeling sorry for herself right now! She could plan to run again for this stranger whose plight touched her heart. She *could* run for Jan and she *could* run for herself.

'If you could just get out there and finish what you started – perhaps by running the other way around Australia, back to Darwin to complete the loop and finish what you started. You will give me great hope.'

Deborah held her breath. 'If you can run again you might give me the hope that I can, perhaps, survive this disease.'

This email was an epiphany for Deborah, who had been sliding into a big black abyss for days.

'*This* is what the run is about,' she reminded herself. 'It's not about setting records, or about ego, or even being the first woman to run around Australia – it's all about hope!' She sat silently in front of her computer, reassessing everything, suddenly aware of Glyn behind her.

'I've been an idiot,' she said, aloud. 'I've been raising something much more than money, and I almost forgot that until now.'

Glancing at her feet she suddenly felt like a big fraud. What was she worrying about; she hadn't been given three months to live. Even when she'd been diagnosed she hadn't had to sit there and be told she had Stage Four Cancer. In her mind, her Stage Zero cancer was nothing more serious than a virus.

'This poor woman has been given three months to live, and yet she's reaching out and giving hope to someone else,' said Deborah, humbled as she explained the email she'd just received. Hope was such a precious gift, she thought, preparing to reply to this amazing, big-hearted woman.

'I'm going to do this,' Deborah responded. 'Thank you and please watch this space . . . I'm going to do it for you!'

At her next physiotherapy appointment, Deborah shrugged off comments about being a walking miracle. She was not a walking miracle. She was a woman on a mission again.

'I just have something greater to do,' she said when her physio commented on her newfound enthusiasm.

Inspired by Jan's email, Deborah began working even harder during the intensive program of therapy devised for her by former Australian winter Olympian Andrew Wynd.

Her new efforts to rebuild important muscle tone in her legs, which had become significantly wasted since her injury, were dramatically obvious to Andrew, who sensed a new commitment in his patient. While he'd had his doubts about her journey, he now shared his patient's belief that this new dream run of hers was actually possible.

Jan's email had certainly been a life changing moment for Deborah. And she wanted to repay her new Facebook friend with all the hope she needed to help in her battle for survival. If she could do this, Jan might make it too; she had someone other than herself now depending on this dream becoming a reality.

At the next appointment in very late November, Dr Blackney studied Deborah's X-rays again. 'OK,' he said. 'You can start running again, but be gentle.' These were the words Deborah had waited over seven months to hear. 'I will,' she promised.

On Christmas Day, as Glyn, Fran and Ian opened their gifts, Deborah had a present for herself and her very fed-up Director of Greetings, who was as desperate as her owner to escape this enforced retirement.

'Come on, girl,' she called, holding Maggie's leash. 'We're going for a run.' Maggie wagged her tail, excited at the sight of Deborah in her familiar old runners. Glyn cautiously decided to join them. 'This is my Christmas present to *me* from *me*!' said Deborah brightly, as she broke into a gentle one minute run; her first since Darwin.

After exactly 60 seconds, Deborah slowed down, walking slowly for the next four minutes. Then she repeated the exercise three times more, smiling as she breathed in the sea air of Hastings which suddenly smelled far sweeter.

'It's the best Christmas present I've ever had,' she later told Fran and Ian, sitting down for Christmas lunch and toasting herself and Running Pink.

In the New Year of 2010, Deborah saw Dr Blackney again.

'Goodbye,' she said, smiling at him. The doctor shook his head, well aware of her plans to tackle her record-breaking run again.

'If you're going out there to run around Australia again, I'll be seeing you back here in three months!' he warned, his voice more matter of fact than ever. 'Your bones will break!' This time it was Deborah who shook her head.

'No they won't,' she replied, defiantly. 'Remember, I'm a fantastic healer – I'll never see you again thanks.'

Still, she did have a favour to ask of this patient man. 'My nephew wants to be a surgeon,' she said. 'Would you mind if he came to see you?' The doctor smiled.

'No worries,' he agreed.

Dr Blackney hesitated. He had a favour of his own to ask of his most persistent patient ever. 'Would you mind if I take your photograph?' he faltered. 'Perhaps you could even autograph it for my daughter. She's been reading Maggie's blog and following you on Facebook . . .'

Deborah smiled broadly, posing first *with* the doctor, then *for* the doctor. He ought to have known after reading her blog she'd be back on this run again, no matter what!

Walking upright and confidently, the never say never girl turned on her heels and marched out of the surgery, smiling as she passed the nurse on his reception desk. Deborah De Williams never did get around to taking up her offer of that sports shrink who provided therapy for people with broken dreams. She'd found all the therapy she needed in a simple email from a stranger. This time around her run would be all about raising hope – any money she managed to raise to find a cure for breast cancer, and any world record she managed to achieve – would be a bonus.

Jan had given her the hope to chase her dream again – and she planned to repay her with every step she took.

Running for a Cure – Again!

'What do you have to do it again for?' said Karin, looking downright miserable. Deborah printed the email she'd received from Jan.

'This is why,' she said, handing it to her mum. Karin put the email down.

'No you don't. Why can't you just be happy?'

But in Deborah's mind, this was no longer a question of whether she *wanted* a second attempt at a world record. This was a challenge she *had* to attempt.

'I want to come because you're my daughter, but I have to consider my wife's happiness too,' said Owen, aware of Karin's opposition to a second run. Still, he already knew the never say never girl had never taken 'no' for an answer before. And he doubted she would now.

'What about back in Darwin, when you all agreed that you'd be my support crew again when my feet were better?' wheedled Deborah, resorting to a bit of emotional blackmail. Her mum winced, recalling how they'd unanimously agreed that once Deborah's feet had healed they'd be right behind her on a second attempt at the world record.

'Well . . . I'm all healed now,' beamed Deborah. She really hoped Owen would be able to talk Karin around.

Earlier that afternoon she'd returned from the Melbourne specialist's rooms after promising him he'd never see her face again. Yet now, she couldn't help feeling a flutter of anxiety as she recalled his parting words: that if she persisted with this run, she'd be back within three months with smashed feet.

The following week, Karin and Owen had news for their daughter. 'All right, you win!' said Karin, stoically. 'We'll be coming with you on run number 2.' And for the third time, Karin put her leisurely retirement on hold for a dream that apparently couldn't wait.

While the Running Pink crew began to stock up on supplies and sort out the pink convoy in readiness for another crack at the world record, Deborah made an appointment to see Leigh Voss, the helpful bank manager at Westpac Bank, who had been so supportive during both her walk and the previous year's doomed run.

Lee had been so inspired by Deborah's adventures that when she'd discovered this tireless philanthropist had been diagnosed with cancer, she sent her a giant bouquet of flowers, deeply saddened to hear that she faced such a worrying challenge.

But Deborah had such strength of character, thought Lee, as she made arrangements for her to again use her Visa card to fund her new journey, adding the mounting bills to her ever-extending mortgage.

Since there were no more doctor's appointments, Deborah and Glyn returned to Launceston where they pitched the pink van in the front yard of their investment property.

Deborah had already taken the step of announcing her new adventure on her Facebook page as well as in Maggie's blog. Since her injuries, both had been inundated with hundreds of new fans, and with her new run now about to begin she told everyone 'watch this space'.

'What happens if you break your feet again?' a number of friends had cautiously asked.

'I'm a fantastic healer,' replied Deborah, trying not to think about it. But the dark thought did still niggle away in the back of her mind.

Deborah had spent her convalescence reading a number of inspirational books about amazing people who had overcome adversity to achieve their dreams. She'd been particularly impressed by cyclist Lance Armstrong, who had fought his own battle with cancer and gone on to win seven Tour De France races. She'd also been greatly moved by the story of Australian athlete Anna Meares, who had won a silver medal at the Olympics after breaking her back and being told she would not walk again! Such stories reinforced Deborah's belief in miracles.

In March 2010, nine long months after abandoning her first dream run, Deborah and the Running Pink convoy hit the road again. Before she left home, Deborah contacted Jan, the woman whose email had given her such hope.

'I'm doing this for you!' she said. 'I'll keep you posted.'

As Jan had suggested, Deborah's route this time would involve running around Australia clockwise. Unlike the first time where she'd run up the east coast towards Darwin, this time she intended to follow the route she'd taken on her world-record-breaking walk. She would cover Tasmania, the smallest state first, then catch the ferry to mainland Victoria, where she'd run west towards Adelaide and across the Nullarbor again. From Perth she'd head up the coast to Darwin.

Deborah was keeping her fingers crossed that her healed feet would at least carry her back to the city where the adventure had ended so abruptly. That way she could accomplish her goal of circumnavigating the country, albeit in two stages.

Beneath the clear blue skies of a warm autumn day, Deborah's run began once again in Parliament House Gardens in the centre of Hobart, where the Lord Mayor, Rod Valentine, who had waved her off on her walk and on her first run, was waiting with a crowd of supporters.

'I see you've got more than 12,000 friends on Facebook,' he teased, patting her excited Director of Greetings, whose tail wagged wildly as she glimpsed her first crowd of adoring fans in nine months. 'That's more than the entire Liberal Party of Tasmania!'

A gathering of women from breast cancer support groups were there, all wearing pink and holding bobbing pink balloons. Deborah's new Running Pink Facebook page had certainly helped spread the word, and everyone, aware of the broken feet that had ended her first run, now turned out like an army to wave her off on her second attempt at the world record.

Running Pink

The inspirational story of a breast cancer survivor running around Australia to help find a cure for other women had sparked a flurry of media interest, and camera crews and newspaper journalists jostled for interviews and a shot that would make the evening news and the next day's papers.

'Good luck,' said Rod Valentine, who had again obligingly written letters of introduction to fellow mayors around Australia. 'See you in a year.'

Deborah gulped. A whole year . . . it suddenly sounded like such a long time as she nervously began the slow shuffle out of Hobart, secretly worrying about her poor feet. She was joined by a couple of friends on the slow shuffle northwards up the Midlands Highway, through the historic towns of Oatlands and Ross. It was her intention to run up the 'guts' of Tasmania and her running friends, in a show of support, wanted to make sure she had some company.

Ultra-marathon runner Peter Hoskinson, who trained people for marathons, joined her with two of his female friends who were dressed in pink.

'Come on, let's pick up the pace,' he said, and with Maggie trotting beside her owner, they soon caught up with the convoy on the side of the road at Pontville, 32 kilometres north of the city.

Deborah had bought herself a brand new more hi-tech GPS this time around. The Garmin Forerunner 310XT is a multi-sports management timing device which she wore on her arm like a wrist watch. The sophisticated device would calculate every step she took; recording every kilometre, every minute, hour and day of her journey. This was matched each day to the GPS in the car. Deborah also carried a device that recorded the number of steps she would run every day and which could be downloaded throughout the adventure onto her computer. With all this technology, there would be no doubt how far she'd travelled when the adventure was over.

This time even the new GPS device would become so embattled from the extreme weather conditions, that before the run was over, it resembled a train crash. The GPS, exposed to heat, water and cold, would finally fall to pieces outside Brisbane, prompting Owen to pot-rivet another strap onto the device to hold it together.

Deborah checked it obsessively during her run, ensuring she always remembered to charge it each night. There would be occasions ahead, when she'd be so exhausted after a long day on the road that she'd simply crawl into bed forgetting to charge it. This held her up the next morning as she couldn't leave until the device was fully charged.

Deborah was already worrying about Maggie, who had not coped well on the ferry trip to the mainland at the start of the first adventure, or recently on their brief return home.

On their journey to Melbourne for the first run, the terrified dog in her dog box in the cargo hold had become so panic stricken by the incessant barking of all the other anxious four-legged travellers, that Deborah had been forced to take drastic action.

When nobody was looking, Deborah had sneaked her out of her box on the *Spirit of Tasmania* and hidden her in the cosy pink caravan were she hoped she'd be less stressed.

When they had initially landed in Melbourne, Maggie had been like Velcro, as she stuck to Deborah's leg, afraid of being banished back into her box again. A dog box in the cargo hold was no place for her Director of Greetings.

Blisters

The cameras were waiting when Deborah disembarked for a second time at Port Melbourne. This time she made bigger news as journalists honed in on the story of the breast cancer survivor who, after beating the disease, had run 862 kilometres on two broken feet.

Now, against all odds, she was doing it again. Their news editors dispatched an interviewer and camera crew to the docks to make sure they covered this story about an inspirational Aussie who was off to finish what she'd started back in 2008.

On the eight-hour ferry crossing from Melbourne to Devonport and back, Deborah made sure Maggie was coping with the stress of her dog box. But her D.O.G. was now a more seasoned traveller and took the journey in her stride. After running halfway around the country, Maggie was a more accomplished celebrity, too, and obliged the TV crews by wagging her tail and posing for the cameras where she belonged. Deborah watched her basking in the hail of flashlights, lapping up the glory befitting a star of her calibre.

While the flu had dogged the start of Deborah's first world record attempt, this time another unforseen problem threatened her new run. After spending months on her back with each foot in plaster, the soles of her feet were uncharacteristically soft. Before she'd even reached Launceston large blisters had begun to form on the soles of both feet.

The last time Deborah had suffered blisters she'd just arrived in the New South Wales town of Taree on her first run up towards Darwin. While Deborah was nursing her sore feet, Maggie had been revelling in her newfound fame, and happily posing for newspaper photographers as part of her official duties.

It had been Day 101 of the run then, and the Running Pink roadshow had set up camp next to a tidal river where there was a designated swimming area, power and a cold outdoor shower. Deborah had submerged herself in the salty water feeling immediate relief from her throbbing blister. She climbed into bed later that night convinced nature and beauty had helped heal her blister and her soul.

But this time it was going to take far more than salt water to fix these giant blisters and by the time Deborah disembarked from the boat in Melbourne they were already the size of the palm of Glyn's hand and causing great pain as they began to weep and bleed. Running long distances every single day on such enormous blisters was an agony Deborah couldn't even begin to describe.

By the time Deborah ran into Werribee – the town where she'd burst into tears and gone home to bed at the start of her world record walk – she was ready to burst into tears and go home all over again.

'Oh no,' she said, wincing as she struggled to peel off her sweaty socks. She'd only been on the mainland two days and with severe injuries like this, she couldn't imagine how she'd possibly survive, day after day. 'Running every day won't give them a chance to heal,' she groaned, not knowing what to do.

But while angels appeared in the outback on the first run when she'd prayed for a miracle, one was already winging his way towards her now. Malcolm Matthews was a record keeper for the long-distance runs and a good friend of Deborah's. He was aware of her current dilemma from her Facebook postings, and he'd decided to track her down before she left Victoria to offer his help.

'Thought you might need some assistance,' said Malcolm, a fireman in the Melbourne Metropolitan Fire Brigade and part of the support crew for the Fire Department's relay runs around Australia as well as a masseur. He tracked Deborah down on the side of the road at Werribee, convincing her someone had just answered her prayers with the first miracle of her adventure.

Blisters

'Ooooh . . . nasty,' said Malcolm, studying the giant blisters and producing a miracle in the form of two soft floppy jelly pads called Second Skin. He gently slipped the palm-sized gel pads over the weeping blisters, wincing as Deborah slipped her socks back on and stood on them. The pads, consisting of 100 per cent water, would provide a healing cushion between the blisters and the friction of her socks as she ran.

'I've even got blisters under my toenails,' said Deborah miserably. 'They've caused my nails to actually lift!' Seasoned runners were lucky to have any toenails at all, since long distances usually resulted in nails falling off.

'That's what you get for lying on your back,' teased Malcolm, knowing that the months his friend had spent off her feet had been harder on them in the longer term. If she'd been able to run every day, her tough feet would have hardened and she'd have been less susceptible to an injury like this.

'Remember to change them every 20 kilometres,' he reminded her, handing Glyn supplies of the gel pad dressings.

'Goodness knows what this has cost Malcolm,' said Deborah as she changed the pads again that night and collapsed onto the bed in pain. She knew the dressings were costly, but she also appreciated her friends desperately wanted to help her realise her dream.

Another ultra-marathon runner also joined Deborah on her run out of Melbourne that day. David Hughes was a man in his forties who had taken up running to kick start a weight-loss program. But long after he'd shed 45 kilograms, he realised he'd developed a passion for running, soon becoming a regular on the ultra-marathon circuit. He'd been so inspired when he heard Deborah had run 862 kilometres on two broken feet that when he discovered she was attempting her world record a second time, he wanted to offer some moral support.

David found her limping along on the gel pads, her blisters still causing her great pain.

'This running gets in your blood doesn't it,' she said, wincing as she ran.

'Sure does,' agreed David. This lovely man had a friend called Donna Crebbin who was battling breast cancer. 'Would you mind if I give your phone number to her?' he asked. Deborah said she'd be honoured, and they parted ways with David scribbling down the number of her satellite mobile. 'It would do her good to talk to someone who understands,' he said.

Over the coming week, Malcolm continued to call, to check on his friend's progress.

'I'm still in a lot of pain,' she said, now hobbling a reduced number of kilometres which she hoped she'd be able to make up later in the journey. Amidst all the concern about her feet she hadn't even considered it would be blisters that might threaten her new world record attempt.

Malcolm accompanied the convoy as far as Colac, where the two caravans parked beside the road. He checked Deborah's feet again and changed her dressings one last time. She'd completed her run that morning with a woman called Jo, who'd turned up on the road wanting to run along with the pink runner whose Facebook page had sparked her imagination.

The group were sitting around on the roadside having morning tea, when a car pulled up, and a familiar face approached the group.

'You're back on the road then?' grinned Dr John Johnson, the young casualty doctor who'd given Deborah the bad news about her two broken feet.

'Oh my God, it's the doctor from Darwin Hospital!' uttered Deborah, in astonishment.

She told the doctor about her bad blisters. 'But that's better than two broken feet huh?' she said, wryly. The doctor had been travelling to Melbourne on a holiday, when he recognised the familiar Running Pink convoy.

'It had to be you!' he laughed, inquiring about the surgery that had put her back on her feet. Dr Johnson looked genuinely happy to see his former patient and smiled as he witnessed Deborah's log book. This young medic had been so helpful and kind. He'd even managed to get her bone scans done for free — the hospital's own personal contribution to her fundraiser.

'You must have healed really well to be doing this again so soon,' he said. Deborah grinned. But as she watched him drive away she still felt a nervous flutter rising in her chest. How *were* these feet going to stand up to the rigorous challenges of the road ahead?

In Robe, Maggie was the centre of attention as a group of local children gathered around wanting to pat her. After the witness book was signed, a young woman called Pip was excited to discover she had a great deal in common with Deborah. Pip revealed she'd been in a motorcycle accident and it was 16 months before she could walk independently again. 'I had the whole broken feet broken legs scene, and the surgery, plaster, crutches and cam-walker ordeal.'

Deborah shook her head. 'Seven months was enough for me,' she said.

By mid-April Deborah's blistered feet were still hurting as she headed into the South Australian town of Tailem Bend where a policeman came out to meet the runner and her dog.

'I'm your official police escort,' he said. Deborah looked horrified.

'Is this a bad joke?' she asked. 'Because the last time we had a police escort into a town I tripped over my dog and broke my feet.' Maggie wagged her tail and looked from the policeman to her owner as though she understood every word. 'Come on, Maggie, let's go,' she said. And they ran into town together to a sea of pink balloons, and even a few dogs with pink bows around their necks. And nobody got hurt!

Running towards Murray Bridge, Deborah was greeted by the peculiar sight of a man driving an old Massey Ferguson Tractor towing a slide-on camper trailer. The man smiled and waved as he drove by, stopping up ahead at the turnoff. Deborah ran up and introduced herself, thrilled to learn he was a fellow Tasmanian who lived about 30 kilometres north of her. Ken was driving with his pug Millie across the Nullarbor in the tractor.

'I'm going to visit my son in Perth,' he said, blithely. Millie peered down at Maggie from her perch on the tractor. There was more than one star of the show on the open road.

By the time Deborah reached Adelaide, she was running out of dressings and was in so much pain from her weeping blisters that she'd adopted an awkward gait as her body compensated to protect two injured feet.

Shuffling for hundreds of kilometres in this awkward posture soon created pain in her hips and knees. Glyn spent most nights gently massaging his wife's hips to relieve the pain so she could begin her run again next morning.

'Let's check out these blisters again,' said Malcolm, who flew out to Adelaide to check his patient's progress. Malcolm, who had first met Deborah when he was a lap counter at the Colac Six Day Race, had enough experience with runners to know that he wouldn't have expected such blisters to have healed yet, especially given the distance she'd covered in such a short time. Running every single day was certainly not conducive to the healing process. Malcolm had decided at the last minute to make the trip to Adelaide to ensure his friend had a new supply of the dressings that would cushion the blisters and help her on her way.

'They're not a pretty sight,' he said, examining her feet again. 'But this should do you . . . take it easy!'

Malcolm's stay in Adelaide was more eventful than he'd imagined. The friendly fireman was staying with an old female friend who had invited him to use her home as a base from which he could drive out onto the road each day to check on the injured runner's progress. But over the course of his impromptu trip, a romance blossomed with his old friend. The couple soon announced they'd fallen in love, and for the rest of their lives, Malcolm would credit Deborah's blisters and her world record run for bringing them together.

'You were running for a cure, and you ended up playing matchmaker without even knowing it,' he joked.

After Malcolm left, Deborah hobbled on, still battling the pain under her feet. But an unexpected phone call from a past angel took her completely by surprise.

'I'm afraid I've got some bad news,' revealed Nobby, her walking guru. 'My ex-wife has just passed away . . . she had breast cancer.' Deborah's heart sank. She knew from her chats with the grey nomad that he'd opted to give his ex-wife the family home in Sydney, saying he had no particular need for bricks and mortar when he spent his days shuffling from town to town. But now he revealed his own private pain. 'I nursed her till the end,' he told Deborah, sadly.

Nobby had been unaware of Deborah's own battle with breast cancer, but he had heard about her new world record attempt to raise money for research into the disease, and had called to support her after she'd broken her feet. Now he wanted to give her a big pat on the back, more aware than ever of the significance of her important run.

'Go for it girl,' he said. 'You can do it . . . you can do anything.'

Nobby and his ex-wife were very much in Deborah's mind as she shuffled out of Adelaide. She *had* to achieve the world record this time around, she told herself. If she could raise enough money, then perhaps one day there would be a cure for this foul disease and women in future generations would face treatment knowing they were not facing a potential death sentence.

When Deborah was running through Adelaide, her old friend and fellow runner Colin Ricketts turned up on the road to greet her. The meeting was a shock to Deborah, who knew Colin had gone into hospital after volunteering to donate one of his kidneys to his brother who was in dire need of a life-saving transplant. Colin, being the angel that Deborah knew him to be, had not hesitated to be his brother's donor and was in an Adelaide Hospital recovering from his surgery when Deborah arrived in the city of churches.

But nothing was going to keep Colin off the road on 2 May, not even major surgery. When his wife came to collect him from the Royal Adelaide Hospital after the operation, the patient refused to go home as instructed, insisting instead that she drive him straight to the Adelaide foothills, a short drive from his home in Mount Barker, so he could find his friend and wish her good luck.

Deborah wiped tears from her eyes as she watched this wonderful, generous spirit emerge from his car in his post-operative state, determined not to let this momentous occasion pass without being a part of it.

Colin had tears in his own eyes as he recalled that night at his home the previous June, where his friend had cried over her broken feet and questioned her ability to repeat the adventure all over again.

'Here you are, Deb,' he said, smiling. 'I told you that you *could* do this!'

Deborah was so full of adrenalin after her brief reunion with Colin, that in spite of her sore feet, she managed to run the equivalent of a marathon.

While many of her friends competed in marathons, racing in a marathon was not Deborah's idea of fun. Deborah much preferred to shuffle along at a steady pace, competing with nobody but herself. Athletes who ran at fast paces could not keep it up over long distances and over extended periods of time.

The first marathon Deborah ever completed was the Hobart Marathon in January 2008, shortly after her practice run around Tasmania. She ran the marathon with Glyn as part of her training program in preparation for her first attempt at the world record run which would begin in October that year. But since Deborah ran 50 kilometres plus most days, running a marathon was no big deal, though she had no particular desire to *race* towards the finishing line.

In Adelaide Deborah was thrilled when her godmother, Vija came to check on her progress. The Running Pink crew had stopped at an Adelaide caravan park when her mother's dearest friend of 42 years arrived with her husband Joe to greet her lifelong girlfriend and wish her god-daughter good luck.

The Lithuanian couple had met Karin and Owen when they were all young parents forging lives for their families.

It was a day for friends, mused Deborah, as Alistair arrived from Tasmania to help the Running Pink crew negotiate the streets through the city, and to assist with the fundraising. He joined the convoy and their long-term family friends for the hearty barbecue meal that the men had cooked, happy to spend some time with his friends.

The run from Hobart to Adelaide, covering three states on the first leg of the run, had taken Deborah just 30 days. And she'd run almost the entire distance on blisters that would have left most people wanting to quit.

Lucky Money

On 2 May, Deborah was running slowly towards the Nullarbor in the heat, shuffling slowly and barely lifting her feet off the hot road so as to conserve energy. Her blisters had healed by now, making life a little easier, though the rising temperatures made running a hot sticky affair.

As she and Maggie jogged along that morning towards Port Augusta they heard the roar behind them of the Ghan train which makes its way north–south across the continent between Adelaide and Darwin. The stretch of road where Deborah and Maggie ran this morning was the only part where the tracks pass close to the road. Deborah managed to catch a glimpse of the spectacle at very close quarters as it flew by in the direction of Port Augusta. As it passed Deborah looked up and noticed an arm appearing out of the train window. A hand wildly waved a pink hanky at her in a gesture of support.

'See that, Maggie,' said Deborah. 'We are a work in progress. We have supporters everywhere.'

The train wasn't the only spectacular vision that greeted them on their way to the Nullarbor. Deborah soon encountered a couple in a bright red Mercedes campervan. 'Hello,' said the couple, pulling over. The older couple were doing a charity cycle for the Starlight Foundation. Glenda was cycling and her husband, Frank, who had just turned 91 two days earlier, was her sole support crew in the 1966 campervan.

'Bought this before you were born,' he grinned. Deborah

laughed, imagining she'd be the female equivalent of Frank one of these days.

Six days later Deborah arrived in the tiny town of Kimba, which claims to stand halfway across the continent, between Iron Knob and Wudinna.

It was 8 May 2010, and the tiny community was in the midst of a football game where a sausage sizzle had been organised by a local breast cancer survivor. The woman greeted Deborah warmly and armed with a collection tin, rattled it around the spectators in the small crowd saying, 'Come on guys, cough up . . . this is for a great cause.' Everybody put their hands in their pockets and donated.

In many of the small communities that Deborah ran through this was a familiar story. Local people often welcomed Running Pink at pre-planned events like footie games or markets, knowing the crowds that had gathered would give generously to a good cause. They were happy to allow Karin and Owen to rattle their collection tins, and more often than not helped out, encouraging mates and neighbours to support this fundraising run.

Deborah had been greeted at Ceduna Airport by a group of women wearing purple tops with pink bras on the outside. The group were all breast cancer survivors who had been part of the Relay for Life event. A week before Deborah's arrival they had raised money for her charity which they now proudly donated to her, before running with her into their town.

Further along the route, in the town of Minnipa, Deborah glimpsed a familiar local landmark – affectionately known by locals and travellers alike as the Concrete Crapper. While self-explanatory, this giant circular concrete toilet which sits slap-bang in the middle of nowhere is a prominent spectacle on the flat landscape. Deborah laughed as she recalled parking the Britz next to the most remote dunny in Australia during her 2004 walk. She had certainly spread her DNA far and wide across this vast country, she thought.

A few days later, Deborah received a call from her brother.

'Where are you?' asked Adam, who was on the long drive back to Melbourne from Perth. 'Fancy meeting for breakfast?'

Karin was delighted to hear from her son. They arranged to meet Adam in the car park of the Nundroo Roadhouse. Deborah woke on 25 May to find her brother sitting in her mum's van, waiting for his sister to wake. The siblings spent an hour catching up on family gossip over a delicious breakfast of bacon and eggs that their mother happily cooked everyone.

'Can you do me a favour?' asked Deborah, mischievously. 'Can I drive your truck?' She'd always wondered what it felt like to be sitting up in the seat of one of those enormous double D trucks that steamed past her on the road.

Reluctantly Adam agreed, smirking as his little sister sat behind the wheel of his truck and gingerly turned the key in the ignition. She drove it 50 metres around the car park, saying she fancied knowing what the truckies saw when they peered out at her from their windows.

In the past week or so many truck drivers had pulled over to speak with her. 'Still goin'?' they asked in surprise.

'No,' she laughed. 'This is a new run . . . I broke my feet, but now I'm mended I'm back again.' They would usually give her a donation before driving off into the dust.

At Eucla Deborah was greeted by the strange sight of a team of people gathered around a wheelchair which they were pushing along at speed.

'What are you doing?' asked Deborah, bemused. It was usually a question other people asked her.

'We're pushing a wheelchair,' they said, stating the obvious. The team were part of an event called the Big Roll, which involved them pushing a wheelchair all the way from Perth to Sydney. 'It's a fundraiser,' they explained cheerily. The quirky annual event was aimed at raising money to provide needy Australians and their carers with the transport, financial and material support they needed to maintain and enhance their quality of life.

'I heard about you guys back in Mount Barker,' said Deborah. The bush telegraph certainly worked overtime out on the road, where everyone knew what everyone else was up to. This was why Deborah constantly found herself joined by people, or swamped by welcome parties in towns along the way. The bush telegraph was a better communications network than any mobile phone provider.

A storm was threatening as Deborah shuffled towards the Mundrabilla Roadhouse, the first roadhouse after the town of Eucla on the Nullarbor Plain. As she ran, she was stunned to see a sole cyclist pedalling towards her in the distance.

'I thought I'd come and join you,' announced the young female cyclist in a heavy French accent. As she rode alongside on her pushbike, the young woman revealed she worked at the Mundrabilla Roadhouse and had heard about a pink lady running to raise money for breast cancer. When she heard from the truck drivers that Deborah was heading her way she wanted to join her.

'I thought you might like some company out here,' she said.

She rode beside Deborah for several kilometres until the heavens opened and a thunder and lightning show lit up the sky.

'I'll see you at the roadhouse,' she said, looking uneasily at the skies. It wasn't sensible being out in the open with lightning striking around you, and she decided to pedal ahead, leaving Deborah on her own. With nowhere to shelter, Deborah kept going into pitch darkness, relieved to see Glyn driving towards her.

'You can't run on your own in this weather,' he said, driving behind her in the 4WD, his headlights lighting her way.

Deborah finally shuffled into Mundrabilla after another eight kilometres, saturated from the rain and humidity.

'You can have a nice hot shower,' said the Frenchwoman, appearing with a key to the showers. When Deborah prepared to leave at six a.m. the following morning, a surprise awaited her.

'For you,' said the generous French casual worker. She had risen much earlier than Deborah and had baked and iced eight pink cup cakes bearing the words 'Running Pink'. They would make a great morning tea, she said, handing them to the runner.

Deborah was plodding along the Nullarbor when Maggie's ears pricked up. 'What is it Maggie Moo?' asked Deborah, following the dog's gaze, now fixed behind them on a cloud of red dust. A roaring sound heralded the sudden appearance of a strange, colourful convoy of trucks and trailers. The drivers waved out of the windows at Deborah as they tore past bound for Perth. 'It's a circus, Maggie,' said Deborah, pausing to admire the spectacle of Circus Royale. 'Perhaps it will stop and we'll get to see an elephant.' But the circus road show appeared to be in a hurry as it vanished up the road and into the distance.

While towns had been giving generously to Deborah's fundraiser, it wasn't only donation money that Running Pink had begun collecting along the road. 'Have you noticed how many coins you find lying around on the road?' Glyn had observed on their first run. Whether they were in town streets, on highways, in car parks or out in the bush, they could be sure that one of them would walk along and find a dollar lying around. On the previous walk and run, Deborah had put the coins straight into the donation tins. But now, out of curiosity, she decided to put any coins they unearthed into a large jar in the caravan. 'We'll count it up at the end and see how much we've found,' said Deborah.

They nicknamed their growing coin collection 'lucky money' and produced a handful of coins most days which they added to the jar. Running along the road to Whyalla, following the pipeline dirt track beside the road where the soft earth was more gentle on Deborah's still sore feet than the hard surface of the highway, she had observed Glyn running back to meet her. On the short run Glyn had collected seven $1 coins for the jar.

Another time when Deborah nicked into the bush to answer a call of nature, checking the long grass for snakes, she'd found a $10 note. 'I reckon most of this money falls out of men's pockets when they go to the loo,' she said, though she couldn't explain the coins that they found on roads in the middle of nowhere.

By the time the second run ended they'd have accumulated a staggering $700 worth of loose change, many of the coins still covered in sticky tarmac, bent from the heat or gnarled together from the sizzling temperatures.

'One of these days we'll buy a TattsLotto ticket for the $30 million draw,' said Deborah. 'Who knows . . . this is lucky money . . . perhaps we might win!' The past three road trips had certainly been costly affairs. And while they'd been successful fundraisers, Deborah still had her expandable mortgage to cover. 'We could do with a win,' said Glyn.

Angels and Fairies

While still at the other end of the Nullarbor, Deborah was surprised to find a new email in her inbox from an unfamiliar sender. 'My name is Damian Syred and I am the owner of Circus Royale,' wrote the stranger. 'We saw you on the Nullarbor on our way to Perth and would really like to help you.' Damian, who was also the ringmaster of the circus, said the circus would be happy to help Deborah out when she arrived in Perth.

'We could organise your fundraising collection tins to be distributed amongst our audiences,' he offered.

Karin emailed back promising the Running Pink crew would most certainly track the circus down when they arrived in Perth. A circus, like a pink convoy, wouldn't be too hard to find.

Now, as she made her way across the Nullabor she passed through Norseman and recalled that crazy Christmas Day in 2003 at the Railway Hotel, which now had a new owner.

When the tiny Western Australian town of Jerramungup discovered that Deborah was heading their way, a ripple of excitement quickly spread through the closeknit community. Deborah had first shuffled through 'Jerry' on her walk, making many friends who had never forgotten the ambassador for Kids Helpline.

Now aware from Deborah's Facebook page of her battle with breast cancer, and that she was running for a second time to raise money to find a cure for the disease, the small town determined to give her a reception she would never forget.

They'd learned from some local women that Deborah had formed her own charity, Running Pink, and was raising funds for vital medical research. A local woman who had recently lost her sister to the disease, volunteered to organise a fundraiser for Running Pink. She told friends that after witnessing her sister's battle against breast cancer, she wanted to make sure the town gave generously so that no other family would have to endure the pain her family had suffered after her sister's diagnosis.

When Deborah arrived, a pink cheer squad was waiting to escort her to the town's community sports arena where the local women netballers were preparing to play a charity game against the hulking blokes from the senior footie team.

But the real highlight of the match was the half-time entertainment. If Deborah's doctors and friends imagined she was achieving the impossible with her new run, then this gregarious Jerry resident most certainly had.

Standing conspicuously on the field to kick-off the half-time entertainment, the woman had recruited four very large, middle-aged, overweight, hairy men who she'd somehow convinced would look fantastic dressed up in sugar pink fairy costumes. 'Come on guys . . . it's for a great cause,' she'd cajoled, anticipating their mates, their families and anyone else in need of a laugh would pay to see the spectacle.

Now, hoots of laughter swept the crowd as the unlikely troupe of hairy, scary, not-so-dainty sugar plum fairies pranced out onto the court. These good-natured country blokes really got into the spirit of things as people hurriedly donated to see them twirling and flitting around in their fluffy pink dresses – curls of wiry hair from their chests peeking out over the bodices of the frocks, their white wings flapping haphazardly behind them as they danced.

For Deborah it was a most hilarious moment in her adventure and one she'd always remember. For the small, truly remarkable community, it was an astonishing effort; a wonderful gesture of goodwill as the fairies winked at a crowd now in stitches of laughter.

Despite its tiny population of just 5000, the comical fundraiser resulted in a generous donation of $6000 towards Deborah's charity.

She left the town the next day still wearing the biggest smile as she pictured those fairies clumsily doing their bit to help save women's lives.

'See . . . anything is possible,' said the proud organiser, waving Deborah out of the town. 'Now go and chase that dream.' The magic dust from those fairy wands would sparkle for many months to come in Jerry, casting a warm pink cloud over Deborah's pink convoy as it moved its way north.

By the time Deborah headed out of Jerry, she'd contracted such a bad flu that she was struggling to breathe. She spent the ensuing three days running up to 60 kilometres each day, cutting a peculiar sight and looking more like an alien as she trudged along the road wearing a mask soaked in eucalyptus oil to relieve the cold symptoms and help her breathe. One car slowed down to have a closer look at this strange apparition.

'That's a really bad Michael Jackson impersonation you're doing,' shouted the bright spark behind the wheel. Deborah interrupted her coughing fit to laugh at the wisecracking driver.

The fairy dust of Jerry had already sprinkled its way to Albany where Deborah was astonished to find yet another troupe of unlikely pink fairies. Boasting the dubious name of the Fairy Slappers, this group of women who had banded together to raise money for the recent Relay for Life – an event that raises money for people with cancer – waited at the signpost into their town.

In their midst was their 'honorary fairy', their local MP, Peter Watson, who had rather wisely opted for a Relay for Life t-shirt instead of the sugar pink frocks and wings of his lively companions.

'We're going to walk you into town,' said Fairy Slapper Sue Bassett, who looked hilarious in her outfit. Sue had been part of the 24-hour relay fundraiser and led the group of eight fairies back to town. Amongst them were a number of breast cancer survivors who were supportive of Deborah and her cause. As they walked, a group of little girls dressed as fairies also joined them.

'I'm an honorary fairy slapper,' chuckled Peter Watson with a grin. Peter, himself a former Olympic runner, was now in his sixties and had just taken part in his first Relay for Life. When he'd heard about Deborah's cause he had taken up the offer to join Sue and her fairy troupe to welcome their pink guest.

'I've arranged for the school and the Albany Council to host a Pink Day for you,' said Sue. The Fairy Slappers presented Running Pink with a cheque at their local shopping centre.

On Day 93, Sunday 27 June 2010, Deborah ran into Balingup, the same tiny town in Western Australia where on her walk, local resident Wendy Trow had organised a community relay to walk her through the beautiful township, and where locals had given Glyn and Deborah a free night's accommodation in a romantic hilltop cabin. Deborah had remained in contact with Wendy, the Balingup woman being so impressed by the inspirational walker and children's advocate that when she learned about her run for breast cancer in 2008 she'd been delighted at the prospect of seeing her friend again. Sadly, Wendy's excitement was dampened when she'd heard about Deborah's broken feet. She was bitterly disappointed to learn the run had come to an abrupt end and that Deborah would not be able to run through Western Australia or complete her dream.

So in 2010 when she learned Deborah was making a second attempt at the world record, Wendy was so thrilled she wanted to make sure the town rewarded such courage by doing something extra special. Deborah had been due to run into the town at lunchtime, but a chance meeting with another familiar face from her walk had delayed her.

She had been running along the road about 35 kilometres from Bridgetown, on her way to Balingup, when she recognised the woman waiting for her a little way ahead. Back in 2004 Barbara had been the Shire President of Kununurra, a small town in the Kimberleys that was nothing like the pretty town of Bridgetown, which sits amidst cool rolling hills not much different to the scenery of Deborah's home in Tasmania. When Deborah had walked into Kununurra, Barbara Johnson had come out onto the road to welcome her into town.

But Deborah was baffled to now see this former Shire president, thousands of kilometres away from her former territory.

'What are you doing here?' asked Deborah, stopping in amazement. But Barbara, who had been seen a story about the Running Pink lady in the newspapers, knew exactly what Deborah was doing in this far-flung part of south-west Western Australia.

'I live in Bridgetown now,' revealed Barbara, delighted to see Deborah again. 'I did a tree change!' Barbara handed Deborah some photographs. 'I need you to talk to a woman I know in Balingup who lost her sister to breast cancer,' she said. 'I talked to her on the phone but she was too distraught to come out with me to meet you.'

Barbara asked Deborah if she had time for coffee, and though she knew she needed to be in Balingup by early afternoon, it was an offer Deborah couldn't refuse. She finally arrived in Balingup, exhausted and dirty, at six p.m., amazed to find that her welcome committee was still waiting for her.

She'd also been astonished to find that the entire population had, for some reason, returned to the Dark Ages! Wendy Trow, a dynamic woman and a leading light in her small community, had organised for everyone in Balingup to greet Deborah in style. The crowd before her were all wearing elaborate medieval costumes as part of a lavish medieval festival Wendy had arranged in honour of the VIP guest.

Now, instead of welcoming the runner with the usual pink reception committee, Deborah found herself being greeted by a noisy medieval town crier, who rang a bell and shouted loudly: 'Oyez, oyez . . . all ye gather here . . .' Wendy Trow's thrilled face beamed out of the crowd at her friend.

'This is for you,' said Wendy, handing Deborah a certificate which bestowed upon her the special honour of not having to pay taxes whilst in the care of this very friendly shire. Wendy, dressed in the full medieval garb of a maiden, then escorted the dirty pink guest to the town's medieval festival where she read aloud her own 'Ode to Deborah!' to the lively gathering.

Running Pink

Later, Wendy insisted on taking the entire Running Pink crew to her home for a hot shower and a hearty home-cooked dinner.

There were so many familiar faces who were delighted to welcome Deborah back on the road. The long-haul truckies constantly tooted their horns at the sight of the familiar pink runner and her dog as they drove past them along the highways for a second time. Some didn't even realise this was a second attempt and assumed she was like one of the familiar grey nomads who just spent their time trekking around the country.

'You still goin'?' yelled a burly truck driver from the window of his giant road train, slowing down to acknowledge this crazy pink lady plodding along the road in her hat and sunnies with Maggie jogging beside her.

And Deborah stopped and explained that this wasn't the same run, but a new world record attempt.

'Good on youse and good luck with the world record!' he shouted, driving off, tooting loudly as he steamed up the road in a cloud of dust.

The Greyhound bus drivers were also pleased to see Deborah on the road again. 'We saw you the first time in Queensland,' they'd say. 'We heard you were hurt but you're back again!' Even the grey nomads, running into Deborah again, aware of her accident, donated to her cause.

'They don't have two cents to rub together but they gave what they had just the same,' said Deborah, touched by the gesture.

It was impossible not to feel encouraged with such wonderful support from everyone.

By the time Deborah reached Perth on 4 July, Australians had voted in their first-ever female prime minister, Julia Gillard. Deborah was pondering this fact as she ran into the beautiful city where she'd been born. On that sunny Sunday in one of the city's biggest shopping malls it wasn't pink t-shirts that were waiting for Deborah, but a gang of middle aged, fun-loving women wearing purple outfits and incredibly vibrant red hats.

'We're the Red Hat Society,' explained one bubbly woman in

Angels and Fairies

a flamboyant red hat. 'We're your welcome party.'

Deborah had never heard of this group before, but they were certainly enjoying themselves and many had stories of friends whose lives had been touched by breast cancer. The Red Hat Society, which has members around the world, is made up of women over 50 – the age bracket of women who are most at risk of contracting breast cancer. The group was set up by a group of women who decided to greet middle age with verve, humour and élan. Their philosophy is the comic relief of life. But underneath the frivolity, they share a bond of affection, forged by common life experiences and a genuine enthusiasm for wherever life takes them next.

'Where do I join up?' laughed Deborah, surveying their colourful garb which was attracting a good deal of attention and lots of donations to Deborah's cause as Karin began passing the tin around. When the fuss died down, Running Pink was officially welcomed into Perth by the Deputy Lord Mayor, John Tognolini, who received the letter from the Lord Mayor of Hobart on Deborah's behalf.

With her official duties over, Deborah went in search of the circus. They found the Big Top sitting ceremoniously amidst the trucks and caravans that had passed them on the Nullarbor at Langley Park overlooking the Swan River.

'We'll put on a barbecue for you,' offered Damian, the owner and ringmaster of Circus Royale, who had been following Deborah's adventure on Facebook. Damian kept his promise and distributed Running Pink's donation tins amongst their audiences. For a couple of days, the pink convoy took up the invitation to park beside the trucks and trailers of the circus performers.

'When I was a kid I always wanted to run away and join the circus and now I have,' laughed Deborah, who left with a cheque for a $1000 donation and a swag of great memories. It was the most colourful stopover of the adventure so far.

The following day Deborah and Maggie appeared on the Channel Ten TV show *The Circle*. After the interview, Deborah went to a local doctor's for a check-up. She was still nervous about her navicular bones holding up on a rigorous run of 50–60 kilometres a day and had made several appointments on the road ahead just to be safe.

After ending her run at just 23 kilometres, Deborah had driven back to Langley Park in time for the matinee in the Big Top. Maggie's blog that night read:

> Wow what a event. There were ducks, ponies, llamas, people swinging in the air, but who stole the show? Woof, woof . . . who let the dogs out . . . Damian and his dogs. I was so jealous they could do all sorts of tricks I couldn't. I felt like I'd had a neglected childhood. Mind you, I wouldn't want to be in that kind of daily spotlight, I have enough trouble with paparazzi as it is. They follow me wherever I go. Just look at this morning as an example. I was on a national television show. After such a busy day I sneaked off to the pooch palace and enjoyed all the memories of the fabulous Circus Royale.

Pink Pyjamas

Deborah was still in Perth when another of her guardian angels was winging her way across Australia to lend a helping hand. Social worker Merienne Shortridge lived in Victoria and had met Karin and Owen, an amateur wine maker, through the local wine circle in Healesville. Karin and Merienne had become very close friends over the years and Deborah's adventure had sparked the 50-something dynamo to escape her high-pressure job for a taste of freedom on a previous occasion.

On Deborah's walk, Merienne had taken two weeks leave and had flown into the remote outback mining community of Mount Isa in Queensland on a mission to relieve Glyn — who was support crew at the time — of some of his day-to-day duties.

'I can wash and cook and clean,' offered Merienne who dealt with many children from families in crisis, and thought Deborah's Kids Helpline cause was a great one.

'What do you mean you've broken your feet?' she'd groaned, bitterly disappointed to find that her plans to help Deborah on her first run had been scuppered by injury. This time around she'd kept her fingers crossed that the adventure would go to plan so that she could join the road trip again and be part of the Running Pink crew.

In early July, Merienne arrived in Perth ready to roll her sleeves up. 'I'll help with the cooking and washing and you can have a bit of a rest,' she told her grateful friend Karin.

Karin spent long hours fundraising and doing the behind-the-scenes chores and was glad of the help. But the thought of Merienne's cooking was not so appealing to her daughter. Deborah was also familiar with Merienne's washing and drying obsession. On the walk she'd return from a long day on the road to find her undies on a make-shift line blowing in the breeze in full view of all the truck drivers.

Merienne had been ingenious enough to devise a washing line using a piece of string which she'd hooked between the Britz and the nearest tree. Deborah would cringe at the sight of her undies blowing in the afternoon heat alongside Merienne's larger, very unsexy Bridget Jones-style knickers for all the world to see.

'I like things aired,' announced Merienne, pegging more washing on the line. At least the clothes were clean, reasoned Deborah.

Now joining them on the run, the first thing that Merienne organised was the washing line and by the time Deborah caught up with the convoy, the laundry was flapping in the breeze again. But if Deborah could live with the sight of her smalls on display, Merienne's culinary talents were a whole other story. One morning Deborah returned from her early run in time for breakfast, horrified that Merienne had now taken charge of the cooking.

'Baked beans on toast,' announced Karin's mate, shoving a plate filled with rock hard burned toast in front of the ravenous runner. The toast clunked as the plate hit the table. 'I like to keep it warm in the oven,' explained Merienne, as Deborah politely attempted to take a bite of the hard toast she suspected had been in the oven for at least half an hour.

Worse still, the baked beans were stone cold. Deborah loved Merienne and would have hated to hurt her feelings. She was starving hungry and in need of the protein, so she gulped the cold beans down in silence. But running up to 70 kilometres a day on a stomach filled with cold beans and tough toast was not conducive to great energy levels. And what had once been Deborah's favourite food was no longer. It would be at least 12 months after Merienne left before Deborah could bring herself to eat baked beans again.

But what she lacked in culinary expertise Merienne more than made up for in humour. She told the funniest stories and Deborah's enduring memory of her mum's good friend was the day she left when they both paraded around on the highway together wearing hot pink pyjamas and waving at all the passing truckies. The day before Merienne left on 24 July 2010, she gave Deborah a special present. The pink ribbon made of glass with a gold trim came with a poem entitled 'Ribbon of Hope'. It read:

> This ribbon edged in pink and gold
> Holds Hope to find a cure,
> To each survivor this we pray,
> With faith you will endure

The thoughtful gift brought tears to Deborah's eyes. Merienne understood the journey better than most as she had lost two special people to breast cancer, her good friend Sue and her cousin Sue. She left the Running Pink Crew at Carnarvon after spending three weeks of her annual leave helping with the good cause. Deborah watched with tears in her eyes as Merienne's truckie mate, Deeks, turned up on the highway to collect her.

Deeks drove the 3000-kilometre route from Perth to Fortescue Mine and back twice a week and had been tracking the pink convoy up the coast of Western Australia. Merienne now climbed into his big double B and waved furiously from the passenger seat as he drove away.

Deborah lost count of the small community groups and organisations that had offered support on the road. But while some were prepared and waited for her with a welcome committee and a barbecue, others simply stumbled across her on the road.

One such group she encountered on 13 August came by the strange moniker of the Dirty Dog Dingoes and literally happened across Deborah as she ran out of Port Hedland, the town she walked into in 2004 when she played cat and mouse with a cyclone.

'What are you up to?' asked a young guy who pulled over in a 4WD with his pregnant partner. Two more 4WDs parked behind him, and Deborah learned that the group were avid 4WD fanatics from Melbourne who had been travelling around Australia on an adventure driving holiday. 'We call ourselves the Dirty Dog Dingoes,' said the friendly young guy whose name was Matt. 'We've just done the Gibb River Road from Kununurra to Derby – it was one hell of a challenge!' While parts of the road consist of gravel, other parts are nothing more than rocks. 'We got four flat tyres on the route,' he said. 'You'd never manage it in a car and the only buses that can manage it are 4WD buses . . . it's pretty hairy!'

The 4WD thrill-seekers were very curious to know what a sole pink runner was doing in this remote part of Australia.

'Running for charity,' said Deborah, explaining the purpose of her fundraiser.

'We'd better give you this then,' they said, handing her a pink stubby holder that said 'Dirty Dog Dingoes'. They pulled out a camera. 'Mind a photo with us?' they asked. And Deborah posed amongst the group on the side of the highway, wondering how a pregnant woman coped with such an adrenalin-charged adventure.

After the photo the group climbed back into their vehicles and were on their way, looking for a new adventure.

'See ya back in Melbourne,' they shouted as they tore off up the highway. Deborah watched them go, stepping back onto the road in time to see a snake slithering away in the grass nearby. It was minding its own business and she figured she should do the same!

Road Works

In August Deborah began the run through the Kimberleys from Western Australia towards the Northern Territory. On the way the staff at the Pardoo mine, between Port Hedland and Broome, invited them to camp overnight. The men cooked a big barbecue for their unexpected guests who left with $400 that the staff donated to the fundraiser.

As she got closer to Broome, she gave a radio interview to the ABC by phone. They had even 'interviewed' Maggie, who Deborah photographed sitting in the van with her pink tongue slobbering all over the microphone.

As Deborah trudged on, memories of Darwin began to resurface in her mind. When she reached Broome she saw a physiotherapist because her right foot was seriously troubling her.

'What do you think?' she asked.

'I think it's not likely to be a stress injury, more likely a repetitive strain injury,' she said. Deborah felt relieved, but the pain continued to dog her.

The Running Pink convoy had been reunited with Alistair in Broome. He'd flown in for four days, keen to do his turn with the support crew, but turned out to be of very little help due to the bout of flu he bought with him. His constant sneezing and runny nose put paid to any plans he had to assist with fundraising duties. He was feeling much better by the time he left, but by then nobody else was! Everyone, including Deborah, caught the bug he'd brought up from Tasmania and the next few days after his departure were miserable as everyone coughed and spluttered and Deborah struggled to run.

'Thanks a bunch, Alistair,' she said, ringing him in Launceston where he sounded very chipper. 'You left the flu here with us.'

The run through the Kimberleys came to a sudden halt 130 kilometres east of the turnoff to Derby when Deborah found herself confronted by a burly man, holding a lollipop sign saying 'stop.' There were earth movers and heavy machinery in clusters on the road ahead where a number of workers were involved in road works.

'You're going to need an escort through these road works,' he said, eyeing up the pink convoy which looked strangely out of place in this remote neck of the woods.

The man studied the message on the pink caravans and the logo on Deborah's hat and t-shirt.

'You running to raise money for breast cancer then?' he asked. Deborah nodded.

'You'd better grab a bucket then,' he replied, getting on his walkie-talkie radio. 'Hey guys,' he said, alerting the crews up ahead. 'There's a pink lady running through here — she's raising money for breast cancer, make sure you get your money out!'

The lollipop guy handed Deborah his stop sign and took her photo. Then he arranged an escort through the section of road works that were being carried out during the dry season. As Deborah ran with her bucket, the workers crowded onto the road to meet her, their notes and change in their hands. 'Great cause,' shouted another worker as she trudged past. 'Good on yer!' shouted the man on the bulldozer, putting in a $20 note. The road works spanned a five-kilometre stretch of road, and with every step she took, the donations poured in from these generous workers. The road works ended, only to begin all over again the next morning around 35 kilometres further up the highway. Again she was given an escort along the next five kilometres of road works where the workers abandoned their work to put their donations in Deborah's collection tins. 'Our mates down the road radioed ahead . . . we knew you were comin' our way,' explained a man on a giant earth mover. Most of them knew someone who had battled breast cancer, and all of them wanted to support this mission to find a cure.

'Where youse all stayin' tonight?' asked the burly foreman who had the unusual name of Hollywood. He had earned his name because the headlights on his truck shone onto the bumpy roads and pointed into the sky like the spotlights of the Hollywood Hills.

'Dunno,' replied Deborah, sweating in the heat.

'Well,' he said. 'There's a camp about 10 kilometres up the road at Ellendale, why don't you stay with us there? We have power and showers . . . and a few cold beers.' The offer sounded too good to turn down, especially the offer of a free beer. In a 'dry' area like the Kimberleys where alcohol is restricted due to the social issues arising from its abuse, Deborah thought this sounded like a perfect resort.

On that sticky night of 27 August, Deborah and her family were the honorary guests of the work crews who provided them with cool showers, even cooler beers and a barbecue of steak and sausages.

'We've got ice-cream, too,' said one of the workers, producing a carton of vanilla ice-cream for the VIP visitors. It had been ages since Deborah had enjoyed an ice-cream, and as she sat in her fold up seat in the middle of nowhere it couldn't have tasted better.

The crew later retreated to their caravans overwhelmed by the generosity of these construction workers who had dug deep already, only to spoil them some more. The following morning the guys even filled up the tanks of the 4WDs with gallons of free diesel.

'This will save you having to spend your money,' they said.

Acts of random kindness had turned up in the most unlikely places, particularly in the middle of nowhere, mused Deborah, who was rising very early to begin her run before the heat of the day set in.

The burglary at the caravan was very much in Karin's and Deborah's minds as the convoy entered the Western Australian town of Halls Creek. This place held memories of such a low point on Deborah's fundraising walk – it was where she'd almost called it quits.

It was here, later that night, that Deborah received a phone call from a stranger. 'Hi, my name is Donna Crebbin . . . you don't know me, but I know of you,' said the young woman on the other end. Donna was the friend that David Hughes had mentioned to Deborah back in Melbourne in the early weeks of this second run. 'David gave me your phone number and said it would be OK for me to call,' explained Donna, hesitantly.

Donna had been following Deborah's journey on Facebook and wanted to meet this runner David had told her all about. 'I'm not doing so great,' she revealed, explaining that she'd drunk a bottle of sauvignon blanc before working up the courage to pick up the phone. 'I'm still going through chemo at the moment,' she said. 'It's really tough.' Deborah agreed.

Donna explained that she was having chemotherapy to reduce the now five-centimetre lump so she could have surgery to remove it. Donna's biggest issue was that she didn't want to lose her breast. 'My doctors can't tell me if I will lose it or not until after I finish chemo and have had the first operation to remove the lump,' she said sadly.

Deborah knew from her discussions with other young breast cancer survivors, that the loss of one or both breasts is a huge issue. Many of the young mastectomy patients had told her how they struggled with the loss of identity. As if losing a part of their sexuality robbed them of their sense of who they were.

Donna's journey was more problematic because a diagnosis had been difficult to pinpoint, and it had been some time before she'd discovered that the lump she'd found in her breast was cancer.

'Where do you live?' asked Deborah.

'Sydney,' said Donna, despondently.

'Well, I will call you when I get there,' replied Deborah. Hopefully, by the time she made it to Sydney, Donna would be on the last leg of her treatment.

Road Works

On the run up the Great Northern Highway towards the Victoria Highway, the temperatures soared. Deborah was now running on blistering 44-degree days with high humidity of 88 per cent. Because of the extreme weather conditions, Glyn had been doing short bunny-hops ahead of around one kilometre so his wife could catch up for another cool drink and recover for a few moments under the air conditioner.

It was another stinking hot day as Deborah continued her run. The humidity was now a stifling 90 per cent and Deborah was feeling exhausted. For much of the day she had caught up with the vans where her mum had shoved her underneath the air conditioner to cool her down. Now, with only about five kilometres to go until the end of the day, Karin came out onto the road to walk the last distance and help her daughter through. After two kilometres they began to wonder where Owen and Glyn had got to with the convoy.

'Perhaps they are getting us an ice-cream,' joked Deborah. Even as she said it, she imagined how great it would be to actually have an ice-cream to eat out here in the middle of nowhere.

Minutes later she heard Glyn's 4WD approaching. He slowed down as he passed and handed Karin and Deborah an ice-cream cone each.

'Where did you get them?' she asked in amazement.

'Some guy pulled over and gave us free diesel, a cold beer and these ice-creams,' he laughed. Deborah believed more than ever that you attract what you need.

She recalled how, on her practice run, she had told Vlastik how much she wanted to eat fish for dinner . . . only to arrive at the next camping spot where two guys handed them freshly caught trout.

These kind acts just seemed to follow her. She recalled her first run through the Northern Territory, when she'd stopped at an outback station called Soudan Station, which lies about 100 kilometres from the Queensland–Northern Territory border. The owners of the isolated cattle Station welcomed Deborah and her crew into their homes, feeding their visitors on a feast of red meat, which on a shoestring budget, Running Pink certainly could not stretch to.

'What does your dog eat?' asked the kindly owner. 'VIP Working Dog Food,' said Deborah, thankful for the sponsor's contribution to her run. At least the dwindling budget didn't have to cover the cost of dog food for a whole year. The owner laughed out loud. 'That's not dog food,' he said. They later left the cattle station, their small freezer loaded with cuts of prime red meat. The gift included stacks of meat for Maggie of such premium, that Karin could most certainly have fed her family on it. It truly was a gift from heaven.

For more than two weeks before Deborah crossed the border from Western Australia into the Northern Territory for the sixth time, her feet were causing her serious concern. Ongoing numbness and pins and needles had made her unsteady on her feet and she had misplaced her step on a couple of occasions and fallen.

As she trudged in the heat, her hip was hurting so much from her latest fall that she began to feel really worried. For the entire trip she'd taken the precaution of strapping her feet up to support her weakened navicular bones. But with the tingling now creeping up her leg, she wondered if the specialist's predictions might be coming true.

'You don't think it's my naviculars again, do you?' Deborah asked, ringing Jason, her podiatrist, back in Melbourne. She was 1000 kilometres from Broome and felt very anxious that she was unable to feel the sole of her right foot.

But Jason didn't sound concerned. 'Keep on going,' he said. 'It's sounding more like a pinched nerve to me.'

His reassurances didn't allay Deborah's fears for long, as the numbness crept up her leg and she began to worry again that her old problem was rearing its head and threatening to put the brakes on a second time.

By now the soaring temperatures were really getting to Deborah, too. Fortunately the convoy happened to be in the Western Australian town of Kununurra when the 4WD broke down.

'It needs a new part for the clutch,' said a local mechanic, ordering the part from Perth. But it took another five days to fly the part out which meant the caravan was stuck.

Luckily, the owners of the local Kununurra Motel allowed the crew to park their two caravans in their car park for the following days. Deborah's run would begin at four a.m. before temperatures soared into the 40s. For the next four days, Deborah ran the minimum 20 kilometres, with her mother driving ahead in the car in the heat, to save her having to carry her food and drink on her back in such difficult conditions. Then she'd drive her back to the motel again.

In Kununurra, the numbness in Deborah's right food was getting worse and she made an appointment with another physiotherapist who wondered if the underlying cause might be her navicular bone. Deborah panicked.

'You'd need an MRI to be sure,' he said.

But the tingling continued to get worse in the month that followed, giving Glyn had another idea.

'Ring Geoff Thompson in Darwin,' he suggested.

'How far away are you?' asked the doctor who had thrown Deborah a lifeline of hope when he'd told her he believed surgery could put her back on the road again.

Glyn pulled out the map. 'Just over 365 kilometres,' he said.

The doctor's voice sounded flat. 'I'm leaving tomorrow for the World Masters in Alice Springs,' he apologised. 'But if you can get up here by tomorrow morning I'll check you out before I go.'

Deborah was desperate. She went to bed really early that night, setting her alarm for just after midnight. When she and Glyn climbed out of bed she was thrilled to be greeted by a clear beautiful full moon and ran her 21 kilometres minimum in the moonlight, out in the middle of nowhere, eager to keep her record alive.

By 5.30 a.m., Owen had unhooked the van from the 4WD. He waved goodbye to Karin and Maggie, who would remain behind in the van by the side of the road, while the others drove the 730-kilometre round trip to Darwin to see Dr Thompson.

It was mid-morning when they arrived in his clinic. 'No . . . definitely not the naviculars,' said Dr Thompson, looking as pleased as Deborah. 'You've got a pinched nerve in your hip, no wonder your foot is numb.'

The doctor suggested the best remedy would be for Glyn to massage his wife's hip each night using his elbow.

'That should fix it,' he said, waving them off.

'Thanks,' said Deborah, looking greatly relieved.

By the time they arrived back at the van it was dark, and Owen was exhausted from his heavy day of driving.

'What's this?' said Deborah walking in to find a box of Karin's favourite rye bread. 'Where on earth did you get those in the middle of nowhere?'

Karin smiled. Bernice and Bevan, the owners of the supermarket back at Kununurra knew how much Karin enjoyed their delicious rye bread – baked by a local woman. They had found out where the convoy were thanks to the bush telegraph and had dispatched the special delivery hundreds of kilometres up the road right to her door.

Deborah had first encountered the lovely couple on the side of the road as they'd been returning to Kununurra from a camping holiday about six months earlier. It was hard to miss the pink convoy on the road, and the couple had pulled over to talk to Deborah.

They had a personal interest in Deborah's cause. 'Our daughter had breast cancer,' they explained. They were such delightful people that when the convoy finally arrived in their town, Bevan and Bernice had insisted on taking everyone out to dinner. They even organised a fundraiser and donated towards Deborah's run for a cure.

Now, while Deborah was at the doctor's in Darwin, the couple had sent Karin some of her favourite bread. Karin had been amazed when she opened her caravan door in the middle of nowhere to find a driver holding a box of bread.

Deborah marvelled at the number of people who took the time to either drive out, or to stop to wish her well and catch up on her progress. Even the young French girl, who had ridden her bike beside Deborah east of the Mundrabilla Roadhouse as she crossed the Nullarbor in May 2010, had paid Karin a visit in Deborah's absence that day.

'She had left the roadhouse for a holiday,' explained Karin, beaming. 'She saw the pink convoy and pulled over to say hello and wish you luck!' The young foreign well-wisher had also signed her name in Deborah's witness book. Deborah smiled. 'People are just so generous,' she said.

Completing the Loop

After her appointment with Dr Thompson, Deborah continued her run towards Darwin crossing into the Northern Territory on 18 September, feeling far more confident than she'd felt for the last 3000 kilometres. Her pain had now gone, and the doctor's reassurances had been a huge morale booster.

At Adelaide River, where Crusty had joined Deborah on her first run, a bus driver pulled over.

'I do the drive from Broome to Darwin,' he said. 'I've seen you so many times on this road as I pass up and down.' He gave Deborah a donation. By the time she reached Darwin this bus driver would have passed her countless times in the 48 days it took her to run from Broome.

Darwin was in Deborah's sights when her running friend Ken Nash next called.

'I'm coming to join you,' said Ken, and drove down to the very place at Craters Lake Road and the Stuart Highway where she'd ended her run the year before. Aware of the agony Deborah had been in on that first run, Ken wanted to share the joy of this last stretch.

It was 4 October and Alistair, who had also arrived in Darwin a couple of days ahead of the momentous occasion, hired a car and drove down to meet the convoy. Karen, Owen and Glyn all gathered together at the spot marked in pink that had, until now held only bad memories for Deborah.

'I've hired a guy with a video camera to take footage of me on that spot in the road,' said Deborah.

The Northern Territory police also sent two traffic constables to join the group. One of the officers, Erin Simonato, had lost her grandmother to breast cancer and happily witnessed Deborah officially becoming the first female to run the entire distance around Australia (non-continuously).

Now Deborah stood on the same landmark where she had once hobbled through on two broken feet, smiling for the camera and pinching herself in disbelief and joy. Three days earlier had marked the start of National Breast Cancer Month; a fitting month to be one step closer to achieving a goal to raise money for a cure.

'Congratulations,' said Ken, who had arrived with his wife, and now signed his friend's witness book. Deborah, feeling very emotional, wiped a tear from her face as Glyn sprayed the new pink marker as evidence that she'd reached the spot where she'd been forced to stop the first time around, while the video man captured the magical moment.

The spot is about 92 kilometres south of Darwin and at this point, Deborah became the first female and Maggie the first dog to run the entire distance around Australia – though not continuously as she'd planned. Ken and Deborah then ran another seven kilometres as the convoy steamed ahead of them. They joined the crew shortly afterwards for a celebration breakfast of bacon and eggs that Karin had cooked for everyone.

The next morning Ken drove back in the dark from Darwin to join Deborah on her morning run. He joined her again later in the day to run the last five kilometres to the caravan park which was seven kilometres from Darwin's Central Business District. Ken then got up early again the following day to run into Darwin with his friend and join her at the reception with the Lord Mayor.

'I'm really proud of you,' said Ken, who had been there to help when his friend ran into Darwin on her two broken feet, and had been there as she'd waited for the bad news from her doctors. It felt really good to be there when Deborah achieved her goal this time around.

Arriving in Darwin was a surreal experience. Against all odds she had finally run all the way around Australia, back to the place where her dreams had once collapsed. Deborah had placed her trust in her feet that they would get her this far. Now there was something she needed to do.

'Jan,' she said, ringing her friend. 'I did it . . . I'm here, in Darwin.' Jan was delighted.

'I knew you could do it,' she said, thrilled.

Deborah began to cry. 'I didn't just do this for me. I did this for you, Jan . . . you gave me the hope I needed.'

Now it was Jan who softly wept down the phone. 'I'm so very proud of you,' she said in tears. 'I know it's been tough but you did it.'

But Jan had another question for Deborah. 'Are you going to go for the world record then?' she asked. 'You've completed the loop of the country now, but how do you feel about carrying on and breaking the world record of achieving the longest continuous run by a female?'

It was the million-dollar question from a woman who, a year earlier, had been given just three months to live. Jan had said that if Deborah could run again, then perhaps it would give her the hope she needed to believe she could survive. So far Jan had defied the doctor's prognosis.

'Of course I will keep going,' said Deborah. 'I'll finish what I started – for you.'

This time around, Deborah had not been running for records or money. She'd been running to give hope and the journey was far from over.

Pink X-Men

The road down from Darwin retraced the route Deborah had taken on her first run to Darwin. She left the city wishing that Dr Thompson had been there so she could have jogged into his surgery to give him the good news personally.

But by an incredible coincidence she was about to get that opportunity. Deborah was sitting in her fold-up chair beside the highway at Daly Waters when she noticed a car pull up alongside the pink convoy.

At the time she was trying to decide what to have for morning tea, her decision drifting away as the specialist's familiar face approached her.

'I'm on my way back from the Masters Games,' he explained with a smile. He studied Deborah's face and surveyed the caravans – one cancer survivor assessing another. 'I think what you're doing is amazing,' he said, proudly.

Deborah paused. What this wonderful doctor had done for her was even more amazing, she thought.

'You gave me such hope at a time when things looked hopeless,' she said. 'It was that hope that drove me on.'

She had a favour. 'Would you please sign my witness book?' she asked.

'I would be delighted,' said Dr Thompson. What a coincidence, she thought later. Two of the doctors who had been so helpful to her in Darwin and were so much a part of her journey had stumbled across her on the road again as she chased her dream a second time. Both had signed their names in her witness book as evidence that she was, indeed, on track for the world record.

At one stage on the first half of her trip, it had occurred to Deborah that, just for a laugh, she might photograph herself at every 1000-kilometre mark and send the snapshot back to Dr Blackney in Melbourne to prove she was still living her dream. But she'd chickened out, thinking it might be too cheeky. Just the same, she had photographed every 1000-kilometre milestone along the way, using the photographs to inspire herself to keep on going.

On 9 October Deborah was running towards Manton Creek when Ken's mate Darryl, who had run with her for the previous five days, turned up on the road with milk, mangoes, chocolate and other goodies. The following day a man stopped to talk to her.

'My name is Rob Elliott,' he said. 'I am from Melbourne but I work in Darwin. My life has been touched by cancer many times.'

He explained that one of his sisters had died from breast cancer. 'Now my other sister is going through treatment.' It was a familiar story since medical experts have now identified a hereditary rogue gene known to cause breast cancer in families.

'Give your sister this,' said Deborah, taking off one of her pink wrist bands that said 'Run girl run'.

When Deborah arrived in the small outback town of Larrimah nine days later, she was greeted by the sight of a giant pink panther, the permanent mascot of the landmark Pink Panther Hotel. It was an astonishing coincidence, thought the pink runner, who couldn't resist having her photo taken with this bizarre sight.

Thanks to the efficiency of the bush telegraph, it wasn't long before a group of guys wearing hot pink wigs appeared in town flashing pink t-shirts and looking for a pink runner. Deborah was as noticeable as the pink panther outside the local hotel.

'Just the woman,' said one of the men, climbing out of his car and approaching her. 'We've heard all about you.' Deborah was dumbfounded.

'From who?' she asked.

'From the Masters Games in Alice,' they said.

The nine likely lads called themselves the X-Men and were members of the Navy touch football team. At the Games where they were raising money for breast cancer research, they had met Dr Thompson who had told them all about his pink lady patient.

'We wanted to meet you,' said the men, whose approach to fundraising was a little more in-your-face than Deborah's. 'If they didn't hand over money, we squirted them in the face with our water pistols.'

They had left Alice Springs after checking out the Running Pink website to see where Deborah might be heading. They all signed their names on a pink football which they handed to Deborah and posed for photographs with her on the side of the road.

'Good luck,' they shouted, as they headed off.

By 23 October the crew were back at the turnoff to Newcastle Waters, where Deborah had been hobbling in pain after her injuries in Elliott, now just a little further down the highway.

'What's going on?' asked Deborah, glimpsing a camera crew. The cameras were from Channel Ten who were filming a new Top End travel show with popular TV presenter Nicky Buckley. Maggie the Director of Greetings was perfectly comfortable being filmed with her mum.

In Elliott that afternoon, Deborah was greeted by the principal of the town's primary school, Colin Baker, who waited at the entrance to the town with a group of schoolchildren all dressed in pink. A police escort appeared on the horizon, bringing back shades of the sirens that had spooked Maggie into one of her ratty runs and sent her owner sprawling. Deborah was grateful they didn't turn them on this time.

The same smiling CEO that had greeted her last time, waited again amongst the smiling Aboriginal children.

'I broke my feet last time I was here,' said Deborah, explaining why she was running again. The man, a New Zealander, had not been aware of her misfortune.

'But you're back,' he smiled. While Deborah had limped out of Elliott last time in agony, she breezed into the town this time around, linking hands with all the children who had organised a pink party complete with pink iced cup cakes. Unfortunately after drinking gallons of the red cordial that the mums had put out in jugs on the table, the reserved gathering soon resembled a gang of crazy monkeys who barely noticed when their pink guest shuffled out of town a second time.

Two days later was Pink Ribbon Day and after Deborah's speech at a nearby town, she ran back onto the highway to glimpse smoke in the distance from a number of spot fires. It had been intensely hot and in the heat came the swirling of willy-willys – small tornados of dust which swirled upwards in grey columns, looking almost eerie as the air sucked them up to the sky.

At Tennant Creek, Deborah was greeted by an athletic young man who turned out in the heat to run with her into town. The man was Luke Ricketts, the son of Deborah's ultra-marathon mate Colin from Adelaide, who had learned from her website she was heading his way on her route to Queensland.

Like Deborah, Luke had also had cancer. He'd fought his battle as a child, but was now a healthy, fit young man who was as kind and generous as his father. Deborah was honoured that he'd taken the trouble to escort her into town.

'I'll tell dad I met you,' he said as he watched her jog on her way.

Near Soudan Station a car pulled over on the road and a couple handed them a donation and a box of giant mangoes. It was Bevan and Bernice from Kununurra, and they had been following the second run on the internet.

'This is our contribution to your run,' they said, before driving away.

An irrigation worker whose job involved travelling up and down the Barkly Highway pulled over for a chat. He had repeatedly passed Deborah and wanted to know about her run. Before he left he handed her $100 donation. After that, whenever he passed he stopped to inquire about her progress.

Another traveller who had passed Deborah many times on her first run stopped to ask why she was still going.

'It's a new run,' she said. 'I broke my feet.' The guy looked amazed. 'Wow,' he said and promptly donated $50.

October yielded some astonishing news that left Deborah feeling very blessed. A phone call from the Australia Day Council revealed that she was among the four Tasmanian finalists for the presitgious Australian of the Year Awards.

'What an honour,' she said, thrilled to bits with the recognition. 'But why am I nominated when I haven't even completed my run yet?' she asked, puzzled.

The woman explained the nomination had come from the Tasmanian community and was not only about this second run, but acknowledgment for her previous fundraising efforts.

'For your walk and for being inspirational and getting back out there on this second run,' said the woman.

In November, as Deborah headed towards the Queensland border and her friend Ann Stewart-Moore's cattle station at Dunluce, she received an even more thrilling phone call. 'You have been awarded Tasmanian Australian of the Year,' announced the Lord Mayor, Rod Valentine, his voice bubbling with excitement down the phone. Even from the Julia Creek Caravan Park, Deborah could hear the sounds of voices in the background. 'I'm at the awards ceremony in Hobart,' explained Rod. 'Congratulations!'

Deborah could barely believe that she'd been honoured in such a public way. 'We're going out to celebrate,' announced Glyn. And the pink crew crowded into the Julia Creek Hotel, where they bought the only bottle of Jansz Tasmania bubbles – the lady behind the bar looking particularly pleased as Deborah suspected this bottle of her favourite drink had stood idly behind the counter waiting for the right customer to come along!

Back on the road again next day, Deborah called her friend Ann at her cattle station, 700 kilometres from Townsville, the town which had been too far for Ann's treatment.

'Of course you can stay,' said Ann. This time the Running Pink crew met Ann's husband Ninian, who had not been at home when they'd come through on the first run.

'When I first came here I was told by the Mayor that you were just 20 kilometres up the road,' laughed Deborah. 'It might seem like that in a car, but it's actually 32 kilometres from Hughendon.' Wherever she ran, asking directions, locals would point up the road and guess the distance. It was Murphy's Law but they were always miles out. 'Every extra kilometre seems so far at the end of a 12-hour day,' she said.

After hearing about Deborah's broken feet, Ann had been extra surprised to learn she was tackling her adventure all over again. The innovative farmers showed the crew their Maremma dogs that they had introduced to deal with the problem of dingoes. The Maremma breed had been used for centuries to protect sheep and, being extremely territorial, made sure no dingo set foot on the land or attacked the cattle and sheep that the Stewart-Moores raised here.

'They are very protective dogs,' said Ann, who felt this was a more humane solution to the dingo program than shooting and baiting. 'Because they're territorial they establish a boundary around the property and the dingoes won't venture near.' Deborah observed the Maremma dogs snapping at the cattle's heels and rounding up the sheep and could see why. Their pioneering idea had been so successful it was now being widely adopted by other farmers in the region.

The Stewart-Moores treated the crew to the biggest dinner with the best lamp chops they'd had for years. But their working dogs were so territorial that the star of the show spent the overnight stay at Dunluce confined to the caravan!

A Christmas Cyclone

At Cairns, on the Queensland coast, a pleasant-faced woman came over to introduce herself at the fundraising stall.

'Hi, I'm Donna's mum,' she said, mentioning the young woman from New South Wales who had called Deborah back in Halls Creek.

'How's she going?' asked Deborah.

'She's doing it tough,' said her mum, being honest. Deborah hoped Donna would come out to meet her when she finally arrived in Sydney.

As Deborah headed south down the Queensland coast, she contemplated another Christmas Day on the road. At this steady pace, she was estimating that the Running Pink crew might spend Christmas Day in Townsville. Her parents were very much in her mind, too, as she ran along the road that morning. This trip had been such a big sacrifice for her family, who tirelessly went into shopping malls setting up their fundraising stall and coaxing donations out of communities everywhere they went. But it was hard on them, she thought – especially Owen, whose own elderly mum, Thelma, was now in a nursing home back in Adelaide suffering Parkinson's disease. Deborah adored Thelma, who had been so kind to her as a child. She was, in every way, the kind of grandmother every child deserved. Thelma had spent her career nursing other people; now she was a patient herself.

Just before Christmas, Deborah ran into the town of Mareeba in the Atherton Tablelands when Owen received a call from a relative in South Australia.

'Mum's been taken into hospital,' he said, looking very anxious. 'They think she's got pneumonia.' On 12 December 2010, Thelma Drogemuller slipped into a coma following complications which doctors suspected might be internal bleeding.

'You must go to see her right away,' said Deborah, feeling sick with worry for Owen. Her dad looked pale and extremely sad.

'What's the use?' he said. 'She's in a coma, she won't know me.'

Deborah ran the next day and the day after that with a heavy heart. She felt as though the family was in limbo and poor Owen was waiting for bad news from his relatives.

On 20 December, the news he'd been dreading finally came. Deborah was in Cardwell at the Beachcomber caravan park.

'Mum's gone,' he said simply. His face looked resigned, and Deborah's heart broke for this gentle man.

'What about the funeral?' asked Deborah, urging him to go to Adelaide.

'They won't have the funeral until after Christmas,' he said. Christmas Day would have been his mother's 92nd birthday.

Deborah felt distraught for Owen. The last time she'd seen Thelma was when she'd run through Adelaide back in April. Owen's brother Craig and his wife Sharon had collected her from the nursing home and driven her out to the side of the road about 20 kilometres south of Gawler to see the young woman she'd always treated as a granddaughter.

'You take care,' she'd told Deborah. 'And good luck.' Deborah now wept, knowing she'd never see the old lady again.

The day after his mum died, Owen was at the fundraising table in Ingham. Deborah felt heartbroken that her cause had prevented Owen from spending those final days with his mother. This dream of hers came at a price. Thelma's passing cast a shadow over Christmas that year. But other clouds were gathering that were about to plunge Queensland into a state of national disaster.

On Christmas Eve Deborah ran into Townsville where the local Lions Club had a cheque to donate to her fundraising effort. Deborah had written to every Lions Club in every town on her route, and a kindly member of the Lions Club had invited Deborah, Glyn and her parents to have Christmas Day drinks with him. The man had also arranged for the crew to spend Christmas night at the Arts Centre in nearby Giru.

On Christmas Eve they'd checked into the Townsville caravan park where they stayed on the first run and where the generous owners had put on a barbecue and fundraiser for Deborah.

Unfortunately the owners who had supported Deborah then were no longer at the park. The couple, who were in their sixties, had glimpsed Glyn sitting beside the pink caravan waiting for his wife on the road to Darwin and had stopped to ask what he was doing out here in the middle of nowhere all over again. They looked sad as they explained that since Deborah had last run through Townsville they'd been forced to sell the caravan park and would not be around to welcome the convoy when it finally arrived in a few months from now.

'It's my husband,' explained the woman in a low voice. 'He's just been diagnosed with cancer.' Glyn felt very sad to hear the news. 'We've decided to sell up and travel around the country because he wants to see something of the place.'

Deborah felt just as upset for them when Glyn later shared the couple's news. It was amazing how a diagnosis like cancer suddenly made you think of all the things you had ever wanted to do, thought Deborah, who had certainly done a big life reassessment after her diagnosis with breast cancer.

Even before then, there had been times in her life when she'd wondered how she'd feel if her life was coming to an end and she found herself regretting all the things she'd wanted to do but had put off until another time.

'You have to follow your dreams and live for today,' said Deborah, more convinced than ever that procrastinating really was a time bandit.

'He's organised all his chemotherapy appointments at different towns around Australia,' explained Glyn. 'That way he can still follow his dreams.'

On the earlier run where they'd originally met this lovely couple, Deborah recalled running into the town with a woman called Lia who had raised $1000 for Running Pink. Lia had recently spotted Deborah's itinerary on the internet and had decided to run out to look for her.

'I'll run with you out of Townsville to Rollington,' offered Lia, who had kept in regular contact with Deborah, since her doomed first run, by Facebook and emails. On the first run to Rollington, Lia had arrived with her friend Carol, another marathon runner. 'I've never run 52 kilometres before,' she confessed. 'But I'm sure I can do it.'

Deborah had enjoyed a wonderful day, just the three of them running along the road, telling each other stories.

Since her injury, Lia had become a good friend, and when she discovered Deborah was back on the road and in the area, she turned up with two running friends, Trevor Brown and Bernadette Norris. Together they ran from the caravan park 32 kilometres out of Townsville, eventually joining Deborah for breakfast. Deborah then drove back to Townsville for her appointment with the Deputy Mayor, Councillor Jane Lang at the Centro shopping centre, and drinks with the Lions Club representative.

Lia invited Deborah and her family to her home for Christmas Eve drinks.

But the weather outside was horrendous and by the time the Running Pink crew returned to the campsite, the vans were swaying madly in the wind. For Karin and Deborah, who had outrun two cyclones on the walk, this did not appear promising at all.

'This is more than a storm,' predicted Deborah, waking in the early hours of Christmas Day, and studying the wild weather through the van window. The following morning, other travellers at the campsite confirmed Deborah's suspicions. 'How about that weather?' they said. 'We caught the tail end of Tropical Cyclone Tasha!' Early on Christmas morning, while everyone had been sleeping, Cyclone Tasha, a Category One cyclone, had struck the coast north of Townsville. It was a gentle reminder to Deborah to ensure she kept updated on the weather conditions in this part of the country.

As she prepared the duck for yet another traditional Christmas dinner on the road, Karin wondered what it was about Deborah's adventures that kept taking her into the paths of cyclones.

Still, the wild weather didn't stop Deborah enjoying a Christmas Day breakfast of warm croissants and champagne at Alligator Creek with Alistair's brother, Ewan.

Glyn took a photo of Deborah running in the driving rain up to her shins in water smiling in her Christmas hat, Maggie sloshing happily along beside her.

'Get Maggie in the van,' shouted Deborah suddenly, rushing towards the convoy in a panic. Glyn looked surprised.

'She's loving it,' he said as Deborah bundled Maggie into the caravan.

'She might like it, but I just ran past a freshie in the canefields beside the road up there . . . he would eat her for Christmas dinner.' The rain was causing the rivers to flood, and freshwater crocodiles were finding their way onto the highways. Whilst these small metre-long crocs wouldn't pose a particular threat to Deborah, they would certainly manage a dog.

Deborah was running towards Giru where a member of the local Lions Club greeted them with a donation. On the way, Deborah received a call from ABC Radio, wanting to interview her about her Christmas Day on the road. She found it extremely difficult running in such adverse weather, with a gale force wind blowing in her face, trying to talk to the ABC interviewer at the same time.

The bad weather made the Running Pink crew reconsider their plans to have drinks at the home of the lovely Lions Club member who had made a donation to Running Pink when they had arrived in Townsville. Since Karin was already planning to do her traditional roast duck dinner they decided to retire to the Giru Arts Centre and escape the weather for the night.

'Thanks so much for the kind offer,' said Deborah, 'But I am wrecked after running in this weather – I'm going to call it a day.'

The crew had just arrived at the Arts Centre, pleased with the luxury of the shower and surroundings, when a local tapped on the door.

'We've got to get you out of here,' he warned, looking worried. 'The Haughton River is about to burst and if it does it will cause terrible floods here. You can't stay here.'

Karin stared at her husband in alarm. She'd already had a bad experience of cyclones and floods back in Western Australia during her daughter's walk.

'Not again,' she said.

Deborah was more worried about her run getting held up, painfully aware of the problems it had caused at Roebuck Plains during her walk.

'Where can we go?' she asked, panicking.

'To the roadhouse,' said the man. 'It's on higher ground and you will be safer there if the place floods.' Deborah, who had just unstrapped her legs and slipped her aching feet out of her runners, grabbed her shoes and hurriedly laced them up again. While Owen and Glyn led the way, Deborah began the run out of Giru.

As she ran she heard a loud noise roaring towards her, and was stunned to see a black wall of rain hurtling into her path.

'Oh God, this is going to hurt,' she said, bracing herself. The wall hit Deborah so hard she felt the burning of tiny needles stinging her skin. She ran on another nine kilometres, drenched to the skin, until she reached higher ground and the convoy.

'There's no power and it's stinking hot in there,' said Glyn, relieved to see his wife emerging from the torrential rain.

Deborah felt miserable. The Arts Centre had looked like such a comfortable, luxurious place in comparison. But Karin soon cheered everyone up, dishing up the roast duck she'd had cooking in the oven and the special dumplings that Deborah loved. They all sat together around the table in the caravan under the air conditioner, the plastic blow-up Christmas tree staring down on them, thankful for their feast. It would take more than a cyclone to stop Karin's traditional Christmas dinner.

Deborah turned in that night wondering what the morning would hold, and preparing to have to run again in torrential rain. She suspected that she'd not seen the last of this awful weather. What she couldn't have imagined was that the howling wind and rain was poised to plunge the entire state into a disaster of calamitous proportions.

The wild weather that began on Christmas Day 2010 caused a series of floods that would, within days, force thousands of Queenslanders to evacuate their homes in towns and cities across the state. By early January, 200,000 people were affected, with three-quarters of Queensland set to be declared a disaster zone. The cost of the widespread flood damage would soon stand at a staggering $1 billion.

For Deborah, who had already experienced the impact of cyclones and floods on her previous adventures, the prospect of running through such dangerous conditions was nerve wracking. More worrying than running, was *not* being able to run. The thought of being stranded in some out-of-the-way place where she'd be unable to keep her record alive gave her a very sleepless night.

'I *have* to keep going,' she told her concerned family next morning as she dodged the floodwater now spreading rapidly across North Queensland. With the Fitzroy and Burnett Rivers already overflowing, a number of roads were soon blocked off and the continuing rain would cause the Condamine, Ballone and Mary Rivers to burst their banks, adding to the mounting crisis.

'I feel so sorry for all those families whose Christmases are ruined,' said Deborah, setting off on the road again. She had no idea then that the New Year of 2011 would bring far worse.

A few days later, Karin and Owen flew from Townsville to Adelaide for Thelma's funeral, leaving their caravan at the O'Connell caravan park, south of Proserpine.

'We won't charge you to leave it here . . . take as long as you like,' said the generous owners.

A National Disaster

Glyn and Deborah spent New Year on their own in their caravan. After running all day in the worst weather conditions, Deborah was exhausted.

Her thoughts were with Owen, who was still in Adelaide at his mother's funeral, and with such sadness in the air, Deborah wasn't feeling very much like celebrating. She and Glyn spent New Year's Eve in the van, and slept their way into 2011.

The New Year that held so much promise for so many Australians was poised to turn the lives of thousands of Queenslanders upside down as the weather brought heartache and tragedy to many families who would lose loved ones and properties before the week was out. The pouring rain and widespread flooding also started Deborah wondering how she was going to run through Queensland.

After their return from Adelaide and the funeral, Owen and Karin had spent a week at the caravan park recuperating. Deborah had suggested they should take some time out from fundraising, concerned that Owen needed the time to mourn his mother's death. But Owen was as committed to this trip as Deborah and soon they re-joined the convoy again for the trip down the east coast.

Deborah estimated it would take her five good days of running to cover the 300-kilometre stretch from Mackay to Rockhampton. But she was horrified when she discovered the road had already been cut off by the rising floodwaters.

'They're saying it's going to be cut off for at least two weeks,' she said, panicking and studying the map for an alternative route.

Because of the dangerous conditions, Deborah decided to slow her pace down from 50 kilometres a day to the minimum 20 kilometres each day, not wishing to find herself stranded. When she'd last outrun a cyclone and flooding, she'd been lucky enough to be running away from trouble, leaving the disaster behind her. But now, the weather updates on the ABC radio informed her that with flooding ahead of her, she was running into chaos.

On 10 January, Toowoomba and the Lockyer Valley were hit by flooding so severe it was called an 'inland tsunami'. The following day evacuations began in Brisbane itself as the Wyvenhoe Dam, built to control the flow of water into the Brisbane River, reached 190 per cent capacity. By the time the river peaked on 13 January, 25,000 homes and businesses in Brisbane were affected and the Central Business District had been closed.

While the volunteer response was speedy, the Emergency Services were stretched to capacity resulting in the mobilisation of the Australian Defence Forces to help in the evacuation effort and the big clean up. More than 35 people would lose their lives in the floods which impacted upon 70 separate Queensland communities. By Australia Day, 26 January, many people would still be unaccounted for.

Deborah would later discover that the beautiful caravan park at Cardwell where they'd stayed when they heard the bad news about Owen's mum had been flattened by Cyclone Yasi which devastated North Queensland in February.

On Deborah's previous run, the nation had rallied around the victims of Victoria's Black Saturday bushfires. Now, as people donated to the Queensland relief effort, more trouble was unfolding further south. As far away as central Victoria, severe rainfall caused major flooding and hundreds more homes were under threat.

Deborah was painfully aware of the dangers and anxious at the prospect of running into a disaster zone. She did not wish to put her family in danger, nor did she want to get herself into risky situations which would see her becoming a burden on the State Emergency

Services whose resources in the flood-stricken areas were already stretched to the limit.

'Look at these poor people,' she said, gazing at the photographs that filled the newspapers as the death toll mounted. The images of devastation were so distressing, filled with the faces of shocked and traumatised Queenslanders. Deborah was particularly touched by the plight of the elderly who had lost homes in communities where they'd spent entire lifetimes, and worried for the safety of her own parents, who were involved in a road trip that had become fraught with fear and risk.

At her slower pace, she ran into a free campsite called Carmilla Beach, where the 4WD became bogged in the floodwater. Everything seems to be against me, thought Deborah.

Queensland Floods

'Where are you now?' asked the radio journalist, ringing again from the ABC. The reporter who had interviewed Deborah about her not-so-merry Christmas on the road was now part of the team of journalists covering the disaster caused by the Queensland floods. She rang Deborah on her mobile, concerned for her safety and hoping for a story update.

But Deborah felt her story paled into insignificance in the scheme of things.

Deborah's slow run saw her arriving near a small town south of St Lawrence, a few kilometres north of the bigger town of Rockhampton where Glyn's fall from the Britz ladder had once almost brought Deborah's earlier walk to a grinding halt.

With severe flooding in Rockhampton, and many areas under water, the convoy were struggling to find a campsite for the night. 'Would you mind if we parked our van outside your home?' Glyn asked an elderly woman who he spotted in her front yard on the edge of the town.

He explained the reason for the pink convoy and how Deborah was running around Australia.

'Come around the back,' said the woman, directing the convoy to the rear of her property. 'You can connect your cable to my power supply,' she offered generously.

The woman, who lived alone, embraced four total strangers, in spite of the drama unfolding around her. She invited them into her home the next morning to watch the horrific images on the *Sunrise* breakfast show, capturing the surge of water that ripped through the small Queensland town of Toowoomba, leaving destruction and death in its wake.

The footage of people losing their homes and people they loved, was too shocking to countenance.

'How can I complain about being delayed when people are losing their families, their homes and everything else they hold dear?' Deborah whispered to her parents as they left the house. It was deeply concerning knowing that everywhere she ran she was leaving flood-stricken towns and grieving people behind her. Worse still, she was heading into other devastated towns where the mop-up exercise would take many weeks to restore any kind of normality to families whose lives would never be the same. This truly was a disaster of epic proportions, and Deborah was running right through the middle of it.

Deborah left next day feeling more conscious than ever of the safety of her family. The days she spent running through the floods would, before she knew it, turn into weeks. All she could do was reschedule some of her appointments in towns that were now without power and basic necessities and dealing with homelessness and tragedy.

With the whole of Australia now rallying around to raise vital funds for the victims of these terrible floods – and outpourings of sympathy from around the world from those who had witnessed the unfolding tragedy on TV – Deborah felt these disaster-struck communities were in more urgent need of money for the relief effort than any other cause.

Deborah had been heading into Julia Creek on the Barkly Highway when she received a telephone call reminding her about the Australia Day Awards which were due to take place on 25 January. The Prime Minister, Julia Gillard, would be presenting the national awards in each category.

'Is that Deborah De Williams?' asked a woman from the Australia Day Council. Now the woman told her, 'There is to be a presentation in Canberra. We hope you will be able to make it.'

Deborah explained that she was still out on the open roads and that it would be months yet before she was anywhere near Canberra. But the Australia Day Council wanted her there, and Deborah continued to receive calls as she moved through Queensland.

She had no idea how she could possibly make it. Even if she won, which she strongly doubted, it would be impossible to keep her daily record alive and attend the awards. Now it was January and in the midst of the Queensland crisis, she was more concerned how she'd manage to keep her record alive at all. By now, the widespread flooding that had left most of the state under water meant that just completing her run every day was risky business.

'Do I have to be there?' she asked, worried, taking another call from the Council.

'Well, obviously it's a great honour,' said the caller testily.

Deborah continued her run that day feeling even more stressed. 'How am I going to get to the nearest airport?' she asked Glyn. 'Where is the nearest airport anyway?' Glyn looked on the map.

'Mackay,' he said. His wife looked more stressed and dismayed.

'I'm definitely not going back there,' she said. 'What if I get stuck?' With many roads closed off behind them, as well as ahead of them, she wasn't going to backtrack.

With the awards just one week away on 25 January, the eve of Australia Day, Deborah wondered if it was possible to run further down the coast to another airport.

'Rockhampton has a small airport,' said Glyn, studying the map, and went off to make a phone call to see if he could arrange flights for Deborah and her mum to Canberra. When he returned his face was clouded.

'Rocky Airport is a metre underwater,' he said, as his wife groaned. Her other option was to run further south to Bundaberg.

'I'd have to run 60–70 kilometres a day for three days to reach the airport there,' she said. She would also have to figure out how to manage a minimum daily run, then catch a plane to Canberra and get back again in time to resume the run in Bundaberg. It was all sounding very hard and incredibly stressful.

'Even if I make it there in time, I don't have a thing to wear for a swanky luncheon with the PM,' she moaned. 'I can't really turn up to meet the Prime Minister in my pink shorts and runners!'

Janelle Larkin, her friend from the breast cancer network in Hobart had a suggestion when Deborah rang. 'Order something online,' she said, 'and have it delivered to you.' So Deborah hopped on her laptop and ordered a beautiful vintage 1950s dress in her favourite green and arranged for it to be delivered to Alistair in Launceston.

'Collect it from a post office box in Rockhampton on your way to Bundaberg,' suggested Alistair, who had posted the package on to her next destination, hoping the floods wouldn't stop her making it there on time.

Heading towards Rockhampton the devastation caused by the floods was everywhere. Thick brown sludge and mud covered parks that had been green when Deborah ran through on her first run. Even the landmark of the giant bull that stood on the grass on a roundabout outside Rockhampton was knee-deep in thick brown mud. Glyn had posed for a photo there dressed in a Cheapa Chickenfeed suit the first time around, as evidence for Deborah's sponsors – the Tasmanian Chicken Feeders Discount Variety Store – that she was advertising their chooks all around the country. They now compared the photograph with the one they took as they drove through the floods, revealing no sign of the lush green grass on which the bull had stood.

Running through Rockhampton proved to be one of the most sobering experiences of Deborah's entire life. The town had been badly hit by the floods but Deborah, upon hearing that the road had finally been re-opened, upped her pace to run 60 kilometres that day. She'd been told by the weather bureau that another wet front was coming through and she was desperate to get through Rockhampton before there were more problems.

As she entered the town, a woman on the side of the road rushed up to Deborah and hugged her tightly.

'I don't know what to do,' wept the elderly woman, breaking down on Deborah's shoulder. 'I just lost my husband to cancer at

Christmas – now this!' Deborah comforted the woman, feeling sick as she observed the flood damaged property that had once been her family home. 'I don't know what to do,' repeated the distraught widow. Deborah had no words to comfort her. She had no idea what this poor Queenslander was going to do. Having a disaster of this magnitude following hot on the heels of such a painful private tragedy, only magnified the loss. 'I'm so sorry,' was all Deborah could manage.

Coming out of Rockhampton, the battered, water-damaged homes with gardens covered in thick brown sludge made a miserable sight. Many front yards were filled with piles of ruined carpet and furniture. Piles of rubbish lined the road out of town. The trail of disaster that marked Deborah's route south was far more grim in the cold light of day than anything she'd witnessed on the TV news.

The inconsolable widow and her double tragedy played heavily on Deborah's mind as she trudged out of town not knowing what lay ahead.

As she ran, Deborah came across an old bow-legged man stacking up the sodden contents of his life in his front yard. The elderly Queenslander was struggling to lift a water-damaged armchair onto the rubbish pile. This man looked very traumatised, thought Deborah.

'Can I help you with that?' she shouted. The man nodded, and Deborah walked over and helped the man lift the chair onto the pile of flood-damaged furniture.

The old man's tanned weathered face was expressionless as he stared at the rubbish pile with tears in his eyes.

'What are you doin' out here?' he asked, suddenly aware of Deborah's pink t-shirt and its Running Pink slogan. Deborah blinked back at him.

'I'm raising money for breast cancer by running around the country,' she replied.

And before she could say more, the old man began to cry. Large silent tears trickled down his face, and instinctively Deborah put her arms around him and hugged him gently.

'I lost my wife five years ago to breast cancer,' he sobbed. 'That chair up there was *her* chair.' He pointed to the chair Deborah had just helped him pile onto the rubbish. 'She always sat in that chair when she was alive,' he continued, taking a deep breath. 'I've spent the last five years of my life talking to that empty chair . . . talking to my wife as if she were still with me.'

If words had escaped Deborah during her run into Rockhampton, they certainly eluded her now.

'Somehow, everything that's happened in the floods, my wife's chair getting ruined and going on the rubbish, has brought the whole thing back,' he said sadly. 'It's like losing her all over again!'

Perhaps that's how it felt for the other poor woman, pondered Deborah, holding onto the man and trying her hardest not to cry with him. But suddenly the old Aussie battler pushed Deborah roughly away.

'That's enough of all that!' he snapped, straightening himself up and wiping away his tears. And with that he hurried away from the pink stranger into his house and closed the door behind him.

Deborah trudged away with a heavy heart. These were just two stories that gave this awful disaster a human face, she thought sadly. There were undoubtedly many thousands of victims with heartbreaking tales of their own. The realisation made Deborah feel so small and invisible; she was no more than a tiny blip on a landscape of destruction where losses were mounting by the day.

'What's wrong?' asked Glyn startled to observe Deborah climbing into the caravan where she burst into tears.

'I'm losing it,' she sobbed, by now completely hysterical. She wept for the lonely ones grieving lost partners, for the Queenslanders who'd lost loved ones, pets and homes; for the sick women like Jan, and for all the women she was running for – from the patients enduring chemotherapy in hospitals or leaving hospital without breasts, or the survivors battling to pick up the pieces of lives that would never be the same again.

Later she cried for herself, because this challenge suddenly felt way too hard. Instinctively, Maggie, sensing her owner's pain, sidled up to Deborah and pressed a black wet nose against her hand, her brown eyes staring sympathetically across at her. Even Maggie had lost the wag in her tail today.

'I'll put the kettle on,' said Glyn as Deborah hiccupped another sob.

Deborah was sipping her coffee when Glyn had a suggestion. 'Why don't you just do the minimum and see the day out?' he said.

But Deborah was ready to give up. 'It's too hard . . . I've had enough,' she sniffed. She rang Janelle Larkin, her friend who had worked for the NBCF in Tasmania as a Regional Development Officer.

'Deborah how are you?' she asked. Across the silence Deborah had a question.

'Janelle . . . what am I doing here?' Janelle had not heard Deborah sound this bad, not even when she'd telephoned to say her feet were broken. In tears, Deborah told her about the floods, the two old people who'd lost people they loved, the man's wife through breast cancer.

'That's why you're there, Deborah,' said Janelle softly. 'You are there doing what you are doing, so that nobody else in future will have to lose a mum or a wife.'

Deborah hung up the phone. Then she ran out of the caravan and shuffled for another 33 kilometres until she reached the next camping site. Her talk with Janelle hadn't just saved the day, she thought that night. It had saved the run. She really had hit a wall that day, and with a friend she'd never met now in a hospice, she'd felt too sad to keep going.

The following morning she started her run early, turning on her iPod and listening again to yet another book in the magical Harry Potter saga. Over the past months, she'd listened to her favourite music, refocussing herself with her favourite John Lennon single, 'Imagine', and the motivational tapes that occupied her thoughts for hours after.

But when she felt like escaping, nothing beat the series of Harry Potter stories. Over the course of her second run, Deborah had listened to all seven books in J.K. Rowling's magnificent series. She loved the characters and while she hadn't listened to the stories every day, she had the habit of using these tales as a special treat — a distraction when the going got too tough. After the past few days, she really needed to catch up on another Harry Potter story.

Deborah particularly liked the magical notion of dreams and possibilities within these stories. She liked that the hero, Harry Potter, had come from humble beginnings not unlike her own, and she adored Hermione Granger, the heroine, identifying with this smart powerful girl and the whole dynamic between the wizard students who worked together as a unit to help each other achieve a common good. In Deborah's mind Running Pink's crew was not that different; her family all worked together like a dynamic little powerhouse towards the greater good. This run was such a team effort, she thought. This was not just about Deborah De Williams at all, because without her support crew this run just couldn't have happened.

Meeting the Prime Minister

'We're going to call you the rain genie,' joked Glyn, watching Deborah pull off her soaking runners. There were days when the rain was so torrential that she ran in a plastic mac, and other days when she put plastic bags on her feet and squeezed them into her runners. But the weather in Queensland was like nothing she had ever experienced.

Despite the chaos, there were other odd things about Queensland that Deborah had registered amidst the torrential rain – such as the fact that there appeared to be more highway signs than cars. And most of them, by coincidence, seemed to be advertising food, which was ironic since the floods had created food shortages in the devastated communities.

For a hungry runner who spent most of her time craving food that was in short supply, just the glimpse of a McDonald's sign was enough to spark a craving for chicken McNuggets or a Happy McMeal that would encourage Deborah to pick up her pace and head for the next town drive-through.

In the bleak days ahead, Deborah trudged down the coast through stricken communities, following a sign pointing to the nearest McDonald's – a staggering 200 kilometres away! She trudged on for days, fantasizing about chicken nuggets and when she got there, was bitterly disappointed to find it was closed. Even where food was available, the flood waters of these devastated communities left customers in short supply too.

'Did you see that?' she said to Glyn, when the road to Rockhampton finally opened and the trucks slowly began to slosh into the stricken town. 'They're carrying important supplies,' she smiled wryly. 'Beer and food!'

Still, Deborah's belief that you attracted what you wished for prevailed as she recalled her run down the coast to St Lawrence where the days spent dreaming of mangoes were rewarded after she arrived in town to find a shop selling mango ice-creams.

Now, waiting for the flooded Fitzroy River at Rockhampton to go down so she could continue her run towards Bundaberg, Deborah just hoped that the communities ahead had enough food to feed their families. She was finally given the go-ahead on 17 January. While she ran that day she heard she had appeared on Nicky Buckley's new show *Making Tracks* in the clip she'd filmed on her run into Elliott.

'Perhaps you'll get spotted by an agent, Maggie,' she laughed, as her dog ran along beside her, anticipating that the re-opening of the Bruce Highway the following day would allow them a clear run to Bundaberg.

Being out on the road had meant that she'd already missed the Tasmania presentation of her award as one of the four Tasmanian Australians of the Year for 2011. She had had to email a thank-you speech to a friend in her breast cancer network who had attended the awards ceremony on her behalf. She hadn't yet seen the blue glass commemorative trophy or the certificate that was presented to the other finalists.

Now it looked like she would miss out on the prestigious final presentation in Canberra too.

'You *must* go Deborah,' said Karin. 'It is such an honour.'

On 25 January, Deborah climbed out of bed just after midnight and ran in the dark from her marker on the corner of Rosedale Road, Horwood to Bundaberg, completing a run of 21.9 kilometres to keep her record arrive. She ran straight into the car park at Bundaberg Airport where her convoy were already waiting.

While Glyn sprayed a pink marker on the wet tarmac, Deborah pulled off her runners and grabbed a quick shower in her parents' van. Then she headed into the tiny terminal with her mum, who was accompanying her daughter to the momentous occasion in Canberra.

They hurriedly changed flights in Sydney, heading on to Canberra where a limousine driver was waiting in arrivals holding a card bearing Deborah's name.

'We're VIPs, Mum,' she laughed, still feeling harried.

By the time Deborah arrived at the awards luncheon she had already missed the celebratory breakfast with the Prime Minister, Julia Gillard, and the previous night's cocktail party that the finalists were invited to with the Governor General at Yarralumla. The PM and the other finalists were already on the stage outside the front of Parliament House when Deborah hurried in, just in time to shake the PM's hand and hear her announce that the winner was a Victorian lawyer.

'You must be the woman running around Australia for breast cancer,' observed the PM, greeting an out-of-breath Deborah, who shook her hand, feeling harried and strangely out of place amongst all these dignitaries and significant Australians. She felt even more out of place wearing a dress and proper shoes! After nine months on the road it felt peculiar being in anything other than runners and a pink t-shirt.

Deborah had missed the official part of the awards, and was embarrassed when she realised that the ringing mobile she could hear was her satellite phone – she'd forgotten to turn it off. Deborah and Karin took their seats at the swanky luncheon.

'You must be the runner,' said an Australian of the Year from South Australia.

'Yes . . . I'm her,' she smiled uneasily.

The opera singer who was providing entertainment began to sing and Deborah, like the others at the luncheon, hurriedly turned off her phone and began to listen. 'Sssh,' hissed a snooty-looking woman, partner of one of the other significant Aussies. Deborah looked bemused; she wasn't doing anything! The woman turned to her.

'I don't suppose you've ever heard opera before,' she snipped. Deborah felt her skin bristle.

'Well actually, the last time I heard opera was at the Met in New York,' she snipped back. Cheek! she thought.

'You must be the pink runner who is running around the country for breast cancer research,' said another, equally snooty middle-aged man. Barely looking at her, he went on to relate the story of a colleague who had been diagnosed with breast cancer. 'She found a lump after banging herself while carrying some books to a lecture,' he continued. '*She* was a *professor* you know!' Deborah wondered whether the guy's amazed tone meant he assumed breast cancer was a disease that only afflicted the masses. Yes, she thought, *they* can get it too. But she bit her tongue and sipped on another cup of tea.

During the later festivities, when celebrity chef Maggie Beer approached Deborah, she got in first. 'I'm *just* the woman who ran around the country for breast cancer,' she joked.

The two women made an instant connection, as Maggie's passion for food rivalled Deborah's passion for the open road.

'What did Aussies give you to eat when you were running around the country?' she asked curiously.

'Good old Aussie fare,' laughed Deborah, recalling the hundreds of sausage sizzles where she'd consumed tens of thousands of sausages with tomato sauce. 'Snags and barbecued steak of course!'

'Yep,' agreed Maggie. 'Traditional Aussie cuisine at its finest!' They walked together into a courtyard where they promptly looked at each other and burst out laughing. On the barbecue was a true-blue Aussie feast. The snags might look posher, mused Deborah. But they were still snags!

What Deborah didn't know, while she mingled and chatted, was that her mum was doing some mingling of her own. Karin had been chatting to a man called Jeremy who turned out to be a media advisor to the PM herself. She'd quietly slipped his business card, bearing his private phone extension, into her handbag without saying a word to her daughter. You never know who you might need, thought Deborah's mum. After all her fundraising, she knew it didn't hurt to network.

Deborah and Karin spent the night at an upmarket hotel, courtesy of the Australia Day Council, before rushing back to the airport for the dash back to Bundaberg where the run would have to be resumed immediately.

'I reckon I've only had about six hours sleep in the past 48 hours,' said Deborah, looking exhausted.

Within a couple of hours she was back in her runners, her posh frock stuffed into a cupboard in the caravan, standing beside the pink road marker at Bundaberg Airport. She had a little chuckle to herself as she headed back into the flood stricken area, wondering how long the big pink ribbon marker would remain at Bundaberg airport to greet other travellers arriving at the small terminal. Glyn usually spray painted a big pink 'X' on the road, but this time, despite the early start, he'd been particularly artistic, she thought.

'I've got to keep going forward,' she said, climbing into bed exhausted after another day of running through heavy rain and roads covered in water.

Only that morning she'd received a text from her friend Phil Essam, another ultra-marathon runner and former military policeman, who had been watching the unfolding crisis on TV.

'Just drive forward and forget about the run,' advised Phil, a historian for the Australian Ultra-marathon Association. He didn't want his running friend putting herself in danger. But Deborah's mind could not be changed.

A man had joined Deborah on the road towards Gympie when she received a phone call she had been dreading.

'I am so sorry I have to tell you this, but Jan has been taken into a hospice,' explained her sick friend's mother, aware Jan had been monitoring Deborah's progress. 'She's very gravely ill.'

Deborah welled up with tears, not wanting to reveal the content of this intensely private call to the man running beside her. She tried to keep it together as Jan's mum revealed that this amazing young woman, who had inspired Deborah at her own lowest point to keep her dream alive, was now clinging to life herself. 'We thought you should know,' continued her mum. 'You have given her such hope with your run.' Jan's mother was in tears. 'We are so thankful that you have given our beautiful girl so much hope and she has lived so much longer than anyone expected.'

Deborah choked back her own tears. 'Your beautiful girl has given me so much more than you could imagine too,' she said, sadly. She hung up and continued to run, while the man beside her jogged along, innocently chatting about his life.

Deborah was still trying to hold herself together when she ran into a local shopping centre where a breast care nurse waited with a group of people to welcome her. The scene felt strangely unreal as she battled to keep up her spirits for this kindly group that had turned out to support her. Afterwards she kept an appointment she'd organised to join the sister of her Tasmanian friend Sarah Clarke for coffee, all the time her stomach churning from the bad news.

While people chatted around her, Deborah's thoughts were on Jan, and what her mum had said about how much joy Deborah's adventure had brought to her daughter, how courageously she'd born this disease, and how, even now, she was still hoping against hope that somehow she could survive it. She had also explained how happy and proud she'd been for Deborah, a woman she felt she knew but had never met; a pink runner running around the country for thousands of women just like her.

Deborah felt so helpless. She badly wanted to achieve this world record for her friend, and had imagined herself arriving in Jan's hometown of Melbourne, crossing her fingers that the news that she had fulfilled a dream might somehow give Jan the hope she needed to survive. Now, with Jan in a hospice and the floods in Queensland delaying her journey, Deborah felt the clock was ticking and the weight of her responsibility was unbearable.

'Come over for dinner,' suggested Sarah's sister, who was delighted to see Deborah. But Deborah needed some time to process what she'd been told.

'I'd love to,' she said. 'But I have to go to the caravan park first.'

After the events of the day, she really needed a space to collect her thoughts.

'It's too hard . . . everything is against me,' she sobbed, as she collapsed on her bed in the caravan. All day she'd swallowed her sadness, but now her tears were unstoppable. Glyn put his arms around his wife.

On the Sunshine Coast, close to the health retreat where Deborah had once stayed after her practice run around Tasmania, Deborah met a woman who had been following her adventure on Facebook.

'Why don't you let me organise a fundraising lunch for you,' Janine suggested in an email. Deborah was not going to pass on this offer. Janine Langer lived in the beautiful town of Caloundra, and had a restaurant where she intended to put on a proper luncheon. This would be the only feed Deborah had been given that did not involve a barbie!

Once a month Janine organised a lunch in her local community which she used as a fundraiser for various causes. This time she wanted to donate the money towards Running Pink.

'I would love that,' said Deborah. She came off the phone thinking how much the woman appeared to love her husband. 'She mentioned his name quite a few times,' said Deborah, suddenly wondering if the name Alfie Langer was significant or if the woman just adored his little cotton socks so much that she couldn't help herself talking about him. 'Alfie will help do this or that,' Janine had blithely said.

Now Deborah wondered if she'd been missing something. She rang Alistair, who used to live in Brisbane and would know if this guy was someone whose name she should have recognised.

'Hey Alistair,' she said. 'Have you heard of someone called Alfie Langer?'

Alistair paused. 'What have you done now?' he said. 'Of course I've heard of Alfie Langer . . . he's only a God up there in rugby circles. Didn't you know who he was?' Deborah felt sheepish.

'Er . . . no,' she confessed.

When Janine called again as Deborah ran towards Caloundra, she came clean.

'I am so sorry I sounded so vague,' she said. 'I had no idea who your hubby was – never heard of him!' Janine exploded into fits of laughter.

'That's hilarious,' she giggled. But Deborah soon came face to face with the rugby God himself when she arrived at the Moo Bar and Grill for the posh lunch Janine had arranged and where a number of prominent women – including former Olympian Raelene Boyle, herself a cancer survivor – now waited.

'You won't have heard of me,' he grinned. 'But for the record, I'm Alfie Langer!' And they both laughed together.

Deborah left with a smile on her face and a cheque in her hand. It had been a great day and these people were fantastic folks who just happened to be famous.

On the run down Steve Irwin Way, now named after the TV star and conservationist who had been killed by a stingray in 2006, Deborah was joined by ultra-marathon legend Gary Parsons, another round-Australian runner.

'I'll run a short distance with you,' said Gary who doesn't run much any more. Deborah was honoured as he signed her witness book and exchanged one of his Run Around Australia t-shirts for a Running Pink one.

In 1999–2000 Gary ran 19,031 kilometres in 274 days, setting the record for the longest distance in the shortest time around Australia. Gary's run raised awareness for Legacy and raised tens of thousands of dollars for the organisation.

Two days later, when Deborah ran over the Story Bridge in Brisbane she stopped and caught her breath. She had a panoramic view of the devastation wrought by the floods below her. Even the ferry terminals had been washed away.

She was pleased to see Alistair's smiling face as he arrived in Brisbane to help the crew negotiate the city streets. In Brisbane the 4WD broke down again. In previous breakdowns they had been helped by generous people who donated time and parts to fix their problems and send them on their way. On Deborah's first run through Brisbane, the axle on the caravan went and the mechanic, aware of the reason for the run, mended it for nothing.

Once again, in Brisbane the Running Pink crew's transport was put at the top of the priority list by the mechanic who performed the work for free.

But the city proved a difficult one for a runner who was banned from travelling along the main freeways and had to follow a labyrinth of back streets where Glyn continually took wrong turns and got lost.

'Every time you head off on the wrong road, I have to follow you until you turn around and get back on track,' said Deborah. She had to follow the exact route that Glyn followed to ensure the co-ordinates on their GPS systems matched exactly at the end of each day. But she was putting lots of extra kilometres in having to follow him when he got lost.

Luckily, Alistair used to live in Brisbane and his local knowledge came in very handy as they passed through the city, though they still got lost even with his help.

The Boob Flasher

Travelling down the coast towards the border of New South Wales, Deborah sighed with relief. She was lucky, she thought. She was able to leave the disaster zone behind her, but for those poor Queenslanders whose homes and lives had been washed away, there was no escaping.

Deborah was running into Maitland when John Hogno appeared on the side of the road with a home-made flag that he now waved enthusiastically as she passed. He gave her the thumbs up again.

'Good to see you . . . knew you could do it!' he shouted brightly. God bless John, she thought. He was such a lovely inspirational man. She had eventually drunk his bottle of celebratory bubbly at the 6000-kilometre mark on her first run, just as she'd promised herself she would, toasting John for his encouragement and positivity.

Some distance out of Maitland, the convoy found a dog friendly caravan park that would welcome Maggie. But on closer inspection, they soon concluded that the campers at this park were more of the permanent resident variety.

'I reckon if you had a gun you'd be sleeping with it under your pillow tonight,' observed Deborah, nervously.

She had a speaking engagement in the town that day, and ran back to the park afterwards, which looked dodgier than when she'd left earlier that afternoon.

As Deborah made her way to the caravan, she noticed a large unkempt-looking woman in her dressing gown clearly trying to engage Glyn in some sort of conversation. Deliberately avoiding the woman's gaze, Deborah dashed past and into the caravan.

She was sitting at the table attending to her emails, when through the window she noticed Glyn trying to edge his way back to the caravan. But the woman, who was now dragging on a cigarette – her eyes glazed – was slowly following him.

Glyn bolted inside, and Deborah, feeling very tired, smelled trouble. The woman, a resident of the park, continued to hang around outside, another fag hanging uneasily on her bottom lip.

'This woman wants to talk to you,' said Owen, sticking his head through the caravan door, where Deborah was intentionally hiding, and avoiding eye contact with the woman through the window.

Deborah sighed. Not wishing to be impolite, she emerged from the caravan, Glyn following.

'Hi,' she said, brightly.

'Hey,' responded the woman, dragging on the smoke that now had an inch of ash hanging precariously on its tip.

'Seen what youse all doin',' she drawled, pointing to the two pink vans. Deborah nodded.

'Yes,' she said, unsure about where this conversation was going.

'I think I got breast cancer!' blurted the woman, her voice slurred. Deborah was stunned. This woman seemed so flippant about the possibility of having this awful disease. If she was worried, she certainly didn't appear it.

The woman continued in a slow, vague voice: 'I've got these funny lumps on me boobs,' she announced.

Glyn shifted, uncomfortably. 'You'd better go to your doctor and get them checked out,' he suggested, edging away.

The woman nodded, turning to Deborah with eyes that suggested she was affected by some kind of prescription drug. Deborah had no doubt from her spaced-out behaviour that she was affected by *something*.

'I got breast cancer I reckon,' she rambled on, shuffling backwards and forwards in her slippers and dragging on her fag again. 'I've got funny lumps,' she repeated. Deborah suggested a medical professional might be her best bet.

The Boob Flasher

'Gotta check these things,' said Deborah, eyeing Glyn up.

The woman stared from Glyn to Deborah and back again. 'Do you wanna 'ave a look?' she asked, lifting up her top and exposing a giant, floppy white breast which swung uneasily in front of Deborah's shocked face like an old sagging cow's udder!

'I still think you need to see your doctor,' continued Deborah, trying to retain some composure. Glyn walked slowly away shaking his head as the obviously drugged woman pulled her t-shirt back down over her sagging belly and trudged off. Deborah bolted into her parents' caravan, unable to comprehend what she'd just seen.

'Dad – you . . . you . . . Glyn, you bugger!' she said, slamming the van door behind her. 'What are you doing calling me out to deal with that?'

Owen stared in bewilderment as Deborah peered out of the window, ensuring that the coast was clear. Over the course of this journey she had met hundreds of women whose lives had been genuinely affected by breast cancer and who had struggled to share their experiences. But Deborah doubted very much that this woman had anything wrong with her at all, and was simply so out of it that she probably wouldn't even remember the conversation in the morning.

Later, Glyn observed the resident boob flasher hanging around again as they made their way to Owen and Karin's caravan for dinner.

'She's nuts,' said Deborah. 'I'm not going to the showers if she's in there.'

Just to be safe, she had her shower that evening in the privacy of her parents' van. But she and Glyn would later have a chuckle as they recalled the bizarre encounter.

***

Deborah was making her way south from Maitland when she encountered a genuine breast cancer battler whose sobering story would haunt her forever afterwards. Louise was a young mum in her early thirties who had been following Deborah's Facebook postings as she made her way down the east coast. She had been so keen to meet this inspirational runner that she had emailed asking Deborah when she would be arriving in Victoria so she could come out and welcome her.

She was on a holiday in New South Wales with her husband and young son when she discovered from Facebook that Deborah about to pass through Maitland.

'Come on,' she said to her husband. 'It's only 70 kilometres away . . . we can drive up there.'

Arriving in Macksville they had instantly spotted the pink caravan but, finding nobody home, had driven into the town where Louise recognised Glyn from the Facebook photographs.

'Hi, I'm Louise,' she said, introducing herself to Deborah when they followed Glyn out onto the highway to find the pink runner. Louise was clearly still on treatment, thought Deborah, observing her 'chemo-face' – the pale and puffy tell-tale sign of chemotherapy. She had very little hair, too, and told Deborah she was feeling very unwell from the side effects of her treatment.

'I was a former triathlete,' said Louise wistfully. 'I really wanted to meet you.'

Louise wanted to run with Deborah the following day, and made arrangements to meet her. The next day Louise arrived in her runners and began the slow run with Deborah along the road. They stopped a few times for Louise to recover her breath but, in spite of her treatment, she completed 10 kilometres. 'I loved it,' she told Deborah, beaming with joy.

During the run Louise told a sobering story of her diagnosis. 'I was in my early thirties, fit and athletic when I was diagnosed,' she explained. After the birth of her son Jordan, she had discovered a lump in her breast. Her doctor examined her, and organised an ultrasound which was inconclusive. He made no attempt to investigate further and did not do the biopsy that had diagnosed Deborah's lump as a tumour.

But the lump continued to grow and Louise returned to the doctor's on two or three more occasions.

'He said I was being ridiculous,' she said. 'He told me again it was nothing and I should stop worrying . . . he made me feel like I was being silly.'

The family then moved to another area where Louise became pregnant. Her husband accompanied her on her next appointment to the new GP's surgery. The doctor examined her and determined the pregnancy was progressing well.

'Do you have any other concerns?' he asked. Louise said she hadn't. But the doctor overheard her husband say: 'What about the lump?' The doctor's head swung around. 'What lump?' he asked, looking worried. And Louise showed him the enormous lump on her breast. The doctor instantly ordered the biopsy her previous doctor had not thought necessary.

'I'm afraid it is a tumour,' said her doctor at the next appointment. 'In fact it's Stage Three breast cancer.' Louise was distraught. The cancer that could easily have been detected in its earlier stages had now escalated to a third stage tumour and Louise's life was in danger. Since pregnancy sees an escalation in hormones, an aggressive breast cancer in a young woman can quickly spread and treatment is vital.

'What about my baby?' she asked, terrified. Scans to determine if the cancer had spread were very dangerous to Louise's unborn baby, as was the surgery she needed and the ongoing chemotherapy and radiotherapy she would require to save her life.

'That is your choice to make,' said the doctor, sympathetically.

But with a little boy depending on her and a husband who loved and needed her, there really was no choice. At nine weeks, Louise made the heartbreaking decision to terminate her unborn baby and save her own life.

'I wouldn't have gone ahead with another pregnancy and had to make that choice if only my previous doctor had ordered that biopsy,' she said sadly.

Since the termination of a baby she now grieved for, Louise had undergone a mastectomy and gruelling treatment for her aggressive cancer. By the time they reached Kempsey, Deborah was choked with tears and furious with that irresponsible doctor for not following up the lump with further investigation. Deborah had heard similar stories from other young women on her journey who had been diagnosed with breast cancer at more advanced stages because their doctors had not been thorough – wrongly assuming that young fit women were less likely to be candidates for breast cancer because of their age. As a result, young women were being failed.

'I would have been in Louise's position if my doctor had not been so thorough,' she told Glyn that night. Later, Louise's husband ran with Deborah and expressed his fury at the doctor's neglect of his wife.

'I'd like to shoot the bastard,' he said, enraged. But the meeting with this lovely young woman would stay with Deborah forever.

'I'll keep in touch,' promised Deborah.

In the countdown to Sydney, Deborah put a posting on her Facebook page, informing her supporters that she intended to hold a tribute walk in Sydney for all the survivors and the women who had lost their lives to breast cancer.

'I want to honour those women who have been affected by breast cancer,' she said. The meeting place would be the north side of the Sydney Harbour Bridge, she announced. She hoped people would come, and particularly hoped she might meet Donna Crebbin, whose mother she had met in Cairns but who she'd only spoken to by telephone from the Kimberleys.

To Deborah's amazement a group of around 30 men and women were already there when she arrived very early in the morning waiting to walk with her into the city. Among the group was a familiar face from her breast cancer network in Tasmania, who had travelled up to hand her the Tasmanian Australian of the Year Award her friend had collected on her behalf. And there was an unfamiliar face belonging to a voice she recognised.

'Hi, I'm Donna Crebbin,' said the woman who had telephoned Deborah in the Kimberleys after loading herself with 'Dutch courage'.

'I want to run with you as far as the airport,' said Donna, when the Tribute Walk ended at Martin Place in Sydney's CBD. Donna knew that the route south that Deborah intended to follow would take her past Sydney airport and felt she could manage the seven kilometres out of town.

'I read in the local newspaper that you ran all the way through your chemo,' said Donna, who had seen a story on Deborah, and was thrilled because she too, was maintaining her running program throughout her own treatment.

The pair set off together, the convoy passing them as they ran. As the airport came into sight, Deborah checked her GPS.

'We've done seven kilometres,' she informed her running partner. 'How do you feel?'

Donna smiled: 'I feel all right and will run a bit more,' she replied.

Before they knew it, they'd covered 15 kilometres. 'You only need to run a few more kilometres to have completed a half marathon,' said Deborah, encouraging her new running mate. 'What do you reckon?'

Donna looked amazed. 'I'll try,' she said.

By the time they reached the 21.1-kilometre mark, Donna, in her forties, surprised herself by achieving her first half marathon. She was exhausted, but exhilarated.

'I did it,' she said, beaming from ear to ear. 'I've only ever run as far as eight kilometres in the past,' she said. It had only been four weeks since she'd finished radiotherapy, which leaves so many cancer patients exhausted. 'This has been the best day of my life,' she said, hugging Deborah and choking back tears. 'I've just run half a marathon and if I can do that I can beat this disease – I can do anything!'

Long after Donna left, Deborah continued to feel inspired by this great fighter's spirit and her wonderful achievement. The experience had opened her eyes about the goals that can be achieved after cancer; about the possibilities that might exist for Running Pink in the future.

Deborah had gained far more from this run, she thought as she ran on, than anything she might have given to these wonderful women she kept meeting.

Their camping site that night was the unlikely setting of a suburban cul-de-sac in Miranda where they set up the pink convoy on the grass nature strip outside the home of a beautiful Greek couple called Jim and Mary Stamell. Deborah had originally met Mary Stamell during her first run when she had spoken with Karin in a suburban shopping centre. Karin had been fundraising at the time and the Running Pink crew had been struggling to find campsites in the heart of the city, since most tend to be outside the suburbs along the coast.

Deborah's first run through Sydney had seen the convoy arriving in the capital city on the weekend of Australia Day, 26 January, and Karin had been telling Mary how hard it was to find anywhere in the city that would take their Director of Greetings.

'You don't happen to know where there are any camping sites around here?' asked Karin. Mary had a better idea.

'You can come home with me and park your vans outside my place,' she said brightly. The pink convoy made a peculiar sight as it trailed up the suburban cul-de-sac to Mary's home. Mary's generous Greek nature shone through as she offered the grubby crew the use of her showers, introduced them to her beautiful daughters, and insisted on cooking them mountains of Greek food.

When Mary learned Deborah was running around Australia on her second attempt, she insisted they should stay again. The pink vans and their pink 4WDs looked just as out of place, but meeting Mary again was like meeting an old friend, just as it had been with Wendy Trow and Barbara Johnson. Anyway, who would be stupid enough to turn down a chance to sample Mary's delicious Greek cooking?

Deborah was running out of Sydney when the call she'd been dreading finally came.

'I am sorry to tell you, but Jan has passed away,' said Jan's sister, choking on tears. Deborah was stunned. 'She fought a brave battle . . . your run gave her such hope,' she said.

Deborah began to cry. All through this journey, Deborah had run picturing herself arriving in Melbourne and finally meeting this young woman who had helped her realise her dream. She would hug her and say thank you. A part of her hoped that her run might really help Jan find the hope she needed to win this terrible fight against cancer. Now those hopes were gone.

'I'm so sorry,' she wept.

'Those bloody Queensland floods,' she sobbed that night. 'They held me up for three whole weeks . . . if I hadn't been delayed I'd have been in Melbourne by now. I'd have been there to say goodbye.'

Friends in High Places

Deborah headed into Canberra with a heavy heart. Something had broken in her after hearing about Jan's death. But she had promised her friend she would complete her run and now that world record was something she *had* to achieve at all costs.

As she approached Canberra for the second time in a matter of months, she jokingly told her crew: 'We should get the PM to sign my witness book,' Karin's eyes lit up.

'I'll organise it,' she said.

'And who are you going to ring to organise this?' laughed Deborah.

'Jeremy,' said Karin, as casually as if she were ringing an old girlfriend.

'Who's Jeremy?' asked Deborah, shocked. To her amazement her mum produced the business card with her new friend's private number and made the call.

'My daughter will be running into Canberra and we thought the PM might want to meet her again,' said Karin, up-front as ever. She chatted a while and came off the phone looking pleased with herself. 'Done,' she said, and carried on washing up without batting an eyelid.

On 24 March, Deborah ran into Canberra with a smile on her face. Her old mum had just organised a meeting with the most important woman in Australia as easily as if she'd been organising a dental appointment. Deborah's friend Phil Essam was waiting at the Old Parliament House with the CEO of Canberra, Gary Byles to welcome the pink runner.

Deborah had anticipated a brief two-minute meet-and-greet with the PM in a private room. So Deborah was amazed to find a swag of around 50 photographers gathered in the courtyard at Parliament House with their flashlights and cameras, all waiting to capture the meeting between the pink philanthropist and the nation's Prime Minister.

'How are you, Deborah?' asked the PM, as Health Minister Nicola Roxon introduced herself.

'Great,' said Deborah, eyeing up Karin, who was smiling sweetly and looking especially pleased with herself. It certainly did help having such powerful new connections!

'So I hear you've been running 50 kilometres a day,' said the PM, looking very impressed. But not as impressed as Deborah, as she glanced at her mum, as a reminder that this surreal scene with the country's most important woman, was really happening.

'For you,' said Deborah presenting the PM with a silver ribbon brooch which she'd had engraved with the words 'Running Pink'. The PM put it on her jacket immediately.

'Would you mind signing my witness book?' she asked.

'Certainly,' said the PM, taking her pen out and signing with a flourish. Deborah was thrilled. She really is a very gracious woman, thought Deborah.

'Thanks for giving me your time,' she said, shaking the PM's hand once again, as her assistants began to check their watches.

'My apologies, but I have to attend Question Time,' said the PM. The meeting had lasted about 15 minutes, amidst a hail of flashing cameras, and Deborah left smiling in disbelief at her mother's cheek.

'You're such a dark horse, Mum,' she laughed.

Deborah was delighted when she realised the PM would be wearing her silver brooch that symbolised the fight against breast cancer for a TV audience of thousands. Running Pink had certainly raised its profile that night, she thought.

'Thanks, Mum,' she said, hugging her mum who looked like the cat who'd got the cream for the rest of the day.

Deborah was escorted out by two security guards – one of them revealing that his life had been touched by breast cancer too. Deborah ran on to the suburb of Hall, where Phil and his wife joined the Running Pink crew at a community barbecue.

When Deborah crossed the border into Victoria, 13 days later, it was bittersweet. She should have been running with happiness in her heart to meet the friend this run was all about. Now Jan had gone that goal felt very empty.

Running through Gippsland, passing the landmark chimneys of the big power station, Deborah received a call from her friend Ken Nash.

'I'm down there on an army exercise,' he said. 'Where are you? I'll come and run with you.' Deborah was thrilled. Ken always seemed to turn up when she needed him most and right now, as she ran towards the home of a friend she would never meet, she really needed her guardian angel.

By now Deborah was aware she needed to put some extra kilometres onto her journey so she could beat the record that had been set 21 years earlier. She needed to beat the time and the distance that the former record holder had set.

For this reason she had run that day in a loop, returning that night to the east Gippsland town where she had begun the run that morning. The following morning, Ken joined her on the road.

They were jogging together talking about Jan's death and the plight of other breast cancer battlers when they glimpsed a figure up ahead running towards them.

'That looks like Colin.' Deborah stared at the man.

'Nah. . .' said Ken. 'That won't be Col . . . what would he be doing down here?'

But the figure got closer. 'It bloody well is Col,' said Deborah, delighted. Colin ran towards them smiling, now fully recovered from his donor surgery.

'What are you doing here?' asked Deborah, amazed to see her angel again.

'Thought I'd surprise you,' said their mutual mate. 'I thought it would be good to run towards Melbourne on the last lap home with you.' Deborah was thrilled and the trio clung together in a group hug that Glyn photographed. It was a magical moment. These guys always turned up when she really needed a mate.

As they ran together, Deborah's spirit lifted for the first time since hearing about Jan's death.

'How did you find me?' she asked.

'Easy,' said Colin. 'I rang your mum and dad and they told me where you'd be.' But it hadn't been *that* easy. Deborah had been doing her loop and wasn't running on the highway where he'd expected to find her.

That day, with her friends beside her, Deborah ran 55.6 kilometres. 'Three mates all affected by cancer in some way,' she said that night. Deborah had beaten the disease, Ken's wife had succumbed to it, and Colin's son had survived it. The thought put a spring in Deborah's step as she headed for home.

As Deborah ran through Pakenham, John Hughes – the ultra-marathon runner who had joined her on the run out of Melbourne when she'd been hobbling on blistered feet – dispatched his wife Bernadette to meet her. Bernadette brought a friend with her.

'Hi, I'm Kirrily,' said the friend.

Deborah observed Kirrily's bald head and lack of eyebrows, and was not at all surprised when Kirrily revealed she was battling breast cancer.

'Would you mind if I ran with you?' she asked. Deborah said she would be delighted.

They jogged along for five kilometres that morning, chatting about Kirrily's journey and Deborah's incredible run which would soon be at an end, hopefully with a new world record under her belt.

'I have to go to chemo later,' explained Kirrily as Bernadette drove up the road to collect her. She waved to Deborah who stood in silence. She felt such admiration for the courage of these young women who came to run with her to show their support when they were sick, on chemotherapy and struggling with their lives. These were moments that left her feeling very humbled. In many ways this mammoth adventure was as much of an honour run as her run with the Queen's baton had been at the Commonwealth Games.

David Hughes, the ultra-marathoner who had joined Deborah on her run out of Melbourne near the start of her journey, joined her the following day as she headed closer to the city. The night before her run into Melbourne, Deborah camped in the upmarket seaside suburb of Black Rock. When she reached the trendy city suburb of St Kilda, she recognised a friendly face that stood waiting for her.

'I thought I'd run with you into town,' said Matt from the Dirty Dog Dingoes. After their photo with her on the Western Australian Coast, the 4WD fan had promised he'd see her again. And he was as good as his word.

Matt accompanied Deborah on her run around the Bay and up into Federation Square in the city centre, where his partner was standing waiting for Deborah with a smile and a baby in her arms. She had been pregnant when they had met Deborah four months ago, and their baby was now smiling.

There were also a few other familiar faces amongst the large crowd that had gathered to cheer Deborah on. Her nephews, Adam's children Nathan, William, Jarrod and Travis cheered loudly as their aunt ran into view.

Another pink crowd cheered her on amidst the media scrum for stories and photographs as Deborah headed down to the docks at Port Melbourne to join her crew for the ferry trip to Tasmania and the last leg of her journey. Would she beat the world record? asked the media. 'I hope so,' she said.

A New World Record

Deborah ran off the boat checking her GPS again. 'Oh no . . .' groaned Glyn, realising he'd made a big mistake. While Deborah was on track to beat the previous world record set by Sarah Fulcher, an American woman, 21 years earlier, he suddenly realised her previous record had been in miles!

'But we've been calculating it in kilometres,' he said. 'That means you will have to do an extra 400 kilometres on top of what you'd estimated, in order to beat the record.'

Deborah had originally estimated she would be back in Hobart on Saturday 30 April. But after being delayed by the Queensland floods she now cringed at the thought of having to add another 400 kilometres onto her run. She was already feeling so sad about Jan, and exhausted from everything that she couldn't imagine how she could up her pace to make Hobart on 30 April.

'To make it into Hobart for the 30th I'd have to run 87 kilometres a day every day for two whole weeks . . . it can't be done,' she said.

Since Jan had died she no longer had the incentive to run another 400 kilometres on top of what she'd done. 'I'm not doing it,' she said. 'I don't care about the record.' Glyn wasn't so sure. 'Come on,' he said. 'After running all this way, thousands of kilometres, for over a year, you would not forgive yourself if you stopped now!'

'You've already run more than 17,000 kilometres; you are going to say at some stage down the track, I should have gone for the record!'

He's right, thought Deborah.

Deborah now had to add a week to run her additional kilometres to beat the record which would see her arriving home in Hobart, probably on the same day as the Mother's Day Classic. It seemed fortuitous that the Mother's Day Classic is an event that raises money and awareness about breast cancer. It was a perfect end to a world record run. She had to do it.

'If I'm going to add some kilometres, I'll run to Burnie,' she said, putting on her runners again and running off the boat at Devonport. In Burnie, her friend Ian Edwards, Tasmania's local hero of the year was waiting with a gang of children. Ian works for a charity called Kommunity Kids which does a great deal of work for underprivileged children. 'You can stay the night at the police barracks,' he offered. There were benefits to knowing a policeman, she thought.

'I'm going to run with you,' offered Deborah's friend Vlastik, turning up next morning. This was his hometown and he figured Deborah could do with the company.

The elderly runner ran with Deborah for seven kilometres towards Devonport, where she'd made her mind up to wind her way down to Hobart by doing loops around the place to add vital kilometres onto her record. She ran onwards to Deloraine and then to Launceston doing a loop up into the Tamar Valley and back again to Launceston.

'We'll stay here for a few days and I can run from here every day,' Deborah told Alistair, as Glyn parked the van on the front drive.

Over the coming days she ran another loop around the Tamar, Deborah's old training ground and then ran from Launceston to Hobart covering the 200-kilometre distance in just three days. This is the same route that Deborah had done in 24 hours before her cancer diagnosis. Then she ran the loop around the channel where she finished the loop back in Hobart, running on to New Norfolk.

On Adam's birthday, Friday 6 May 2011, five kilometres out of New Norfolk at exactly 1.12 p.m. and after running 406 consecutive days, Deborah finally broke the world record surpassing the one set by American Sarah Fulcher in her home country. While Sarah had run 11,134 miles (17,918 kilometres) in 438 days of continuous running, by the time Deborah's run ended two days later, her new world record meant she'd run 18,026 kilometres in 408 days of non-stop running every single day.

'How does it feel?' asked a journalist, as Deborah stopped at her record-breaking moment outside New Norfolk and celebrated her victory with a bottle of passion pop given to her six weeks earlier by the Crookwell Lions club to have at this very moment. 'Tired but elated,' she replied, squirting the drink all over herself for the benefit of the cameras from the Hobart *Mercury*.

But the triumph lacked the effervescent bubbles it deserved. 'My bloody passion pop's flat – wouldn't you know it!' she laughed.

Two days after that celebration, on Sunday 8 May, right on schedule, Deborah arrived at the Mother's Day Classic in Hobart, running from Richmond into the city where her dream began 408 days earlier. Her final run of the day had begun at two a.m. that morning from the caravan park in Richmond where the convoy had parked overnight. She jogged along in the dark, complaining that it wasn't fair to be running in the dark *and* the rain! 'I am the rain genie to the very end,' she said.

She ran into the Domain where the Mother's Day Event was taking place and where the local Dragon's Abreast Tassie paddlers formed a guard of honour with their pink paddles. Deborah ran underneath the oars to the warmest welcome as scores of women in pink clapped and cheered.

Then, almost unnoticed, she and her friend David Hughes ran a 12.2-kilometre loop of Hobart, to her final destination at Parliament House where David's wife, Bernadette, waited with Glyn and Deborah's parents.

There, away from the crowds, surrounded by people she loved, and who had helped her achieve her dream, Deborah turned her GPS off for the very last time. 'Do the honours David?' she said, and David witnessed his name in the book at the end of her record run. It was a perfect way to end a perfect day, she thought.

With her journey at an end, she returned to the caravan site, and went straight to bed.

Royal Bragging Rights

The following morning, the new world record holder woke in agony. After running along the road for hours each day non-stop for 408 days, Deborah couldn't face the thought of the short jog she would need to keep doing for a few days, so her body could adjust to life off the road.

It was pouring with rain all day and after the floods of Queensland and the rain in Tasmania, Deborah was too exhausted to face another day on the road getting soaked.

The result of stopping abruptly had its consequences, she thought. But she never dreamed that the lactic acid now building up in her muscles would cause such agony. She spent the whole day, curled up in a foetal position, unable to eat and crippled by the effects of this acid build up, wishing she hadn't gone cold turkey.

'I'm so stupid,' she groaned, as her mother observed her writhing on the sofa looking more sick than she'd ever been in her life. 'You have to make yourself go out tomorrow for a run even if it is only a short one,' advised her mum, looking worried. Deborah dug out the Wheatgrass Balm that her ultra-marathon friend Malcolm had given her before beginning her run. It worked like magic when it came to soothing sore muscles.

The next day she managed a slow jog, the pain slowly subsiding by the end of the afternoon. 'I did it,' said Deborah, on the phone to Jan's mother. 'I would not have achieved this if it hadn't been for her.' Jan's mother understood. Deborah had a special request of the bereaved family. 'I address a lot of women when I talk about breast cancer,' she said. 'I would like to be able to talk about Jan's story and her impact on my life and on this run . . . I wondered if you would mind.' The family gave their consent with one request. 'For her privacy we would prefer it if you did not reveal her real name.' Deborah understood.

Over the coming weeks, at every gathering she attended, Deborah spoke about the friend she never managed to meet, who had been the inspiration for her adventure. It remains a story to this day, that she cannot detail without tears. Her journey of hope became part of Jan's journey.

Deborah finally wrote out cheques for $200,000 for breast cancer research, a slightly lower total than the amount she'd optimistically written on her original Running Pink cheque, and posted them off. This amazing amount represented all the donations she had received from equally amazing and generous Australians. Those donations were now being passed on in full towards finding a cure for the disease that claimed Jan's life. Perhaps one day it might save someone else's, she thought.

'I can't stand it,' said Deborah, making her first trip to the crowded supermarket in over a year. After spending 408 days out on the open roads often in the middle of nowhere, the lines of shoppers milling around and the noisy traffic in the car park, felt surreal. It was hideous, and Deborah rushed out of the place, gasping for air. It felt positively claustrophobic after her simple life on the road.

She missed the road already and now the adrenalin had subsided using all her spare energy reserves for that last lap home, Deborah felt herself slowly sinking into a black empty hole. The days that followed were miserable, as she sat on the sofa not knowing what to do with herself or her life.

Even reliving her adventure, in front of eager groups of women, or community organisations, left her gripped with a deep sense of longing. If Maggie missed her fans, Deborah missed the great open spaces of a wonderful country.

The radio interviews soon died down, and Deborah quietly went about her business. But now requests were pouring in from different community groups and particularly schools, whose principals were keen to hear this inspirational Tasmanian Australian of the Year inspiring young Aussies to follow their dreams.

She told them the story of Steve Irwin. 'It doesn't matter if people think your dream is crazy, you should do it anyway,' she said. The children adored Maggie as much as she loved the attention. Deborah often thought about the crowds that had gathered along the road to pat Maggie or give her a welcome treat. The cupboard at home was still filled with supplies of those treats that would last for months to come. But watching the line of children snaking around the classroom as they waited turns to stroke the star of the show, still brought a smile to Deborah's face.

Some weeks after her run, Deborah's friend Mark Dabner, handed her a quote he'd found in the unlikely setting of an old folks' home. 'This reminded me so much of you,' said the designer of her Running Pink website.

> 'Courage doesn't always roar. Sometimes courage is the quiet voice at the end of the day saying, "I will try again tomorrow".' – Mary Anne Radmacher

He said it sounded like it could have been written for Deborah.

On 17 October, Deborah was driving to Smithton at the invitation of her Bosom Buddies' friend Judy King when she received a phone call out of the blue that left her speechless. Judy had invited Deborah to address a group of women about her inspirational walk, and to talk to some elderly residents at a local retirement village when the mobile rang in her car.

'Deborah??' her friend Ian's voice sounded urgent. 'That's me,' said Deborah, whose phone had not stopped since her return to Tasmania and her successful run. 'Have you got an invitation to visit the Queen?' he asked, breathlessly. Deborah laughed out loud. 'No,' she replied cautiously. 'Guess she must have forgotten me!'

Australians, especially the older generation Aussies adored the

British Royalty, especially Queen Elizabeth 2 whose long reign over their country as head of the Commonwealth remained a source of ongoing pride. Now she was heading to Australia on her first tour since opening the Commonwealth Games in Melbourne in 2006 and was holding a reception in Canberra for significant Australians. That VIP guest list included the names of the various Australians of the Year from each state. 'I would have expected you to be on the list,' said Ian, puzzled. 'You should have something in the mail.'

Now it was Deborah's turn to be puzzled. 'Ring the Australia Day Council,' urged Ian. Deborah dialled the official number, wondering where the hottest ticket in town might be. 'There is an invitation in the post,' said the woman on the other end of the line. Deborah was more flustered than exited.

'Mum . . . guess what,' she said, immediately ringing Karin, who was the biggest royal fan. 'What?' said Karin, suspiciously. Finally, after three years of adventures, Karin had managed to get that leisurely retirement trip she'd postponed so many times. Deborah's 'guess what's' always suggested she was about to announce another crazy plan and whatever it might be, Karin wasn't interested in having her own peace and quiet interrupted again. Now in Port Augusta with her husband, on their own road trip, Karin felt nervous. 'Guess who I'm going to meet?' announced Deborah. 'Her Majesty The Queen!' There was a huge silence, then Karin's voice could be heard on the other end telling her husband the news. 'You are joking?' she said, now speaking with Deborah again. 'Nope . . . all true,' replied her daughter.

But Deborah was flustered as she pondered the VIP invitation. 'I don't think I can go, Mum . . . after my trip I'm broke . . . and I don't even have a dress to wear!'

Karin was horrified. 'You have to go, Deborah . . . You *must* go . . . It's a chance of a lifetime.' It certainly is, thought Deborah hanging up. And it gave her mum the biggest bragging rights amongst her older friends. Of course she would go.

Deborah continued the drive to Smithton, pulling the caravan that had been their home in the front yard of the investment place in Launceston. Now back at their home in Midway Point, their peculiar pink 4WD and van sat redundantly outside Alistair's place in Launceston, a very lairy and easily recognisable landmark.

With prior engagements in Smithton, Deborah would need to get a posh frock as soon as possible. She would have put her foot down, but speeding with a caravan in tow did not seem like a great idea.

News of the royal invitation to visit the Queen who was in Australia with her husband, Prince Phillip The Duke of Edinburgh on official duties which included attending a heads of Commonwealth meeting in Perth and the opening Melbourne's multi-million dollar new Royal Children's Hospital, came as a shock to Deborah who had been nominated by the Tasmanian Community. Raising $200,000 for breast cancer research was an achievement the whole state was proud about.

The VIP invitation certainly provided Deborah with another highlight in her illuminating talk about achieving her dream. She suspected it would be an even bigger hit at the forthcoming address to residents of the elderly people's home in Smithton where the Queen would be bound to have a royal fan following amongst people who had fought for Queen and Country.

With Deborah's mail being sent to their house in Launceston, she rang Alistair to find out if the invitation had arrived. He opened it. 'Yep,' he said. But there was another unexpected surprise on the unexpected invitation. The invitation from Her Majesty was for Deborah De Williams *and* Karin Drogemuller! Deborah gulped. Talk about bragging rights now!

She rang her mum and dad again. 'Would you like even bigger bragging rights Mum?' asked Deborah, the excitement bubbling in her voice. 'Well Mum, your name is on the list to see the Queen too!' Deborah knew Karin never missed a chance to boast to her sister about her children's achievements. This time Karen's voice sounded more urgent and shrill. 'Owen . . . Owen . . . turn the car around. . .turn the car around right now! I have to meet the Queen!' With the big meet and greet just three days away on 21 October

Owen put his foot down and headed back from South Australia towards the Australian Capital Territory.

As Deborah suspected, news of her royal invitation was a big hit at the elderly retirement home where she encountered her first heckler. One of the elderly residents was suffering from dementia, and he yelled and heckled at the top of his voice throughout her talk, leaving Deborah wanting to laugh. 'Shut her up,' he shouted across the rows of grey heads in her audience. 'Rubbish, rubbish . . . get her off . . . shut up!' It wasn't quite a hit with *everyone,* she smiled on the drive home.

While Deborah made hurried arrangements for the flight to Canberra from Tasmania, Owen was racing towards Canberra with a highly agitated Karin. Deborah met her mum at Canberra airport and they raced off to buy some clothes fit to the meet the Queen in. Deborah found a formal dress while Karin bought a very posh top. 'We'll do,' smiled Deborah.

They arrived at Parliament Gardens outside Parliament House where the meeting would take place.

'What?' said Deborah, observing a senior politician pushing past her mum, to get a better look at the Queen. Cheek! she said to herself. Deborah crossly escorted her mum out of the hall and back in through another door where they had a better view of the proceedings. 'That man just pushed my mum,' she told the man standing ahead of them, next to security, indicating the politician. The man looked unimpressed. 'Here . . .' he said making room for pint-sized Karin. 'I've got a mum too . . . stand right here by me!' The man introduced himself as Peter Marshall, and he stood aside to give Karin a clear view of the proceedings. He smiled at Deborah. 'I know how important it is to please your mum,' he added.

As Her Majesty made her way from the podium with the Prime Minister, towards the gathering, people fell into two lines. The monarch began to work her way down the lines, shaking hands politely and chatting to her subjects.

Suddenly, a familiar face appeared in the crowd. 'It's Jeremy,' said Karin, addressing the PM's media aide as though they were old friends. Jeremy spotted the pair and hurried over. As the PM and the Queen moved to speak to some people in the line opposite, he stepped forward and said to the PM: 'No . . . over here.' He stealthily directed the two most important women in the room towards the two other most 'important' women guests at the bash. Karin looked totally overawed.

'This is a very special Australian,' said the PM, introducing the diminutive Queen to Deborah. 'Deborah ran all around Australia to raise money for breast cancer research.' So . . . Julia Gillard remembers me, thought Deborah, amazed. The Queen shook Deborah's hand, looking visibly surprised. 'And how long did it take you?' she asked, amazed. '408 days and I ran 18,026 kilometres,' explained Deborah. The Queen looked more astonished. 'Well, I've flown over Australia and it's an *awfully* long way,' she said shaking her royal head in astonishment.

Then Deborah addressed the Queen. 'Her Majesty . . . I would like to introduce a very special person, my mum Karin Drogemuller . . . my support crew on the run.' Karin was a very special Australian too, thought her daughter and was just about the same size as the Queen. Karin stood dumbstruck as the Queen shook her hand. 'You must be very proud,' said the Queen. 'I am,' said Karin in a low voice. Bragging rights forever, thought Deborah smiling at her mum's face – right royal bragging rights! And the Queen moved on.

Deborah savoured the magical moment for herself, but even more for her German-born mum, a long-term royal fan. After everything her mum had done for her, this was Deborah's gift. This feisty little woman had been brave enough to drive through cyclones, through storms and floods and even across deserts. She had put her retirement on hold three times now, and she may not have wanted to go on either of the two record breaking runs, but once there she never complained. She endured burglars and breakdowns on some of the most remote roads in the world, without complaint; patiently waiting long hours in the pink caravan on an outback road while Owen made the 700-kilometre trip to Darwin and back in a single day.

Deborah only wished she'd had the chance to tell Her Majesty all this. But just watching her mum's proud face as she finally met the monarch who had graced the glossy mags for years when Karin had been a young mum herself, was the best thank-you she could ever have given her mum.

'I might have run the kilometres,' whispered Deborah, as they mixed with the cream of the country at the reception. 'But this was definitely a team effort. I couldn't have done it without Running Pink and especially without you Mum!' Karen shrugged. 'I still never want to see another shopping centre,' she said, dismissively. After setting up fundraising stalls in every single shopping centre on Highway One on Deborah's Australian run, she was never doing another road trip again!

At the reception Deborah had determined she would keep a low profile, wondering what these important people made of a crazy woman who had met the Queen for running around the country with her dog! She pre-empted people's introductions, when they said: 'You're just the runner who ran around the country.' Deborah would have felt slightly embarrassed if her attention hadn't been drawn to a very famous runner in the midst of the gathering.

As she turned away from the Queen, Deborah noticed Robert De Castella, an Olympic marathon runner who had for years been on Deborah's wish list. Deborah approached the well-known athlete, telling him about her plans to compete in the New York Marathon the following month. 'I am taking a team of young indigenous Australians,' he said. 'I have been training them to run the New York Marathon.'

Deborah was very impressed. 'Why don't you come to the reception we are organising at the Australian Counsel General's Office in New York. Deborah left the meeting wishing she'd had her witness book on her, so that 'Deeks' could sign his famous name in it.

No Comedy Clubs in Berlin!

Deborah was running again when Donna Crebbin, the young survivor who had run half a marathon in Sydney, flew to Tasmania for a stop-over.

They had been discussing a plan which now saw them sitting at Deborah's table where they designed a pink ribbon which they now took into Launceston with them.

'We want this symbol tattooed on us,' they told the tattoo artist. Deborah had hers tattooed on the inside of her lower arm, watching while Donna had hers tattooed across her lower back. They left like blood-sisters, happy with their new tatts. Cancer had been the bond that had brought these women together and this symbol would remind them that they had both survived the journey. If Deborah had never had cancer she would never have been inspired to follow this dream. 'Think of all the people I would never have met,' she said. 'And think of all the amazing stories I would never have shared.'

'Are you still running?' Deborah asked Donna. Since completing that half marathon with Deborah in Sydney Donna was now convinced she could do anything.

It then occurred to Deborah that the inspiration she'd given this cancer battler might be something that would appeal to other survivors too. On her Facebook page she posted a general invitation to anyone who wanted to come with her to London for the ultimate marathon event in April 2012. They would be the Running Pink contestants!

'I would love to come,' responded survivor Mandy Giblin, a fellow Tasmanian and survivor. Mandy, a former Commonwealth Middle Distance Runner explained in her email that she was a mum of two children and lived in Glenorchy. She believed the run wouldn't just be a personal challenge but that it would help Running Pink to create awareness and educate other women. 'A little over two years ago I was planning to run the Seattle Marathon for my 35th birthday,' she told Deborah. 'Instead I was recovering from surgery after having a mastectomy the previous day.' Mandy's plans were on hold and so was her life.

'The London Marathon will be my first opportunity to run a marathon,' said the keen runner. 'I will definitely be in this.'

Another young mum from Adelaide, Teresa Mitchell, who had been diagnosed in June 2008 at the age of 34, also contacted Deborah. When Teresa's cancer had been discovered it was so large and aggressive that within days she was in surgery and having the tumour removed.

'The oncologist told me he was giving me the strongest form of chemotherapy,' she explained to Deborah. "But he told me there were no guarantees and that since it had spread I should go home and immediately get my affairs in order, especially regarding my children.'

But Teresa's fighting spirit saw her training for the New York Marathon a few months away in November. Her goal after that would be to run the London Marathon. 'We all have a story,' she said. 'This is just mine.'

'But I want to be able to use it by turning it into something positive . . . to raise awareness, funds and hope for a cure. Running Pink has the same wish and message,' she said. 'We are showing everyone you can do it if you set your mind to it and there is life after a cancer diagnosis.'

Deborah was addressing a gathering of women in Geelong at the request of her bank manage, Leigh, when another potential London Marathon competitor approached her. 'I was 57 when I was diagnosed,' explained Deb Watson, a mum of three grown-up children and a grandmother to a 12-year-old grandson.

The idea of running in the London Marathon the day after her 59th birthday really appealed to this plucky survivor. 'What a great thing to do before I turn 60,' she said, inspired by the idea of running for a cure. 'I'm in.' She later told Deborah she had been so inspired by her enthusiasm to do something about this disease that she just *had* to be part of this charity run.

Deborah also had an email from a local Tasmanian man. Paul Taranto, 42, lived in Mount Nelson near Hobart, and had no problems being the only guy running in pink! 'My mother battled breast cancer when I was 14,' he told Deborah, sadly. 'In those days we were made to visit her from behind a pane of glass, when all I wanted to do was hug her. I am sure all she wanted to do was cuddle us, but it wasn't allowed.'

It was an image that continued to haunt him, long after his mum's recovery. 'I want to join this run for a cure,' he said. 'And I definitely want to be in the largest fundraising race on the planet . . . if I'm a thorn between the pink roses, I'm fine with that.' This run would be Paul's way of honouring his mother and all the other women touched by this disease.

Deborah was delighted that she'd found her Running Pink team. Like Mandy she was already in training and wanted to take part in the New York Marathon that November. For years it had been her dream to run in the New York Marathon, the most prestigious marathon in the world, but Deborah realised she would not get into the event at such short notice by going through the normal channels.

Instead she sent a cheeky letter to the Lance Armstrong Foundation asking if she could run for his charity in the ultimate marathon race. 'I'm a cancer survivor too,' she wrote 'My dream is to run in the New York Marathon and wondered if I could join your team.' Her reply had been swift. 'You certainly can,' said the organisers.

The trip got off to a bad start. The night before Deborah and Glyn were due to leave for the US, Qantas grounded their entire fleet around the world in a workplace dispute.

'What are we going to do?' said Deborah, who arrived in Sydney to find herself grounded too. But the travel agency back in Tasmania were sorting the travel plans out. Qantas put all stranded travellers in hotels and the travel agents, aware of the reason for Deborah's trip, organised to book them onto a United Airlines flight for the following day.

'Remember coming here with Alistair,' said Glyn as they sat by Sydney Opera House where they'd sat with their friend on Deborah's first run to Darwin in 2008. Deborah laughed as she recalled Alistair buying himself and Maggie a Mr Whippy ice-cream, but not bothering about anyone else!

Deborah now stared up at the imposing Sydney Harbour Bridge remembering her tribute walk into Sydney earlier in the year where she'd first met Donna. It already seemed like a distant dream now.

'Where are you?' asked Deborah's friend from Tasmania's ABC radio. The journalist was covering the Qantas crisis and knew Deborah would be caught up in it. Deborah sounded breathless. 'What are you doing?' asked the reporter, curious. 'I'm running around the road outside the airport terminal,' said Deborah. 'Of course you are!' laughed the journalist.

Eventually, Deborah and Glyn boarded the flight to San Francisco, where they had missed their connection to New York. Two hours later they were on their way again arriving at New York at two a.m. tired and bedraggled. But there was another 'Deborah' moment, as they arrived at the apartment. 'The key won't work,' she said, ready to cry.

They rang the person who had allocated them the key. 'It won't work,' she howled. An hour later they stood inside the apartment, where Deborah wanted a drink and a shower. 'Bugger that,' said Glyn opening a bottle of duty free Scotch.

With all the travelling and delays, and the lack of sleep, Deborah had a sore throat when she woke next morning. After a day of sightseeing, that had turned into a cold, which turned into full blown flu.

On the day of the marathon, Deborah felt sick as a dog. Her legs burned as she ran over the Queensborough Bridge coughing all the way. She sucked on lozenges and struggled to breathe as she completed the prestigious marathon in six and a half hours, raising $10,000 for the Lance Armstrong Foundation, knowing she'd normally run this distance in four hours 10 minutes. On Deborah's mammoth run around the country, she ran at least a marathon on most days.

'I was beaten by some M and Ms and a man in a chicken suit,' she laughed. These guys had really dressed up for the event which was cheered on by thousands of New Yorkers who lined the route where runners from around the world would compete. One of Deborah's survivors, now in training for the London marathon, competed in the event.

From New York they flew to Paris where, at the top of the Eiffel Tower, a notice caught Deborah's eye. The notice board bore the names of far flung places listing their distances from this city landmark. The distance from Paris to Christchurch in New Zealand was just 100 kilometres further than the distance she had run all around Australia. On a plane you could have done it in 24 hours. On foot, Deborah ran that distance in 407 days!

But there was one more destination on their stop that Deborah had promised herself. A few days later, they boarded a plane for Berlin.

'This is the apartment where my mother grew up,' said Deborah, pointing to the old apartment block in Helensi, where the Haufe family had once lived. The sight of two strangers staring at the apartment block, attracted the attention of a resident. 'Can I help you?' asked a woman coming out. 'My family once lived here,' explained Deborah. 'Before the war.' The woman introduced herself as a resident there and a doctor. She wondered if the old lady living in the top apartment remembered Karin or the family. Sadly the woman did not.

'So you're a Berliner,' she said, smiling. 'No – Australian,' explained Deborah.

But she felt strangely at home in this beautiful city in a way she could not put into words. It was as though she *belonged* here. It was a connection she could not explain, she even looked like she belonged here. In Australia, nobody ever noticed a tall dark haired woman with green eyes. Deborah had never identified to the Aussie ideal of the blonde, blue-eyed surfer chick.

Yet in Berlin, she observed men checking her out. 'Why are they staring at me?' she asked Glyn, feeling awkward. 'Because you are a beautiful woman that's why,' he said. She felt at home in a city where she even looked like she belonged.

Deborah had just one more thing to do before they left for Australia. 'Just as I thought,' she laughed. She hadn't found a single comedy club in Berlin!

She had been home in Hobart four days when Running Pink officially announced its pink contenders for the 2012 London Marathon. She was still coughing when the team members gathered in Parliament House Gardens where Will Hodgman, the Liberal opposition leader, launched a public appeal for the new fundraiser – to 'pink' the most renowned Marathon event in the world.

'I can't jog with you for the launch of the Running Pink Team for the Marathon,' said the politician. 'I've burned my foot!' Deborah laughed to herself. Try running on two broken feet and blisters the size of your hand for miles every day, she thought. But the Liberal leader did her a favour just the same, announcing the new fundraiser and urging Tasmanians to dig deep and help donate money towards the cost of the $26,000 trip. In the past Deborah had funded everything herself, raising money for a cause that did not include herself!

But the politician hoped people would lend a hand to this worthy Australian by raising funds for the team which would be stepping out in London in April 2012; showing a united front for Australian breast cancer survivors at the world renowned event.

As the cameras clicked and the team stepped out in their Running Pink t-shirts Deborah thought of the lessons she'd learned from her world record breaking-run and from Jan, the friend she'd sadly never get to know. She had learned that hope and dreams are central to survival and believed this would be the new direction of Running Pink, as it led the charge to show survivors that there is a future after cancer; that anything is possible and that possibilities are endless.

'There is so much support for people whilst they are on treatment,' she told Will Hodgman. 'But there is not the same support for women when the journeys end.' Women needed survivorship and mentor programs to help them identify their goals and dreams and to encourage them to pursue them.

Cancer patients are often told when their treatment ends to 'get on' and live 'normal' lives. But those lives have been forever changed by the disease and their experience and many struggle to rebuild lives where 'normal' will never be the same 'normal' they knew before diagnosis. So many women on the road had told Deborah 'I just want to get back to normal,' not knowing what that meant to them any more.

Running Pink would lead the way, determined Deborah, to show people that even though lives might not return to the safe normality they'd once known, that *different* could be even more fulfilling.

And as her pink team members drifted back to their lives to prepare for the new challenge, Deborah was already plotting a bigger, far more challenging adventure after London. She'd secretly begun a new training schedule, more rigorous than anything she'd ever done before. Now, as she scribbled in giant black letters on the white board in her office, a new goal to aim for, she wondered how long it would take for her to persuade her mum to abandon her retirement once again and join her on this challenge of a lifetime.

'Watch this space,' wrote Maggie in her blog. 'D's just had another Deborah moment!'

The greatest achievement was at first and for a time a dream. The oak sleeps in the acorn; the bird waits in the egg; and in the highest vision of the soul a waking angel stirs. Dreams are the seedlings of realities.

— James Allen

Author Acknowlegements

A special thanks to Deborah for entrusting me with her journey through cancer and her amazing adventures along the road as she ran for a cure. Deborah, writing this story has been a great privilege. It has been both uplifting and inspirational being the last recruit to the Running Pink crew. I have enjoyed every minute of this book, and have shared yours and Glyn's great sense of humour which allowed me to thicken this soup which has been a work-in-progress.

Thanks to my beautiful husband, Steve, for his love and support – and the hundreds of cups of coffee – during the late nights spent crafting this astonishing story.

To my good friend, Maureen Wilson, a big thank you for making me take time out to walk my dogs, and to my journalist colleague and long-time friend, Leigh Reinhold, for the late night brainstorming and personal encouragement which helped me believe I could meet this incredibly tight deadline.

Most of all, thanks to my sister, Glenys, in England for helping me address my computer woes, and my parents, Tom and Muriel, for the endless snacks while I spent much of my holiday fact-checking and proofing. Thank you to my friend Sonya Roberts for organising repeated printings of the revised manuscript.

And to everyone in the team at The Five Mile Press for believing in this story – especially to our commissioning editor, Julia Taylor, for her endless patience, and to our editor, Linda Funnell, who sacrificed a glorious summer holiday – at incredibly short notice – to turn this story into an entertaining read.

Deborah's Acknowledgements

Achieving the dream that has inspired this story could never have happened without the love, help and support of a cast of literally thousands. In truth, there are so many people I need to thank and acknowledge, that listing all their names would fill a book bigger than the White Pages. So I want to say a big thank you, not just to my family and friends who formed the Running Pink crew, but to my ultra-marathon friends and 'angels' who turned out on the road to help me through my lowest points and who gave me the courage and strength to keep on going; to the hundreds of community-spirited Australians who turned out in their droves to open their arms and their hearts to welcome me into their towns and who offered us everything from food to accommodation, to petrol and free car repairs; and to the hundreds of brave and courageous women who have beaten breast cancer, or who continue to battle a disease that continues to impact on the lives of so many. And a huge thank you and pat on the back to all those battlers who turned out along the road to keep me company and who entrusted me with their stories. I salute you all – you know who you are, and I will not forget your love and generosity. This book is as much a tribute to you and to your stories.

Thanks to Megan Norris who in a mad flurry wrote this book in record time and gave herself swollen feet in the bargain from hours sitting at her computer. I especially wanted to thank Megan's 'support crew', her husband Steve, for his patience and providing Megan with the much needed coffee, Also to Megan's close friends Leigh Reinhold for her late night advice and support and Maureen Wilson for dragging Megan away from her computer to walk her dogs so Megan could return with fresh eyes and more long hours of typing.

Thanks to the team at The Five Mile Press who helped turn this story into a book.

And finally to my beautiful running companion 'Miss Maggie Moo' whose soft brown eyes have always reflected great love and support.

For more information about
Deborah De Williams
or to donate to Running Pink, visit:

www.runningpink.com.au

www.firstfemaletorunaroundaustralia.com

www.deborahdewilliams.com.au

List of sponsors

Running Pink – Running for a Cure, Run around Australia – 2nd attempt

Regent Caravans	VIP Petfoods
Think Big Printing	Telstra
Bloo Goo	Saucony
Chicken Fed	Anaconda
Lululemon Athletica	Taxi Combined Services
Taxi Blue	Launceston Taxi Management
Gunnersen	Camec
Bowhouse	Domestic
Tasmania Alkaloids	Solar Force
G & S Chassis	S & J Plumbing
Flash Images	Dr Wheatgrass
Healed	Cripps Nubake

Walk around Australia – A Journey for Kids

Brtiz Australia	Optus Mobile Sat
Saucony	Ice Breaker
Moores Water	Ozhosting
Michaels Camera, Video, Digital	San Remo Pasta
Victoria Camper Trailers	Spirit of Tasmania
Toucan Display Systems	Tyrepilers
Australian Clothing Company	Webpanache

Running Pink – Running for a Cure, Run around Australia – 1st attempt

Regent Caravans	VIP Petfoods
Think Big Printing	Telstra
Bloo Goo	Saucony

Chicken Fed
Cooroy Mountain Water
Taxi Combined Services
Gunnersen
Bowhouse
Tasmania Alkaloids
G & S Chassis
Cripps Nubake
S & J Plumbing

Anaconda
Spirit of Tasmania
Taxi Blue
Camec
Domestic
Solar Force
S & J Plumbing
G & S Chassis

Logs

Weekly Summary
World Record – Walk around Australia – A journey for kids
17/10/2003

Week	Dates	Weekly kms	Avg/kms	Total kms
1	17/10/2003–23/10/2003	264.9	37.8	264.9
2	24/10/2003–30/10/2003	249.9	35.7	514.8
3	31/10/2003–6/11/2003	294.8	42.1	809.6
4	7/11/2003–13/11/2003	247.5	35.4	1057.1
5	14/11/2003–20/11/2003	255	36.4	1312.1
6	21/11/2003–27/11/2003	325.9	46.6	1638
7	28/11/2003–4/12/2003	296.5	42.4	1934.5
8	5/12/2003–11/12/2003	302.2	43.2	2236.7
9	12/12/2003–18/12/200	334.9	47.8	2571.6
10	19/12/2003–25/12/2003	282.5	40.4	2854.1
11	26/12/2003–1/1/2004	207.1	29.6	3061.2
12	2/01/2004–8/1/2004	277.9	39.7	3339.1
13	9/1/2004–15/1/2004	265.2	37.9	3604.3
14	16/1/2004–22/1/2004	239.6	34.2	3843.9
15	23/01/2004–29/1/2004	218.6	31.2	4062.5
16	30/1/2004–5/2/2004	267.6	38.2	4330.1
17	6/2/2004–12/2/2004	217.4	31.1	4547.5
18	13/02/2004–19/2/2004	315.8	45.1	4863.3
19	20/2/2004–26/2/2004	324.3	46.3	5187.6
20	27/2/2004–4/3/2004	207.6	29.7	5395.2
21	5/3/2004–11/3/2004	323.5	46.2	5718.7
22	12/3/2004–18/3/2004	322.6	46.1	6041.3
23	19/3/2004–25/3/2004	299.1	42.7	6340.4

Running Pink

Week	Dates	Weekly kms	Avg/kms	Total kms
24	26/3/2004–1/4/2204	325.2	46.5	6665.6
25	2/4/2004–8/4/2004	223.8	32.0	6889.4
26	8/2/2004–15/4/2004	321.1	45.9	7210.5
27	16/4/2004–22/4/2004	329.6	47.1	7540.1
28	23/4/2004–29/4/2004	321.9	46.0	7862
29	30/4/2004–6/5/2004	350.6	50.1	8212.6
30	7/05/2004–13/5/2004	422.7	60.4	8635.3
31	14/05/2004–20/5/2004	389	55.6	9024.3
32	21/5/2004–27/5/2004	444	63.4	9468.3
33	28/5/2004–3/6/2004	310.5	44.4	9778.8
34	4/6/2004–10/6/2004	382.4	54.6	10161.2
35	11/06/2004–17/6/2004	374.7	53.5	10535.9
36	18/4/2004–24/4/2004	350.5	50.1	10886.4
37	25/4/2004–1/7/2004	363.3	51.9	11249.7
38	2/7/2004–8/7/2004	268.2	38.3	11517.9
39	9/7/2004–15/7/2004	391.2	55.9	11909.1
40	16/7/2004–22/7/2004	395	56.4	12304.1
41	23/7/2004–29/7/2004	250.7	35.8	12554.8
42	30/7/2004–5/8/2004	299.9	42.8	12854.7
43	6/8/2004–12/8/2004	416	59.4	13270.7
44	13/8/2004–19/8/2004	391.5	55.9	13662.2
45	20/8/2004–26/8/2004	400.1	57.2	14062.3
46	27/8/2004–2/9/2004	385.3	55.0	14447.6
47	3/9/2004–9/9/2004	419.4	59.9	14867
48	10/9/2004–16/9/2004	398.6	56.9	15265.6

23/9/2004: Broke Nobby's World Walk Record at 15669.1km @ 4.40am

49	17/9/2004–23/9/2004	403.5	57.6	15669.1
50	24/9/2004–30/9/2004	288.9	41.3	15958
51	1/10/2004–7/10/2004	352.9	50.4	16310.9
52	8/10/2004–15/10/2004	373.1	53.3	16684

15/10/2004: New Ultra Marathon Walk Record for the longest continuous walk 16684kms in 365 days

Before the World Walk attempt around Australia, Deborah did a trail walk in Tasmania 11/9/2003–19/9/2003 covering 295kms in 9 days

Logs

Weekly Summary
Running Pink – Running for a Cure – Run Around Australia – 1st Attempt
25/10/2008–5/6/2009

Week	Dates	Weekly kms	Avg/kms	Total kms
1	25/10/2008–31/10/2008	277.1	39.6	277.1
2	1/11/2008–7/11/2008	328.4	46.9	605.5
3	8/11/2008–14/11/2008	291.1	41.6	896.6
4	15/11/2008–21/11/2008	264.4	37.8	1161
5	22/11/2008–28/11/2008	310.8	44.4	1471.8
6	29/11/2008–5/12/2008	311.3	44.5	1783.1
7	6/12/2008–12/12/2008	306.1	43.7	2089.2
8	13/12/2008–19/12/2008	369.2	52.7	2458.4
9	20/12/2008–26/12/2008	337.8	48.3	2796.2
10	27/12/2008–2/1/2009	418.7	59.8	3214.9
11	3/1/2009–9/1/2009	391.4	55.9	3606.3
12	10/1/2009–16/1/2009	330	47.1	3936.3
13	17/1/2009–23/1/2009	357.3	51.0	4293.6
14	24/1/2009–30/1/2009	298.4	42.6	4592
15	31/1/2009–6/2/2009	355.7	50.8	4947.7
16	7/2/2009–13/2/2009	309.1	44.2	5256.8
17	14/2/2009–20/2/2009	300.4	42.9	5557.2
18	21/2/2009–27/2/2009	352.7	50.4	5909.9
19	28/2/2009–6/3/2009	351.3	50.2	6261.2
20	7/3/2009–13/3/2009	355.2	50.7	6616.4
21	14/3/2009–20/3/2009	334.9	47.8	6951.3
22	21/3/2009–27/3/2009	367.7	52.5	7319
23	28/3/2009–3/4/2009	380.9	54.4	7699.9
24	4/4/2009–10/4/2009	399.5	57.1	8099.4
25	11/4/2009–17/4/2009	424	60.6	8523.4
26	18/4/2009–24/4/2009	429.8	61.4	8953.2
27	25/4/2009–1/5/2009	447.5	63.9	9400.7
28	2/5/2009–8/5/2009	402.6	57.5	9803.3

During week 29, on 11/5/2009 at Elliot, NT, Deborah tripped over Maggie and broke both her feet but continued to run

Running Pink

Week	Dates	Weekly kms	Avg/kms	Total kms
29	9/5/2009–15/5/2009	315.4	45.1	10118.7
30	16/5/2009–22/5/2009	223.1	31.9	10341.8
31	23/5/2009–29/5/2009	266.7	38.1	10608.5
32	30/5/2009–5/6/2009	216.4	30.9	10824.9

5/6/2009: Journey ended due to broken feet–1st female to run continuously from Hobart to Darwin

Daily Summary
Running Pink – Running for a Cure – World Record Run Around Australia – 2nd Attempt, 27/3/2010–8/5/2011

Day	Date	Daily start location, with GPS coordinates	Daily finish location, with GPS coordinates	Km	Total Km
Tasmania					
1	Sat	27/03/2010	Parliament House Gardens Hobart S 42°53.156' E 147°19.855'	Road Side Stop, 2km Nth Pontville, Midlands Hwy S 42°40.416' E 147°15.615'	30.1	30.1
2	Sun	28/03/2010	Road Side Stop, 2km Nth Pontville, Midlands Hwy S 42°40.416' E 147°15.615'	Caravan Stop Over Park, Lake Dulverton Oatlands S 42°17.995' E 147°22.631'	55.3	85.4
3	Mon	29/03/2010	Caravan Stop Over Park, Lake Dulverton Oatlands S 42°17.995' E 147°22.631'	Ross Caravan Park S 42°01.835' E 147°29.452'	36.7	122.1
4	Tue	30/03/2010	Ross Caravan Park S 42°01.835' E 147°29.452'	Road Side Stop, 9km Nth Epping Forest, Midlands Hwy S 41°41.076' E 147°16.623'	46.2	168.3
5	Wed	31/03/2010	Road Side Stop, 9km Nth Epping Forest, Midlands Hwy S 41°41.076' E 147°16.623'	Private Residence, Vaux St West Launceston S 41°27.695' E 147°08.004'	38.6	206.9
6	Thu	1/04/2010	Private Residence, Vaux St West Launceston S 41°27.695' E 147°08.004'	Deloraine Caravan Park S 41°31.663' E 146°39.114'	48.9	255.8
7	Fri	2/04/2010	Deloraine Caravan Park S 41°31.663' E 146°39.114'	Spirit of Tasmania Dock, East Devonport S 41°10.602' E 146°21.984'	52.4	308.2
Victoria					
8	Sat	3/04/2010	Spirit of Tasmania Dock, East Melbourne S 37°50.591' E 144°55.926'	33–39 Cherry Lane, Laverton Nth, S 37.49.992' E 144°48.318'	21	329.2
9	Sun	4/04/2010	33–39 Cherry Lane, Laverton Nth, S 37.49.992' E 144°48.318'	Little River Hotel S 37°57.916' E 144°29.816'	43.9	373.1
10	Mon	5/04/2010	Little River Hotel S 37°57.916' E 144°29.816'	Waurns Pond Hall, Princes Hwy S 38°12.452' E 144°16.675'	41	414.1
11	Tue	6/04/2010	Waurns Pond Hall, Princes Hwy S 38°12.452' E 144°16.675'	Road Side Stop, 12km E Colac, Princes Hwy, Warncoort Rail Crossing S 38°18.677' E 143°43.511'	51	465.1
12	Wed	7/04/2010	Road Side Stop, 12km E Colac, Princes Hwy, Warncoort Rail Crossing S 38°18.677' E 143°43.511'	Road Side Stop, 3041 Princes Hwy, 10km E Camperdown S 38°15.743' E 143°16.878'	46.7	511.8
13	Thu	8/04/2010	3041 Princes Hwy, 10km E Camperdown S 38°15.743' E 143°16.878'	Terang Caravan Park S 38°14.542' E 142°54.553'	36.6	548.4

Running Pink

Day	Date	Daily start location, with GPS coordinates	Daily finish location, with GPS coordinates	Km	Total Km
14	Fri 9/04/2010	Terang Caravan Park S 38°14.542' E 142°54.553'	Road Side Stop, Cnr Princes Hwy/ Banyan St, Warrnambool S 38°22.893' E 142°29.307'	44.6	593
15	Sat 10/04/2010	Road Side Stop, Cnr Princes Hwy/ Banyan St, Warrnambool S 38°22.893' E 142°29.307'	Road Side Stop, Yambuk Rest Area, Cnr Lindsay St/Princes Hwy, S 38.18.873' E 142°03.840'	46.8	639.8
16	Sun 11/04/2010	Road Side Stop, Yambuk Rest Area, Cnr Lindsay St/Princes Hwy, S 38.18.873' E 142°03.840'	Henty Bay Caravan Park S 38°17.931' E 141°37.337'	47.4	687.2
17	Mon 12/04/2010	Henty Bay Caravan Park S 38°17.931' E 141°37.337'	Pinewood Caravan Park Heywood S 38°07.433' E 141°38.039'	28	715.2
18	Tue 13/04/2010	Pinewood Caravan Park Heywood S 38°07.433' E 141°38.039'	Road Side Stop, Cnr Woodbine Rd. & Princes Hwy S 37°55.421' E 141°10.305'	51.2	766.4
19	Wed 14/04/2010	Road Side Stop, Cnr Woodbine Rd, & Princes Hwy S 37°55.421' E 141°10.305'	Chris White Memorial Reserve Mt Gambier S 37°48.374' E 140°43.794'	46.3	812.7

South Australia

Day	Date	Daily start location, with GPS coordinates	Daily finish location, with GPS coordinates	Km	Total Km
20	Thu 15/04/2010	Chris White Memorial Reserve Mt Gambier S 37°48.374' E 140°43.794'	Lakeside Caravan Park Millicent S 37°35.463' E 140°20.345'	46.8	859.5
21	Fri 16/04/2010	Lakeside Caravan Park Millicent S 37°35.463' E 140°20.345'	Beachport Caravan Park S 37°28.705' E 140°01.012'	35	894.5
22	Sat 17/04/2010	Beachport Caravan Park S 37°28.705' E 140°01.012'	Lakeside Caravan Park Robe S 37°09.964' E 139°46.190'	51.5	946
23	Sun 18/04/2010	Lakeside Caravan Park Robe S 37°09.964' E 139°46.190'	Kingston Caravan Park, Kingston SE S 36°50.225' E 139°50.759'	45.3	991.3
24	Mon 19/04/2010	Kingston Caravan Park, Kingston SE S 36°50.225' E 139°50.759'	Road Side Stop, 4km W Start of Coorong National Park, Princes Hwy S 36°28.905' E 139°49.250'	43.6	1034.9
25	Tue 20/04/2010	Road Side Stop, 4km W Start of Coorong National Park, Princes Hwy S 36°28.905' E 139°49.250'	Coorong Waters Bistro, Policeman's Point S 36°03.450' E 139°35.461'	53.5	1088.4
26	Wed 21/04/2010	Coorong Waters Bistro, Policeman's Point S 36°03.450' E 139°35.461'	Lake Albert Caravan Park, Meningie S 35°41.393 E 139°19.793'	52.7	1141.1
27	Thu 22/04/2010	Lake Albert Caravan Park, Meningie S 35°41.393 E 139°19.793'	Westbrook Caravan Park, 7km MW Tailem Bend S 35°13.118' E 139°24.341'	62	1203.1
28	Fri 23/04/2010	Westbrook Caravan Park, 7km MW Tailem Bend S 35°13.118' E 139°24.341'	Princes Hwy Caravan Park, 5km W Murray Bridge S 35°08.151' E 139°13.984'	24.6	1227.7

Logs

Day		Date	Daily start location, with GPS coordinates	Daily finish location, with GPS coordinates	Km	Total Km
29	Sat	24/04/2010	Princes Hwy Caravan Park, 5km W Murray Bridge S 35°08.151' E 139°13.984'	Contour Woman's Fitness Kookaburra Lane, Little Hampton, via Callington S 35°03.243' E 138°51.123'	44.5	1272.2
30	Sun	25/04/2010	Contour Woman's Fitness Kookaburra Lane, Little Hampton, via Callington S 35°03.243' E 138°51.123'	Windsor Gardens Caravan Park, Windsor Gardens Adelaide S 34°52.663' E 138°38.840'	48.6	1320.8
31	Mon	26/04/2010	Windsor Gardens Caravan Park, Windsor Gardens Adelaide S 34°52.663' E 138°38.840'	Gawler Caravan Park S 34°35.468' E 138°44.734'	39.6	1360.4
32	Tue	27/04/2010	Gawler Caravan Park S 34°35.468' E 138°44.734'	Tarlee Institute & Post Office, Tarlee, North Rd S 34°16.353' E 138°46.160'	37.9	1398.3
33	Wed	28/04/2010	Tarlee Institute & Post Office, Tarlee, North Rd S 34°16.353' E 138°46.160'	Clare Caravan Park S 33°51.886' E 138°37.303'	50.9	1449.2
34	Thu	29/04/2010	Clare Caravan Park S 33°51.886' E 138°37.303'	Yackamoorundie Park, Yacka, North Rd S 33°34.119' E 138°26.694'	43	1492.2
35	Fri	30/04/2010	Yackamoorundie Park, Yacka, North Rd S 33°34.119' E 138°26.694'	Crystal Brook Caravan Park S 33°20.808' E 138°12.223'	40.7	1532.9
36	Sat	1/05/2010	Crystal Brook Caravan Park S 33°20.808' E 138°12.223'	Port Pirie Beach Caravan Park S 33°10.942' E 138°01.399'	27.8	1560.7
37	Sun	2/05/2010	Port Pirie Beach Caravan Park S 33°10.942' E 138°01.399'	Roadside Stop, 6km N Mambray Creek, Eyre Hwy S 32°47.341' E 137°57.467'	50.8	1611.5
38	Mon	3/05/2010	Roadside Stop, 6km N Mambray Creek, Eyre Hwy S 32°47.341' E 137°57.467'	Shoreline Caravan Park, Port Augusta S 32°28.428' E 137°45.759'	43.2	1654.7
39	Tue	4/05/2010	Shoreline Caravan Park, Port Augusta S 32°28.428' E 137°45.759'	Road Side Stop, Half Way Rest Area, 40km S Port Augusta, Lincoln Hwy S 32°43.575' E 137°30.656'	40	1694.7
40	Wed	5/05/2010	Road Side Stop, Half Way Rest Area, 40km S Port Augusta, Lincoln Hwy S 32°43.575' E 137°30.656'	Whyalla Foreshore, Caravan Park S 33°02.526' E 137°34.720'	37.3	1732
41	Thu	6/05/2010	Whyalla Foreshore, Caravan Park S 33°02.526' E 137°34.720'	Iron Knob Roadhouse S 32°43.536' E 137°08.935'	57	1789
42	Fri	7/05/2010	Iron Knob Roadhouse S 32°43.536' E 137°08.935'	Road Side Stop, Kimba East Rest Area, 52km SW of Iron Knob, Eyre Hwy S 33°02.931' E 135°46.163'	52.8	1841.8

Running Pink

Day		Date	Daily start location, with GPS coordinates	Daily finish location, with GPS coordinates	Km	Total Km
43	Sat	8/05/2010	Road Side Stop, Kimba East Rest Area, 52km SW of Iron Knob, Eyre Hwy S 33°02.931' E 135°46.163'	Kimba Caravan Park Kimba S 33°08.776' E 136°24.807'	37.4	1879.2
44	Sun	9/05/2010	Kimba Caravan Park Kimba S 33°08.776' E 136°24.807'	Road Side Stop, Darkes Memorial Rest Area, 56km E Kimba, Eyre Hwy S 33°09.937' E 135°53.200'	56.3	1935.5
45	Mon	10/05/2010	Road Side Stop, Darkes Memorial Rest Area, 56km E Kimba, Eyre Hwy S 33°09.937' E 135°53.200'	Wudinna Caravan Park S 33°03.360' E 135°28.022'	45	1980.5
46	Tue	11/05/2010	Wudinna Caravan Park S 33°03.360' E 135°28.022'	Apex Park, Eyre Hwy, Minnipa S 32°51.263' E 135°09.033'	39.8	2020.3
47	Wed	12/05/2010	Apex Park, Eyre Hwy, Minnipa S 32°51.263' E 135°09.033'	Chandada Pioneer Park, 15km W of Poochera, Poochera/Streaky Bay Rd S 32°45.262' E 134°40.413'	50.7	2071
48	Thu	13/05/2010	Chandada Pioneer Park, 15km W of Poochera, Poochera/Streaky Bay Rd S 32°45.262' E 134°40.413'	Foreshore Pioneer Caravan Park, Streaky Bay S 32°47.820' E 134°11.820'	48.1	2119.1
49	Fri	14/05/2010	Foreshore Pioneer Caravan Park, Streaky Bay S 32°47.820' E 134°11.820'	Perlubie Beach Camp Site, 21km N of Streaky Bay, Flinders Hwy S 32°39.652' E 134°17.678'	23.7	2142.8
50	Sat	15/05/2010	Perlubie Beach Camp Site, 21km N of Streaky Bay, Flinders Hwy S 32°39.652' E 134°17.678'	Road Side Stop, Cnr of Koppi Tucka Dr/Flinders Hwy S 32°19.681' E 133°55.431'	56.2	2199
51	Sun	16/05/2010	Road Side Stop, Cnr of Koppi Tucka Dr/Flinders Hwy S 32°19.681' E 133°55.431'	Road Side Stop, Cnr of Poynton/ McKenzie St, Ceduna S 32°07.568' E 133°40.438'	35	2234
52	Mon	17/05/2010	Road Side Stop, Cnr of Poynton/ McKenzie St, Ceduna S 32°07.568' E 133°40.438'	Road Side Stop, Watraba Rest Area, 25km E Penong, Eyre Hwy S 31°56.445' E 133°16.175'	48.1	2282.1
53	Tue	18/05/2010	Road Side Stop, Watraba Rest Area, 25km E of Penong, Eyre Hwy S 31°56.445' E 133°16.175'	Road Side Stop, 29km W Penong, Eyre Hwy S 31°49.913' E 132°44.641'	53.8	2335.9
54	Wed	19/05/2010	Road Side Stop, 29km W Penong, Eyre Hwy S 31°49.913' E 132°44.641'	Nundroo Roadhouse, Caravan Park S 31°47.553' E 132°13.544'	52.3	2388.2
55	Thu	20/05/2010	Nundroo Roadhouse, Caravan Park S 31°47.553' E 132°13.544'	Road Side Stop, 10km E Yalata @ 10km Yalata Green Rd Sign, Eyre Hwy S 31°32.090' E 131°54.604'	43.2	2431.4
56	Fri	21/05/2010	Road Side Stop, 10km E Yalata @ 10km Yalata Green Rd Sign, Eyre Hwy S 31°32.090' E 131°54.604'	Road Side Stop, 222k Peg Rest Area, 51km W Yalata, Eyre Hwy S 31°21.639' E 131°18.832'	61.3	2492.7

Logs

Day		Date	Daily start location, with GPS coordinates	Daily finish location, with GPS coordinates	Km	Total Km
57	Sat	22/05/2010	Road Side Stop, 222k Peg Rest Area, 51km W Yalata, Eyre Hwy S 31°21.639' E 131°18.832'	Nullarbor Roadhouse S 31°26.974' E 130°53.831'	41.8	2534.5
58	Sun	23/05/2010	Nullarbor Roadhouse S 31°26.974' E 130°53.831'	Road Side Stop, 43.8km W Nullarbor Roadhouse, Eyre Hwy S 31°33.631' E 130°28.252'	43.8	2578.3
59	Mon	24/05/2010	Road Side Stop, 43.8km W Nullarbor Roadhouse, Eyre Hwy S 31°33.631' E 130°28.252'	Road Side Stop, 88.7km W Nullarbor Roadhouse, Eyre Hwy S 31°34.302' E 130°00.508'	44.9	2623.2
60	Tue	25/05/2010	Road Side Stop, 88.7km W Nullarbor Roadhouse, Eyre Hwy S 31°34.302' E 130°00.508'	Road Side Stop, 148.9km W Nullarbor Roadhouse, Eyre Hwy S 31°38.309' E 129°23.312'	60.2	2683.4

Western Australia

Day		Date	Daily start location, with GPS coordinates	Daily finish location, with GPS coordinates	Km	Total Km
61	Wed	26/05/2010	Road Side Stop, 148.9km W Nullarbor Roadhouse, Eyre Hwy S 31°38.309' E 129°23.312'	Eucla Caravan Park Eucla S 31°40.720' E 128°52.887'	51.1	2734.5
62	Thu	27/05/2010	Eucla Caravan Park Eucla S 31°40.720' E 128°52.887'	Mundrabilla Roadhouse S 31°49.004' E 128°13.551'	66	2800.5
63	Fri	28/05/2010	Mundrabilla Roadhouse S 31°49.004' E 128°13.551'	Road Side Stop, @ Entrance to Mundrabilla Homestead, Eyre Hwy S 31°52.493' E 127°51.447'	36.9	2837.4
64	Sat	29/05/2010	Road Side Stop, @ Entrance to Mundrabilla Homestead, Eyre Hwy S 31°52.493' E 127°51.447'	Road Side Stop, Moodini Pass Parking Bay, 27km E Madura, Eyre Hwy S 31°54.615' E 127°17.244'	55.1	2892.5
65	Sun	30/05/2010	Road Side Stop, Moodini Pass Parking Bay 27km E Madura, Eyre Hwy S 31°54.615' E 127°17.244'	Road Side Stop, Olwolgin Bluff Rest Area 23km W Madura, Eyre Hwy S 31°55.685' E 126°46.718'	50.3	2942.8
66	Mon	31/05/2010	Road Side Stop, Olwolgin Bluff Rest Area, 23km W Madura, Eyre Hwy S 31°55.685' E 126°46.718'	Cocklebiddy Caravan Park S 32°02.288' E 126°05.878'	67.8	3010.6
67	Tue	1/06/2010	Cocklebiddy Caravan Park S 32°02.288' E 126°05.878'	Road Side Stop, Jillbunya Rockhole Rest Area, 21km E Caiguna, Eyre Hwy S 32°10.425' E 125°40.451'	45.1	3055.7
68	Wed	2/06/2010	Road Side Stop, Jillbunya Rockhole Rest Area 21km E Caiguna, Eyre Hwy S 32°10.425' E 125°40.451'	Road Side Stop, Domblegabby Rest Area, 39km W Caiguna, Eyre Hwy S 32°19.295' E 125°04.460'	60.6	3116.3
69	Thu	3/06/2010	Road Side Stop, Domblegabby Rest Area, 39km W Caiguna, Eyre Hwy S 32°19.295' E 125°04.460'	Road Side Stop, Woorlba East Rest Area, 132km W Caiguna, Eyre Hwy S 32°23.652' E 124°28.340'	57.6	3173.9

Running Pink

Day	Date	Daily start location, with GPS coordinates	Daily finish location, with GPS coordinates	Km	Total Km
70	Fri	4/06/2010	Road Side Stop, Woorlba East Rest Area, 132km W Caiguna, Eyre Hwy S 32°23.652' E 124°28.340'	Road Side Stop, Driveway to Woorlba Station, 175km W Caiguna, Eyre Hwy S 32°26.720' E 124°01.462'	43	3216.9
71	Sat	5/06/2010	Road Side Stop, Driveway to Woorlba Station, 175k W Caiguna, Eyre Hwy S 32°26.720' E 124°01.462'	Road Side Stop, Parking Bay, 10km W Balladonia, Eyre Hwy S 32°18.474' E 123°31.761'	52.5	3269.4
72	Sun	6/06/2010	Road Side Stop, Parking Bay, 10km W Balladonia, Eyre Hwy S 32°18.474' E 123°31.761'	Road Side Stop, Parking Bay, @ Newman Rocks Rd Sign, 50km W Balladonia, Eyre Hwy S 32°07.288' E 123°09.991'	40.3	3309.7
73	Mon	7/06/2010	Road Side Stop, Parking Bay, @ Newman Rocks Rd Sign, 50km W Balladonia, Eyre Hwy S 32°07.288' E 123°09.991'	Fraser Range Caravan Park S 32°01.767' E 122°47.690'	40.3	3350
74	Tue	8/06/2010	Fraser Range Caravan Park S 32°01.767' E 122°47.690'	Road Side Stop, @ 60km E Norseman Green Rd Sign, Eyre Hwy S 32°03.729' E 122°20.467'	46.5	3396.5
75	Wed	9/06/2010	Road Side Stop, @ 60km E Norseman Green Rd Sign, Eyre Hwy S 32°03.729' E 122°20.467'	Norseman Caravan Park S 32°11.370' E 121°46.598'	59.2	3455.7
76	Thu	10/06/2010	Norseman Caravan Park S 32°11.370' E 121°46.598'	Road Side Stop, @ Railway Line Access Rd 63.7km S Norseman, Coolgardie – Esperance Hwy S 32°41.316' E 121°32.388'	63.7	3519.4
77	Fri	11/06/2010	Road Side Stop, @ Railway Line Access Rd 63.7km S Norseman, Coolgardie – Esperance Hwy S 32°41.316' E 121°32.388'	Grass Patch Caravan Park S 33°13.726' E 121°42.866'	64	3583.4
78	Sat	12/06/2010	Grass Patch Caravan Park S 33°13.726' E 121°42.866'	Gibson Soak Hotel Motel S 33°39.107' E 121°48.839'	52.6	3636
79	Sun	13/06/2010	Gibson Soak Hotel Motel S 33°39.107' E 121°48.839'	Road Side Stop, Parking Bay 165km E Ravensthorpe, South Coast Hwy S 33°44.536' E 121°42.133'	44.4	3680.4
80	Mon	14/06/2010	Road Side Stop, Parking Bay 165km E Ravensthorpe, South Coast Hwy S 33°44.536' E 121°42.133'	Road Side Stop, Parking Bay 100.7km E Ravensthorpe South Coast Hwy S 33°45.808' E 121°02.895'	64.3	3744.7
81	Tue	15/06/2010	Road Side Stop, Parking Bay 100.7km E Ravensthorpe South Coast Hwy S 33°45.808' E 121°02.895'	Road Side Stop, Parking Bay 47.1km E Ravensthorpe South Coast Hwy S 33°39.364' E 120°30.263'	53.6	3798.3
82	Wed	16/06/2010	Road Side Stop, Parking Bay 47.1km E Ravensthorpe South Coast Hwy S 33°39.364' E 120°30.263'	Ravensthorpe Caravan Park S 33°34.693' E 120°03.262'	45.9	3844.2

Logs

Day	Date	Daily start location, with GPS coordinates	Daily finish location, with GPS coordinates	Km	Total Km
83	Thu	17/06/2010	Ravensthorpe Caravan Park S 33°34.693' E 120°03.262'	Fitzgerald Rest Area, 61.9km W Ravensthorpe, South Coast Hwy S 33°45.447' E 119°26.874'	61.9	3906.1
84	Fri	18/06/2010	Fitzgerald Rest Area, 61.9km W Ravensthorpe, South Coast Hwy S 33°45.447' E 119°26.874'	Jerramungup Caravan Park S 33°56.617' E 118°55.232'	54.6	3960.7
85	Sat	19/06/2010	Jerramungup Caravan Park S 33°56.617' E 118°55.232'	Boxwood Hill Roadhouse S 34°21.771' E 118°44.924'	59.6	4020.3
86	Sun	20/06/2010	Boxwood Hill Roadhouse S 34°21.771' E 118°44.924'	Road Side Stop, @ entrance to Kaola Station, 116km S Jerramungup, South Coast Hwy S 34°40.788' E 118°19.920'	56	4076.3
87	Mon	21/06/2010	Road Side Stop, @ entrance to Kaola Station, 116km S Jerramungup S 34°40.788' E 118°19.920'	Road Side Stop, 3.1km from Esperance/ Entrance Main, Roundabout on Denmark Rd S 35°00.008' E 117°49.984'	66	4142.3
88	Tue	22/06/2010	Road Side Stop, 3.1km from Esperance/ Entrance Main, Roundabout on Denmark Rd S 35°00.008' E 117°49.984'	Denmark River Caravan Park S 34°58.234' E 117°22.024'	49.1	4191.4
89	Wed	23/06/2010	Denmark River Caravan Park S 34°58.234' E 117°22.024'	Road Side Stop, Parking Bay @ Boat Harbour Rd 26.2km W Denmark S 34°59.473' E 117°06.491'	27.7	4219.1
90	Thu	24/06/2010	Road Side Stop, Parking Bay @ Boat Harbour Rd 26.2km W Denmark S 34°59.473' E 117°06.491'	Road Side Stop, John Rate Lookout, 5km W Walpole, South Western Hwy S 34°59.112' E 116°40.706'	46.8	4265.9
91	Fri	25/06/2010	Road Side Stop, John Rate Lookout, 5km W Walpole, South Western Hwy S 34°59.112' E 116°40.706'	Road Side Stop, Parking Park, 55km W Walpole, South Western Hwy S 34°39.192' E 116°29.749'	49.6	4315.5
92	Sat	26/06/2010	Road Side Stop, Parking Park, 55km W Walpole, South Western Hwy S 34°39.192' E 116°29.749'	Manjimup Caravan Park S 34°13.330' E 116°09.194'	68	4383.5
93	Sun	27/06/2010	Manjimup Caravan Park S 34°13.330' E 116°09.194'	Balingup Transit Park S 33°46.933' E 115°59.163'	61.5	4445
94	Mon	28/06/2010	Balingup Transit Park S 33°46.933' E 115°59.163'	Donnybrook Transit Park S 33°34.223' E 115°49.205'	32.9	4477.9
95	Tue	29/06/2010	Donnybrook Transit Park S 33°34.223' E 115°49.205'	Australind Caravan Park S 33°18.271' E 115°42.213'	40.6	4518.5
96	Wed	30/06/2010	Australind Caravan Park S 33°18.271' E 115°42.213'	Myalup Caravan Park S 33°06.156' E 115°41.457'	26.8	4545.3
97	Thu	1/07/2010	Myalup Caravan Park S 33°06.156' E 115°41.457'	Lake Clifton Caravan Park S 32°47.221' E 115°40.284'	40.3	4585.6

Running Pink

Day		Date	Daily start location, with GPS coordinates	Daily finish location, with GPS coordinates	Km	Total Km
98	Fri	2/07/2010	Lake Clifton Caravan Park S 32°47.221' E 115°40.284'	Hilltop Caravan Park Mandurah S 32°31.582' E 115°43.474'	35.8	4621.4
99	Sat	3/07/2010	Hilltop Caravan Park Mandurah S 32°31.582' E 115°43.474'	Road Side Stop, 4.2km from Cnr Ennis Ave/Paterson Rd, Rockingham S 32°14.214' E 115°46.614'	35.6	4657
100	Sun	4/07/2010	Road Side Stop, 4.2km from Cnr Ennis Ave/Paterson Rd, Rockingham S 32°14.214' E 115°46.614'	Langley Park, Riverside Drive, Perth S 31°57.630' E 115°51.933'	39.5	4696.5
101	Mon	5/07/2010	Langley Park, Riverside Drive, Perth S 31°57.630' E 115°51.933'	6980 West Swan Rd, Swan Valley S 31°50.158' E 115°59.535'	23.2	4719.7
102	Tue	6/07/2010	6980 West Swan Rd, Swan Valley S 31°50.158' E 115°59.535'	Road Side Stop, 66km N Perth, Brand Hwy S 31°30.479' E 115°56.755'	42.8	4762.5
103	Wed	7/07/2010	Road Side Stop, 66km N Perth, Brand Hwy S 31°30.479' E 115°56.755'	Road Side Stop, Parking Bay, Brand Hwy, 10km S Regans Ford, Roadhouse S 31°03.816' E 115°44.586'	56.9	4819.4
104	Thu	8/07/2010	Road Side Stop, Parking Bay, Brand Hwy, 10km S Regans Ford, Roadhouse S 31°03.816' E 115°44.586'	Road Side Stop, @ Cooljarloo Mine Turnoff, 15km N Cataby, Brand Hwy S 30°39.055' E 115°27.960'	55.5	4874.9
105	Fri	9/07/2010	Road Side Stop, @ Cooljarloo Mine Turn off, 15km N Cataby, Brand Hwy S 30°39.055' E 115°27.960'	Badgingarra Caravan Park S 30°23.593' E 115°30.010'	30.4	4905.3
106	Sat	10/07/2010	Badgingarra Caravan Park S 30°23.593' E 115°30.010'	Road Side Stop, Parking Bay, Brand Hwy, 10km N Halfway Mill Roadhouse S 29°58.988' E 115°18.131'	54.8	4960.1
107	Sun	11/07/2010	Road Side Stop, Parking Bay, Brand Hwy, 10km N Halfway Mill Roadhouse S 29°58.988' E 115°18.131'	Road Side Stop, Arrowsmith Rest Area, 30km N Eneabba, Brand Hwy S 29°34.750' E 115°08.135'	53.1	5013.2
108	Mon	12/07/2010	Road Side Stop, Arrowsmith Rest Area, 30km N Eneabba, Brand Hwy S 29°34.750' E 115°08.135'	Dongara Seaspray, Caravan Park S 29°15.177' E 114°55.289'	51.1	5064.3
109	Tue	13/07/2010	Dongara Seaspray, Caravan Park S 29°15.177' E 114°55.289'	Central Greenough Café & Visitor Centre Car Park S 28°56.657' E 114°44.727'	42.7	5107
110	Wed	14/07/2010	Central Greenough Café & Visitor Centre Car Park S 28°56.657' E 114°44.727'	Road Side Stop, Cnr Coronation Beach Rd/North West Coastal Hwy S 28°32.743' E 114°37.826'	51.5	5158.5
111	Thu	15/07/2010	Road Side Stop, Cnr Coronation Beach Rd/North West Coastal Hwy S 28°32.743' E 114°37.826'	Road Side Stop, 18.9km N Northampton PO, North West Coastal Hwy S 28°11.542' E 114°38.215'	43	5201.5

Logs

Day	Date	Daily start location, with GPS coordinates	Daily finish location, with GPS coordinates	Km	Total Km
112	Fri	16/07/2010	Road Side Stop, 18.9km N Northampton PO, North West Coastal Hwy S 28°11.542' E 114°38.215'	Road Side Stop, Galena Bridge Parking Bay, 13km N Kalbarri Turnoff S 27°49.667' E 114°41.329'	43.3	5244.8
113	Sat	17/07/2010	Road Side Stop, Galena Bridge Parking Bay, 13km N Kalbarri Turnoff S 27°49.667' E 114°41.329'	Road Side Stop, 60km S Billabong Roadhouse @ Green Rd Sign, North West Coastal Hwy S 27°20.477' E 114°37.245'	58	5302.8
114	Sun	18/07/2010	Road Side Stop, 60km S Billabong Roadhouse @ Green Rd Sign, North West Coastal Hwy S 27°20.477' E 114°37.245'	Billabong Roadhouse, Caravan Park S 26°49.069' E 114°36.875'	61	5363.8
115	Mon	19/07/2010	Billabong Roadhouse, Caravan Park S 26°49.069' E 114°36.875'	Road Side Stop, 12km N Overland Roadhouse, North West Coastal Hwy S 26°18.193' E 114°25.376'	60.7	5424.5
116	Tue	20/07/2010	Road Side Stop, 12km N Overland Roadhouse, North West Coastal Hwy S 26°18.193' E 114°25.376'	Wooramel Roadhouse, Caravan Park S 25°46.269' E 114°17.628'	63.4	5487.9
117	Wed	21/07/2010	Wooramel Roadhouse, Caravan Park S 25°46.269' E 114°17.628'	Edaggee Rest Area S 25°27.542' E 114°03.531'	43.4	5531.3
118	Thu	22/07/2010	Edaggee Rest Area S 25°27.542' E 114°03.531'	Road Side Stop, @ 40km S Carnarvon, Green Rd Sign, North West Coastal Hwy S 25°08.185' E 113°50.662'	42.9	5574.2
119	Fri	23/07/2010	Road Side Stop, @ 40km S Carnarvon, Green Rd Sign, North West Coastal Hwy S 25°08.185' E 113°50.662'	Road Side Stop Parking Bay, @ 120k S Minilya Roadhouse, Green Rd Sign, North West Coastal Hwy S 24°47.075' E 113°45.798'	48.4	5622.6
120	Sat	24/07/2010	Road Side Stop Parking Bay, @ 120k S Minilya Roadhouse, Green Rd Sign, North West Coastal Hwy S 24°47.075' E 113°45.798'	Road Side Stop @, Entrance to Boologoora Station, 80km N Carnarvon, North West Coastal Hwy S 24°20.136' E 114°01.637'	61	5683.6
121	Sun	25/07/2010	Road Side Stop @, Entrance to Boologoora Station, 80km N Carnarvon, North West Coastal Hwy S 24°20.136' E 114°01.637'	Minilya Roadhouse Transit Park S 23°48.910' E 114°00.631'	60.3	5743.9
122	Mon	26/07/2010	Minilya Roadhouse Transit Park S 23°48.910' E 114°00.631'	Lyndon River East Parking Bay, 49.3km Nminilya Roadhouse, North West Coastal Hwy S 23°28.965' E 114°16.548'	49.3	5793.2
123	Tue	27/07/2010	Lyndon River East Parking Bay, 49.3km Nminilya Roadhouse, North West Coastal Hwy S 23°28.965' E 114°16.548'	Road Side Stop, 57.6km N Lyndon River, North West Coastal Hwy S 23°03.566' E 114°31.938'	57.6	5850.8

Running Pink

Day		Date	Daily start location, with GPS coordinates	Daily finish location, with GPS coordinates	Km	Total Km
124	Wed	28/07/2010	Road Side Stop, 57.6km N Lyndon River, North West Coastal Hwy S 23°03.566' E 114°31.938'	Barradale Rest Area Yannarie River 70km S Nanutarra Roadhouse, North West Coastal Hwy S 22°51.795' E 114°57.274'	50.8	5901.6
125	Thu	29/07/2010	Barradale Rest Area Yannarie River 70km S Nanutarra Roadhouse, North West Coastal Hwy S 22°51.795' E 114°57.274'	Road Side Stop, 12.3km S Nanutarra Roadhouse, North West Coastal Hwy S 22°37.787' E 115°24.449'	57.7	5959.3
126	Fri	30/07/2010	Road Side Stop, 12.3km S Nanutarra Roadhouse, North West Coastal Hwy S 22°37.787' E 115°24.449'	Road Side Stop, Onslow Turnoff Parking Bay, North West Coastal Hwy S 22°09.029' E 115°32.460'	59.5	6018.8
127	Sat	31/07/2010	Road Side Stop, Onslow Turnoff Parking Bay, North West Coastal Hwy S 22°09.029' E 115°32.460'	Road Side Stop, 60km S Fortescue River Roadhouse, North West Coastal Hwy S 21°43.053' E 115°48.756'	58.7	6077.5
128	Sun	1/08/2010	Road Side Stop, 60km S Fortescue River Roadhouse, North West Coastal Hwy S 21°43.053' E 115°48.756'	Fortescue River Roadhouse S 21°17.712' E 116°08.311'	60.8	6138.3
129	Mon	2/08/2010	Fortescue River Roadhouse S 21°17.712' E 116°08.311'	Road Side Stop, 58.6km N Fortescue River Roadhouse, North West Coastal Hwy S 20°54.056' E 116°26.748'	58.6	6196.9
130	Tue	3/08/2010	Road Side Stop, 58.6km N Fortescue River Roadhouse, North West Coastal Hwy S 20°54.056' E 116°26.748'	Road Side Stop, @ driveway to Broadcast Transmitting station 3km E Karratha Turnoff, North West Coastal Hwy S 20°47.671' E 116°53.589'	50.2	6247.1
131	Wed	4/08/2010	Road Side Stop, @ driveway to Broadcast Transmitting station 3km E Karratha Turnoff, North West Coastal Hwy S 20°47.671' E 116°53.589'	Harding River Caravan Park Roebourne S 20°46.524' E 117°09.047'	31.3	6278.4
132	Thu	5/08/2010	Harding River Caravan Park Roebourne S 20°46.524' E 117°09.047'	Road Side Stop, @ Entrance to Sherlock Station 50km N Roebourne, North West Coastal Hwy S 20°56.208' E 117°33.939'	50.2	6328.6
133	Fri	6/08/2010	Road Side Stop, @ Entrance to Sherlock Station 50km N Roebourne, North West Coastal Hwy S 20°56.208' E 117°33.939'	Road Side Stop, Peawah River West Parking Bay, North West Coastal Hwy S 20°50.858' E 118°04.098'	60.5	6389.1
134	Sat	7/08/2010	Road Side Stop, Peawah River West Parking Bay, North West Coastal Hwy S 20°50.858' E 118°04.098'	Road Side Stop, Cnr North West Coastal Hwy/Great Northern Hwy S 20°34.160' E 118°26.254'	50.2	6439.3

Logs

Day	Date	Daily start location, with GPS coordinates	Daily finish location, with GPS coordinates	Km	Total Km
135	Sun	8/08/2010	Road Side Stop, Cnr North West Coastal Hwy/Great Northern Hwy S 20°34.160' E 118°26.254'	Port Hedland Caravan Park S 20°22.445' E 118°38.041'	34.8	6474.1
136	Mon	9/08/2010	Port Hedland Caravan Park S 20°22.445' E 118°38.041'	Road Side Stop, @ Entrance Atlas Pardoo Mining Camp, Great Northern Hwy S 20°20.904' E 119°05.939'	51.9	6526
137	Tue	10/08/2010	Road Side Stop, @ Entrance Atlas Pardoo Mining Camp, Great Northern Hwy S 20°20.904' E 119°05.939'	Road Side Stop, 31km N Pardoo Mining Camp, Great Northern Hwy S 20°18.550' E 119°22.336'	30.7	6556.7
138	Wed	11/08/2010	Road Side Stop, 31km N Pardoo Mining Camp, Great Northern Hwy S 20°18.550' E 119°22.336'	Pardoo Road House, Caravan Park S 20°03.314' E 119°49.663'	58.5	6615.2
139	Thu	12/08/2010	Pardoo Road House, Caravan Park S 20°03.314' E 119°49.663'	Road Side Stop, 37km Nth Pardoo Roadhouse, Great Northern Hwy S 19°58.521' E 120°09.816'	37.5	6652.7
140	Fri	13/08/2010	Road Side Stop, 37km Nth Pardoo Roadhouse, Great Northern Hwy S 19°58.521' E 120°09.816'	Road Side Stop, @ 50km S Sandfire, Green Rd Sign, Great Northern Hwy S 19°51.360' E 120°38.114'	52.4	6705.1
141	Sat	14/08/2010	Road Side Stop, @ 50km S Sandfire, Green Rd Sign, Great Northern Hwy S 19°51.360' E 120°38.114'	Sandfire Roadhouse, Caravan Park S 19°46.164' E 121°05.512'	50.6	6755.7
142	Sun	15/08/2010	Sandfire Roadhouse, Caravan Park S 19°46.164' E 121°05.512'	Road Side Stop, 45km Nth Sandfire, Great Northern Hwy S 19°31.491' E 121°24.113'	45.1	6800.8
143	Mon	16/08/2010	Road Side Stop, 45km Nth Sandfire, Great Northern Hwy S 19°31.491' E 121°24.113'	Road Side Stop, @ Entrance to Nita Downs Station, Great Northern Hwy S 19°04.712' E 121°39.175'	58.7	6859.5
144	Tue	17/08/2010	Road Side Stop, @ Entrance to Nita Downs Station, Great Northern Hwy S 19°04.712' E 121°39.175'	Road Side Stop, Cnr Great Northern Hwy/Bidyadanga Station Turnoff S 18°43.244' E 121°52.800'	48	6907.5
145	Wed	18/08/2010	Road Side Stop, Cnr Great Northern Hwy/Bidyadanga Station Turnoff S 18°43.244' E 121°52.800'	Road Side Stop, 56km N Bidyadanga Turnoff, Great Northern Hwy S 18°20.028' E 122°12.663'	56.2	6963.7
146	Thu	19/08/2010	Road Side Stop, 56km N Bidyadanga Turnoff, Great Northern Hwy S 18°20.028' E 122°12.663'	Road Side Stop, 26km S Roebuck Plains Roadhouse, Great Northern Hwy S 18°02.951' E 122°35.479'	54.3	7018
147	Fri	20/08/2010	Road Side Stop, 26km S Roebuck Plains Roadhouse, Great Northern Hwy S 18°02.951' E 122°35.479'	Road Side Stop, 400m E Broome Turnoff, Great Northern Hwy, @ Green Rd Sign S 17°50.856' E 122°30.362'	26.9	7044.9

Running Pink

Day		Date	Daily start location, with GPS coordinates	Daily finish location, with GPS coordinates	Km	Total Km
148	Sat	21/08/2010	Road Side Stop, 400m E Broome Turnoff, Great Northern Hwy, @ Green Rd Sign S 17°50.856' E 122°30.362'	Road Side Stop, @ Entrance to Radio Tower, @ 60km East Broome, Green Rd Sign, Great Northern Hwy S 17°49.212' E 122°44.410'	26.1	7071
149	Sun	22/08/2010	Road Side Stop, @ Entrance to Radio Tower, @ 60km East Broome, Green Rd Sign, Great Northern Hwy S 17°49.212' E 122°44.410'	Road Side Stop, @Entrance to Kimberley Stone, 5km E Nillibubbica Rest Area, Great Northern Hwy S 17°38.435' E 123°10.300'	50.6	7121.6
150	Mon	23/08/2010	Road Side Stop, @Entrance to Kimberley Stone, 5km E Nillibubbica Rest Area, Great Northern Hwy S 17°38.435' E 123°10.300'	Road Side Stop, 23km E Willare Bridge, @ 80km Derby Green Rd Sign, Great Northern Hwy S 17°40.351' E 123°27.878'	32.1	7153.7
151	Tue	24/08/2010	Road Side Stop, 23km E Willare Bridge, @ 80km Derby Green Rd Sign, Great Northern Hwy S 17°40.351' E 123°27.878'	Road Side Stop, Parking Bay @ Derby Turnoff, Great Northern Hwy S 17°38.088' E 123°44.545'	37.8	7191.5
152	Wed	25/08/2010	Road Side Stop, Parking Bay @ Derby Turnoff, Great Northern Hwy S 17°38.088' E 123°44.545'	Road Side Stop, 47km SE Derby Turnoff, @ Derby 90km Green Rd Sign, Great Northern Hwy S 17°48.809' E 124°06.471'	46.7	7238.2
153	Thu	26/08/2010	Road Side Stop, 47km SE Derby Turnoff, @ Derby 90km Green Rd Sign, Great Northern Hwy S 17°48.809' E 124°06.471'	Road Side Stop, @ Entrance Blina Station, Great Northern Hwy S 17°50.853' E 124°34.020'	49.5	7287.7
154	Fri	27/08/2010	Road Side Stop, @ Entrance Blina Station, Great Northern Hwy S 17°50.853' E 124°34.020'	Ellendale Roadwork's Camp, Great Northern Hwy S 17°57.749' E 124°50.313'	34.5	7322.2
155	Sat	28/08/2010	Ellendale Roadwork's Camp, Great Northern Hwy S 17°57.749' E 124°50.313'	Road Side Stop, @ Jubliee Downs Station Turnoff, Great Northern Hwy S 18°00.154' E 125°17.334'	49.2	7371.4
156	Sun	29/08/2010	Road Side Stop, @ Jubliee Downs Station Turnoff, Great Northern Hwy S 18°00.154' E 125°17.334'	Fitzroy River Lodge Caravan Park, Fitzroy Crossing S 18°12.542' E 125°35.033'	41	7412.4
157	Mon	30/08/2010	Fitzroy River Lodge Caravan Park, Fitzroy Crossing S 18°12.542' E 125°35.033'	Road Side Stop, 36.3km SE Fitzroy Crossing, 500m W Outcamp Creek, Great Northern Hwy S 18°27.170' E 125°45.133'	36.3	7448.7
158	Tue	31/08/2010	Road Side Stop, 36.3km SE Fitzroy Crossing, 500m W Outcamp Creek, Great Northern Hwy S 18°27.170' E 125°45.133'	Road Side Stop, Mt Pierre Station & Mimbi Caves Turnoff, Great Northern Hwy S 18°45.526' E 126°03.916'	54	7502.7

Logs

Day	Date	Daily start location, with GPS coordinates	Daily finish location, with GPS coordinates	Km	Total Km
159	Wed	1/09/2010	Road Side Stop, Mt Pierre Station & Mimbi Caves Turnoff, Great Northern Hwy S 18°45.526' E 126°03.916'	Road Side Stop, @ Entrance to Radio Tower, @ 150km W Halls Creek, Green Rd Sign, Great Northern Hwy S 18°47.517' E 126°30.034'	47.6	7550.3
160	Thu	2/09/2010	Road Side Stop, @ Entrance to Radio Tower, @ 150km W Halls Creek, Green Rd Sign, Great Northern Hwy S 18°47.517' E 126°30.034'	Mary Pool Camp Site, @ Mary River, 180km E Fitzroy Crossing, Great Northern Hwy S 18°43.592' E 126°52.333'	43	7593.3
161	Fri	3/09/2010	Mary Pool Camp Site, @ Mary River, 180km E Fitzroy Crossing, Great Northern Hwy S 18°43.592' E 126°52.333'	Road Side Stop, 33km E Mary Pool, @ cattle loading area, Great Northern Hwy S 18°34.414' E 127°05.731'	33.1	7626.4
162	Sat	4/09/2010	Road Side Stop, 33km E Mary Pool, @ cattle loading area, Great Northern Hwy S 18°34.414' E 127°05.731'	Road Side Stop, Truck Parking Bay, 20.6km W Halls Creek, Great Northern Hwy S 18°20.630' E 127°31.284'	56.3	7682.7
163	Sun	5/09/2010	Road Side Stop, Truck Parking Bay, 20.6km W Halls Creek, Great Northern Hwy S 18°20.630' E 127°31.284'	Road Side Stop, 9.6km E from, Halls Creek Police Station, Great Northern Hwy S 18°09.284' E 127°42.754'	30.6	7713.3
164	Mon	6/09/2010	Road Side Stop, 9.6km E from Halls Creek Police Station, Great Northern Hwy S 18°09.284' E 127°42.754'	Road Side Stop, 51km E Halls Creek, @ Mains Rds WA Reference Station Mark : HC 4173, Great Northern Hwy S 17°50.569' E 127°49.029'	41.4	7754.7
165	Tue	7/09/2010	Road Side Stop, 51km E Halls Creek, @ Mains Rds WA Reference Station Mark : HC 4173, Great Northern Hwy S 17°50.569' E 127°49.029'	Road Side Stop, Gravel Pitt 500m E of Whydam 290km Green Rd Sign, 80km E Halls Creek, Great Northern Hwy S 17°35.229' E 127°48.994'	31	7785.7
166	Wed	8/09/2010	Road Side Stop, Gravel Pitt 500m E of Whydam 290km Green Rd Sign, 80km E Halls Creek, Great Northern Hwy S 17°35.229' E 127°48.994'	Road Side Stop, 2.4km E of Whydam 240km Green Rd Sign, Great Northern Hwy S 17°14.651' E 128°05.119'	51.9	7837.6
167	Thu	9/09/2010	Road Side Stop, 2.4km E of Whydam 240km Green Rd Sign, Great Northern Hwy S 17°14.651' E 128°05.119'	Warrum/Turkey Creek, Caravan Park S 17°00.978' E 128°13.015'	30.5	7868.1
168	Fri	10/09/2010	Warrum/Turkey Creek, Caravan Park S 17°00.978' E 128°13.015'	Road Side Stop, @ March Fly Creek, 49.4km NE Turkey Creek, Great Northern Hwy S 16°39.522' E 128°12.833'	49.4	7917.5
169	Sat	11/09/2010	Road Side Stop, @ March Fly Creek, 49.4km NE Turkey Creek, Great Northern Hwy S 16°39.522' E 128°12.833'	Road Side Stop, Cnr Great Northern Hwy & Mandangala Rd Turn Off S 16°15.548' E 128°18.268'	50.5	7968

Running Pink

Day		Date	Daily start location, with GPS coordinates	Daily finish location, with GPS coordinates	Km	Total Km
170	Sun	12/09/2010	Road Side Stop, Cnr Great Northern Hwy & Mandangala Rd Turn Off S 16°15.548' E 128°18.268'	Road Side Stop, Cockburn Rest Area, Cnr Great Northern Hwy/ Victoria Hwy S 15°52.130' E 128°22.329'	51.9	8019.9
171	Mon	13/09/2010	Road Side Stop, Cockburn Rest Area, Cnr Great Northern Hwy/Victoria Hwy S 15°52.130' E 128°22.329'	Road Side Stop, @ W side of Ord River Dam, 5km W Kununurra, Victoria Hwy S 15°47.609' E 128°41.545'	39.4	8059.3
172	Tue	14/09/2010	Road Side Stop, @ W side of Ord River Dam, 5km W Kununurra, Victoria Hwy S 15°47.609' E 128°41.545'	Road Side Stop, @ Four Mile Creek, 28.4km E Kununurra, Victoria Hwy S 15°53.926' E 128°56.168'	33.7	8093
Northern Territory						
173	Wed	15/09/2010	Road Side Stop, @ Four Mile Creek, 28.4km E Kununurra, Victoria Hwy S 15°53.926' E 128°56.168'	Road Side Stop, 8km E NT Border, @ 50km Kununurra, Green Rd Sign, Victoria Hwy S 16°01.089' E 129°03.701'	22.9	8115.9
174	Thu	16/09/2010	Road Side Stop, 8km E NT Border, @ 50km Kununurra, Green Rd Sign, Victoria Hwy S 16°01.089' E 129°03.701'	Road Side Stop, 37km E NT Border, @ Entrance to Newry Station, Victoria Hwy S 16°03.406' E 129°15.733'	24.7	8140.6
175	Fri	17/09/2010	Road Side Stop, 37km E NT Border, @ Entrance to Newry Station, Victoria Hwy S 16°03.406' E 129°15.733'	Road Side Stop, @ 100km Kununurra, Green Rd Sign, Victoria Hwy S 16°00.216' E 129°28.660'	24.9	8165.5
176	Sat	18/09/2010	Road Side Stop, @ 100km Kununurra, Green Rd Sign, Victoria Hwy S 16°00.216' E 129°28.660'	Road Side Stop, @ Entrance to Bullo River Station, Victoria Hwy S 15°55.912' E 129°43.296'	30.1	8195.6
177	Sun	19/09/2010	Road Side Stop, @ Entrance to Bullo River Station, Victoria Hwy S 15°55.912' E 129°43.296'	Road Side Stop, @ Entrance to Avuergne Station, Victoria Hwy S 15°45.895' E 130°01.595'	40	8235.6
178	Mon	20/09/2010	Road Side Stop, @ Entrance to Avuergne Station, Victoria Hwy S 15°45.895' E 130°01.595'	Road Side Stop, Bradshaw Bridge, 8km W Timber Creek, Victoria Hwy S 15°36.831' E 130°24.452'	48.3	8283.9
179	Tue	21/09/2010	Road Side Stop, Bradshaw Bridge, 8km W Timber Creek, Victoria Hwy S 15°36.831' E 130°24.452'	Road Side Stop, Gravel Pitt between Skull Creek Minor & Skull Creek Major, Victoria Hwy S 15°43.957' E 130°45.270'	50.1	8334
180	Wed	22/09/2010	Road Side Stop, Gravel Pitt between Skull Creek Minor & Skull Creek Major, Victoria Hwy S 15°43.957' E 130°45.270'	Victoria River Roadhouse, Caravan Park S 15°37.005' E 131°07.718'	51.2	8385.2
181	Thu	23/09/2010	Victoria River Roadhouse, Caravan Park S 15°37.005' E 131°07.718'	Road Side Stop, 31.6km E Victoria River, Victoria Hwy S 15°30.455' E 131°20.130'	31.6	8416.8

Logs

Day	Date	Daily start location, with GPS coordinates	Daily finish location, with GPS coordinates	Km	Total Km
182	Fri	24/09/2010	Road Side Stop, 31.6km E Victoria River, Victoria Hwy S 15°30.455' E 131°20.130'	Road Side Stop, 17km W Buntine Hwy Turnoff, @ 2.4km SW 140km Katherine Green Rd Sign, Victoria Hwy S 15°25.385' E 131°29.381'	21.7	8438.5
183	Sat	25/09/2010	Road Side Stop, 17km W Buntine Hwy Turnoff, @ 2.4km SW 140km Katherine Green Rd Sign, Victoria Hwy S 15°25.385' E 131°29.381'	Road Side Stop, 35km E Buntine Hwy Turnoff, @ 0.5km SW 90km Katherine Green Rd Sign, Victoria Hwy S 15°03.518' E 131°45.262'	52.7	8491.2
184	Sun	26/09/2010	Road Side Stop, 35km E Buntine Hwy Turnoff, @ 0.5km SW 90km Katherine Green Rd Sign, Victoria Hwy S 15°03.518' E 131°45.262'	Road Side Stop, Limestone Creek, Victoria Hwy S 14°48.623' E 131°55.326'	35.6	8526.8
185	Mon	27/09/2010	Road Side Stop, Limestone Creek, Victoria Hwy S 14°48.623' E 131°55.326'	Riverview Caravan Park, Katherine S 14°29.110' E 132°15.363'	53.3	8580.1
186	Tue	28/09/2010	Riverview Caravan Park, Katherine S 14°29.110' E 132°15.363	Road Side Stop, @ 70km S Pine Creek, Green Road Sign, Stuart Hwy S 14°21.216' E 132°08.276'	22.1	8602.2
187	Wed	29/09/2010	Road Side Stop, @ 70km S Pine Creek, Green Road Sign, Stuart Hwy S 14°21.216' E 132°08.276'	Road Side Stop, @ Entrance to Claravale Station, Stuart Hwy S 14°00.222' E 131°55.694'	47.4	8649.6
188	Thu	30/09/2010	Road Side Stop, @ Entrance to Claravale Station, Stuart Hwy S 14°00.222' E 131°55.694'	Road Side Stop, 15km N Pine Creek Turnoff, Stuart Hwy S 13°43.994' E 131°43.331'	40.5	8690.1
189	Fri	1/10/2010	Road Side Stop, 15km N Pine Creek Turnoff, Stuart Hwy S 13°43.994' E 131°43.331'	Hayes Creek Caravan Park S 13°35.009' E 131°27.448'	39.6	8729.7
190	Sat	2/10/2010	Hayes Creek Caravan Park S 13°35.009' E 131°27.448'	Road Side Stop, @ 350m N 20km Adelaide River, Green Rd Sign,. Stuart Hwy S 13°21.693' E 131°12.876'	38	8767.7
191	Sun	3/10/2010	Road Side Stop, @ 350m N 20km Adelaide River, Green Rd Sign,. Stuart Hwy S 13°21.693' E 131°12.876'	Road Side Stop, Cnr Ringwood Rd/ Stuart Hwy, 18km N Adelaide River S 13°04.938' E 131°06.412'	38	8805.7
192	Mon	4/10/2010	Road Side Stop, Cnr Ringwood Rd/ Stuart Hwy, 18km N Adelaide River S 13°04.938' E 131°06.412'	Road Side Stop, Acacia Store S 12°47.931' E 131°07.350', via GPS co-ordinates S 13°03.130' E 131°06.663',	33.7	8839.4

The Point when Deborah became the 1st female to run the entire distance around Australia

| 193 | Tue | 5/10/2010 | Road Side Stop, Acacia Store S 12°47.931' E 131°07.350' | Luprechaun Caravan Park Darwin S 12°25.566' E 130°52.167' | 57.4 | 8896.8 |

Running Pink

Day	Date	Daily start location, with GPS coordinates	Daily finish location, with GPS coordinates	Km	Total Km
194	Wed 6/10/2010	Luprechaun Caravan Park Darwin S 12°25.566' E 130°52.167'	Road Sign Stop, 14km S Darwin, @ Lagoon Rd Sign S 12°26.206' E 130°55.963'	21.8	8918.6
195	Thu 7/10/2010	Road Sign Stop, 14km S Darwin, @ Lagoon Rd Sign S 12°26.206' E 130°55.963'	Road Side Stop, Cnr Arnhem & Stuart Hwy, @ Humpty Doo Turnoff S 12°33.955' E 131°04.422'	22	8940.6
196	Fri 8/10/2010	Road Side Stop, Cnr Arnhem & Stuart Hwy, @ Humpty Doo Turnoff S 12°33.955' E 131°04.422'	Road Side Stop, @ Entrance to Manton Dam Recreation Area, Stuart Hwy S 12°50.171' E 131°08.022'	32	8972.6
197	Sat 9/10/2010	Road Side Stop, @ Entrance to Manton Dam Recreation Area, Stuart Hwy S 12°50.171' E 131°08.022'	Adelaide River, Caravan Park S 13°14.321' E 131°06.433'	47.5	9020.1
198	Sun 10/10/2010	Adelaide River, Caravan Park S 13°14.321' E 131°06.433'	Road Side Stop, @ 90km Pine Creek, Green Rd Sign, Stuart Hwy S 13°22.580' E 131°14.548'	23.5	9043.6
199	Mon 11/10/2010	Road Side Stop, @ 90km Pine Creek, Green Rd Sign, Stuart Hwy S 13°22.580' E 131°14.548'	Hayes Creek, Caravan Park S 13°35.006' E 131°27.447'	34.8	9078.4
200	Tue 12/10/2010	Hayes Creek, Caravan Park S 13°35.006' E 131°27.447'	Lazy Lizard Caravan Park, Pine Creek S 13°49.250' E 131°50.121'	56	9134.4
201	Wed 13/10/2010	Lazy Lizard Caravan Park, Pine Creek S 13°49.250' E 131°50.121'	Road Side Stop, 51.7km S Pine Creek, Caravan Park, Stuart Hwy S 14°12.575' E 132°02.378'	51.7	9186.1
202	Thu 14/10/2010	Road Side Stop, 51.7km S Pine Creek, Caravan Park, Stuart Hwy S 14°12.575' E 132°02.378'	Katherine Information Centre S 14°28.013' E 132°15.950'	40	9226.1
203	Fri 15/10/2010	Katherine Information Centre S 14°28.013' E 132°15.950'	Road Side Stop, King River Rest Area, 47.7km S Katherine Information Centre, Stuart Hwy S 14°38.673' E 132°37.998'	47.7	9273.8
204	Sat 16/10/2010	Road Side Stop, King River Rest Area, 47.7km S Katherine Information Centre, Stuart Hwy S 14°38.673' E 132°37.998'	Road Side Stop, Truck Parking Bay, @ 90km Katherine, Green Rd Sign Stuart Hwy S 14°49.613' E 132°57.247'	42.3	9316.1
205	Sun 17/10/2010	Road Side Stop, Truck Parking Bay, @ 90km Katherine, Green Rd Sign, Stuart Hwy S 14°49.613' E 132°57.247'	Road Side Stop, Truck Parking Bay, 29.5km S Mataranka, Stuart Hwy S 15°10.676' E 133°05.712'	45.7	9361.8
206	Mon 18/10/2010	Road Side Stop, Truck Parking Bay, 29.5km S Mataranka, Stuart Hwy S 15°10.676' E 133°05.712'	Larrimah Caravan Park S 15°34.454' E 133°12.922'	46.2	9408

Logs

Day	Date	Daily start location, with GPS coordinates	Daily finish location, with GPS coordinates	Km	Total Km
207	Tue	19/10/2010	Larrimah Caravan Park S 15°34.454' E 133°12.922'	Road Side Stop, 39.3km S Larrimah, @ Alexander Forrest Commerative Cairn, Stuart Hwy S 15°51.555' E 133°24.264'	39.3	9447.3
208	Wed	20/10/2010	Road Side Stop, 39.3km S Larrimah, @ Alexander Forrest Commerative Cairn, Stuart Hwy S 15°51.555' E 133°24.264'	Daly Waters Pub, Caravan Park S 16°15.262' E 133°22.199'	53.8	9501.1
209	Thu	21/10/2010	Daly Waters Pub, Caravan Park S 16°15.262' E 133°22.199'	Road Side Stop, 35.8km S Daly Waters, Caravan Park, Stuart Hwy S 16°33.046' E 133°21.444'	35.8	9536.9
210	Fri	22/10/2010	Road Side Stop, 35.8km S Daly Waters, Caravan Park, Stuart Hwy S 16°33.046' E 133°21.444'	Road Side Stop, Truck Parking Bay, 36.8km S Dunmarra, Stuart Hwy S 17°00.340' E 133°26.244'	53.1	9590
211	Sat	23/10/2010	Road Side Stop, Truck Parking Bay, 36.8km S Dunmarra, Stuart Hwy S 17°00.340' E 133°26.244'	Elliot Caravan Park, @ United Petrol, Stuart Hwy S 17°33.236' E 133°32.637'	65	9655
212	Sun	24/10/2010	Elliot Caravan Park, @ United Petrol, Stuart Hwy S 17°33.236' E 133°32.637'	Road Side Stop, Gravel Pitt, 32km S Elliot, @ 220km Tenant Creek, Green Rd Sign, Stuart Hwy S 17°48.444' E 133°40.388'	32.7	9687.7
213	Mon	25/10/2010	Road Side Stop, Gravel Pitt, 32km S Elliot, @ 220km Tenant Creek, Green Rd Sign, Stuart Hwy S 17°48.444' E 133°40.388'	Renner Springs, Caravan Park, Stuart Hwy S 18°19.147' E 133°47.770'	60.1	9747.8
214	Tue	26/10/2010	Renner Springs, Caravan Park, Stuart Hwy S 18°19.147' E 133°47.770'	Road Side Stop, 40.1km S Renner Springs, @ 500m S Muckaty Station Turnoff, Stuart Hwy S 18°38.190' E 133°56.951'	40.1	9787.9
215	Wed	27/10/2010	Road Side Stop, 40.1km S Renner Springs, @ 500m S Muckaty Station Turnoff, Stuart Hwy S 18°38.190' E 133°56.951'	Road Side Stop, Attack Creek Rest Area, 47km N Threeways Roadhouse, Stuart Hwy S 19°01.487' E 134°08.533'	49	9836.9
216	Thu	28/10/2010	Road Side Stop, Attack Creek Rest Area, 47km N Threeways Roadhouse, Stuart Hwy S 19°01.487' E 134°08.533'	Road Side Stop, 15km N Threeways Roadhouse, @ 40km Tenant Creek, Green Rd Sign, Stuart Hwy S 19°18.075' E 134°11.144'	32.3	9869.2
217	Fri	29/10/2010	Road Side Stop, 15km N Threeways Roadhouse, @ 40km Tenant Creek, Green Rd Sign, Stuart Hwy S 19°18.075' E 134°11.144'	Road Side Stop, 14km E Threeways Roadhouse, @ 420km QLD Green Rd Sign Barkly Hwy S 19°26.450' E 134°20.246'	29.6	9898.8
218	Sat	30/10/2010	Road Side Stop, 14km E Threeways Roadhouse, @ 420km QLD Green Rd Sign, Barkly Hwy S 19°26.450' E 134°20.246'	Road Side Stop, 41 Mile Bore Rest Area, 70km E Threeways Roadhouse, Barkly Hwy S 19°19.242' E 134°51.072'	57.3	9956.1

Running Pink

Day		Date	Daily start location, with GPS coordinates	Daily finish location, with GPS coordinates	Km	Total Km
219	Sun	31/10/2010	Road Side Stop, 41 Mile Bore Rest Area, 70km E Threeways Roadhouse Barkly Hwy S 19°19.242' E 134°51.072'	Road Side Stop, Frewena Rest Area, 55km W Barkly Homestead Barkly Hwy S 19°25.963' E 135°24.096'	62.1	10018.2
220	Mon	1/11/2010	Road Side Stop, Frewena Rest Area, 55km W Barkly Homestead Barkly Hwy S 19°25.963' E 135°24.096'	Barkly Homestead, Caravan Park S 19°42.699' E 135°49.632'	55.5	10073.7
221	Tue	2/11/2010	Barkly Homestead, Caravan Park S 19°42.699' E 135°49.632'	Road Side Stop, Wonarah Bore Rest Area, 40km E Barkly Homestead Barkly Hwy S 19°50.544' E 136°09.385'	40.6	10114.3
222	Wed	3/11/2010	Road Side Stop, Wonarah Bore Rest Area, 40km E Barkly Homestead Barkly Hwy S 19°50.544' E 136°09.385'	Road Side Stop, 52.3km E Wonarah Bore Barkly Hwy S 19°58.943' E 136°36.623'	52.3	10166.6
223	Thu	4/11/2010	Road Side Stop, 52.3km E Wonarah Bore Barkly Hwy S 19°58.943' E 136°36.623'	Soudan Station, Barkly Hwy S 20°03.089' E 137°01.075'	49.4	10216
224	Fri	5/11/2010	Soudan Station, Barkly Hwy S 20°03.089' E 137°01.075'	Avon Downs Police Station, Rest Area, Barkly Hwy S 20°01.490' E 137°29.340'	51.4	10267.4
225	Sat	6/11/2010	Avon Downs Police Station, Rest Area, Barkly Hwy S 20°01.490' E 137°29.340'	Road Side Stop, 46km E Avon Downs, @ Western Creek, Barkly Hwy S 19°55.947' E 137°54.162'	46.4	10313.8

Queensland

Day		Date	Daily start location, with GPS coordinates	Daily finish location, with GPS coordinates	Km	Total Km
226	Sun	7/11/2010	Road Side Stop, 46km E Avon Downs, @ Western Creek, Barkly Hwy S 19°55.947' E 137°54.162'	Camooweal Caravan Park S 19°55.341' E 138°07.148'	23.4	10337.2
227	Mon	8/11/2010	Camooweal Caravan Park S 19°55.341' E 138°07.148'	Road Side Stop, Gravel Pit, Barkly Hwy, 44.8km E Camooweal S 19°59.598' E 138°31.521'	44.8	10382
228	Tue	9/11/2010	Road Side Stop, Gravel Pit, Barkly Hwy, 44.8km E Camooweal S 19°59.598' E 138°31.521'	Road Side Stop, David Searing Hall Parking Bay, 92.3km E Camooweal, Barkly Hwy S 20°11.365' E 138°53.883'	47.5	10429.5
229	Wed	10/11/2010	Road Side Stop, David Sterling Hall Parking Bay, 92.3km E Camooweal, Barkly Hwy S 20°11.365' E 138°53.883'	Road Side Stop, World War 2 Rest Area, 137.9km E Camooweal, Barkly Hwy S 20°22.389' E 139°15.840'	45.6	10475.1
230	Thu	11/11/2010	Road Side Stop, World War 2 Rest Area, 137.9km E Camooweal, Barkly Hwy S 20°22.389' E 139°15.840'	Mt Isa Caravan Park S 20°43.445' E 139°30.571'	56.7	10531.8

Logs

Day	Date	Daily start location, with GPS coordinates	Daily finish location, with GPS coordinates	Km	Total Km
231	Fri	12/11/2010	Mt Isa Caravan Park S 20°43.445' E 139°30.571'	Road Side Stop, Dingo Creek Kua Floodway Flinders Hwy S 20°42.313' E 139°41.826'	21.5	10553.3
232	Sat	13/11/2010	Road Side Stop, Dingo Creek Kua Floodway, Flinders Hwy S 20°42.313' E 139°41.826'	Road Side Stop, Gravel Pitt, Flinders Hwy, 47.1km E Dingo Creek S 20°48.462' E 140°03.964'	47.1	10600.4
233	Sun	14/11/2010	Road Side Stop, Gravel Pitt, Flinders Hwy, 47.1km E Dingo Creek S 20°48.462' E 140°03.964'	Gilbert Park Caravan Park Cloncurry S 20°42.472', E 140.31.721'	53.7	10654.1
234	Mon	15/11/2010	Gilbert Park Caravan Park Cloncurry S 20°42.472', E 140.31.721'	Road Side Stop, Gravel Pitt, @ 100km Julia Creek, Green Rd Sign, Flinders Hwy S 20°40.293', E 140.50.083'	36	10690.1
235	Tue	16/11/2010	Road Side Stop, Gravel Pitt, @ 100km Julia Creek, Green Rd Sign, Flinders Hwy S 20°40.293', E 140.50.083'	Road Side Stop, @ Entrance to Station 55.2 km W Julia Creek PO, Flinders Hwy S 20°37.655' E 141°14.697'	44.8	10734.9
236	Wed	17/11/2010	Road Side Stop, @ Entrance to Station 55.2km W Julia Creek PO, Flinders Hwy S 20°37.655' E 141°14.697'	Julia Creek Caravan Park S 20°39.159' E 141°44.744'	56.5	10791.4
237	Thu	18/11/2010	Julia Creek Caravan Park S 20°39.159' E 141°44.744'	Road Side Stop, @ Telecom & QLD Rail Station Pole No. 5039254, 36.7 km E Julia Creek, Flinders Hwy S 20°39.021' E 142°05.335'	36.7	10828.1
238	Fri	19/11/2010	Road Side Stop, @ Telecom & QLD Rail Station Pole No. 5039254, 36.7 km E Julia Creek, Flinders Hwy S 20°39.021' E 142°05.335'	Road Side Stop, @ Floodway 87km E Julia Creek, Flinders Hwy S 20°42.185' E 142°33.005'	50.3	10878.4
239	Sat	20/11/2010	Road Side Stop, @ Floodway 87km E Julia Creek, Flinders Hwy S 20°42.185' E 142°33.005'	Richmond Caravan Park S 20°44.120' E 143°08.797'	63.9	10942.3
240	Sun	21/11/2010	Richmond Caravan Park S 20°44.120' E 143°08.797'	Road Side Stop, 40.1km E Richmond, Flinders Hwy S 20°51.179' E 143°29.622'	40.1	10982.4
241	Mon	22/11/2010	Road Side Stop, 40.1km E Richmond, Flinders Hwy S 20°51.179' E 143°29.622'	Dunluce Station, 37km W Hughendon, Flinders Hwy S 20°52.446' E 143°51.360' S 20°52.446' E 143°51.360'	39.5	11021.9
242	Tue	23/11/2010	Dunluce Station, 37km W Hughendon, Flinders Hwy S 20°52.446' E 143°51.360'	Hughenden Caravan Park S 20°50.981' E 144°11.755'	38.7	11060.6
243	Wed	24/11/2010	Hughenden Caravan Park S 20°50.981' E 144°11.755'	Prairie Hotel S 20°52.256' E 144°35.995'	45.7	11106.3

Running Pink

Day		Date	Daily start location, with GPS coordinates	Daily finish location, with GPS coordinates	Km	Total Km
244	Thu	25/11/2010	Prairie Hotel S 20°52.256' E 144°35.995'	Private Residence, 42 Torrens St, Torrens Creek S 20°46.133' E 145°01.048'	45.9	11152.2
245	Fri	26/11/2010	Private Residence, 42 Torrens St, Torrens Creek S 20°46.133' E 145°01.048'	Pentland Caravan Park S 20°31.262' E 145°24.096'	52.9	11205.1
246	Sat	27/11/2010	Pentland Caravan Park S 20°31.262' E 145°24.096'	Homestead General Store S 20°21.722' E 145°39.267'	33.1	11238.2
247	Sun	28/11/2010	Homestead General Store S 20°21.722' E 145°39.267'	Balfes Creek Caravan Park S 20°12.961' E 145°54.560'	31.5	11269.7
248	Mon	29/11/2010	Balfes Creek Caravan Park S 20°12.961' E 145°54.560'	Charters Towers Caravan Park S 20°05.637' E 146°15.673'	41.4	11311.1
249	Tue	30/11/2010	Charters Towers Caravan Park S 20°05.637' E 146°15.673'	Fletcher View, Vet Research Station, James Cook University, Greogory Development Rd S 19°53.067' E 146°10.747'	30.4	11341.5
250	Wed	1/12/2010	Fletcher View, Vet Research Station, James Cook University, Greogory Development Rd S 19°53.067' E 146°10.747'	Road Side Stop, @ Entrance to Hillgrove Station, Greogory Development Rd S 19°35.719' E 145°46.085'	61.6	11403.1
251	Thu	2/12/2010	Road Side Stop, @ Entrance to Hillgrove Station, Greogory Development Rd S 19°35.719' E 145°46.085'	Road Side Stop, Cnr Gregory Development Rd/Clark River Lagoons Turnoff, Greogory Development Rd S 19°12.867' E 145°25.529'	60.2	11463.3
252	Fri	3/12/2010	Road Side Stop, Cnr Gregory Development Rd/Clark River Lagoons Turnoff S 19°12.867' E 145°25.529'	Greenvale Caravan Park S 19°00.043' E 144°59.041'	59	11522.3
253	Sat	4/12/2010	Greenvale Caravan Park S 19°00.043' E 144°59.041'	Road Side Stop, 40.7km N Greenvale, @ Call Point No 23 Sign, Gregory Development Rd S 18°56.845' E 144°38.907'	40.7	11563
254	Sun	5/12/2010	Road Side Stop, 40.7km N Greenvale, @ Call Point No 23 Sign, Greogory Development Rd S 18°56.845' E 144°38.907'	Road Side Stop, Gravel Pitt, Kennedy Hwy, @ 40km Lynd Junction, Green Rd Sign S 18°35.829' E 144°43.440'	53.2	11616.2
255	Mon	6/12/2010	Road Side Stop, Gravel Pitt, Kennedy Hwy, @ 40km Lynd Junction, Green Rd Sign S 18°35.829' E 144°43.440'	Road Side Stop, @ Entrance to Meadowbank Station, Kennedy Hwy S 18°14.347' E 144°45.961'	42.4	11658.6
256	Tue	7/12/2010	Road Side Stop, @ Entrance to Meadowbank Station, Kennedy Hwy S 18°14.347' E 144°45.961'	Road Side Stop, Truck Parking Bay, 55.5km N Meadow Bank Station Turnoff, Kennedy Hwy S 17°49.097' E 144°57.302'	55.4	11714

Logs

Day		Date	Daily start location, with GPS coordinates	Daily finish location, with GPS coordinates	Km	Total Km
257	Wed	8/12/2010	Road Side Stop, Truck Parking Bay, 55.5km N Meadow Bank Station Turnoff, Kennedy Hwy S 17°49.097' E 144°57.302'	Innot Hot Springs Caravan Park S 17°39.968' E 145°14.308'	41.9	11755.9
258	Thu	9/12/2010	Innot Hot Springs Caravan Park S 17°39.968' E 145°14.308'	Road Side Stop, Windy Hill Farm, Kennedy Hwy, Viewing Carpark Ravenshoe S 17°35.413' E 145°31.752'	36.3	11792.2
259	Fri	10/12/2010	Road Side Stop, Windy Hill Farm, Kennedy Hwy, Viewing Carpark Ravenshoe S 17°35.413' E 145°31.752'	RedHill Farm, 6 Dawson Rd Atherton S 17°14.797' E 145°28.712'	49.8	11842
260	Sat	11/12/2010	RedHill Farm, 6 Dawson Rd Atherton S 17°14.797' E 145°28.712'	Riverview Caravan Park Mareeba S 17°00.079' E 145°25.700'	35.2	11877.2
261	Sun	12/12/2010	Riverview Caravan Park Mareeba S 17°00.079' E 145°25.700'	Road Side Stop, @ Entrance to Ergon Energy Yalkula Sub Station, Peninsula Development Rd S 16°41.681' E 145°20.523'	38.7	11915.9
262	Mon	13/12/2010	Road Side Stop, @ Entrance to Ergon Energy Yalkula Sub Station, Peninsula Development Rd S 16°41.681' E 145°20.523'	Mossman Riverside, Leisure Park S 16°27.264' E 145°22.330'	38.1	11954
263	Tue	14/12/2010	Mossman Riverside, Leisure Park S 16°27.264' E 145°22.330'	Road Side Stop, Gravel Pitt, Captian Cook Hwy, 46.3km S Mossman S 16°42.766' E 145°38.105'	46.3	12000.3
264	Wed	15/12/2010	Road Side Stop, Gravel Pitt, Captian Cook Hwy, 46.3km S Mossman S 16°42.766' E 145°38.105'	Road Side Stop, Cnr James St/ Captain Cook Hwy, Cairns S 16°54.526' E 145°45.641'	31.6	12031.9
265	Thu	16/12/2010	Road Side Stop, Cnr James St/ Captain Cook Hwy, Cairns S 16°54.526' E 145°45.641'	Road Side Stop, Gordonvale Rest Area, Mulgrave River S 17°05.979' E 145°47.236'	30.5	12062.4
266	Fri	17/12/2010	Road Side Stop, Gordonvale Rest Area, Mulgrave River S 17°05.979' E 145°47.236'	Mirriwinni Hotel S 17°23.879' E 145°54.586'	40.9	12103.3
267	Sat	18/12/2010	Mirriwinni Hotel S 17°23.879' E 145°54.586'	August Moon Caravan Park Innisfail S 17°33.460' E 146°02.137'	27.9	12131.2
268	Sun	19/12/2010	August Moon Caravan Park Innisfail S 17°33.460' E 146°02.137'	Greenway Caravan Park Tully S 17°55.911' E 145°55.710'	49	12180.2
269	Mon	20/12/2010	Greenway Caravan Park Tully S 17°55.911' E 145°55.710'	Beachcombers Caravan Park Cardwell S 18°15.330' E 146°01.104'	43.3	12223.5
270	Tue	21/12/2010	Beachcombers Caravan Park Cardwell S 18°15.330' E 146°01.104'	Palm Tree Caravan Park Ingham S 18°40.623' E 146°09.231'	60.1	12283.6

Running Pink

Day	Date	Daily start location, with GPS coordinates	Daily finish location, with GPS coordinates	Km	Total Km
271	Wed	22/12/2010	Palm Tree Caravan Park Ingham S 18°40.623' E 146°09.231'	Rollingston Hotel S 19°02.792' E 146°23.443'	55.4	12339
272	Thu	23/12/2010	Rollingston Hotel S 19°02.792' E 146°23.443'	Coral Coast Caravan Park, Townsville S 19°15.697' E 146°44.917'	46.2	12385.2
273	Fri	24/12/2010	Coral Coast Caravan Park, Townsville S 19°15.697' E 146°44.917'	Road Side Stop, Alligator Creek Vehicle Inspection Bay, Bruce Hwy S 19°23.468' E 146°57.812'	31.6	12416.8
274	Sat	25/12/2010	Road Side Stop, Alligator Creek Vehicle Inspection Bay, Bruce Hwy S 19°23.468' E 146°57.812'	Road Side Stop, Greenacres Roadhouse, via Giru S 19°33.794' E 147°09.268'	39.9	12456.7
275	Sun	26/12/2010	Road Side Stop, Greenacres Roadhouse via Giru S 19°33.794' E 147°09.268'	Cascade Caravan Park Ayr S 19°34.827' E 147°24.134'	30.1	12486.8
276	Mon	27/12/2010	Cascade Caravan Park Ayr S 19°34.827' E 147°24.134'	Inkerman Caravan Park S 19°45.014' E 147°29.483'	23.9	12510.7
277	Tue	28/12/2010	Inkerman Caravan Park S 19°45.014' E 147°29.483'	Road Side Stop, Guthalungra Roadhouse, Rest Area, Bruce Hwy S 19°55.382' E 147°50.578'	43.4	12554.1
278	Wed	29/12/2010	Road Side Stop, Guthalungra Roadhouse, Rest Area, Bruce Hwy S 19°55.382' E 147°50.578'	Road Side Stop, Bowen Rest Area, Bruce Hwy, Opposite Big Mango S 20°02.776' E 148°13.773'	50.1	12604.2
279	Thu	30/12/2010	Road Side Stop, Bowen Rest Area, Bruce Hwy, Opposite Big Mango S 20°02.776' E 148°13.773'	Gunna Go Caravan Park, 6km N Proserpine S 20°21.085' E 148°33.343'	52.8	12657
280	Fri	31/12/2010	Gunna Go Caravan Park, 6km N Proserpine S 20°21.085' E 148°33.343'	Seabreeze Caravan Park, Airlie Beach S 20°16.590' E 148°42.192'	28.2	12685.2
281	Sat	1/01/2011	Seabreeze Caravan Park, Airlie Beach S 20°16.590' E 148°42.192'	Proserpine Caravan Park S 20°24.254' E 148°34.304'	25.7	12710.9
282	Sun	2/01/2011	Proserpine Caravan Park S 20°24.254' E 148°34.304'	O'Connell Caravan Park, 22km S Proserpine S 20°33.878' E 148°36.921'	22.8	12733.7
283	Mon	3/01/2011	O'Connell Caravan Park, 22km S Proserpine S 20°33.878' E 148°36.921'	Road Side Stop, Bloomsbury Caltex Service Station, Bruce Hwy, via Midge Point S 20°42.341' E 148°35.795'	29.9	12763.6
284	Tue	4/01/2011	Road Side Stop, Bloomsbury Caltex Service Station, Bruce Hwy, via Midge Point S 20°42.341' E 148°35.795'	St Helens Caravan Park Calen S 20°54.285' E 148°46.692'	32.7	12796.3
285	Wed	5/01/2011	St Helens Caravan Park Calen S 20°54.285' E 148°46.692'	Road Side Stop, Kuttabul General Store S 21°02.427' E 148°54.618'	21.7	12818

Logs

Day	Date	Daily start location, with GPS coordinates	Daily finish location, with GPS coordinates	Km	Total Km
286	Thu	6/01/2011	Road Side Stop, Kuttabul General Store S 21°02.427' E 148°54.618'	Road Side Stop, Cnr Ashburton Rd/Bruce Hwy, 10km N Mackay S 21°06.034' E 149°05.306'	21.3	12839.3
287	Fri	7/01/2011	Road Side Stop, Cnr Ashburton Rd/Bruce Hwy, 10km N Mackay S 21°06.034' E 149°05.306'	The Parks Caravan Park, Bruce Hwy Mackay S 21°11.095' E 149°09.180'	21.2	12860.5
288	Sat	8/01/2011	The Parks Caravan Park, Bruce Hwy Mackay S 21°11.095' E 149°09.180'	Sarina Masonic Centre, Cnr Phillip St/Bruce Hwy S 21°25.220' E 149°12.998'	31.1	12891.6
289	Sun	9/01/2011	Sarina Masonic Centre, Cnr Phillip St/Bruce Hwy S 21°25.220' E 149°12.998'	Koumala Caravan Park S 21°36.597' E 149°14.814'	22.9	12914.5
290	Mon	10/01/2011	Koumala Caravan Park S 21°36.597' E 149°14.814'	Private Residence, 86065 Bruce Hwy Orkabie S 21°48.328' E 149°22.187'	28.6	12943.1
291	Tue	11/01/2011	Private Residence, 86065 Bruce Hwy Orkabie S 21°48.328' E 149°22.187'	Carmila Beach Camp Area, 6km E Carmila Roadhouse S 21°55.076' E 149°27.822'	21.5	12964.6
292	Wed	12/01/2011	Carmila Beach Camp Area, 6km E Carmila Roadhouse S 21°55.076' E 149°27.822'	Clairview Caravan Park S 22°07.290' E 149°32.152'	36.2	13000.8
293	Thu	13/01/2011	Clairview Caravan Park S 22°07.290' E 149°32.152'	St Lawrence Recreation Reserve S 22°21.015' E 149°31.221'	32.1	13032.9
294	Fri	14/01/2011	St Lawrence Recreation Reserve S 22°21.015' E 149°31.221'	Road Side Stop, Truck Parking Bay, Bruce Hwy, 18.5km S Waverly Creek, Rest Area S 22°35.634' E 149°32.110'	33.2	13066.1
295	Sat	15/01/2011	Road Side Stop, Truck Parking Bay, Bruce Hwy, 18.5km S Waverly Creek, Rest Area S 22°35.634' E 149°32.110'	Marlborough Caravan Park S 22°49.501' E 149°53.719'	48.3	13114.4
296	Sun	16/01/2011	Marlborough Caravan Park S 22°49.501' E 149°53.719'	Road Side Stop, Gravel Pitt, Bruce Hwy, 6.5km N Yaamba S 23°06.990' E 150°18.852'	62.4	13176.8
297	Mon	17/01/2011	Road Side Stop, Gravel Pitt, Bruce Hwy, 6.5km N Yaamba S 23°06.990' E 150°18.852'	Parkhurst Caravan Park Rockhampton S 23°17.820' E 150°30.902'	33.7	13210.5
298	Tue	18/01/2011	Parkhurst Caravan Park Rockhampton S 23°17.820' E 150°30.902'	Kangaroo Ground Caravan Park, 59741 Bruce Hwy S 23°29.551' E 150°32.475'	25	13235.5
299	Wed	19/01/2011	Kangaroo Ground Caravan Park, 59741 Bruce Hwy S 23°29.551' E 150°32.475'	Road Side Stop, Cnr Horrigan Rd & Bruce Hwy, 8km S Mount Larcom S 23°41.963' E 150°47.345'	37.8	13273.3
300	Thu	20/01/2011	Road Side Stop, Cnr Horrigan Rd & Bruce Hwy, 8km S Mount Larcom S 23°41.963' E 150°47.345'	Gladstone Showgrounds S 23°50.991' E 151°15.300'	58.9	13332.2

Running Pink

Day	Date	Daily start location, with GPS coordinates	Daily finish location, with GPS coordinates	Km	Total Km
301	Fri	21/01/2011	Gladstone Showgrounds S 23°50.991' E 151°15.300'	Road Side Stop, Truck Parking Bay, Bruce Hwy, 38.2km S Gladstone S 24°05.239' E 151°24.550'	38.2	13370.4
302	Sat	22/01/2011	Road Side Stop, Truck Parking Bay, Bruce Hwy, 38.2km S Gladstone S 24°05.239' E 151°24.550'	Road Side Stop, Gravel Pitt, 3km S Miriam Vale, Angus Water – 1770 Rd S 24°19.859' E 151°34.731'	36.8	13407.2
303	Sun	23/01/2011	Road Side Stop, Gravel Pitt, 3km S Miriam Vale, Angus Water – 1770 Rd S 24°19.859' E 151°34.731'	Rosedale Hotel Caravan Park S 24°37.793' E 151°54.992'	59.6	13466.8
304	Mon	24/01/2011	Rosedale Hotel Caravan Park S 24°37.793' E 151°54.992'	Road Side Stop, Cnr Rosedale/ Horwood Rd S 24°48.573' E 152°11.942'	41	13507.8
305	Tue	25/01/2011	Road Side Stop, Cnr Rosedale/ Horwood Rd S 24°48.573' E 152°11.942'	Bundaberg Airport Carpark S 24°53.546' E 152°19.070'	21.9	13529.7
306	Wed	26/01/2011	Bundaberg Airport Carpark S 24°53.546' E 152°19.070'	Road Side Stop, @ Entrance Bundaberg, Gliding Club, Bundaberg Childers Rd S 25°02.333' E 152°13.363'	21.9	13551.6
307	Thu	27/01/2011	Road Side Stop, @ Entrance Bundaberg, Gliding Club, Bundaberg Childers Rd S 25°02.333' E 152°13.363'	Sugar Bowl Caravan Park Childers S 25°14.151' E 152°15.883'	26.6	13578.2
308	Fri	28/01/2011	Sugar Bowl Caravan Park Childers S 25°14.151' E 152°15.883'	Burrum River Caravan Park, 141 Old Bruce Hwy Howard S 25°19.795' E 152°34.725'	35.7	13613.9
309	Sat	29/01/2011	Burrum River Caravan Park, 141 Old Bruce Hwy Howard S 25°19.795' E 152°34.725'	Hervey Bay Surf Club, Cnr Macks Rd/Charlton Esplanade Torquay S 25°17.022' E 152°52.548'	41.6	13655.5
310	Sun	30/01/2011	Hervey Bay Surf Club, Cnr Macks Rd/Charlton Esplanade Torquay, via Hervey Bay & back S 25°17.022' E 152°52.548'	Maryborough Caravan Park S 25°33.379' E 152°40.169'	49	13704.5
311	Mon	31/01/2011	Maryborough Caravan Park S 25°33.379' E 152°40.169'	Road Side Stop, Cnr Bruce Hwy/ Molteno Rd S 25°52.901' E 152°35.833'	39.8	13744.3
312	Tue	1/02/2011	Road Side Stop, Cnr Bruce Hwy/ Molteno Rd S 25°52.901' E 152°35.833'	Twin Lakes Caravan Park Gympie S 26°13.376' E 152°41.513'	48.9	13793.2
313	Wed	2/02/2011	Twin Lakes Caravan Park Gympie S 26°13.376' E 152°41.513'	Pomona Showgrounds, Caravan Park S 26°21.554' E 152°51.550'	33.9	13827.1
314	Thu	3/02/2011	Pomona Showgrounds, Caravan Park S 26°21.554' E 152°51.550'	Yandina Caravan Park S 26°33.993' E 152°57.307'	31.6	13858.7

Logs

Day	Date	Daily start location, with GPS coordinates	Daily finish location, with GPS coordinates	Km	Total Km
315	Fri	4/02/2011	Yandina Caravan Park S 26°33.993' E 152°57.307'	Road Side Stop, Outside Cotton Tree, Aquatic Centre, Maroochydore S 26°39.253' E 153°05.941	22.3	13881
316	Sat	5/02/2011	Road Side Stop, Outside Cotton Tree, Aquatic Centre, Maroochydore S 26°39.253' E 153°05.941'	Road Side Stop, Cnr Ridgewood/ Caloundra Rd Caloundra S 26°47.094' E 153°05.422'	22.7	13903.7
317	Sun	6/02/2011	Road Side Stop, Cnr Ridgewood/ Caloundra Rd Caloundra S 26°47.094' E 153°05.422'	Caboolture Showgrounds S 27°03.902' E 152°56.829'	45.5	13949.2
318	Mon	7/02/2011	Caboolture Showgrounds S 27°03.902' E 152°56.829'	Road Side Stop, Chermside Lions Park, Cnr Gympie/Webster Rd Chermside S 27°22.361' E 153°01.385'	40.4	13989.6
319	Tue	8/02/2011	Road Side Stop, Chermside Lions Park, Cnr Gympie/Webster Rd Chermside S 27°22.361' E 153°01.385'	Sheldon Caravan Park, Holmead Rd Eight Mile Plains S 27°34.242' E 153°05.594'	29.1	14018.7
320	Wed	9/02/2011	Sheldon Caravan Park, Holmead Rd Eight Mile Plains S 27°34.242' E 153°05.594'	Road Side Stop, Cnr Ramu St/Fryer Rd Eagleby S 27°42.829' E 153°12.662'	24.4	14043.1
321	Thu	10/02/2011	Road Side Stop, Cnr Ramu St/Fryer Rd Eagleby S 27°42.829' E 153°12.662'	Gold Coast Holiday Park, Siganto Dr, Helensvale S 27°53.947' E 153°19.015'	26.2	14069.3
322	Fri	11/02/2011	Gold Coast Holiday Park, Siganto Dr, Helensvale S 27°53.947' E 153°19.015'	Road Side Stop, Cnr Maxwell Ave/. Northcliffe Tce, Surfers Paradise S 28°00.483' E 153°25.882'	21.4	14090.7

New South Wales

Day	Date	Daily start location, with GPS coordinates	Daily finish location, with GPS coordinates	Km	Total Km
323	Sat	12/02/2011	Road Side Stop, Cnr Maxwell Ave/. Northcliffe Tce, Surfers Paradise S 28°00.483' E 153°25.882'	River Retreat Caravan Park, Tweed Heads S 28°11.655' E 153°31.215'	30.4	14121.1
324	Sun	13/02/2011	River Retreat Caravan Park, Tweed Heads S 28°11.655' E 153°31.215'	Wooyong Caravan Park S 28°27.346' E 153°33.146'	40.5	14161.6
325	Mon	14/02/2011	Wooyong Caravan Park S 28°27.346' E 153°33.146'	Byron Bay Tourist Village S 28°38.226' E 153°35.632'	31.9	14193.5
326	Tue	15/02/2011	Byron Bay Tourist Village S 28°38.226' E 153°35.632'	Lismore Palm Caravan Park S 28°48.097' E 153°17.203'	47.6	14241.1
327	Wed	16/02/2011	Lismore Palm Caravan Park S 28°48.097' E 153°17.203'	Road Side Stop, Cnr Naughtons Gap/Stone Rd Casino S 28°48.301' E 153°05.708'	39.2	14280.3
328	Thu	17/02/2011	Road Side Stop, Cnr Naughtons Gap/ Stone Rd Casino S 28°48.301' E 153°05.708'	Lismore Palm Caravan Park S 28°48.094' E 153°17.203'	23.3	14303.6

Running Pink

Day	Date	Daily start location, with GPS coordinates	Daily finish location, with GPS coordinates	Km	Total Km
329	Fri	18/02/2011	Lismore Palm Caravan Park S 28°48.094' E 153°17.203'	Ballina Waterfront Village Caravan Park S 28°51.924' E 153°31.437'	30.4	14334
330	Sat	19/02/2011	Ballina Waterfront Village Caravan Park S 28°51.924' E 153°31.437'	Broadwater Stopover, Tourist Park S 29°01.170' E 153°25.430'	23.2	14357.2
331	Sun	20/02/2011	Broadwater Stopover, Tourist Park S 29°01.170' E 153°25.430'	Maclean Riverside, Caravan Park S 29°26.945' E 153°12.091'	62.3	14419.5
332	Mon	21/02/2011	Maclean Riverside, Caravan Park S 29°26.945' E 153°12.091'	Glenwood Tourist Park, Heber St Sth Grafton S 29°42.875' E 152°56.758'	49.6	14469.1
333	Tue	22/02/2011	Glenwood Tourist Park, Heber St Sth Grafton S 29°42.875' E 152°56.758'	Road Side Stop, Lions Park, Cnr Pullen St/Pacific Hwy Woolgoolga S 30°06.788' E 153°11.405'	57.1	14526.2
334	Wed	23/02/2011	Road Side Stop, Lions Park, Cnr Pullen St/Pacific Hwy Woolgoolga S 30°06.788' E 153°11.405'	Bellingen Showgrounds S 30°26.814' E 152°53.921'	64	14590.2
335	Thu	24/02/2011	Bellingen Showgrounds S 30°26.814' E 152°53.921'	Private Residence, 296 Valla Rd Valla S 30°35.652' E 152°57.923'	33.7	14623.9
336	Fri	25/02/2011	Private Residence, 296 Valla Rd Valla S 30°35.652' E 152°57.923'	Road Side Stop, Paddy's Rest Area, 5km S Warrell Creek, Pacific Hwy S 30°48.852' E 152°52.288'	33.7	14657.6
337	Sat	26/02/2011	Road Side Stop, Paddy's Rest Area, 5km S Warrell Creek, Pacific Hwy S 30°48.852' E 152°52.288'	Kempsey Tourist Village S 31°06.115' E 152°49.925'	42.7	14700.3
338	Sun	27/02/2011	Kempsey Tourist Village S 31°06.115' E 152°49.925'	Leisure Caravan Park, Port Macquarie S 31°25.513' E 152°52.488'	42.6	14742.9
339	Mon	28/02/2011	Leisure Caravan Park, Port Macquarie S 31°25.513' E 152°52.488'	Bonny Hills Holiday Park S 31°35.449' E 152°50.402'	30.1	14773
340	Tue	1/03/2011	Bonny Hills Holiday Park S 31°35.449' E 152°50.402'	Road Side Stop, Groki Wharf, Cnr Ferry Rd/Barton St Croki S 31°52.620' E 152°35.627'	50.6	14823.6
341	Wed	2/03/2011	Road Side Stop, Groki Wharf, Cnr Ferry Rd/Barton St Croki S 31°52.620' E 152°35.627'	Great Lakes Holiday Park Tuncurry, via Taree S 32°11.054' E 152°29.498'	52.8	14876.4
342	Thu	3/03/2011	Great Lakes Holiday Park Tuncurry, via Taree S 32°11.054' E 152°29.498'	Road Side Stop, Bungwahl Top of the Myall, Rest Area, Lakes Way S 32°22.923' E 152°26.858'	36.4	14912.8
343	Fri	4/03/2011	Road Side Stop, Bungwahl Top of the Myall, Rest Area, Lakes Way S 32°22.923' E 152°26.858'	Road Side Stop, Nerong Bus Stop, Pacific Hwy S 32°30.689' E 152°12.697'	49.6	14962.4

Logs

Day		Date	Daily start location, with GPS coordinates	Daily finish location, with GPS coordinates	Km	Total Km
344	Sat	5/03/2011	Road Side Stop, Nerong Bus Stop, Pacific Hwy S 32°30.689' E 152°12.697'	Road Side Stop, Medowie Rd Rest Area, 12km N Karuah S 32°40.183' E 151°50.110'	44.9	15007.3
345	Sun	6/03/2011	Road Side Stop, Medowie Rd Rest Area, 12km N Karuah S 32°40.183' E 151°50.110'	Bellhaven Caravan Park, Raymond Terrace S 32°46.831' E 151°44.155'	61.5	15068.8
346	Mon	7/03/2011	Bellhaven Caravan Park, Raymond Terrace S 32°46.831' E 151°44.155'	Coach Stop Caravan Park Maitland S 32°44.554' E 151°33.895'	27.4	15096.2
347	Tue	8/03/2011	Coach Stop Caravan Park Maitland S 32°44.554' E 151°33.895'	Road Side Stop, Intersection Old Pacific Hwy/Newcastle Inner City Bypass Bennetts Green, via Newcastle S 32°59.541' E 151°41.385'	42.2	15138.4
348	Wed	9/03/2011	Road Side Stop, Intersection Old Pacific Hwy/Newcastle Inner City Bypass Bennetts Green, via Newcastle S 32°59.541' E 151°41.385'	Budgewoi Holiday Park S 33°14.061' E 151°34.017'	35.5	15173.9
349	Thu	10/03/2011	Budgewoi Holiday Park S 33°14.061' E 151°34.017'	Road Side Stop, Cnr Brookhill Lane/, Central Coast Hwy, West Gosford S 33°25.615' E 151°25.259'	28.5	15202.4
350	Fri	11/03/2011	Road Side Stop, Cnr Brookhill Lane/, Central Coast Hwy, West Gosford S 33°25.615' E 151°25.259'	Road Side Stop, Cnr Peats Ridge Rd South/Old Pacific Hwy, Calga S 33°25.916' E 151°13.604'	29	15231.4
351	Sat	12/03/2011	Road Side Stop, Cnr Peats Ridge Rd South /Old Pacific Hwy, Calga S 33°25.916' E 151°13.604'	Road Side stop, Killard Railway Station Carpark, Cnr Lorne Ave/ Culworth Ave, Killard S 33°45.950' E 151°09.647'	52	15283.4
352	Sun	13/03/2011	Road Side stop, Killard Railway Station Carpark, Cnr Lorne Ave/ Culworth Ave, Killard S 33°45.950' E 151°09.647'	Private Residence, 7 Castle Place Sylvania Sydney S 34°01.278' E 151°05.761'	40.9	15324.3
353	Mon	14/03/2011	Private Residence, 7 Castle Place Sylvania Sydney S 34°01.278' E 151°05.761'	Road Side Stop, Cnr Garie Rd/Sir Bertrum Stevens Dr Royal National Park Sydney S 34°10.227' E 151°03.004'	25.4	15349.7
354	Tue	15/03/2011	Road Side Stop, Cnr Garie Rd/Sir Bertrum Stevens Dr Royal National Park Sydney S 34°10.227' E 151°03.004'	Sharkey's Beach Car Park S 34°17.644' E 150°56.617'	28.9	15378.6
355	Wed	16/03/2011	Sharkey's Beach Car Park S 34°17.644' E 150°56.617'	Kendalls Beach Holiday Park Kiama S 34°40.874' E 150°51.189'	53.7	15432.3

Running Pink

Day	Date	Daily start location, with GPS coordinates	Daily finish location, with GPS coordinates	Km	Total Km
356	Thu	17/03/2011	Kendalls Beach Holiday Park Kiama S 34°40.874' E 150°51.189'	Road Side Stop, Cnr Bolong Rd/ Back Forest Rd, @ Broughton Creek, Nowra/Bomaderry S 34°51.265' E 150°40.756'	30.9	15463.2
357	Fri	18/03/2011	Road Side Stop, Cnr Bolong Rd/ Back Forest Rd, @ Broughton Creek, Nowra/Bomaderry S 34°51.265' E 150°40.756'	Palm Beach Caravan Park, Sanctuary Point S 35°06.837' E 150°38.010'	44	15507.2
358	Sat	19/03/2011	Palm Beach Caravan Park, Sanctuary Point S 35°06.837' E 150°38.010'	Beach Haven Holiday Park, Ulladulla S 35°22.709' E 150°27.577'	54.6	15561.8
359	Sun	20/03/2011	Beach Haven Holiday Park, Ulladulla S 35°22.709' E 150°27.577'	Batesman Bay North, Tourist Park S 35°40.404' E 150°13.353'	44.5	15606.3
360	Mon	21/03/2011	Batesman Bay North, Tourist Park S 35°40.404' E 150°13.353'	Road Side Stop, Cnr Western Distributor Rd/, Kings Hwy, Currowan State Forest S 35°35.217' E 150°03.396'	26.4	15632.7
361	Tue	22/03/2011	Road Side Stop, Cnr Western Distributor Rd/, Kings Hwy, Currowan State Forest S 35°35.217' E 150°03.396'	Braidwood Showgrounds S 35°25.284' E 149°47.498'	41.3	15674
362	Wed	23/03/2011	Braidwood Showgrounds S 35°25.284' E 149°47.498	Road Side Stop, Brooks Hill Rest Area, Kings Hwy S 35°18.650' E 149°24.333'	53.3	15727.3

Australian Capital Territory

Day	Date	Daily start location	Daily finish location	Km	Total Km
363	Thu	24/03/2011	Road Side Stop, Brooks Hill Rest Area, Kings Hwy S 35°18.650' E 149°24.333'	Road Side Stop, Cnr Bellenden St/ Barton Hwy Hall via Canberra S 35°13.166' E 149°07.118'	41.8	15769.1

New South Wales

Day	Date	Daily start location	Daily finish location	Km	Total Km
364	Fri	25/03/2011	Road Side Stop, Cnr Bellenden St/ Barton Hwy Hall via Canberra S 35°13.166' E 149°07.118'	Yass Caravan Park S 34°50.019' E 148°54.481'	52.4	15821.5
365	Sat	26/03/2011	Yass Caravan Park S 34°50.019' E 148°54.481'	Boorowa Caravan Park S 34°26.027' E 148°43.198'	53.6	15875.1
366	Sun	27/03/2011	Boorowa Caravan Park S 34°26.027' E 148°43.198'	Road Side Stop, Water Tank Fill up Station, 51.75km E Boorowa, Boorowa/Crookwell RD S 34°25.568' E 149°08.864'	51.7	15926.8
367	Mon	28/03/2011	Road Side Stop, Water Tank Fill up Station, 51.75km E Boorowa, Boorowa/Crookwell RD S 34°25.568' E 149°08.864'	Crookwell Caravan Park S 34°27.279' E 149°28.045'	36.1	15962.9
368	Tue	29/03/2011	Crookwell Caravan Park S 34°27.279' E 149°28.045'	Road Side Stop, Intersection Braidwood Rd/, Hume Hwy, Goulburn, Braidwood Rd S 34°46.516' E 149°42.660'	48	16010.9

Logs

Day	Date	Daily start location, with GPS coordinates	Daily finish location, with GPS coordinates	Km	Total Km
369	Wed	30/03/2011	Road Side Stop, Intersection Braidwood Rd/, Hume Hwy, Goulburn, Braidwood Rd S 34°46.516' E 149°42.660'	Tarago Sports & Recreation Grounds, S 35°04.091' E 149°39.345'	34.7	16045.6
370	Thu	31/03/2011	Tarago Sports & Recreation Grounds S 35°04.091' E 149°39.345'	Torpys Motel Braidwood S 35°26.359' E 149°47.999'	48.3	16093.9
371	Fri	1/04/2011	Torpys Motel Braidwood S 35°26.359' E 149°47.999'	Road Side Stop, Gravel Pitt, Kings Hwy, 58.1km E Braidwood S 35°41.143' E 150°10.772'	58.1	16152
372	Sat	2/04/2011	Road Side Stop, Gravel Pitt, Kings Hwy, 58.1km E Braidwood S 35°41.143' E 150°10.772'	River Breeze Tourist Park Moruya S 35°54.250' E 150°04.737'	29.8	16181.8
373	Sun	3/04/2011	River Breeze Tourist Park Moruya S 35°54.250' E 150°04.737'	Surf Beach Holiday Park Narooma S 36°13.416' E 150°08.319'	45	16226.8
374	Mon	4/04/2011	Surf Beach Holiday Park Narooma S 36°13.416' E 150°08.319'	Road Side Stop, @ Jack Thomas Commerative Plaque, 2636 Bermagui – Tathra Rd S 36°33.501' E 150°01.991'	52.4	16279.2
375	Tue	5/04/2011	Road Side Stop, @ Jack Thomas Commerative Plaque, 2636 Bermagui – Tathra Rd S 36°33.501' E 150°01.991'	Sapphire Valley Caravan Park Merimbula S 36°52.999' E 149°54.152'	51.3	16330.5
376	Wed	6/04/2011	Sapphire Valley Caravan Park Merimbula S 36°52.999' E 149°54.152'	Road Side Stop, Cnr Edrom Rd/ Princes Hwy, Ben Boyd National Park S 37°11.444' E 149°50.939'	45.6	16376.1

Victoria

Day	Date	Daily start location, with GPS coordinates	Daily finish location, with GPS coordinates	Km	Total Km
377	Thu	7/04/2011	Road Side Stop, Cnr Edrom Rd/ Princes Hwy, Ben Boyd National Park S 37°11.444' E 149°50.939'	Road Side Stop, @ Mallacoota Turnoff, Genoa S 37°28.543' E 149°35.616'	44.6	16420.7
378	Fri	8/04/2011	Road Side Stop, @ Mallacoota Turnoff, Genoa S 37°28.543' E 149°35.616'	Cann River Caravan Park S 37°34.011' E 149°08.809'	48	16468.7
379	Sat	9/04/2011	Cann River Caravan Park S 37°34.011' E 149°08.809'	Road Side Stop, @ Bemm River Turnoff, Princes Hwy S 37°40.349' E 148°47.693'	40.1	16508.8
380	Sun	10/04/2011	Road Side Stop, @ Bemm River Turnoff, Princes Hwy S 37°40.349' E 148°47.693'	Road Side Stop, Snowy River Rest Area 2, via 4 km N Marlo, Marlo Rd S 37°46.061' E 148°32.221'	45.4	16554.2
381	Mon	11/04/2011	Road Side Stop, Snowy River Rest Area 2, via 4 km N Marlo, Marlo Rd S 37°46.061' E 148°32.221'	Private Residence, Regal Park Stud Park, 621 Princes Hwy, Lakes Entrance S 37°50.122' E 148°01.906'	62.4	16616.6

Running Pink

Day	Date	Daily start location, with GPS coordinates	Daily finish location, with GPS coordinates	Km	Total Km
382	Tue	12/04/2011	Private Residence, Regal Park Stud Park, 621 Princes Hwy, Lakes Entrance S 37°50.122' E 148°01.906'	Road Side Stop, Cnr Redcournt Lane/, Princes Hwy, 15km W Bairnsdale S 37°51.961' E 147°29.538'	58.6	16675.2
383	Wed	13/04/2011	Road Side Stop, Cnr Redcournt Lane/, Princes Hwy, 15km W Bairnsdale S 37°51.961' E 147°29.538'	Sale Holiday Village Park, Sale via Maffra S 38°06.818' E 147°03.392'	68.4	16743.6
384	Thu	14/04/2011	Sale Holiday Village Park, Sale via Maffra S 38°06.818' E 147°03.392'	Road Side Stop, Intersection Gippsland Hwy/, Hyland Hwy, Yarram S 38°32.767' E 146°42.028'	70.7	16814.3
385	Fri	15/04/2011	Road Side Stop, Intersection Gippsland Hwy/, Hyland Hwy, Yarram S 38°32.767' E 146°42.028'	Gormandale Football Oval S 38°17.551' E 146°42.071'	36.4	16850.7
386	Sat	16/04/2011	Gormandale Football Oval S 38°17.551' E 146°42.071'	Moe Garden Caravan Park S 38°10.594' E 146°15.034'	55.6	16906.3
387	Sun	17/04/2011	Moe Garden Caravan Park S 38°10.594' E 146°15.034'	Warragul Gardens, Caravan Park S 38°09.810' E 145°55.520'	40	16946.3
388	Mon	18/04/2011	Warragul Gardens, Caravan Park, via Warragul CBD & back S 38°09.810' E 145°55.520'	Pakenham Caravan Park S 38°04.340' E 145°29.629'	52.4	16998.7
389	Tue	19/04/2011	Pakenham Caravan Park S 38°04.340' E 145°29.629'	Road Side Stop, Black Rock Car Park, Beach Rd S 37°57.940' E 145°00.699'	51.1	17049.8
390	Wed	20/04/2011	Road Side Stop, Black Rock Car Park, Beach Rd S 37°57.940' E 145°00.699'	Spirit of Tasmania Dock East Melbourne, via Melbourne CBD S 37°50.568' E 144°55.897'	30.4	17080.2

Tasmania

Day	Date	Daily start location, with GPS coordinates	Daily finish location, with GPS coordinates	Km	Total Km
391	Thu	21/04/2011	Spirit of Tasmania Dock East Devonport S 40°10.728' E 146°22.113'	Wivenhoe Police Compound, via Burnie S 41°04.109' E 145°56.229'	59.6	17139.8
392	Fri	22/04/2011	Wivenhoe Police Compound, via Burnie S 41°04.109' E 145°56.229'	Road Side Stop, Blackburn Drive, Turners Beach S 41°09.708' E 146°14.663'	34.2	17174
393	Sat	23/04/2011	Road Side Stop, Blackburn Drive, Turners Beach S 41°09.708' E 146°14.663'	Road Side Stop, Caltex Service Station, Bass Hwy Elizabeth Town S 41°27.162' E 146°33.938'	51.8	17225.8
394	Sun	24/04/2011	Road Side Stop, Caltex Service Station, Bass Hwy Elizabeth Town S 41°27.162' E 146°33.938'	Private Residence, Vaux St West Launceston S 41°27.673' E 147°08.023'	60.7	17286.5
395	Mon	25/04/2011	Private Residence, Vaux St West Launceston S 41°27.673' E 147°08.023'	Grubb St Recreation Ground, Beaconsfield S 41°11.969' E 146°49.300'	53	17339.5

Logs

Day	Date	Daily start location, with GPS coordinates	Daily finish location, with GPS coordinates	Km	Total Km
396	Tue	26/04/2011	Grubb St Recreation Ground, Beaconsfield S 41°11.969' E 146°49.300'	Private Residence, Vaux St West Launceston S 41°27.675' E 147°08.024'	49.9	17389.4
397	Wed	27/04/2011	Private Residence, Vaux St West Launceston S 41°27.675' E 147°08.024'	Road Side Stop, @ Front of Catholic Church, King St Campbell Town S 41°55.837' E 147°29.702'	66.7	17456.1
398	Thu	28/04/2011	Road Side Stop, @ Front of Catholic Church, King St Campbell Town S 41°55.837' E 147°29.702'	Caravan Stop Over Park, Lake Dulverton Oatlands S 42°18.018' E 147°22.562'	49.5	17505.6
399	Fri	29/04/2011	Caravan Stop Over Park, Lake Dulverton Oatlands S 42°18.018' E 147°22.562'	Hobart Showgrounds, Brooker Hwy Hobart S 42°49.917' E 147°17.094'	77.5	17583.1
400	Sat	30/04/2011	Hobart Showgrounds, Brooker Hwy Hobart S 42°49.917' E 147°17.094'	Hobart Showgrounds, Brooker Hwy Hobart, via loop around East Side Derwent River & Hobart CBD S 42°49.876' E 147°17.243'	26.8	17609.9
401	Sun	1/05/2011	Hobart Showgrounds, Brooker Hwy Hobart, via loop around East Side Derwent River & Hobart CBD S 42°49.876' E 147°17.243'	Private Residence, 181 Howden Rd, Howden S 43°00.753' E 147°17.302'	44.9	17654.8
402	Mon	2/05/2011	Private Residence, 181 Howden Rd, Howden S 43°00.753' E 147°17.302'	Cygnet Holiday Park S 43°09.384' E 147°04.478'	63.9	17718.7
403	Tue	3/05/2011	Cygnet Holiday Park S 43°09.384' E 147°04.478'	Road Side Stop, @ Carpark behind Geeveston Information Centre S 43°09.801' E 146°55.598'	61.5	17780.2
404	Wed	4/05/2011	Road Side Stop, @ Carpark behind Geeveston Information Centre S 43°09.801' E 146°55.598'	Road Side Stop, @ Carpark behind Geeveston Information Centre, via loop around Surges Bay, Police Point, Dover Waterloo S 43°09.810' E 146°55.574'	54.1	17834.3
405	Thu	5/05/2011	Road Side Stop, @ Carpark behind Geeveston Information Centre, via loop around Surges Bay, Police Point, Dover Waterloo S 43°09.810' E 146°55.574'	Hobart Showgrounds, Brooker Hwy Hobart S 42°49.881' E 147°17.246'	67.1	17901.4

6/5/2011: GPS co-ordinates S 42°46,435' E 147°07.591', the point @ 17, 975km Deborah broke the existing 21 year record for the longest continuous run by a female

| 406 | Fri | 6/05/2011 | Hobart Showgrounds, Brooker Hwy Hobart S 42°49.881' E 147°17.246' | Road Side Stop, Cnr Church/Boyer Rd, Dromedary S 42°43.917' E 147°10.602' | 43.8 | 17945.2 |
| 407 | Sat | 7/05/2011 | Road Side Stop, Cnr Church/Boyer Rd, Dromedary S 42°43.917' E 147°10.602' | Richmond Caravan Park S 42°44.241' E 147°25.555' | 38.4 | 17983.6 |

Running Pink

Day	Date	Daily start location, with GPS coordinates	Daily finish location, with GPS coordinates	Km	Total Km
408	Sun	8/05/2011	Richmond Caravan Park S 42°44.241' E 147°25.555'	Parliament House Gardens Hobart, Including 4km run in Mother's Day Classic Hobart S 42°53.159' E 147°19.848'	42.8	18026.4

New Ultra Marathon Record for the longest continuous run by a female, 18026.4kms in 408 days*

*At time of going to print the record has been submitted but yet to be verified